THE BATTLE BOOK

Crucial Conflicts in History
from
1469 BC to the Present

BRYAN PERRETT

ARMS AND
ARMOUR

Arms and Armour Press
An imprint of the Cassell Group
Wellington House, 125 Strand, London WC2R 0BB

Distributed in the USA by Sterling Publishing Co. Inc.,
387 Park Avenue South, New York, NY 10016-8810

Distributed in Australia by Capricorn Link (Australia) Pty. Ltd.,
2/13 Carrington Road, Castle Hill, NSW 2154

First published 1992
Reprinted 1993
This paperback edition 1996

British Library Cataloguing-in-Publication Data: a catalogue record
for this book is available from the British Library

ISBN 1-85409-328-2

Designed and edited by DAG Publications Ltd.
Designed by David Gibbons; edited by Roger Chesneau;
typeset by Ronset Typesetters, Darwen, Lancashire; printed and bound
in Great Britain by Hartnolls Limited, Bodmin.

INTRODUCTION

I F WAR is one of the four great locomotives of history (the others being power, wealth and sex), then battles represent the mileposts along its route. At first, such mileposts were comparatively few and far between, but as the centuries passed they became more and more frequent until, during the two World Wars of the twentieth century, fighting was continuous. Indeed, since the end of the Second World War there have been few days, let alone weeks, when an armed struggle was not taking place somewhere around the globe. Superficially, this might suggest the depressing view that mankind, far from evolving, is actually reverting into barbarism, yet the evidence is that human nature remains unaltered. What has made the size, frequency and intensity of battles inevitable is the growth in population coupled with the industrial and agricultural revolutions of the last two centuries which, together, have made it possible to maintain, arm and equip very large armies in the field for as long as they are needed.

The object of this book is to provide an easy-to-use source of information on some 560 engagements which have taken place, from Megiddo (1469 BC), the first fully documented battle in history, to the Gulf War of 1990–1991, the most recent major conflict at the time of writing. It was Rudyard Kipling who wrote that the sum total of his knowledge was acquired from six honest serving men whose names were What and Why and When, and How and Where and Who. For the military historian, the researcher and the student, these same six are masters rather than servants, and every effort must be made to satisfy them. For this reason, therefore, the book has been arranged as a series of numbered entries in alphabetical order, each set out in tabulated form from which information can be extracted quickly from the sub-headings **Date**, **Location**, **War and campaign**, **Opposing sides**, **Object**, **Forces engaged**, **Casualties** and **Result**.

It should be noted that the **Location** of a battle does not always coincide with the placename which it has generally been accorded. Sometimes the placename has been changed by the passage of time, and sometimes it has been altered for political or demographic reasons (this is particularly common in Eastern Europe). The placenames quoted are, therefore, those in use today and easily identified on a modern map.

The identities of the commanders responsible for the conduct of engagements will be found under **Opposing sides**. In the case of the largest battles, involving several armies or corps, the identity of subordinate commanders has, where appropriate, been incorporated in the information contained in **Forces engaged**. With regard to the latter, a degree of caution is necessary regarding some battles of remote antiquity or the Dark Ages where the chroniclers have inflated both the size of the armies and the casualties incurred,

5

hoping to confer prestige on their masters. It is, perhaps, dangerous to place too much emphasis on the importance of casualties, firstly because body counts are notoriously suspect and secondly because it will be found that the victorious army sometimes sustained the heavier losses – although such figures do provide an indication of the intensity of the fighting.

The majority of entries provide notes relating to the action and many also incorporate references to related battles in CAPITAL LETTERS, indicating that these can also be found in the text. A further means of placing a battle in context can be found in Appendix A, which provides a chronological list of battles within wars, with entry numbers. For those interested in personalities, the more important commanders and their battles are listed in Appendix B. Tactical analyses with, where relevant, technical innovations, can be found in Appendix C.

Finally, it will be appreciated that, within a work covering three-and-a-half millennia of land warfare, limitations of space alone make it impossible to produce a specific bibliography, since this would entail the listing of thousands of volumes. However, a select general bibliography has been provided, and the majority of these books themselves contain extensive bibliographies which, if followed through, will lead the researcher to more specific works.

Bryan Perrett, February 1992

ENTRY NUMBERS

9

Aachen

Date: 4 October to 1 December 1944.
Location: Within the German frontier with Belgium and Holland along a front stretching from the Huertgen Forest through Aachen to beyond Geilenkirchen.
War and campaign: Second World War: North-West Europe.
Opposing sides: (a) General Omar Bradley commanding the US 12th Army Group; Field Marshal Walter Model commanding the German Army Group B.
Objective: The Allies sought to break through the defences of the Siegfried Line (West Wall) to Cologne on the Rhine, and also into the Roer valley.
Forces engaged: (a) Thirteen American and one British infantry divisions and four American and one British armoured divisions – total approximately 300,000 men and 750 tanks; (b) eleven infantry and five panzer divisions – total approximately 250,000 men and 500 tanks.
Casualties: (a) About 85,000; (b) about 70,000
Result: Although breaches were effected in the Siegfried Line, the attempt to reach Cologne was abandoned after the failure of the US First Army's attempts to capture the Roer dams near Schmidt.

Fighting in defence of their own soil, Model's men were fiercely motivated and the battle was one of the most bitter attritional struggles of the entire war. In the south, the difficult terrain of the Huertgen Forest favoured the defenders, but Aachen was captured after a week's heavy fighting, from 13 to 20 October. It was the first major German city to fall to the Allies, the result being simultaneously to effect the first breach in the Siegfried Line. In the north the British XXX Corps succeeded in capturing Geilenkirchen. Although the Americans continued to make slow progress towards the Roer valley and were within 25 miles of Cologne, they were fully committed and further progress was inhibited not only by an unshaken German defence but also by atrocious weather and widespread flooding which made movement difficult. On 1 December Bradley, recognizing that further attempts to secure the Roer dams would result in heavy losses for negligible gains, abandoned the offensive. Despite the heavy casualties incurred by both sides, the battle was indecisive, for, although the Allies secured some of their objectives, the tenacity of the defence encouraged the German High Command to launch its counter-offensive on the Ardennes sector later in December (see BULGE, THE).

Abensburg

Date: 19–20 April 1809.
Location: 18 miles south-west of Regensburg (Ratisbon), Bavaria, Germany.
War and campaign: War of the Fifth Coalition, 1809: Campaign against Austria.
Opposing sides: (a) The Emperor Napoleon I commanding the Grand Army; (b) the Archduke Charles commanding the Austrian Army.
Objective: The Austrians, invading Bavaria, attempted unsuccessfully to trap the French III Corps (Davout), but at Abensburg ran into the rapidly assembled Grand Army.
Forces engaged: (a) 90,000; (b) 80,000.
Casualties: (a) 2,000 killed and wounded; (2) 2,800 killed and wounded plus 4,000 captured.

Result: Napoleon smashed through the Archduke's centre with Lannes' corps, 25,000 strong. The effect of this was to split the Austrian army into two wings which Napoleon then defeated in detail at Landeshut (21 April), Eckmuhl (22 April) and Regensburg (23 April). In total, these actions cost the Austrians some 30,000 casualties plus much artillery and equipment lost, while French casualties amounted to approximately 15,000. Nevertheless, while Charles was able to preserve his army and withdraw into Austria, he was unable to prevent Napoleon from occupying Vienna (13 May). See ASPERN-ESSLING.

Aboukir 3

Date: 25 July 1799.
Location: Between Alexandria and the Nile Delta, Egypt.
War and Campaign: French expedition to Egypt, 1798–1801.
Opposing sides: (a) General Napoleon Bonaparte; (b) the identity of the Turkish commander is uncertain.
Objective: Following his victory at the Battle of THE PYRAMIDS, Bonaparte consolidated his hold over Egypt and then embarked on an abortive foray into Palestine and Syria (January–June 1799). Shortly after his return a Turkish army was shipped from Rhodes under British naval escort and entrenched itself at Aboukir. Concentrating as many troops as possible, Bonaparte marched to meet it.
Forces engaged: (a) 6,000; (b) 18,000.
Casualties: (a) 900 killed and wounded; (b) 12,000 killed, wounded or drowned plus 6,000 captured.
Result: The Turkish army was destroyed and driven into the sea when its entrenchments were stormed. The following month, as Egypt now seemed secure, Bonaparte handed over command to General Jean-Baptiste Kleber and returned to France, where he took part in the *coup* which resulted in his being appointed First Consul. See ALEXANDRIA.

Abu Klea 4

Date: 17 January 1885.
Location: On the track Korti–Gakdul–Metemmeh, cutting across the base of the Great Bend of the Nile, Sudan.
War and campaign: Sudan Campaigns: Gordon Relief Expedition.
Opposing sides: (a) General Lord Wolseley; (b) the Mahdi Mohammed Ahmed.
Objective: A British flying column had been despatched across the shorter desert route in the hope that it would be able to relieve General Charles Gordon, besieged in KHARTOUM.
Forces engaged: (a) 1,500 men, three guns and one Gardner machine gun, commanded by Brigadier-General Sir Herbert Stewart; (b) about 12,000 dervishes.
Casualties: (a) 76 killed and 82 wounded; (b) 1,100 killed and a greater number wounded.
Result: While at one point it penetrated the British square, the dervish attack was beaten off and the column resumed its march. See ABU KRU.

Abu Kru

Date: 19 January 1885.
Location: On the track Korti–Gakdul–Metemmeh, cutting across the base of the Great Bend of the Nile, Sudan.
War and campaign: Sudan Campaigns: Gordon Relief Expedition.
Opposing sides: (a) General Lord Wolseley; (b) the Mahdi Mohammed Ahmed.
Objective: A British flying column had been despatched across the shorter desert route in the hope that it would be able to relieve General Charles Gordon, besieged in KHARTOUM. Despite having been heavily engaged at ABU KLEA two days earlier, the column was continuing to fight its way forward.
Forces engaged: (a) 1,400 men, three guns and one Gardner machine gun, commanded by Brigadier-General Sir Herbert Stewart; (b) about 20,000 dervishes.
Casualties: (a) 23 killed (including Stewart) and 98 wounded; (b) unknown but far heavier.
Result: The dervish attack was beaten off and the column, now commanded by Colonel Sir Charles Wilson, reached the Nile later that day and was met by two of Gordon's tiny steamers. Having embarked a token force, these fought their way to within sight of Khartoum on 28 January, but the Mahdists, alarmed by the approach of Stewart's column, had stormed the city two days earlier. Wolseley was ordered to withdraw.

Admin Box

Date: 6–25 February 1944.
Location: East of the Ngakyedauk Pass between Maungdaw and Buthidaung, Arakan, Burma.
War and campaign: Second World War: Burma Campaign, Second Arakan Offensive.
Opposing sides: (a) Lieutenant-General A. F. P. Christison commanding XV Corps; (b) Lieutenant-General Hanaya commanding the 55th Division.
Objective: (a) The British sought to defeat a Japanese counter-offensive and resume their advance; (b) the Japanese sought to isolate the British forward units, compelling a hasty withdrawal, which they intended to follow up with an advance on Chittagong.
Forces engaged: (a) 5th, 7th and 26th Indian Divisions, 81st West African Division and one armoured regiment equipped with Lees; (b) 55th Division, reinforced by elements of the 54th Division.
Casualties: (a) Moderate, given the nature of the fighting; (b) unknown, but crippling.
Result: A complete defeat for the Japanese.

Having defeated an earlier British offensive in the Arakan by means of infiltration tactics, the Japanese attempted to repeat their success. By early 1944, however, they had lost air supremacy and Christison ordered his isolated forward units to stand fast and supplied them by air. The hub of the fighting was the Admin Box, which contained the headquarters of the 7th Indian Division. The garrison of the box included a single infantry battalion and an armoured regiment, but the bulk of its strength consisted of administrative and line-of-communications troops. These threw back repeated assaults until the box was relieved. The Japanese, who had already sustained serious casualties, were thus denied the rations they had counted on capturing and, starving and diseased, they were forced to withdraw; indeed, only by committing fresh troops were they able to maintain their presence in the Arakan. The British advance was resumed and only halted when the onset of the monsoon brought movement to a standstill. The battle is important in that it not only provided the first clear-cut British victory over the Japanese but also demonstrated that tanks could be used effectively in the Burmese jungle.

Adowa 7

Date: 1 March 1896.
Location: Abyssinian (Ethiopian) town in mountainous country close to the border with Eritrea, then an Italian colony.
War and campaign: Italo-Abyssinian War, 1895–1896.
Opposing sides: (a) General Oreste Baratieri; (b) the Emperor Menelek.
Objective: The Italians were attempting to extend their possessions in East Africa.
Forces engaged: (a) 20,000; (b) approximately 100,000.
Casualties: (a) 6,500 killed or wounded and 2,500 prisoners; (b) unknown.
Result: Italy recognized the independence of Abyssinia.

The dispersed Italian columns were defeated in detail. At the time Adowa was the most serious reverse ever sustained by the regular, well-equipped troops of a colonial power at the hands of irregulars; the Italian losses would have been even heavier had the Abyssinians conducted a vigorous pursuit.

Adrianople 8

Date: 9 August 378.
Location: Near modern Edirne, Turkey-in-Europe, close to the Greek and Bulgarian frontiers.
War and campaign: Gothic invasion of the Roman Empire.
Opposing sides: (a) The Emperor Valens; (b) Fritigern commanding the combined Visigoth/Ostrogoth army.
Objective: The Roman intention was to suppress the Goths – who had been permitted to settle in Thrace – because of friction and disorder.
Forces engaged: (a) 40,000 infantry and 20,000 cavalry – total 60,000; (b) 50,000 infantry and 50,000 cavalry – total 100,000.
Casualties: (a) 40,000 killed, including Valens; (b) unknown, but far lighter.
Result: The Roman army was destroyed. Although briefly pacified in 383, the Goths retained their tenure and were soon in revolt against the Empire again.

Valens unwisely ordered a general assault on Fritigern's wagon fort before all his infantry had come up and without knowing that the greater part of the Gothic cavalry was approaching the battlefield. This force then fell on the flank of the Roman cavalry and drove it from the field. The entire Visigoth army then surrounded Valens' legions and slaughtered them.

Adwalton Moor

Date: 30 June 1643.
Location: 5 miles east of Bradford, Yorkshire.
War and Campaign: First Civil War, 1642–1646.
Opposing sides: (a) William Cavendish, Duke of Newcastle, commanding the Royalists; (b) Lord Ferdinando Fairfax commanding the Parliamentarians.
Objective: The Royalists intended to eliminate the Parliamentary presence in Yorkshire.
Forces engaged: (a) 10,000; (b) 4,000.
Casualties: (a) Light; (b) 2,000 killed, wounded, captured and missing.
Result: The Parliamentary army was destroyed, leaving Yorkshire, with the exception of Hull, under Royalist control. While small in scale, the battle had important strategic consequences. Parliament, its fortunes at their lowest ebb (see also ROUNDWAY DOWN and CHALGROVE FIELD), concluded the Solemn League and Covenant with the Scots on 25 September. Under the terms of this the latter agreed to supply military support in return for subsidies and the virtual establishment of the reformed religion throughout Britain. The arrival of Scottish troops in January 1644 radically altered the complexion of the war in the north of England – see MARSTON MOOR.

Agincourt

Date: 25 October 1415.
Location: East of the village of Agincourt, approximately halfway between Abbeville and Calais.
War and campaign: Hundred Years' War, 1337–1457: English Invasion of France, 1415.
Opposing sides: (a) Henry V; (b) Charles d'Albret, Constable of France.
Objective: The English, having besieged and captured Harfleur, were retreating to Calais, where they intended spending the winter; at Agincourt they found further progress barred by the French army.
Forces engaged: (a) 4,950 archers and 750 men-at-arms – total 5,700; (b) 3,000 crossbowmen, 7,000 mounted and 15,000 dismounted men-at-arms and several guns – total approximately 25,000.
Casualties: (a) Approximately 400 killed, including the Duke of York; (b) approximately 8,000 killed, including d'Albret, three dukes, 90 nobles and 1,560 knights, and 200 captured.
Result: A major English victory. Henry resumed his march to Calais but did not exploit the strategic potential of his success. The battle cost France half her nobility.

D'Albret had planned to adopt a defensive stance which would have compelled the English, weary and short of rations, to attack with little chance of success. However, the more impetuous of the French nobles insisted that he should attack, confident that with their numerical superiority they could rout the little English army.

The English took up a position across the narrowest gap between the woods of Agincourt and Tramcourt, with their archers on the flanks and in two wedges in the centre, behind a line of iron-tipped stakes. As successive French attacks came in, their frontage was inevitably compressed by the converging tree-lines, and at length a point was reached where the compression was so great that the attackers were unable to use their weapons. The English, men-at-arms and archers alike, then charged into this struggling mass to slaughter at will. Numerous prisoners were taken for ransom, although some were killed on Henry's orders when, confronted by the uncommitted French reserve, which alone outnumbered his army, he learned that his camp, a mile to the rear, had been attacked. The French, finally disheartened, were easily driven off the field and the threat to the camp was revealed as being nothing more serious than a crowd of plundering peasants.

Agincourt, together with CRÉCY and POITIERS, forms the trio of famous victories for which the English archers are best remembered.

Agordat   11

Date: 21 December 1893.
Location: Town in central Eritrea, then an Italian colony.
War and campaign: Sudan Campaigns.
Opposing sides: (a) General Arimondi; (b) the Emir Ahmed Ali.
Objective: The Italians were resisting a Mahdist invasion from the Sudan.
Forces engaged: (a) 20,000; (b) 11,500.
Casualties: (a) 250; (b) approximately 3,000.
Result: The Mahdists withdrew.

Ain Jalut   12

Date: 3 September 1260.
Location: Near Nazareth, Israel.
War and Campaign: Mongol Invasion of Syria, 1258–1260/Wars of the Crusader States.
Opposing sides: (a) Kitboga and Prince Bohemond VI of Antioch; (b) Sultan Qutuz commanding the Mamelukes.
Objective: Following the death of Khakhan Mangu, most of the Mongols returned to Karakorum to elect his successor, leaving a detachment to hold the conquered territory in Syria. This allied itself with a Crusader faction but soon found itself opposed by a Mameluke army.
Forces engaged: (a) 10,000 Mongols and a small Crusader contingent; (b) 12,000 Mamelukes and an unknown number of infantry.
Casualties: (a) Unknown, but heavy (Kitboga was captured and executed); (b) moderate.
Result: The Mongols and their allies were decisively defeated.

The Mamelukes tightened their grip on Syria while the Crusaders' hold on their remaining territory was proportionately weakened.

Aisne, The

Date: 13–27 September 1914.

Location: Along the line of the Aisne river between Rheims and Compiègne.

War and campaign: First World War: Western Front.

Opposing sides: (a) General Joseph Joffre, Commander-in-Chief of the French armies; (b) General Erich von Falkenhayn, Chief of the German General Staff.

Objective: Following the FIRST BATTLE OF THE MARNE, the Allies intended crossing the Aisne in pursuit of the Germans.

Forces engaged: (a) The French Fifth Army (Franchet d'Esperey), the British Expeditionary Force (French) and the French Sixth Army (Manoury); (b) The German First Army (von Kluck), Seventh Army (von Heeringen) and Second Army (von Bulow).

Casualties: Unknown, but heavy on both sides.

Result: Although the Allies succeeded in crossing the Aisne, stiffening German resistance halted their advance on the plateau beyond. Both sides, exhausted, began entrenching their positions. See also YPRES, FIRST BATTLE OF.

The battle marked the beginning of static warfare on the Western Front.

Alamein, First Battle of

Date: 1–27 July 1942.

Location: Approximately 65 miles west of Alexandria, Egypt.

War and campaign: Second World War: North Africa.

Opposing sides: (a) General Sir Claude Auchinleck, Commander-in-Chief Middle East Land Forces, in personal command of the British Eighth Army; (b) nominally Marshal Ugo Cavallero, Supreme Commander Axis Forces in North Africa, *de facto* Field Marshal Erwin Rommel commanding Panzerarmee Afrika.

Objective: (a) The British strove to halt the Axis advance, then break through to the west; (b) the Axis forces were attempting to break through to Cairo and Alexandria.

Forces engaged: On 1 July: (a) approximately 20,000 men and 252 tanks (plus an estimated 232 more in workshops); (b) possibly 15,000 men and 85 tanks (plus an estimated 300 more in workshops). Both sides received substantial reinforcements throughout the battle, their respective personnel strength on 27 July being 124,000 and 57,000.

Casualties: (a) About 13,000 men and 193 tanks; (b) about 22,000, including 7,000 prisoners (tank losses uncertain but probably less than 100).

Result: The British succeeded in halting the Axis drive but were unable to achieve a breakthrough with any of their counter-attacks.

Both sides, tired and in some confusion after the previous month's fighting at GAZALA and TOBRUK, reached the Alamein position at the same time. A series of hard-fought encounters followed, centred on Ruweisat Ridge and Tel el Eisa, but while each side received reinforcements neither was strong enough to impose its will on the other. By 27 July both armies were exhausted and the battle had ended in apparent stalemate. However, the British were in the better strategic situation, being close to their bases, and were being reinforced at a rate which the Axis forces, with their over-extended supply lines, were unable to match. See ALAM HALFA.

Alamein, Second Battle of   15

Date: 23 October to 4 November 1942.
Location: Approximately 65 miles west of Alexandria, Egypt.
War and campaign: Second World War: North Africa.
Opposing sides: (a) General Sir Harold Alexander, Commander-in-Chief Middle East Land Forces; (b) nominally Marshal Ugo Cavallero, Supreme Commander of Axis Forces in North Africa, *de facto* Field Marshal Erwin Rommel, commander of Panzerarmee Afrika.
Objective: The British Eighth Army was determined to destroy its Axis opponents.
Forces engaged: (a) Lieutenant-General Bernard Montgomery commanding the Eighth Army with 195,000 men, 1,029 tanks (with 200 in immediate reserve and a further 1,000 in workshops) and 2,311 artillery weapons; (b) General Georg Stumme 23/24 October, General Ritter von Thoma 24/26 October, Field Marshal Erwin Rommel for the remainder of the battle, commanding Panzerarmee Afrika and other Axis formations with 104,000 men (50,000 German and 54,000 Italian), 520 tanks and 1,219 artillery weapons.
Casualties: (a) 2,350 killed, 8,950 wounded and 2,260 missing, plus 500 tanks disabled (the majority reparable) and 111 artillery weapons; (b) 10,000 killed, 15,000 wounded, 30,000 captured and all but a small proportion of tanks and artillery destroyed or lost.
Result: A decisive British victory which, coupled with the Anglo-American landing in Algeria and Morocco on 8 November (Operation 'Torch'), spelt the end of Axis hopes in the North African theatre of war.

Aware that his opponents were critically short of fuel, Montgomery decided to fight what he described as a 'crumbling' battle, switching the emphasis of his attack from point to point, thereby compelling the Axis armour to react. The first phase involved a diversionary attack by XIII Corps on the southern sector while, further north, the infantry of XXX Corps fought to secure two corridors through the enemy minebelts in the area of Miteiriya and Kidney Ridges, through which the 1st and 10th Armoured Divisions could be passed. Progress was slow and on 26 October the 9th Australian Division attacked on the coast, isolating a number of Axis units and provoking a heavy armoured counter-attack. Montgomery immediately shifted the emphasis of the battle back to the Kidney Ridge area and a major tank battle took place at Tel el Aqqaqir on 2 November. In this the British sustained the heavier losses but the Axis could not cope with their own rate of attrition and by the evening of 3 November only 30 serviceable German tanks remained. In obedience to Hitler's directives, Rommel hung on a little longer, but he began to extract the remnants of his army the following day. The British pursuit was slow to develop and was hindered by torrential rain and fuel shortages, enabling Rommel to disengage.

Alam Halfa   16

Date: 30 August to 2 September 1942.
Location: Ridge some 15–20 miles south-east of El Alamein station.

War and campaign: Second World War: North Africa.
Opposing sides: (a) General Sir Harold Alexander, Commander-in-Chief Land Forces Middle East; Lieutenant-General Bernard Montgomery commanding the Eighth Army; (b) nominally Marshal Ugo Cavallero, Supreme Commander of Axis Forces in North Africa, *de facto* Field Marshal Erwin Rommel, commanding Panzerarmee Afrika.
Objective: Axis attempt to break through the southern sector of the British defences at ALAMEIN and resume its advance on Cairo and Alexandria.
Forces engaged: (a) Eighth Army, with some 700 tanks available to meet the attack (the brunt of which fell on XIII Corps); (b) Panzerarmee Afrika with 203 German and 243 Italian tanks.
Casualties: (a) 1,640 killed and wounded, plus 68 tanks and 18 anti-tank guns; (b) 3,000 personnel (including Major-General von Bismarck, commanding 21st Panzer Division, killed on the first night), 49 tanks, 60 artillery weapons and 400 lorries.
Result: The Axis attempt was defeated and, because his fuel supplies had been consumed during the fighting, Rommel found himself in a strategic straitjacket from which he could neither advance nor retreat. Meanwhile, Montgomery's Eighth Army, its self-confidence restored after the victory, prepared methodically for the decisive SECOND BATTLE OF ALAMEIN.

While Rommel succeeded in forcing his way through the British minebelts, when he turned north towards the coast he was halted south of Alam Halfa Ridge by a co-ordinated defence in which tanks, artillery, anti-tank guns and ground-attack aircraft all played a part. On 2 September he acknowledged that further progress was impossible and withdrew.

Albuera   17

Date: 16 May 1811.
Location: Village 14 miles south-east of Badajoz, Spain.
War and campaign: Peninsular War, 1807–1814: Campaign of 1811.
Opposing sides: (a) Lieutenant-General Sir William Beresford (Field Marshal and Commander-in-Chief of the Portuguese Army); (b) Marshal Nicholas Jean-de-Dieu Soult.
Objective: The French were attempting to relieve the frontier fortress of Badajoz, which was besieged by an Allied army.
Forces engaged: (a) 35,000 (7,000 British, 13,300 Portuguese and 14,700 Spanish); (b) 24,600.
Casualties: (a) 6,200 killed, wounded and missing plus one gun captured; (b) approximately 8,000 killed and wounded.
Result: The French were defeated and BADAJOZ was reinvested, although the siege was abandoned in June; the fortress did not fall into Allied hands until April 1812.

Soult, intending to envelop the Allied right, feinted at the centre, but Beresford, recognizing the real threat, redeployed. Unfortunately the Spanish, holding the Allied right, were both slow to react and unreliable and were driven off the vital high ground. The first British brigade to reach the scene was overrun by French cavalry before it could form a square. The arrival of further British and Portuguese units stabilized the situation, and the French assault was bloodily repulsed. Of the 7,000 British troops who bore the brunt of this desperate struggle, only 1,700 remained on their feet when the battle ended.

Alesia 18

Date: 52 BC.
Location: Mont Auxois, east of Alise-Sainte-Reine, near Dijon, Côte d'Or, France.
War and campaign: Caesar's Gallic War, 58–52 BC.
Opposing sides: (a) Julius Caesar; (b) Vercingetorix.
Objective: Caesar was besieging the stronghold in order to force the Gallic chieftain Vercingetorix to surrender, thereby bringing the war to an end.
Forces engaged: (a) Approximately 70,000; (b) within the fortress, 80,000 infantry and 15,000 cavalry; with the relief army, possibly 250,000 infantry and 8,000 cavalry; total 353,000.
Casualties: Unknown.
Result: The defeat of the Gallic relief army followed by the surrender of Vercingetorix completed the Roman conquest of Gaul.

Caesar enclosed the fortress within an 11-mile line of contravallation, but before this was completed Vercingetorix, already worried by supply shortages, sent out his cavalry with an appeal for the Gallic tribes to come to his assistance. On the approach of the relief army, Caesar built an outer ring of fortifications (circumvallation) 14 miles long. The Gauls repeatedly tried to break through this while Vercingetorix attempted to break out. Following the final defeat of the relief army, Vercingetorix, whose men were starving, capitulated.

Aleutian Islands 19

Date: 11 May to 15 August 1943.
Location: Chain of islands lying between Alaska and the Asian mainland.
War and Campaign: Second World War, Northern Pacific Theatre.
Opposing sides: (a) Rear Admiral Francis D. Rockwell's North Pacific Amphibious Force; (b) Japanese garrisons of Attu and Kiska.
Objective: Allied recapture of the two most westerly islands, Attu and Kiska, which had been occupied by the Japanese in June 1942 as part of their diversionary manoeuvres prior to the Battle of Midway.
Forces engaged: (a) US 7th Infantry Division; (b) 2,500-strong garrison on Attu.
Casualties: (a) 561 killed and 1,136 wounded; (b) all but 29 of the Attu garrison killed in 18 days of fighting.
Result: Atta was recaptured.

On 15 August a joint American-Canadian force of 34,000 men landed on Kiska to find that the 5,000-strong enemy garrison had already been evacuated.

Alexandria

Date: 21 March 1801.
Location: Outside Alexandria, Egypt.
War and campaign: French expedition to Egypt, 1798–1801.
Opposing sides: (a) General Sir Ralph Abercromby; (b) General Jacques Menou (Kléber, designated commander of the French troops in Egypt by Bonaparte on his return to France, had been assassinated the previous June).
Objective: The British and the Turks had decided to eliminate the French presence in Egypt (see PYRAMIDS, THE, and ABOUKIR). On 8 March they succeeded in effecting a landing at Aboukir Bay in the teeth of fierce opposition. A period of deadlock ensued, with both sides holding defensive positions, but on 21 March the French attacked.
Forces engaged: (a) 15,000; (b) approximately 20,000.
Casualties: (a) 1,376 killed and wounded, including Abercromby, mortally wounded; (b) estimated 3,000 killed and wounded.
Result: The French were defeated.

There was little serious fighting after Alexandria. Menou, isolated by British sea power from France, capitulated on 31 August and was granted passage home for his 26,000 men.

Aliwal

Date: 28 January 1846.
Location: Village in the Punjab 6 miles west of Ludhiana.
War and campaign: First Sikh War, 1845–1846.
Opposing sides: (a) Major-General Sir Harry Smith; (b) Ranjur Singh.
Objective: Recovering from their defeats at MUDKI and FEROZESHAH, the Sikhs despatched a strong force south of the Sutlej to ravage British territory in the Ludhiana area. The British intention was to destroy this.
Forces engaged: (a) 12,000 British and Indian troops with 32 guns; (b) 15,000 men with 67 guns.
Casualties: (a) 151 killed, 422 wounded and 25 missing; (b) in excess of 3,000 killed, including a number drowned as they fled across the Sutlej, plus all artillery, stores and supplies captured.
Result: Ranjur Singh's army was destroyed.

Smith's attack went so exactly to plan that Aliwal has been described as 'the battle without a mistake'. See also SOBRAON.

Alkmaar, Siege of

Date: 21 August to 8 October 1573.
Location: Fortified town 23 miles north-west of Amsterdam.
War and campaign: Eighty Years' War (War of Dutch Independence), 1568–1648: Campaign of 1573.

Opposing sides: The Patriot garrison; (b) Don Frederic de Toledo.
Objective: The Spanish intention was to capture the town and put its inhabitants to the sword as an example to other Dutch Patriots.
Forces engaged: (a) 800 trained soldiers and 1,300 armed citizens; (b) five *tercios* and ample artillery – total 16,000.
Casualties: Assault of 18 September: (a) 24 soldiers and 13 armed citizens killed; (b) approximately 1,000 killed.
Result: After his assault had been repulsed, Don Frederic abandoned the siege when the Dutch threatened to open the dykes and flood the entire area.

The failure at Alkmaar was a serious blow to Spanish prestige and raised the morale of the Dutch insurgents.

Alma, Battle of the 23

Date: 20 September 1854.
Location: 15 miles north of Sevastopol, Crimea.
War and campaign: Crimean War, 1854–1855.
Opposing sides: (a) Field Marshal Lord Raglan and Marshal Armand de Saint-Arnaud in joint command of the Allied army; (b) General Prince Alexander Menshikov commanding the Russian army in the Crimea.
Objective: Having effected a successful landing at Calamita Bay, the Anglo-French-Turkish army was marching on Sevastopol when its advance was contested by the Russian army holding the high ground beyond the River Alma.
Forces engaged: (a) 27,000 British, 25,000 French and 8,000 Turks; (b) 37,000.
Casualties: (a) British – 362 killed and 1,621 wounded; French – approximately 500 killed and wounded; (b) 1,800 killed and 3,700 wounded.
Result: The Russians were driven from their positions.

The Allies went on to besiege SEVASTOPOL.

Almanza 24

Date: 25 April 1707.
Location: Near Almansa, 40 miles north-west of Alicante, south-eastern Spain.
War and campaign: War of Spanish Succession 1701–1714: Spanish Campaign of 1707.
Opposing sides: (a) The Earl of Galway commanding the Allied army; (b) the Duke of Berwick commanding the Franco-Spanish army.
Objective: An Allied army advancing on Madrid from Valencia was intercepted by a Franco-Spanish army south of Almansa.
Forces engaged: (a) 25 infantry battalions, 17 cavalry squadrons and 30 guns – total 15,000 (British, Dutch and Portuguese); (b) 72 infantry battalions, 76 cavalry squadrons and 40 guns – total 30,000.
Casualties: (a) 4,000 killed and wounded and 5,000 prisoners; (b) 2,000 killed and 4,000 wounded.

> **Result:** Galway's troops were decisively defeated and the Allied cause in Spain sustained a blow from which it never fully recovered.

A curious feature of the battle was the relative background of the two commanders. Galway was an exiled French Huguenot, Henri de Massue de Ruvigny, who had entered the service of William III. Berwick, otherwise named James FitzJames, was an English Jacobite exile who had entered the service of Louis XIV; his natural parents were James II and Arabella, sister of the Duke of Marlborough.

Altendorf (Alte Veste) 25

Date: 31 August to 4 September 1632.
Location: Village, castle and ridge above the Rednitz river near Furth, west of Nuremberg, Bavaria.
War and campaign: Thirty Years' War, 1618–1648: German Campaign of 1632.
Opposing sides: (a) Gustavus Adolphus, King of Sweden; (b) Maximilian I of Bavaria and General Albrecht von Wallenstein commanding the Imperialist/Catholic army.
Objective: The Swedish Army, close to starvation, faced the alternatives of attacking the more numerous Imperialists in their entrenched positions or withdrawing to the north; the former was chosen.
Forces engaged: (a) 40,000; (b) 50,000.
Casualties: (a) 2,300; (b) 2,700.
Result: Despite repeated attacks, Gustavus Adolphus sustained a rare defeat, largely because the broken ground and scrub covering Wallenstein's well-chosen position made it impossible to deploy the Swedish cavalry and artillery to best advantage.

The Swedes disengaged and withdrew northward; Wallenstein did not pursue. See also LÜTZEN (1632).

Amiens 26

Date: 8–11 August 1918.
Location: East of Amiens, France, along a 10-mile frontage.
War and campaign: First World War: Western Front.
Opposing sides: (a) Marshal Ferdinand Foch, Allied Supreme Commander; (b) General Erich Ludendorff, First Quartermaster-General of the German Army.
Objective: To remove the threat to Amiens by means of a massed tank attack which would achieve an Allied breakthrough and force the Germans into a withdrawal.
Forces engaged: (a) General Sir Henry Rawlinson commanding the British Fourth Army, including the Australian and Canadian Corps, with a total of thirteen infantry divisions, the Cavalry Corps with three divisions and the Tank Corps (324 Mk V tanks, 96 Whippet light tanks, 42 tanks in reserve, 120 supply tanks, 22 gun carriers and one armoured car battalion), plus a diversionary operation on the right flank mounted by the French First Army (General M. Eugene Debeney) with, initially, two divisions; (b) General Georg von der Marwitz and General Oskar von Hutier commanding, respectively, the German Second and Eighteenth Armies with eleven divisions in the line and eight in reserve on the threatened sector.

Casualties: (a) British – 22,000 killed, wounded and missing, with 109 tanks knocked out by German gunfire during the first day; French – 24,232 up to 15 August and including First and Third Army (Humbert) losses as the advance was taken up to the south of the original penetration; (b) over 75,000, including 29,873 prisoners.
Result: The great tank attack achieved complete surprise and penetrated to a depth of 7½ miles; thereafter progress became slower as the number of serviceable tanks dropped. The principal result of the battle, however, was to reveal the extent to which the German Army was affected by war-weariness.

Coming as it did on the heels of his reverse during the SECOND BATTLE OF THE MARNE, the defeat profoundly depressed Ludendorff, who described 8 August as 'The Black Day of the German Army' and advised the Kaiser that victory was no longer possible. Amiens initiated the slow but sustained Allied advance which continued for the remainder of the war.

Amoaful

Date: 31 January 1874.
Location: 20 miles south of Kumasi, Gold Coast (now Ghana) West Africa.
War and campaign: Second Ashanti War, 1873–1874.
Opposing sides: (a) Major-General Sir Garnet Wolseley; (b) King Coffee Calcalli.
Objective: A British punitive expedition marching on Kumasi was intercepted by the Ashanti army at Amoaful.
Forces engaged: (a) Approximately 2,000 with a battery of mountain artillery and rocket tubes in support; (b) approximately 10,000.
Casualties: (a) Four killed and 194 wounded; (b) estimated 800 to 1,000 killed and the same number wounded.
Result: The Ashanti were defeated and Wolseley destroyed Kumasi.

On 13 February Coffee signed a treaty of submission and paid a modest indemnity.

Antietam (Sharpsburg)

Date: 17 September 1862.
Location: Antietam, Sharpsburg, Maryland (now a National Battlefield).
War and campaign: American Civil War: Lee's First Invasion of the North.
Opposing sides: (a) Major-General George B. McClellan commanding the Army of the Potomac; (b) General Robert E. Lee commanding the Confederate Army of North Virginia.
Objective: Following his victory at SECOND BULL RUN, Lee sought to carry the war to the North and inflict a decisive defeat on the Federal Army of the Potomac.
Forces engaged: (a) 75,000; (b) 38,000.
Casualties: (a) 12,401; (b) 10,318.
Result: Lee won a narrow tactical victory, but his severe losses, coupled with those incurred at SECOND BULL RUN the previous month, caused him to abandon his invasion of the North and retire across the Potomac into Virginia. This outcome

restored President Lincoln's confidence sufficiently for him to issue his Preliminary Emancipation Proclamation on slavery (23 September), which effectively doomed the Confederacy's hopes of recognition by foreign governments. At the political and strategic levels, therefore, it was the Federal Government which benefited most from the battle, making it one of the most decisive engagements of the war. McClellan's lack of energy in following up Lee's withdrawal led to his being replaced on 7 November by the more aggressive Major-General Ambrose E. Burnside. Antietam was the bloodiest battle of the war, accounting for more American casualties in a single day than any other engagement before or since.

McClellan opened the battle with a heavy attack against the Confederate left and, while this held, Lee was forced to commit troops from his right to contain the threat. As the day wore on, the fighting spread towards the centre and became focused on a sunken road later named Bloody Lane. Mistaken orders resulted in the Confederates abandoning this and retreating, but McClellan failed to follow up his advantage. Meanwhile, on the Federal left, Burnside's corps fought its way over a bridge spanning Antietam Creek and deployed to assault Sharpsburg. Quite possibly this attack might have succeeded, as the Confederate line had been stripped dangerously thin to meet the demands of others sectors, but at the critical moment Major-General A. P. Hill's division, having made a forced march from HARPER'S FERRY, where it had been guarding Federal prisoners, fell on Burnside's flank and drove him back until darkness ended the fighting. Although McClellan retained ample reserves throughout the battle, he made no attempt to exploit his unexpected success at Bloody Lane, nor did he support Burnside as the latter deserved. Both sides remained in their positions the following day, but McClellan declined to renew the contest and Lee withdrew unmolested.

Antioch (The·Orontes) 29

Date: 28 June 1098.	
Location: Near modern Antakya, on the Turkish border with north-eastern Syria.	
War and campaign: First Crusade, 1096–1099.	
Opposing sides: (a) Duke Bohemond of Taranto; (b) Kerboga, Emir of Mosul, commanding the Moslem army.	
Objective: The Crusaders, having besieged and captured Antioch, were in turn besieged by a Moslem army and reduced to desperate straits. They were, however, inspired by the somewhat dubious discovery of the Holy Lance used to pierce Christ's side during the Crucifixion and mounted a fierce sortie across the Orontes to attack the Moslems.	
Forces engaged: (a) 1,000 cavalry and 14,000 infantry; (b) 75,000.	
Casualties: (a) Moderate; (b) heavy.	
Result: Kerboga's army was defeated.	

Bohemond and his men established the Principality of Antioch, but the remaining Crusaders resumed their advance into the Holy Land. See JERUSALEM, SIEGE OF.

Anzio 30

Date: 22 January to 23 May 1944.	
Location: 30 miles south of Rome.	

War and campaign: Second World War: Italy.
Opposing sides: (a) Lieutenant-General Mark Clark commanding the US Fifth Army and Major-General John P. Lucas commanding US VI Corps; (b) Field Marshal Albert Kesselring, Commander-in-Chief Italy, and General Eberhard von Mackensen commanding the German Fourteenth Army.
Objective: Allied attempt to outflank the Gustav Line and break the apparent impasse at CASSINO by effecting an amphibious landing behind the German lines.
Forces engaged: (a) Initially British 1st and US 3rd Infantry Divisions plus supporting armour and artillery – total approximately 50,000 men (subsequently reinforced); (b) initially four German divisions, rising to nine by mid-February – total about 90,000 men.
Casualties: (a) Approximately 40,000; (b) approximately 35,000.
Result: The beach-head was quickly contained by the rapid German response to the landing, but on 23 May VI Corps broke out, simultaneously effecting a junction with the US II Corps advancing from the south and spearheading the Allied drive on Rome.

Codenamed 'Shingle', the initial landings lost much of their impact when the cautious Lucas consolidated his perimeter defences rather than advancing inland to secure the Alban Hills. The beach-head was subjected to heavy counter-attacks which resulted in some of the most desperate fighting of the entire war. On 23 February Lucas was replaced by Major-General Lucien K. Truscott.

Appomattox Court House 31

Date: 9 April 1865.
Location: 21 miles east of Lynchburg, Virginia.
War and campaign: American Civil War: Grant's Virginia Campaign of 1865.
Opposing sides: (a) General Ulysses S. Grant, the US Army's General-in-Chief, in the field with Major-General George C. Meade's Army of the Potomac; (b) General Robert E. Lee commanding the Army of Northern Virginia.
Objective: Lee, withdrawing from Petersburg after the Battle of FIVE FORKS, was hoping to retire southwards and effect a junction between his army and that of Lieutenant-General Joseph E. Johnston, but he found that Grant's troops had already cut his line of retreat.
Forces engaged: (a) 63,285; (b) 31,900.
Casualties: (a) 164; (b) 500 killed and wounded, 28,231 surrendered and paroled.
Result: With the exception of 2,400 cavalry, the Army of Northern Virginia was unable to fight its way out of the trap and Lee met Grant to agree terms of surrender.

Grant was magnanimous, permitting officers to retain their side arms, and men who owned horses serving with the army were allowed to return home with them for the spring ploughing; he also provided badly needed rations. Although the last Confederate troops in the field did not lay down their arms until May, to all intents and purposes Lee's surrender at Appomattox Court House marked the end of the war.

Arbela (Guagamela)

Date: 1 October 331 BC.
Location: On the Plain of Guagamela near modern Mosul, northern Iraq.
War and campaign: Conquests of Alexander the Great: Campaign of 331 BC.
Opposing sides: (a) Alexander the Great; (b) Darius III, King of Persia.
Objective: Following his conquest of Asia Minor, Syria and Egypt, Alexander invaded the heartland of the Persian Empire. He was opposed by the Persian army near the site of ancient Nineveh, some 70 miles west of Arbela (now Arbil).
Forces engaged: (a) 7,000 cavalry and 40,000 infantry – total 47,000; (b) 45,000 cavalry, 200,000 infantry, 200 scythe-chariots and 15 elephants – total approximately 250,000.
Casualties: (a) 500 killed; (b) the more realistic estimates vary between 40,000 and 90,000 killed.
Result: The Persian army was destroyed and Alexander continued his march into Asia. See HYDASPES, THE.

To counter Darius's great numerical superiority Alexander deployed his army in two lines, the second of which was used to defeat the Persian cavalry's attempts at a double envelopment. The Persian scythe-chariots were unable to penetrate the hedge of Macedonian spearpoints and were routed by Alexander's light troops. Alexander, perceiving a weakness in the Persian left-centre, mounted a concentrated counter-attack and broke through close to Darius, who fled the field. At this the Persian army broke and was completely dispersed by the vigorous Macedonian pursuit. Darius was murdered by his own nobles, leaving Alexander the undisputed ruler of the Persian Empire.

Arcola

Date: 15–17 November 1796.
Location: Village on the Alpone river, 15 miles south-east of Verona, northern Italy.
War and campaign: War of the First Coalition, 1792–1798: Campaign in Italy, 1796–1797.
Opposing sides: (a) General Napoleon Bonaparte; (b) General Baron Josef Alvintzy.
Objective: Following their defeat at BASSANO, the Austrians mounted a further attempt to relieve their besieged garrison at Mantau, advancing on two fronts against the French covering force. The French intention was to defeat both Austrian armies in detail before they could combine.
Forces engaged: (a) 18,000; (b) 20,000.
Casualties: (a) Approximately 4,600; (b) approximately 6,000.
Result: After three days of attritional fighting, Napoleon secured river crossings and attacked Alvintzy's rear, forcing him to withdraw. He then turned on the second and smaller Austrian army, commanded by General Paul Davidovich, and drove it back. See also RIVOLI.

Arnhem

Date: 17–25 September 1944.

Location: Holland, on the north bank of the Neder Rijn.

War and campaign: Second World War: North-West Europe.

Opposing sides: (a) Field Marshal Sir Bernard Montgomery commanding the 21st Army Group; (b) Field Marshal Walter Model commanding Army Group B.

Objective: The final phase of an Allied attempt to secure a bridge over the Neder Rijn, so turning the northern flank of the Siegfried Line in preparation for a drive into Germany itself.

Forces engaged: (a) British 1st Airborne Division and 1st Polish Parachute Brigade at Arnhem, US 101st Airborne Division at Eindhoven and Veghel, US 82nd Airborne Division at Grave and Nijmegen and British XXX Corps – total about 100,000 men; (b) elements of First Paratroop Army, II SS Panzer Corps and numerous *ad hoc* battlegroups and contingents drawn from garrison troops – total about 85,000 men.

Casualties: (a) British 1st Airborne Division – 7,200; (b) German troops at Arnhem – about 3,300.

Result: The gallant failure of the 1st Airborne Division postponed the crossing of the Rhine until March 1945, although the capture of Nijmegen proved to be of great value in the operations leading up to this.

The landing zone selected for Major-General Roy Urquhart's 1st Airborne Division was too far to the west of Arnhem and only one battalion group managed to reach the principal objective, the road bridge in the town itself, where it held out for several days. The remainder of the division was contained in the suburb of Oosterbeek by troops of II SS Panzer Corps, which was refitting in the Arnhem area after the fighting in Normandy. Elsewhere, while the British XXX Corps relieved the American airborne divisions it was unable to break through to Arnhem because of a strong defensive front some miles north of Nijmegen. On 21 September the 1st Polish Parachute Brigade was dropped at Driel on the south bank of the Neder Rijn, opposite Oosterbeek, where it was joined next day by part of the 43rd (Wessex) Division, which had fought its way past the flank of the main German defences. On the 25th Montgomery decided to withdraw the survivors of the 1st Airborne Division and that night a mere 2,163 men were ferried from Oosterbeek to the south bank. In addition to poor planning and ill luck, communications failures and limited air support caused by bad flying weather also contributed to the failure.

Aroghee (Magdala)

Date: 31 April 1868.

Location: Three miles north of Magdala, northern Abyssinia (Ethiopia).

War and campaign: Anglo–Abyssinian War, 1867–1868.

Opposing sides: (a) General Sir Robert Napier; (b) the Emperor Theodore.

Objective: The British were mounting a punitive expedition following the imprisonment of their consular officials.

Forces engaged: (a) 4,000 British and Indian troops, including 460 cavalry, two mountain batteries and one rocket battery; (b) approximately 5,000, including a large proportion with muskets, and some 20 guns.

Casualties: (a) 30 wounded; (b) over 500 killed plus an unknown number of wounded and all guns captured.	
Result: Theodore's army was defeated and he committed suicide when his fortress at Magdala was stormed, virtually without loss, three days later.	

Napier's achievement lay not so much in defeating the enemy but in overcoming the logistic problems posed by the 379-mile march through difficult country from his landing place near Massawa on the Red Sea to Theodore's mountain fortress; about 27,000 animals were employed, including elephants, camels, mules and bullocks and, as was usual at the time, the army was outnumbered by its camp-followers. Of the 10,000 soldiers at Napier's disposal, the majority were engaged in maintaining the line of communication. Aroghee was the first occasion on which British troops used breech-loading rifles and, while the firepower of these was in itself decisive, the enemy was also seriously unsettled by the rockets, which were manned by a naval detachment.

Arras 36

Date: 21 May 1940.
Location: Valley of the River Scarpe, north-eastern France.
War and campaign: Second World War: France, 1940
Opposing sides: (a) Major-General H. E. Franklyn commanding Frank Force and attached units; (b) Major-General Erwin Rommel commanding the 7th Panzer Division.
Objective: Allied attempt to drive into the flank of the German advance to the Channel coast.
Forces engaged: (a) 1st Army Tank Brigade (4 and 7 RTR), 6th and 8th Battalions Durham Light Infantry and supporting artillery, elements of French 3rd *Division Légère Mécanique*; (b) 7th Panzer Division, elements of 3rd SS Motorized Division *Totenkopf*.
Casualties: (a) 220 men and 57 tanks; (b) 378 men and some 30 tanks.
Result: Although the Allied counter-strike was ultimately contained, it created such alarm that the German high command halted the drive of its panzer divisions to the coast for 24 hours, thereby contributing to the success of the DUNKIRK evacuation.

When the Allied attack struck the flank of Rommel's division, the German 37mm anti-tank guns proved useless against the thick armour of the British Matilda Is and IIs and two motor rifle regiments were overrun. The resulting panic communicated itself to the neighbouring SS Motorized Division *Totenkopf*, part of which also bolted. By concentrating the fire of his divisional artillery and 88mm anti-aircraft guns, Rommel was able to halt the advance, but he reported that he was being attacked by 'hundreds' of tanks and this caused serious concern at the higher German command levels; in fact the strength of 1st Army Tank Brigade amounted to 58 Matilda Is and 16 Matildas IIs, although the French 3rd DLM still retained a few of its tanks. During the evening Rommel's rallied division counter-attacked and Frank Force retired to the area of its start line on Vimy Ridge.

Arras/Vimy Ridge 37

Date: 9–15 April 1917.

Location: North, north-east and south-east of Arras.
War and campaign: First World War: Western Front.
Opposing sides: (a) General Sir Douglas Haig commanding the British armies in France and Belgium; (b) General Erich Ludendorff, First Quartermaster-General of the German Army.
Objective: British attack intended to attract German reserves prior to the launching of the NIVELLE OFFENSIVE.
Forces engaged: (a) General Sir Edmund Allenby and General Sir Henry Horne commanding, respectively, the British Third and First Armies; (b) General Baron von Falkenhausen commanding the German Sixth Army.
Casualties: (a) Approximately 20,000; (b) approximately 27,000.
Result: A British tactical victory in which all objectives were captured, including Vimy Ridge.

The principal reason for the British success was the meticulous planning which went into the preparation of the attack. With 5,000 guns, the British artillery outnumbered the German by four to one; in addition, the position of the German batteries was known and most were neutralized while the effectiveness of the others was greatly reduced by a newly developed gas shell. Miles of tunnels had also been constructed in which the assault troops sheltered prior to the attack. Sixty tanks were available and although the majority got bogged down in the muddy, shell-torn ground, the appearance of others was decisive. The capture of Vimy Ridge by the Canadian Corps, commanded by Lieutenant-General Sir Julian Byng, was one of the war's most notable feats of arms; having lost the summit, the Germans were forced to withdraw from their positions below its reverse slopes, as these had become untenable. Only the British cavalry fared badly, the attempt by two brigades to exploit a breach in the line at Monchy-le-Preux being stopped with heavy casualties by concentrated machine-gun fire. Ludendorff, angered by a clear German defeat, gave orders for its circumstances to be examined by a Court of Inquiry.

Arsuf   38

Date: 7 September 1191.
Location: On the coast to the north of modern Tel Aviv, Israel.
War and campaign: Third Crusade, 1189–1192.
Opposing sides: (a) Richard I, King of England; (b) Salah-al-din Yusuf ibn-Ayub (Saladin).
Objective: The Crusaders, having taken Acre, were marching south towards Jerusalem when their column was ambushed by the Saracens.
Forces engaged: Numbers uncertain, but believed approximately 25,000 on each side.
Casualties: (a) 700; (b) 7,000.
Result: The Saracens were defeated and driven off with heavy losses. Saladin, recognizing that Richard was a commander of exceptional ability, never engaged him again in open battle. Instead, he pursued a scorched-earth policy which prevented the Crusaders from laying siege to Jerusalem. In 1192 the two concluded a treaty which granted rights and privileges to Christian pilgrims travelling to Jerusalem.

Richard, determined to avoid the mistakes which had resulted in the disaster at HATTIN, imposed strict discipline on his army. The Crusader column was flanked by its infantry, which contained a high proportion of crossbowmen who were able to keep the mounted Saracen archers at a distance and were protected by padded surcoats capable of absorbing the penetrative power of the latter's short arrows. Only when pressure on the rearguard became unbearable did Richard give the signal permitting his knights to pass through the infantry screen in a concentrated counter-charge. The effect on the over-confident Saracens was devastating. After pursuing their beaten enemy for a limited distance, the knights rallied and returned to the column.

Ascalon 39

Date: 12 August 1099.
Location: South of modern Ashqelon on the coast of Israel.
War and campaign: First Crusade, 1096–1099.
Opposing sides: (a) Godfrey de Buillon, Guardian of Jerusalem; (b) the Emir al-Afdal.
Objective: A Fatimid army had set out from Egypt to relieve JERUSALEM but halted at Ascalon when it learned that the city had fallen. The Crusader army marched south to engage it.
Forces engaged: (a) 1,200 cavalry and 9,000 infantry; (b) 50,000.
Casualties: (a) Light; (b) unknown, but heavy.
Result: The Crusaders launched a surprise dawn attack on the Fatimid camp, driving their opponents into the sea.

The victory consolidated the Crusaders' hold on Palestine and brought the First Crusade to an end. The majority of its participants returned to Europe.

Ashingdon (Assandune) 40

Date: 18 October 1016.
Location: Between the rivers Crouch and Roach, 5 miles north of Southend-on-Sea, Essex.
War and campaign: Danish Conquest of England.
Opposing sides: (a) King Edmund Ironside; (b) Cnut (Canute).
Objective: The English, having driven the Danes into Essex, forced a battle on them.
Forces engaged: Unknown, although it is unlikely that either side could have fielded more than 7,000 men.
Casualties: Unknown, but those of the English were undoubtedly the greater.
Result: Edmund was defeated and made peace with Cnut, remaining king of an independent Wessex until his death the following month. The Witan then elected Cnut king of the entire country, initiating a 20-year period of strong rule and prosperity.

The battle might have had a different outcome had it not been for the treachery of Edmund's brother-in-law, Eadric of Mercia, who deliberately kept the English right wing out of the fight. This enabled the Danes to outflank Edmund's centre, but despite this the battle was hard-fought and Edmund managed to withdraw with part of his army. Many important members of the English nobility were killed in the fighting.

Asiago (Trentino Offensive) 41

Date: 15 May to 17 June 1916.
Location: The Trentino Alps, northern Italy, between Arco and Cavalese, extending southwards in a salient to Asiago.
War and campaign: First World War: Italy.
Opposing sides: (a) Field Marshal Count Conrad von Hotzendorff, Chief of the Austro-Hungarian General Staff; (b) General Luigi Cadorna, Chief of the Italian General Staff.
Objective: By achieving a breakthrough and advancing towards the Adriatic coast, the Austrians hoped to outflank the Italian armies on the ISONZO sector and compel them to withdraw.
Forces engaged: (a) The Archduke Eugen's army group with the Austro-Hungarian Eleventh (General Viktor Dankl) and Third (General Kovess von Kovesshaza) Armies; (b) Lieutenant-General Count Pecori-Giraldi commanding the Italian First Army.
Casualties: (a) Approximately 30,000, including 2,000 prisoners; (b) approximately 52,000, including 40,000 prisoners and 300 guns captured.
Result: The Austrians gained some ground but difficult terrain and the arrival of Italian reinforcements finally halted the offensive on 10 June. Some of the gains were lost when the Italians counter-attacked and the battle ran down when Conrad was forced to rush troops to the Eastern Front in response to the BRUSILOV OFFENSIVE.

Aspern-Essling 42

Date: 21–22 May 1809.
Location: Villages on the north bank of the Danube some 5 miles east of Vienna.
War and campaign: War of the Fifth Coalition, 1809: Campaign against Austria.
Opposing sides: (a) The Emperor Napoleon commanding the Grand Army; (b) the Archduke Charles commanding the Austrian army.
Objective: Although Napoleon had captured Vienna, the Austrian army still remained in being after its defeats at ABENSBERG and he decided to destroy it after forcing a crossing of the Danube via Lobau Island. The Austrians immediately counter-attacked the French bridgehead.
Forces engaged: (a) 48,000 infantry, 7,000 cavalry and 144 guns – total approximately 60,000; (b) 85,000 infantry, 5,000 cavalry and 300 guns – total approximately 95,000.
Casualties: (a) 21,000 killed and wounded, including Marshal Lannes killed; (b) 23,000 killed and wounded.
Result: Unable to make further progress after two days of savage fighting in which the village of Aspern changed hands no fewer than ten times, the French withdrew to Lobau Island when the bridge connecting it with the south bank was swept away.

This was the first serious check sustained by Napoleon and he was forced to re-plan the battle. See WAGRAM.

Assaye

Date: 23 September 1803.
Location: Village in Berar located between the confluence of the Juah and Kaitna rivers, approximately 250 miles north-east of Bombay.
War and campaign: Second Maratha War: Deccan Campaign.
Opposing sides: (a) Major-General Sir Arthur Wellesley (later Duke of Wellington); (b) Dowlut Rao Scindia and the Rajah of Berar.
Objective: The British intention was to destroy the Maratha field army in the Deccan.
Forces engaged: (a) 4,520 British and Indian troops, including 2,170 infantry and 1,200 cavalry, and a small number of guns; (b) 30,000 cavalry, 17,000 infantry (including 10,500 regulars) and 190 guns.
Casualties: (a) 428 killed and 1,156 wounded or missing; (b) approximately 6,000 killed and wounded and 98 guns captured.
Result: The defeat of the Maratha army which, coupled with a further defeat at LASWARI in Hindustan, caused Scindia to sue for peace. Nevertheless, hostilities between the British and Marathas continued until 1805. Assaye revealed Wellesley's potential as a field commander.

The Maratha army had been disciplined and trained by French instructors, although at Assaye it was a German officer named Pohlmann who commanded its infantry. Wellesley was well aware that to pit his tiny force against the enemy host in open country would be to court disaster, but he observed two villages facing each other on opposite banks of the Kaitna, some way beyond the Maratha left, and correctly deduced that they were connected by a ford. Using broken ground for concealment, he led his troops across this and then deployed to face the enemy with his right protected by the Juah and his left by the Kaitna. This forced the Marathas to turn towards him, but because the front narrowed as the two rivers flowed towards their confluence, they were able to deploy only a fraction of their strength. The British took the initiative and, despite local checks, after three hours had driven the Maratha army off the field. Wellington was later to comment that Assaye had been his greatest victory, and proportionately the bloodiest action he ever witnessed, for although his casualties might be regarded as light, given the nature of his achievement, they amounted to one-third of his force. Napoleon was to sneer that Wellington was a sepoy general, but it is interesting to speculate what his own solution to the problem might have been.

Atbara River

Date: 8 April 1898.
Location: At the confluence of the Nile and Atbara rivers, Sudan.
War and campaign: Sudan Campaigns: Reconquest of the Sudan.
Opposing sides: (a) General Sir Herbert Kitchener (the Sirdar); (b) the Emirs Mahmud and Osman Digna.

Objective: The Mahdists were opposing the advance of the Anglo-Egyptian army up the Nile towards their capital, Omdurman.
Forces engaged: (a) 14,000 men, including an Egyptian infantry division, a British brigade, eight squadrons of Egyptian cavalry, four field artillery batteries, a rocket battery and Maxim machine guns; (b) 12,000 entrenched infantry and 3,000 cavalry.
Casualties: (a) 570 killed and wounded; (b) 3,000 killed and 2,000 captured, including Mahmud.
Result: The Mahdist force was destroyed and the advance on OMDURMAN continued.

Atlanta   45

Date: 20 July to 31 August 1864.
Location: Atlanta, Georgia.
War and campaign: American Civil War: Sherman's Campaign in Georgia.
Opposing sides: (a) Major-General William T. Sherman commanding an army group consisting of Major-General George H. Thomas's Army of the Cumberland, Major-General James B. McPherson's Army of the Tennessee and Major-General John M. Schofield's Army of the Ohio; (b) General John B. Hood commanding the reinforced Army of Tennessee.
Objective: Sherman's intention was to encircle and capture Atlanta, one of the Confederacy's most important railway and supply centres.
Forces engaged: (a) Approximately 100,000; (b) approximately 60,000.
Casualties: (a) Approximately 8,000; (b) approximately 15,000.
Result: Hood evacuated Atlanta during the night of 31 August. On 15 November Sherman began his march to SAVANNAH, some 300 miles distant, carving a 50-mile-wide swathe of destruction across Georgia. At the political level the capture of Atlanta removed the threat to President Lincoln from the Peace Democrats.

Hood conducted a vigorous defence, mounting aggressive counter-attacks at Peachtree Creek (20 July), Atlanta, during which McPherson was killed (22 July), Ezra Church (28 July) and Jonesboro (31 August), but was unable to sustain the rate of attrition and, with his army in danger of being isolated, was forced to withdraw. The comparatively low casualties incurred during the capture of Atlanta itself conceal the fact that since leaving CHATTANOOGA on 5 May the Federals had sustained losses amounting to 22,000 men, while those of the Confederates amounted to 27,000. See also NASHVILLE.

Aughrim   46

Date: 12 July 1691.
Location: Village near Ballinasloe, County Galway, Eire.
War and campaign: War of the League of Augsburg, 1688–1697: Jacobite Campaign in Ireland, 1689–1691.
Opposing sides: (a) General Godert de Ginkel commanding the Williamite army; (b) the Earl of Lucan and the Marquis de St-Ruth commanding the Jacobite army.

Objective: Following its victory at THE BOYNE, the Williamite army steadily consolidated its hold on Ireland. At Aughrim the Jacobite army was brought to battle.
Forces engaged: (a) 18,000 (English, Irish Protestant, Dutch and French Huguenot); (b) 25,000 (Irish Catholic and French).
Casualties: (a) 700 killed and wounded; (b) up to 7,000 killed, including St-Ruth, the majority during the ruthless pursuit.
Result: The Jacobite army was destroyed. Limerick, the last Jacobite stronghold, surrendered on terms in October, bringing the war in Ireland to an end.

The Jacobite position was protected by a bog and at first Ginkel's troops could make no impression on the enemy. However, a panic flight ensued when the Williamite cavalry discovered a way round and launched a flank attack.

Austerlitz ('The Battle of the Three Emperors')

Date: 2 December 1805.
Location: Slavkov (formerly Austerlitz) village, 5 miles east of Brno, Czechoslovakia.
War and campaign: War of the Third Coalition, 1805–1806: Campaign in Austria, 1805.
Opposing sides: (a) The Emperor Napoleon I; (b) the Emperor Francis II of Austria and Tsar Alexander of Russia, *de facto* commander General Mikhail Kutuzov.
Objective: Having destroyed an Austrian army at ULM and occupied Vienna, Napoleon marched north and successfully tempted the combined Austro-Russian army into fighting a battle on ground of his own choosing.
Forces engaged: (a) 73,100 men with 139 guns; (b) 85,700 men with 278 guns.
Casualties: (a) Approximately 8,500 killed and wounded, plus 570 prisoners; (b) 16,000 killed and wounded, 11,000 prisoners and 185 guns captured.
Result: A crushing defeat for the Austro-Russian army. Although the United Kingdom and Russia remained at war with Napoleon, Austria sued for peace immediately and the Coalition collapsed.

Kutuzov began the battle with an assault on the French right, hoping to sever Napoleon's communications with Vienna. With the arrival of Davout's corps the threat was contained and Kuruzov committed more troops to this sector. On the French left, however, Lannes and Murat repulsed Austro-Russian attacks and then took the initiative, pushing the Allies steadily eastwards. In the light of this Napoleon, observing that the steady movement of troops southward across the Pratzen Plateau had weakened the Allied centre, launched Soult's corps in a concentrated thrust which took the high ground. Kutuzov counter-attacked with the Russian Guard, but, while this forced Napoleon to commit his own reserve in response, the French not only retained their gains but extended their advance as far as the village of Austerlitz, cutting the Allied army in two. Napoleon then directed Soult against the rear of the Allied troops which were already engaged with Davout. Now surrounded, these attempted to escape across frozen lakes but the ice, weakened by French gunfire, broke and many were drowned.

Badajoz, Siege and Storming of

Date: 16 March to 6 April 1812.
Location: Fortress city near the Spanish/Portuguese frontier, located on the Guadiana river due east of Lisbon.
War and campaign: Peninsular War, 1807–1814: Campaign of 1812.
Opposing sides: (a) General the Earl of Wellington commanding the Allied army; ((b) General Armand Phillipon commanding the French garrison.
Objective: Having captured CIUDAD RODRIGO on 19 January, Wellington now sought possession of this second frontier fortress, which covered the southern invasion route from Portugal, with a view to mounting offensive operations in French-occupied Spain.
Forces engaged: (a) Approximately 32,000; (b) approximately 5,000.
Casualties: (a) Approximately 4,000 British and 1,000 Portuguese killed and wounded; (b) approximately 1,500 killed and wounded, plus 3,500 prisoners.
Result: The fortress was stormed and Wellington advanced into Spain (see SALAMANCA).

The investment of the town was completed on 16 March. During night of 24 March the outlying bastion of Fort Picurina was captured, enabling the artillery to start opening breaches in the main walls. These were stormed at several points in a bitterly contested night assault on 6 April. Such was the ferocity of the defence and so great the Allied casualties that Wellington's troops were out of hand for the next three days, only the threat of capital punishment serving to restore discipline.

Baghdad

Date: 13 December 1916 to 11 March 1917.
Location: From south of Kut-al-Amara northwards up the Tigris to beyond Baghdad.
War and campaign: First World War: Mesopotamia.
Opposing sides: (a) General Sir Frederick Stanley Maude commanding the Tigris Army; (b) Khalil Pasha commanding the Turkish Sixth Army.
Objective: The British intention was to avenge the defeat at KUT-AL-AMARA and capture Baghdad.
Forces engaged: (a) I Indian Corps (Lt-General A. S. Cobbe) and III Indian Corps (Maj-General W. R. Marshall), plus a cavalry division – total 45,000 men; (b) initially Kiazam Karabekir Bey's Turkish XVIII Corps with three divisions (20,000 men), joined latterly by Ali Ishan Pasha's Turkish XIII Corps (14,000 men).
Casualties: (a) Estimated 10,000; (b) the Sixth Army was so badly mauled that it no longer presented a serious threat (XVIII Corps was all but destroyed, losing about 9,000 men as prisoners alone).
Result: Kut-al-Amara was abandoned by the Turks and on 11 March Baghdad was captured. The latter event restored British prestige in the Middle East while that of Turkey was severely damaged.

Khali's victory at KUT-AL-AMARA had made him contemptuous of his opponents and, leaving Kiazam Karabekir with a covering force to hold what he believed to be impregnable positions downstream, he left with the rest of the Sixth Army to deal with a Russian incursion into northern Persia. Maude, however, worked his way steadily up the right bank of the Tigris, which was less well defended. In danger of being surrounded, Kiazim abandoned his position and withdrew towards Baghdad, having already sustained serious losses. Too late, Khalil despatched Ali Ishan's corps back along the Diyala valley, but Maude easily fended off the threat and took Baghdad without the need for a pitched battle, concentrating thereafter on pushing the enemy beyond striking distance of the city. Throughout this model campaign, Maude had employed the indirect approach, crossing and re-crossing the Tigris to outflank Turkish positions. For his part, Khalil was handicapped by the fact that reinforcements destined for the Mesopotamian Front were diverted to Palestine (see GAZA, THIRD BATTLE OF).

'Bagration', Operation   50

Date: 22 June to 27 August 1944.
Location: Byelorussia and Eastern Poland.
War and campaign: Second World War: Russian Front.
Opposing sides: (a) General I. K. Bagramyan commanding the 1st Baltic Front, General Ivan Chernyakhoski commanding the 3rd Byelorussian Front, General G. F. Khakarov commanding the 2nd Byelorussian Front and General Konstantin Rokossovsky commanding the 1st Byelorussian Front; (b) Field Marshal Ernst Busch commanding Army Group Centre.
Objective: The intention of the Soviet High Command was to drive the Germans out of Byelorussia and inflict crippling losses on Army Group Centre.
Forces engaged: (a) 1,200,000 men, 4,000 tanks, 28,600 artillery weapons and 5,300 aircraft; (b) 1,200,000 men, 900 tanks, 10,000 artillery weapons and 1,300 aircraft.
Casualties: (a) Unknown, but described by the Soviet commanders themselves as 'appalling', particularly during the break-in phase; (b) the equivalent of between 25 and 28 divisions destroyed, with 350,000 men lost, including 21 generals captured and ten killed.
Result: Byelorussia was liberated, the German Army Group Centre was effectively destroyed and as a direct consequence of this the neighbouring Army Group North was isolated.

Busch, aware of the Soviet preparations, requested permission to withdraw behind the Berezina river so that the initial weight of the Russian blow would land in empty space, thereby dislocating the timetable for the offensive and creating conditions for a counter-stroke. Hitler dismissed the idea and ordered Army Group Centre to hold its ground. While the Germans undoubtedly fought hard and inflicted terrible casualties, large numbers were cut off at Vitebsk on 27 June, at Mogilev on the 28th, at Bobruysk on the 29th and east of Minsk on 3 July. No fewer than 40 Soviet tank brigades and numerous cavalry mechanized groups swept on into what had formerly been eastern Poland, reaching Wilno on 13 July, Lublin on the 23rd and Brest-Litovsk on the 28th. When the offensive finally ran down as it approached the Vistula during the last week of August, it had torn a 250-mile gap in the German line and advanced some 450 miles. Operation 'Bagration' is regarded by Russian historians as the decisive battle of the Great Patriotic War and the methods employed are still studied by the Soviet Army. Certainly, it dealt the Wehrmacht a blow from which it never fully recovered. Whether, during its final stages, the Soviets still possessed the means or the will to assist the concurrent rising by the Polish Home Army in Warsaw remains the subject of debate.

Balaklava 51

Date: 25 October 1854.
Location: 6 miles south of Sevastopol, Crimea.
War and campaign: Crimean War.
Opposing sides: (a) Field Marshal Lord Raglan; (b) General Prince Alexander Menshikov.
Objective: The Russians were attempting to cut the communications of the British portion of the Allied army besieging SEVASTOPOL by attacking Balaklava harbour.
Forces engaged: (a) 1,500 infantry, 1,600 British and 150 French cavalry and nine guns – total 3,250; (b) 22,000 infantry, 3,400 cavalry and 78 guns – total 26,000.
Casualties: (a) 615; (b) 627.
Result: The Russian attack was repulsed.

The battle witnessed three remarkable feats of arms: first, the repulse of a portion of the Russian cavalry advancing directly on Balaklava by the 'Thin Red Line' of the 93rd Highlanders, who received the attack in line rather than the more usual square formation; second, the Charge of the Heavy Brigade, which repulsed the main body of the Russian cavalry; and third (and best remembered), the heroic failure of the Charge of the Light Brigade, initiated to recover guns being removed from Turkish redoubts which the Russians had overrun. Thanks to an inaccurate appreciation of terrain factors, coupled with poor staff work and a combination of unfortunate circumstances, the Light Brigade attacked the wrong guns and charged the length of what subsequently became known as the Valley of Death, swept on three sides by enemy fire. The Russian battery was captured but was untenable and the survivors withdrew the way they had come, partially covered by a charge of the French Chasseurs d'Afrique. Of the 670 participants in the charge, 247 were killed or wounded and 475 horses were lost. In effect, the Light Brigade was destroyed and its surviving mounts died of starvation during the subsequent winter. Nevertheless, the ferocity of the British response, and in particular the reckless courage of the Light Brigade, provided a severe shock for the Russians, who did not press the potentially decisive advantage they held during the early stages of the battle.

Ballinamuck 52

Date: 8 September 1798.
Location: Village near Granard, County Longford, Eire.
War and campaign: Rebellion in Ireland, 1798: French attacks on the British Isles. See also FISHGUARD.
Opposing sides: (a) General Lord Charles Cornwallis and Lieutenant-General Gerard Lake commanding the government forces; (b) General Joseph Humbert commanding the French and rebel army.
Objective: After landing at Killala Bay in Mayo on 22 August, a small French force recruited local support and inflicted a surprising defeat on government troops at Castlebar. It then advanced on Dublin but at Ballinamuck was trapped between two British columns and forced to fight.

Forces engaged: (a) 5,000 with Cornwallis and 4,000 with Lake; (b) 850 French and approximately 1,000 rebels.
Casualties: (a) Light; (b) French losses comparatively light, but several hundred rebels killed and 90 captured.
Result: Humbert fought for a token 30 minutes then surrendered, the status of his men as regular troops being respected; the rebels, however, were not so fortunate and most of their casualties were incurred during the pursuit.

Given the size of his force, Humbert had achieved a great deal and his early successes caused considerable alarm. His arrival in Ireland, however, was too late to be of much assistance to the rebellion for most areas were back under government control and the largest rebel army had been destroyed at VINEGAR HILL on 12 June.

Baltimore (Gadfly Wood) 53

Date: 12 September 1814.
Location: 5 miles east of Baltimore on the road to North Point, Chesapeake Bay, Maryland.
War and campaign: War of 1812: Chesapeake Bay theatre.
Opposing sides: (a) Major-General Robert Ross, succeeded by Colonel Arthur Brooke; (b) Senator Samuel Smith.
Objective: The British intention was to capture Baltimore but the advance of the landing force was contested by an American militia brigade at Gadfly Wood.
Forces engaged: (a) Approximately 4,000; (b) approximately 3,200.
Casualties: (a) 319 killed and wounded, including Ross killed; (b) 163 killed and wounded and about 200 captured.
Result: The Americans were driven from their position. Next day Brooke examined the entrenchments covering the city and decided that these could not be assaulted successfully with the small force at his disposal; the decision was a wise one, as the works were held by approximately 13,000 militia. Following the failure of Admiral Sir George Cockburn's covering fleet to subdue the defences of Fort McHenry, the landing force re-embarked on 14 September. See NEW ORLEANS.

Ross, a popular and humane officer, was killed by sniper fire during the early stages of the engagement. A line of sunken hulks prevented Cockburn's ships from engaging Fort McHenry within effective range; little or no damage was sustained by either side during several hours of sustained firing. Nevertheless, the engagement was noisy and spectacular and inspired the American lawyer and poet Francis Scott Key, who witnessed it from the deck of HMS *Minden*, to write the words of *The Star-Spangled Banner*. Curiously, Congress did not adopt the song as the official anthem of the United States until 3 March 1931.

Bannockburn 54

Date: 24 June 1314.
Location: 1 mile south-east of Stirling.
War and campaign: The Anglo-Scottish Wars.
Opposing sides: (a) King Edward II; (b) King Robert the Bruce.

Objective: The English intention was to relieve Stirling Castle; the Scots sought a decisive battle.
Forces engaged: (a) 1,000 cavalry and 17,000 infantry – total 18,000; (b) 500 cavalry and 9,000 infantry – total 9,500.
Casualties: (a) 22 barons, 68 knights and 1,000 infantry (many more were killed or capturing during the pursuit); (b) two knights and approximately 500 infantry. The figures of 15,000 and 4,000 sometimes quoted for the respective English and Scottish losses are unrealistic, given the size of the armies engaged.
Result: Bruce won a decisive victory which secured Scottish independence.

On the day before the battle the English had pushed out two reconnaissance groups in the direction of Stirling Castle, but both were repulsed. During one of these encounters Bruce brained an English knight, Sir Henry de Bohun, who engaged him in single combat. Next morning Bruce formed his army in four schiltrons of pikemen, retaining his cavalry in reserve, and moved forward against the English, who had crossed the Bannock Burn. Edward chose to ignore the clear lessons of FALKIRK (1298), and indeed his entire conduct of the battle was inept. His cavalry, advancing ahead of the infantry, attacked the schiltrons, masking the fire of the English archers in the process, but were unable to penetrate them. The archers were then moved out on to the right flank, from where they opened a galling fire, but Bruce committed his own cavalry reserve and, unsupported, they were ridden down. The schiltrons then advanced into the heart of the English infantry, which was disordered as a result of the repulse of the cavalry. Observing the approach of Scottish reinforcements, Edward's army broke and fled.

Bardia   55

Date: 3–5 January 1941.
Location: Fortified town and harbour in north-eastern Cyrenaica, Libya.
War and campaign: Second World War: North Africa.
Opposing sides: (a) Lieutenant-General Richard O'Connor commanding XIII Corps and Major-General Iven Mackay commanding the 6th Australian Division; (b) General Bergonzoli commanding the Italian garrison.
Objective: The British capture of Bardia.
Forces engaged: (a) 6th Australian Division, 16th British Brigade and one squadron of Matilda II tanks (7 RTR); (b) 1st and 2nd Blackshirt Divisions, elements of 62nd, 63rd and 64th Divisions – total 45,000 men, supported by 400 guns and over 100 tanks.
Casualties: (a) 150 killed and 350 wounded; (b) apart from a handful of men including Bergonzoli, who succeeded in reaching TOBRUK, the entire garrison was killed, wounded or captured, prisoners numbering 38,000 and the booty including 120 tanks, 700 assorted vehicles and all the artillery.
Result: A complete victory for the British, resulting in a further lowering of Italian morale. See also SIDI BARRANI, TOBRUK (FIRST BATTLE OF) and BEDA FOMM.

Barnet   56

Date: 14 April 1471.
Location: Immediately to the north of Barnet, Hertfordshire.

War and campaign: Wars of the Roses, 1455–1485.
Opposing sides: (a) Edward IV commanding the Yorkist army; (b) the Earl of Warwick commanding the Lancastrians.
Objective: Richard Neville, Earl of Warwick (otherwise known as 'The Kingmaker'), had quarrelled with Edward IV and transferred his support to the Lancastrians, releasing Henry VI from captivity and restoring him to the throne. Edward fled abroad briefly but returned to raise an army with which he intercepted Warwick's southward march on London.
Forces engaged: (a) 10,000; (b) 15,000.
Casualties: (a) Approximately 500; (b) approximately 1,000, including Warwick killed.
Result: Warwick's army was defeated, leaving Edward free to deal with a second Lancastrian army raised by Queen Margaret in the west. See TEWKESBURY.

The right wings of both armies were victorious and pursued their opponents off the field, with the result that the central battle had pivoted at right angles to its original axis. However, the fighting took place in thick mist and when the Lancastrian right, under the Earl of Oxford, returned to the battlefield it clashed accidentally but violently with the rear of its own centre, provoking cries of treachery. Edward, observing the confusion, launched his reserve in a counter-attack which completed the Lancastrian rout. Both sides were equipped with artillery, although this seems to have played little part in the battle.

Barrossa (Chiclana)   57

Date: 5 March 1811.
Location: Some miles to the south of Cadiz, Spain.
War and campaign: Peninsular War, 1807–1814: Campaign of 1811.
Opposing sides: (a) Major-General Thomas Graham; (b) Marshal Claude Victor.
Objective: A British seaborne sortie against the rear of the French army besieging Cadiz.
Forces engaged: (a) 5,200 (a 10,000-strong Spanish force under General Lapena was also present but took no part in the action); (b) 7,000.
Casualties: (a) 1,238; (b) 2,062.
Result: A British victory of strategic importance which, while it failed to break the siege of Cadiz, caused the French to commit more troops to the area, to no purpose.

Bassano   58

Date: 8 September 1796.
Location: 30 miles north of Padua, Venezia, Italy.
War and campaign: War of the First Coalition, 1792–1798: Italian Campaign, 1796–1797.
Opposing sides: (a) General Napoleon Bonaparte commanding the Army of Italy; (b) General Count Dagobert Wurmser commanding the Austrian army.

Objective: The Austrians were attempting to relieve Mantua, which was being besieged by the French.
Forces engaged: (a) Approximately 30,000; (b) 26,000.
Casualties: (a) Uncertain, but moderate; (b) 8,000 killed, wounded and missing and 6,000 captured.
Result: An Austrian defeat.

Wurmser and 12,000 men managed to fight their way into Mantua, bringing the garrison's strength to 28,000, but they were unable to break the siege. See also LODI, ARCOLA and RIVOLI.

Bataan

Date: 2 January to 6 May 1942.
Location: Peninsula forming the western side of Manila Bay, Luzon, Philippine Islands.
War and campaign: Second World War: Central Pacific.
Opposing sides: (a) Lieutenant-General Masaharu Homma commanding the Fourteenth Army; (b) General Douglas MacArthur commanding the US/Filipino army until 11 March, then Major-General Jonathan M. Wainwright.
Objective: The Japanese sought to complete their conquest of Luzon, the most important of the Philippine Islands.
Forces engaged: (a) 16th and 48th Divisions, plus two tank regiments and a medium artillery group, reinforced by the 4th Division in March – total about 50,000; (b) I Corps (1st, 11th and 91st Divisions) and II Corps (21st, 41st, 51st and part of 31st Divisions), plus remnants of a two-battalion Provisional Tank Group – total about 80,000 (of whom some 22,400 were American and the remainder Filipino).
Casualties: (a) 12,000 killed and wounded, plus many incapacitated by tropical diseases; (b) 16,000 killed and wounded, the remainder becoming prisoners of war.
Result: A Japanese victory and the largest capitulation in the history of the United States Army.

Although MacArthur possessed the larger army, the majority of his Filipino troops were untrained levies and, with this in mind, his strategy in the event of a Japanese invasion was to withdraw into the Bataan Peninsula, which offered secure flanks, and hold out until the Pacific Fleet arrived with reinforcements. Unfortunately, while he completed the withdrawal successfully, the Pacific Fleet had already been neutralized at Pearl Harbor. Homma launched a major offensive on 9 January, forcing the Americans back to their final defence line (although he incurred heavy casualties in the process), and a comparative lull ensued during which he awaited the arrival of reinforcements. Both armies were now ravaged by tropical diseases, and MacArthur's difficulties were compounded by the fact that his men were already on half-rations; sufficient food had been stockpiled on Bataan to feed 43,000 men for six months, but the 80,000 combatants actually present also had to share their rations with 26,000 civilian refugees from the Manila area. On 11 March MacArthur left the Philippines for Australia in response to a specific order from President Roosevelt. His responsibilities were assumed by Wainwright, and Major-General Edward P. King was appointed field commander on Bataan. Homma launched his final offensive on 3 April, achieving a breakthrough, and King surrendered on 9 April. The captive army was then subjected to a 65-mile march in intense heat, with scant rations or water, to its prison camp at San Fernando; during this, the infamous 'Death March', hundreds who collapsed were simply murdered by their guards, and hundreds more never recovered from the ordeal. About 2,000 men escaped from Bataan to the island fortress of Corregidor, in the mouth of Manila Bay, but this in turn was stormed on 5 May and Wainwright surrendered the following day, instructing his troops in the southern Philippines to conform.

Bautzen   60

Date: 20–22 May 1813.	
Location: Town on the Spree river, 30 miles north-east of Dresden, Germany.	
War and campaign: War of the Sixth Coalition, 1812–1814: Campaign in Germany, 1813.	
Opposing sides: (a) The Emperor Napoleon I commanding the French army; (b) General Ludwig Wittgenstein and Prince Gerhard von Blücher commanding the Allied army.	
Objective: Having captured Dresden on 9 May (see Lützen, 1813), Napoleon followed the Allied army eastwards until he found it occupying a strong defensive position around Bautzen, covered by the Spree. Despatching Ney with one wing of his army on a wide flank march to the north, he mounted a frontal assault with the remainder.	
Forces engaged: (a) 115,000 with Napoleon, 84,000 with Ney; (b) 100,000 Russians and Prussians.	
Casualties: (a) 13,000; (b) 15,000.	
Result: The Allies were defeated but retreated into Silesia. Napoleon, lacking a strong cavalry arm, was unable to make an effective pursuit. Nevertheless, on 4 June he managed to negotiate an armistice and this enabled him to train his army, which now contained a high proportion of young conscripts. The truce lasted until 12 August, when Austria joined the Coalition and declared war on France. See Dresden.	

Napoleon's frontal assault succeeded in forcing crossings of the Spree and capturing Bautzen. Unfortunately, Ney did not read the battle correctly and his flank attack was late in developing. Wittgenstein was thus able to escape from the trap which had been set for him.

Baylen (Bailen), Capitulation of   61

Date: 19 July 1808.	
Location: Town on the Guadalquivir river west of Linares, Cordoba, southern Spain.	
War and campaign: Peninsular War, 1807–1814: Spanish Insurrection of 1808.	
Opposing sides: (a) General Pierre Dupont; (b) General Francisco de Castanos.	
Objective: The Spanish, resenting the imposition of Napoleon's brother Joseph as King of Spain, had risen en masse. Near Bailen a French corps was isolated by a larger force of insurrectos.	
Forces engaged: (a) 20,000; (b) 35,000.	

Casualties: (a) Entire corps killed, wounded or captured; (b) light.

Result: Dupont's corps, short of water, was unable to break out and surrendered on the promise of safe conduct to France. This, the first surrender of a Napoleonic army, not only fuelled the Spanish insurrection but also provided much-needed encouragement for Napoleon's enemies elsewhere in Europe. Strategically, the engagement left the other French army in the Peninsula, commanded by Junot, isolated in Portugal (see VIMEIRO).

Castanos' men were undisciplined levies who promptly violated the surrender terms and massacred most of the unarmed prisoners; the survivors were confined to prison hulks from which few emerged. As a result of this and similar incidents, the Franco-Spanish aspect of the Peninsular War was marked by savage atrocities on both sides, the French taking the view that the *guerrilleros'* activities placed them outside the accepted rules of warfare and the Spanish responding in kind.

Beda Fomm 62

Date: 5–7 February 1941.
Location: 50 miles south-west of Benghazi, Cyrenaica, Libya.
War and campaign: Second World War: North Africa.
Opposing sides: (a) Lieutenant-General Richard O'Connor commanding XIII Corps and Major-General Michael O'Moore Creagh commanding the 7th Armoured Division; (b) Marshal Rodolfo Graziani commanding Italian forces in Libya and General Tellera commanding the Tenth Army.
Objective: The British sought to entrap the remnants of the Italian Tenth Army as it withdrew from Benghazi.
Forces engaged: (a) Elements of the 7th Armoured Division, all seriously below strength; (b) Tenth Army, containing elements of three infantry divisions and one armoured brigade – total about 30,000 men and over 100 tanks.
Casualties: (a) About 50 men and a handful of tanks; (b) about 1,500 killed and wounded and 25,000 prisoners of war, plus 100 tanks, 216 guns and 1,500 wheeled vehicles captured.
Result: The destruction of the Italian Tenth Army and the complete occupation of Cyrenaica by British forces. British morale at home was reinforced by the culminating victory of the brilliant campaign which O'Connor had fought against the numerically superior Italian army in North Africa.

Having ascertained that the Italians intended withdrawing south along the coast road from Benghazi, O'Connor decided to despatch the 7th Armoured Division across the base of the Benghazi Bulge along the axis Mechili–Msus–Antelat with the object of establishing a block at Beda Fomm; simultaneously, the 6th Australian Division was to follow up the Italian withdrawal along the coast, the result being to entrap the Tenth Army between XIII Corps' two major formations. The 7th Armoured Division's advance guard, named Combeforce after its commander, reached Beda Fomm shortly after noon on 5 February and barely had time to emplace its guns when the head of the Italian column appeared. Combeforce beat off several attacks and the 4th Armoured Brigade (2 RTR, 3rd and 7th Hussars) closed in on the enemy flank. Next day the Italians mounted a series of heavy attacks as they strove to break out of the trap. During these Tellera was mortally wounded and General Bergonzoli assumed command of the Tenth Army. The fighting had seriously depleted the strength of the 4th Armoured Brigade, but at the critical moment the 7th Armoured Brigade (1 RTR) arrived, provoking Italian suspicions that the British had adequate reserves in hand; in fact, the 7th Armoured Division had never been able to field more than 32 cruiser and 50 light tanks for this operation, and these figures had been reduced by casualties. At dawn on 7 February a final attempt to break out was repulsed and Bergonzoli surrendered. The battle was a classic example of a numerically inferior force using the indirect approach to trap and destroy a larger army.

Belfort 63

Date: 15–17 January 1871.
Location: On the Lisaine river west of Belfort, a fortress town located in the gap between the Vosges and Jura mountains, Alsace, France.
War and campaign: Franco–Prussian War, 1870–1871.
Opposing sides: (a) General Wilhelm Werder commanding the besiegers; (b) General Charles Bourbaki commanding the relief force.
Objective: A French army was attempting to relieve the besieged fortress.
Forces engaged: (a) 60,000; (b) 150,000.
Casualties: (a) 1,900; (b) 6,000.
Result: The French, inexperienced and largely untrained, failed to break through.

Bourbaki attempted suicide and was replaced by General Justin Clinchant who, in danger of being trapped by the arrival of a fresh German force, led over 80,000 of his men into internment in Switzerland. The 17,600-strong garrison of Belfort, commanded by Colonel Pierre Denfert-Rochereau, continued to resist until the war ended, when it marched out with the honours of war, but only in response to a direct order from the French government.

Belgrade 64

Date: 16 August 1717.
Location: Belgrade city and suburbs south of the Danube, Yugoslavia.
War and campaign: Austro–Turkish War, 1716–1718.
Opposing sides: (a) Prince Eugene of Savoy commanding the Austrian army; (b) Ibrahim Pasha, Grand Vizier of the Ottoman Empire, commanding the Turkish army, and Mustapha Pasha commanding the garrison.
Objective: A Turkish army was attempting to relieve Belgrade, which the Austrians were besieging.
Forces engaged: (a) 40,000 plus 10,000 in the siege lines; (b) approximately 150,000 in the relieving army plus 30,000 within the Belgrade defences.
Casualties: (a) 5,338 killed and wounded; (b) approximately 15,000 killed and wounded.
Result: The Turkish army was routed.

Belgrade surrendered on 21 August.

Berezina River

Date: 26–28 November 1812.
Location: On the banks of the Berezina, near Borisov, Byelorussia.
War and campaign: War of the Sixth Coalition: Napoleon's Invasion of Russia, 1812.
Opposing sides: (a) The Emperor Napoleon I commanding the Grand Army; (b) Generals Mikhail Golenishev-Kutuzov, Prince Ludwig Wittgenstein and Tchichagov commanding the Russian armies.
Objective: Continuing its retreat from Moscow in Arctic conditions (see MALOYAROSLAVETS), the Grand Army, now close to starvation and harried continuously by Cossack irregulars, approached the Berezina only to find that three Russian armies were converging on the area. The French were therefore compelled to fight for control of the crossing sites.
Forces engaged: (a) 31,000 effectives; (b) 72,000.
Casualties: (a) Estimated at 45,000 (the Russians claimed to have recovered 36,000 bodies from the river alone); (b) uncertain, but moderate.
Result: The French fought their way through, but at such terrible cost that the Grand Army was finished as a fighting force. The Russians maintained their pursuit as far as the Niemen.

Fighting took place on both banks of the river as the Russians closed in. Panic contributed to the French casualties but when the Grand Army burned its bridges on the morning of 29 November some 7,000 stragglers were cut off and most of them were massacred. The entire campaign had cost 400,000 French and 300,000 Russian lives. On 5 December Napoleon left for Paris to raise fresh armies but the myth of his invincibility had been shattered and his former allies were about to turn on him, destroying his empire. See LÜTZEN (1813).

Berlin

Date: 16 April to 2 May 1945.
Location: Area stretching from the Baltic coast to the Czechoslovakian frontier.
War and campaign: Second World War: Russian Front.
Opposing sides: (a) Marshal Georgi Zhukov and Marshal Ivan Konev commanding their respective Fronts; (b) Adolf Hitler, Supreme Commander of the remaining German armies.
Objective: The Soviet intention was to destroy the remnants of the German armies in the east and capture Berlin before the Western Allies.
Forces engaged: (a) 2nd Byelorussian Front (Marshal Konstantin Rokossovsky), 1st Byelorussian Front (Zhukov) and 1st Ukrainian Front (Konev) – total 2,500,000; (b) Army Group Centre under Field Marshal Ferdinand Schorner and Army Group Vistula under Colonel-General Gotthard Heinrici – total 1,250,000.
Casualties: (a) Estimated 700,000; (b) estimated 1,000,000.
Result: The capture of Berlin, ending the Second World War in Europe, and the suicide of Hitler.

Following an intense artillery and air bombardment, the Russians smashed through Army Group Centre and advanced westwards. While advanced units probed into Berlin's eastern suburbs, the German capital was isolated by a double envelopment to the west, the jaws of the trap being closed by the 1st Byelorussian Front from the north and the 1st Ukrainian Front from the south. The defences were systematically crushed as the Russians closed in towards the city centre. Hitler, divorced from reality, continued to issue orders to non-existent armies from the depths of the Führerbunker, but at length accepted the situation and took his own life on 30 April. The Reichstag fell on 1 May and next day the German garrison commander, General Weidling, surrendered his remaining 135,000 troops. Their armoured elements and air support having been destroyed in the battle, those German troops who could do so retired rapidly westwards, hoping to surrender to the advancing British and American armies rather than fall into the hands of the Russians.

Betwa, The 67

Date: 1 April 1858.	
Location: Near Jhansi, Central India.	
War and campaign: Indian Mutiny, 1857–1858: Central Indian Campaign.	
Opposing sides: (a) Major-General Sir Hugh Rose commanding the Central India Field Force; (b) Tantia Topi.	
Objective: A large rebel force was advancing to the relief of the Rani of Jhansi, besieged in her capital by the British.	
Forces engaged: (a) 1,500 British and Indian troops, including a contingent from the Nizam of Hyderabad, with three field batteries; (b) 22,000 men and 28 guns.	
Casualties: (a) Light; (b) 1,500 killed, an unknown number of wounded and all artillery captured.	
Result: Tantia Topi's army was routed and set fire to the jungle to cover its flight. Jhansi, held by 12,000 rebels with 40 guns, was stormed on 3 April. Nine months earlier, the city had been the scene of a massacre of European women and children, and the troops showed no mercy to the garrison. The Rani escaped – see GWALIOR.	

The battle provides an astonishing lesson in the superiority of a small, disciplined and highly motivated force over sheer mass. As Tantia Topi's horde surged forward, covered by the fire of its numerous guns, Rose ordered his infantry to lie down in dead ground. Then, at the critical moment, he ordered the whole line, including cavalry, to charge. This was the last thing the enemy expected of this tiny force, and they broke at the first shock, being pursued across the Betwa, in which many of them drowned. Rose only employed a portion of his very limited resources in the battle; the rest of his troops continued with their siege operations.

Bhurtpore, Siege of 68

Date: December 1825 to 18 January 1826.	
Location: Bharatpur, 75 miles south of Delhi.	
War and campaign: British intervention to settle the disputed succession.	

Opposing sides: (a) General Lord Combermere; (b) the illegal Regent of Bhurtpore.
Objective: The fortress, which had successfully withstood a siege in 1805 and was regarded as impregnable by the Indians, had become a symbol of defiance to the East India Company and was again besieged.
Forces engaged: (a) One cavalry and two infantry divisions, plus a large siege train; (b) uncertain.
Casualties: (a) Approximately 1,000 killed and wounded; (b) approximately 8,000 killed and wounded.
Result: The fortress was stormed. The moral effect on Indian opinion was considerable.

As several weeks of sustained gunfire had caused little damage to the massive walls, Combermere decided to resort to mining. Two small mines were exploded and these brought the defenders crowding to the walls to meet the attack. Then a mine containing 10,000lb of gunpowder was detonated beneath them, blowing hundreds into the air and showering the assault columns with shattered masonry. The breach was then stormed in bitter fighting. During this hundreds more of the defenders were forced over the edge of a nullah some sixty feet deep, where their quilted cotton armour was set on fire by burning debris and many perished as a result.

Bilbao

Date: 1 April to 18 June 1937.
Location: City on the northern coast of Spain.
War and campaign: Spanish Civil War, 1936–1939.
Opposing sides: (a) General Emilio Mola, succeeded by General Fidel Davila, in command of the Nationalists; (b) General de la Encomienda.
Objective: Following their defeat at GUADALAJARA, the Nationalists turned north with the intention of eliminating the Republican enclave in the Basque region.
Forces engaged: (a) 50,000; (b) 40,000.
Casualties: (a) Moderate; (b) heavy.
Result: The Republicans abandoned the city after their principal defence line, the so-called 'Ring of Steel', had been breached. Following up, Davila took Santander on 25 August; by the end of the year all of north-western Spain was under Nationalist control. These defeats left the Republicans isolated in central and eastern Spain.

On 25 April, as the Nationalists closed in on Bilbao, the village of Guernica, some miles to the east, was attacked by Luftwaffe aircraft flying in support. The loss of life among the civilian population shocked world opinion and is commemorated in Picasso's painting named after the village.

Bladensburg

Date: 24 August 1814.
Location: Village on the East Branch river, 5 miles north-east of Washington, D.C.

War and campaign: War of 1812: Chesapeake Bay theatre.
Opposing sides: (a) Major-General Robert Ross commanding the landing force; (b) Major-General William Winder.
Objective: A landing force from Admiral Sir George Cockburn's squadron in Chesapeake Bay was put ashore at Bendict on the Patuxent river and began marching on Washington. At Bladensburg it was opposed by a hastily assembled American army consisting mainly of militia regiments.
Forces engaged: (a) Approximately 4,000, with two 3pdr guns and Congreve rockets; (b) approximately 6,500, with some 20 guns.
Casualties: (a) 64 killed and 185 wounded; (b) 26 killed, 51 wounded and about 100 prisoners, plus the artillery captured.
Result: The American army was routed. The public buildings of Washington were burned in reprisal for the burning of York (now Toronto) the previous year and the landing force retired to its ships. See also BALTIMORE.

The battle was witnessed by President James Madison. Major-General Winder, commanding the American army, was a political appointee with limited ability and had already been involved in one disaster (see STONY CREEK) but had been exchanged. The landing force lacked cavalry or worthwhile artillery but solved its difficulties by mounting fifty artillerymen on commandeered horses and substituting easily portable Congreve rockets for guns. Ross's troops were mainly seasoned veterans of the Peninsular War and only their advance guard, about 1,500 strong, was involved in such serious fighting as there was. The untrained American militia, unnerved by the determined advance and alarmed by the erratic flight of the rockets, quickly bolted, leaving some 500 regular marines and seamen under Commodore Joshua Barney to be overrun after a courageous stand. The 'President's palace' was so badly marked by the fire within that it was painted white to conceal the scars and became known as the White House.

Blenheim 71

Date: 13 August 1704.
Location: The village of Blindheim, 10 miles west of DONAUWORTH on the Ulm road, Bavaria.
War and campaign: War of Spanish Succession, 1701–1714: operations in Central Europe, 1704.
Opposing sides: (a) The Duke of Marlborough and Prince Eugene of Savoy in joint command of the Allied army; (b) Marshal Count Camille de Tallard in command of the Franco-Bavarian army.
Objective: The battle was forced on the Franco-Bavarian army by the Allies to break the strategic stalemate on the Danube front.
Forces engaged: (a) 65 infantry battalions, 160 cavalry squadrons and 66 guns – total 52,000 men, including approximately 10,000 British; (b) 79 infantry battalions, 140 cavalry squadrons and 90 guns – total 56,000 men.
Casualties: (a) 12,000 killed and wounded; (b) 20,000 killed and wounded, 14,000 captured, 6,000 desertions and 60 guns lost.
Result: Two-thirds of the Franco-Bavarian army was destroyed, the threat to Vienna was removed and the Allies overran Bavaria.

The Allies' early-morning approach march to the battlefield achieved complete tactical surprise, although this could not be fully exploited because Eugene's Imperial troops had further to go than Marlborough's wing of the army, which contained the British contingent. Tallard's position was protected by the Danube on the right and a range of wooded hills on the left, and most of his infantry was positioned in three villages along his front – Blenheim on the right, Oberglau in the left-centre and Lutzingen on the left. Marlborough, noting that the Franco-Bavarian centre between Blindheim and Oberglau was held by lightly supported cavalry, and that a large area of undefended water meadows lay between the enemy lines and the Nebel stream, decided to mask the villages while his principal thrust tore open Tallard's centre. At 12.30 Marlborough and Eugene advanced simultaneously. At Blindheim Lord Cutts' British battalions failed to break through the defences but caused the local French commander such serious concern that, without informing Tallard, he committed the entire infantry reserve there, with the result that no fewer than 27 infantry battalions were uselessly crammed into the village and contained by a much smaller force. At Oberglau the Allied attack was almost defeated by a determined defence, but Marlborough brought up reinforcements and here, too, the garrison was contained. Likewise, on the Allied right, Eugene's Imperial troops pinned down the Elector's infantry in Lutzingen. In the meantime, British troops had forded the Nebel and begun forming up in the fields beyond. Tallard, suddenly aware of the danger, ordered his cavalry to charge and for a while the issue remained in doubt until Marlborough personally led forward a brigade of cuirassiers which Eugene had made available. This threw back the French counter-attack and by 17.30 the Allies had smashed through the weak French centre. The Bavarians withdrew, pursued by Eugene, and at 23.00 the garrison of Blindheim surrendered. Tallard, together with Marshal de Marsin and several more generals, was captured. Blenheim raised the prestige of British arms, and that of the infantry in particular, to a level not attained since the longbow had dominated the battlefield.

Borodino 72

Date: 7 September 1812.
Location: Village on the Moskva river, 75 miles west of Moscow.
War and campaign: Napoleon's Invasion of Russia, 1812.
Opposing sides: (a) The Emperor Napoleon I commanding the Grand Army; (b) Marshal Prince Mikhail Golenishev-Kutuzov commanding the Russian army.
Objective: The Russians were attempting to halt the French advance on Moscow.
Forces engaged: (a) 56,000 infantry, 28,000 cavalry and 587 guns – total 130,000 men; (b) 82,000 infantry, 24,500 cavalry and 640 guns – total 120,800 men.
Casualties: (a) 30,000 killed and wounded; (b) 40,000 killed, wounded and captured.
Result: Napoleon won a technical victory, albeit at heavy cost, but Kutuzov was able to withdraw his army. The French occupied Moscow on 14 September. See also MALOYAROSLAVETS.

The battle developed into a brutal contest of attrition. Napoleon has been criticized for his reliance on crude frontal attacks which absorbed most of his reserves, and for his failure to commit the Imperial Guard. Although he was still to display flashes of his old brilliance, the lethargy which was to characterize some of his later actions was apparent at Borodino. Above all, however, the battle is best remembered for its horrific casualties, amounting to 28 per cent of those engaged. French losses included no fewer than 43 generals and 110 colonels; Russian losses among senior officers were comparable and included Prince Peter Bagration, mortally wounded.

Bosworth 73

Date: 22 August 1485.
Location: 2 miles south of Market Bosworth, Leicestershire.
War and campaign: Wars of the Roses, 1455–1485.
Opposing sides: (a) The Yorkist king, Richard III; (b) Henry Tudor, Earl of Richmond, the Lancastrian claimant to the throne.
Objective: The Yorkists were attempting to intercept the march of the Lancastrian army on London.
Forces engaged: (a) 12,000 plus a small number of guns; (b) 10,000.
Casualties: (a) 900, including Richard killed; (b) 100.
Result: A decisive Lancastrian victory, following which Richmond was crowned Henry VII; he married Elizabeth, daughter and only surviving child of Edward IV, thereby ending the dynastic quarrel and the Wars of the Roses, although he was to be challenged periodically by Yorkist pretenders (see STOKE).

The Yorkist army was drawn up with its infantry in the centre, flanked by cavalry, with a 'forward' of archers in front. Most of Henry's troops were cavalry, drawn up behind a 'forward' of archers. To the north of the two armies, on Ambion Hill, was a third body of troops under Sir William Stanley, who had promised Henry his support but was not as yet willing to commit himself since Richard, suspecting treachery, was holding his nephew hostage. Following an exchange of arrow flights, the rival armies closed in a general mêlée. Richard led a personal attack on Henry, cutting down his standard bearer, but was himself killed shortly after. At this point Sir William Stanley fell on the Yorkist flank and Richard's army fled. Despite the small numbers involved, Bosworth was one of the most important battles in English history, restoring stability and establishing the strong central administration of the Tudor dynasty.

Bothwell Bridge 74

Date: 22 June 1679.
Location: 7 miles south-east of Glasgow.
War and campaign: Covenanter Rising in Scotland, 1679.
Opposing sides: (a) James Scott, Duke of Monmouth and illegitimate son of Charles II, commanding the Government troops; (b) Robert Hamilton.
Objective: Seriously alarmed by the outcome at DRUMCLOG, the Government quickly assembled a superior force which attacked the Covenanter position at Bothwell Bridge.
Forces engaged: (a) Approximately 5,500 (dragoons, regular infantry and militia); (b) approximately 6,000.
Casualties: (a) Light; (b) over 400 killed and 1,200 prisoners.
Result: The Covenanters were routed and the rising was crushed.

Bouvines

Date: 27 July 1214.
Location: Village south-east of Lille, near the Franco-Belgian border.
War and campaign: Anglo-Imperial Invasion of France, 1214.
Opposing sides: (a) Otto IV, Holy Roman Emperor; (b) Philip Augustus, King of France.
Objective: A pitched battle between the Anglo-Imperial army, advancing on Paris, and the French.
Forces engaged: (a) 6,000 cavalry and 18,000 infantry – total 24,000 (English, Germans and Flemings); (b) 7,000 cavalry and 15,000 infantry – total 22,000.
Casualties: (a) 170 knights and an unknown number of infantry killed, 140 knights and 1,000 infantry captured; (b) light.
Result: A decisive French victory as a result of which Otto lost his throne and King John of England's hopes of regaining territory in northern France were dashed.

Boyne, The

Date: 11 July 1690.
Location: West of Drogheda on the Boyne river, Eire.
War and campaign: War of the League of Augsburg, 1688–1697: Jacobite campaign in Ireland, 1689–1691.
Opposing sides: (a) William III commanding the Williamite army; (b) the former James II commanding the Jacobite army.
Objective: William III forced the battle on the army of the deposed James II, which was withdrawing towards Dublin.
Forces engaged: (a) 26,500 infantry, 8,000 cavalry and 50 guns – total 35,000 (English, Irish Protestant, Dutch and French Huguenot); (b) 18,000 infantry, 5,000 cavalry and six guns – total 23,000 (Irish Catholic and French).
Casualties: (a) 2,000 killed and wounded; (b) 1,500 killed and wounded.
Result: The Jacobites were defeated and James fled to France. The strategic initiative in Ireland was now firmly in the hands of the Williamites – see AUGHRIM.

William launched a frontal attack across the river between Oldbridge and Drybridge, simultaneously sending a force upstream to cross and fall on the Jacobite left flank. Despite offering determined resistance to William's own attack, the Jacobites were unable to resist the pressure of the flanking force and withdrew as soon as it began to threaten their rear.

Brandy Station

Date: 9 June 1863.
Location: Near Culpeper, Virginia.
War and campaign: American Civil War: Lee's Second Invasion of the North.
Opposing sides: (a) Major-General Alfred Pleasanton commanding the cavalry

element of the Army of the Potomac; (b) Major-General J. E. B. Stuart commanding the cavalry element of the Army of Northern Virginia.

Objective: An encounter provoked when Federal cavalry, engaged in an offensive sweep, ran into Confederate cavalry screening the flank of Lee's northward march.

Forces engaged: (a) 11,000; (b) 9,500.

Casualties: (a) 868; (b) 515.

Result: The Confederates had the better of the engagement but Lee's move was detected and Hooker followed with the Army of the Potomac. See GETTYSBURG.

Brandy Station was the largest cavalry engagement of the war.

Brandywine 78

Date: 11 September 1777.

Location: On Brandywine Creek, 25 miles south-west of Philadelphia, Pennsylvania.

War and campaign: American War of Independence, 1775–1783: central theatre of operations.

Opposing sides: (a) Lieutenant-General Sir William Howe; (b) Major-General George Washington.

Objective: A British army had landed near Elkton on Chesapeake Bay and was marching on Philadelphia, the American capital and seat of Congress. At Brandywine Creek it was opposed by Washington's army.

Forces engaged: (a) 13,000; (b) 11,000.

Casualties: (a) 576 killed and wounded; (b) approximately 900 killed and wounded, 300 prisoners and most of the artillery captured.

Result: The Americans were defeated. Howe then outmanoeuvred Washington and entered Philadelphia on 26 September. See GERMANTOWN.

Howe's tactics at Brandywine were similar to those he had used on LONG ISLAND. Noting that Washington's army was covering the lower fords, he directed Lieutenant-General Wilhelm von Knyphausen to mount a holding attack against them with 5,000 men. He then embarked on a wide flank march with the remainder of his troops, crossing the river by its upper fords, and fell on the American right flank, causing Washington to move units from his centre to meet the threat. At this point Knyphausen turned his feint into a real attack, stormed the lower fords and routed the troops covering them.

Breitenfeld, First Battle of 79

Date: 17 September 1631.

Location: 5 miles north of Leipzig.

War and campaign: Thirty Years' War, 1618–1648: German Campaign of 1631.

Opposing sides: (a) Gustavus Adolphus, King of Sweden, and the Elector of Saxony commanding the Protestant army; (b) Count John Tzerklaes de Tilly commanding the Imperialist-Catholic army.

Objective: The Protestants intended recovering Leipzig from the Imperialist-Catholic faction.

Forces engaged: (a) 40,000 Swedes and Saxons, including 248 infantry companies, 170 cavalry squadrons and 60–70 guns; (b) 32,000, comprising 21,000 infantry and 11,000 cavalry, and 30 guns.
Casualties: (a) 4,000 killed and wounded; (b) 7,000 killed and wounded and 6,000 captured; 8,000 subsequently surrendered in Leipzig.
Result: Leipzig was recaptured, the Imperialist-Catholic army was destroyed, the survival of German Protestantism was assured and Sweden emerged as a major military power. See also LÜTZEN.

Tilly gave battle in an area of open, undulating country, deploying his army with fourteen *tercio* blocks in the centre and cavalry on either flank. The Swedish army was similarly deployed, but its smaller units were drawn up with two lines of musketeers supporting the cavalry and the infantry had the immediate support of 42 two-man battalion guns. The smaller but less flexible Saxon contingent was positioned on the Swedish left. The battle commenced at noon with an artillery exchange. Tilly's intention was a double envelopment of the Protestant army and at about 14.00 his left-wing cavalry, commanded by Pappenheim, attempted to turn the Swedish right but was balked when the Swedes simply extended their line by taking units from elsewhere; nor was Pappenheim able to make headway against the Swedish tactics of alternating musketry volleys with counter-charges by their own cavalry, despite fierce fighting which raged for three hours. Simultaneously, the Imperialist *tercios* had also advanced, covered on both flanks by Tilly's right-wing cavalry under Furstenburg, inclining to the right in order to attack the Saxons, who were routed and dispersed by 16.00. Having thus exposed the Swedish left, Tilly seemed certain of victory. However, the commander of the Swedish left wing, Gustaf Horn, promptly mounted a counter-attack which drove some of the Imperialist cavalry back into the infantry *tercios*, which were attempting to reorganize after their successful assault. The time so gained enabled the Swedes to extend their flank, and their counter-attack, combining firepower and shock action, served to compress Tilly's pikemen until the latter were unable to use their weapons. Advancing steadily, the Swedes recaptured the Saxon artillery, then took Tilly's own guns, which were turned on the struggling Imperialist infantry. At about the same time, 18.00, Gustavus Adolphus took the offensive on the right flank and swept the remnants of the Imperial army off the field. The battle demonstrated beyond doubt the supeiority of the Swedish system, combining as it did flexibility, mobility, firepower and shock action, against which the older and more cumbrous cavalry and infantry tactics could not prevail.

Breitenfeld, Second Battle of   80

Date: 2 November 1642.
Location: 5 miles north of Leipzig.
War and campaign: Thirty Years' War, 1618–1648: German Campaign of 1642.
Opposing sides: (a) Field Marshal Lennart Tortensson commanding the Swedish army; (b) Archduke Leopold William commanding the Imperialists.
Objective: The Swedes were forced to abandon their siege of Leipzig on the approach of an Imperialist army, but turned to give battle at Breitenfeld.
Forces engaged: (a) Estimated 25,000; (b) a somewhat larger force.
Casualties: (a) Uncertain, but moderate; (b) 10,000 killed, wounded or captured.
Result: The Imperialists were routed.

A Swedish cavalry attack destroyed Leopold's left wing before it was fully formed. Its flank exposed, the Imperialist infantry was then driven off the field, leaving the isolated right wing to be overwhelmed. For the first time in land warfare, chain shot was employed by the Imperial artillery.

Brody-Dubno 81

Date: 25–30 June 1941.
Location: East of Lvov, Central Ukraine.
War and campaign: Second World War: Russian Front.
Opposing sides: (a) Colonel-General Mikhail Kirponos commanding the South-West Front; (b) Field Marshal Gerd von Rundstedt commanding the German Army Group South.
Objective: The Soviet Army was attempting to halt the German drive into the Ukraine during the opening days of Operation 'Barbarossa'.
Forces engaged: (a) IV, VIII, IX, XV, XIX and XXII Mechanized Corps; (b) General Ewald von Kleist's I Panzer Group (11th, 13th, 14th and 16th Panzer Divisions).
Casualties: (a) The destruction of the major part of the Soviet armour; (b) unknown, but heavier than had been anticipated.
Result: The South-West Front sustained a heavy defeat but imposed a check on Army Group South that was to contribute to the eventual failure of 'Barbarossa'.

Kirponos managed to concentrate a numerically superior force against the armoured spearhead of Army Group South with the result that a fierce tank battle raged over a wide area for a period of four days. The Russians, however, lacked air superiority and much of their strength was written down when the Luftwaffe pounced on the tank columns during their approach march. The rest was squandered in piecemeal, unco-ordinated attacks, while inexperience, poor tactics, breakdowns and fuel shortages also contributed to the severe Soviet losses. Finally, Kirponos extracted the remnants of his corps and retreated to KIEV. Until KURSK (1943), Brody-Dubno was the largest tank battle of the war.

Brunanburgh 82

Date: 937.
Location: Unknown. Possible but unlikely sites suggested include Axminster in Devon, Bromborough on the Mersey and Burnswork in Annandale in Dumfrieshire. The weight of argument, however, favours Brinsworth, near Rotherham, Yorkshire.
War and campaign: Scottish and Norse/Irish Invasion of England, 937.
Opposing sides: (a) Aethelstan; (b) Olaf Guthfrithson in overall command of the allied army.
Objective: King Aethelstan, ascending the throne in 924, had not only continued the policy of his father, Edward the Elder (son of Alfred the Great), and conquered the Danish holdings in England, but he had also campaigned successfully in Scotland and Wales, receiving the homage of their rulers. In 937 the resentful Constantine III, King of the Scots, formed an alliance with Welsh, Norse/Irish and Viking chieftains. These forces effected a concentration at an unknown location in the north and then marched southwards into England with the object of permanent

conquest. Aethelstan waited until he had assembled an army capable of engaging the invaders on equal terms, then marched to meet them.

Forces engaged: Uncertain, but it is probable that each army deployed approximately 18,000 men. For the period, these were very large forces indeed and clearly represented a maximum effort by the participants. The English army is known to have contained a mounted element.
Casualties: The English casualties are unknown but those of the invaders were immense and are said to have included five kings, seven earls and Constantine's son.
Result: The allied army was defeated and the alliance collapsed. The battle not only confirmed England's position as the dominant power within the British Isles, but also ensured that the country would be ruled from the south.

Given the scale and importance of the battle, surprisingly little is known about its course. It can, however, be deduced that the English army occupied a strong position from which it was able to repel the assaults of the allies, and that the latter broke when Aethelstan launched a counter-attack at the critical moment. *The Anglo-Saxon Chronicle* tells us that West Saxon mounted companies carried out a prolonged pursuit in which they inflicted heavy slaughter on the fugitives. The Scots and Scandanavians fled in the direction of their ships in the Humber, while the Norse/Irish contingent headed for the north-west coast.

Brusilov Offensive, The

Date: 4 June to 20 September 1916.
Location: Along a 300-mile front stretching northwards from the Romanian frontier, formerly Austrian Galicia and now part of the western Ukraine.
War and campaign: First World War: Eastern Front.
Opposing sides: (a) Field Marshal Count Conrad von Hotzendorf, Chief of the Austro-Hungarian General Staff; (b) General Alexei Brusilov commanding the South-West Front.
Objective: Mounted in response to Allied requests for help to ease the Central Powers' pressure on the Western and Italian Fronts.
Forces engaged: (a) Austro-Hungarian Seventh Army (Pflanzer-Baltin), Deutsche Sudarmee (Count von Bothmer), Austro-Hungarian Second (Bohm-Ermoli), First (Puhallo) and Fourth (Archduke Josef Ferdinand) Armies; (b) Russian Eighth (Kaledin), Eleventh (Sakharov), Seventh (Shcherbachev) and Ninth (Letchitsky) Armies, joined by the Guards Army (Bezebrazov) in late July.
Casualties: (a) Uncertain, but up to 1,500,000, including a high proportion of prisoners; (b) 1,200,000, plus 212,000 captured.
Result: The South-West Front advanced between 30 and 80 miles. To contain the offensive, the Central Powers were forced to transfer divisions from other sectors of the Eastern Front, the Western Front, Italy and Turkey.

The scale of voluntary surrenders among the Slavic elements of the Austro-Hungarian Army indicated that Austria was close to collapse and that henceforth Germany would carry the burden of the war. The Russian success led Romania to declare war on Germany and Austria on 27 August; unfortunately, she collapsed almost immediately and the Russian armies were forced to extend their own line when they could least afford to do so. Although the Brusilov Offensive was the most effective Russian operation of the war, the Russian Army had sustained over five million casualties even before it started, and the additional losses proved to be insupportable. Unrest and indiscipline had already begun to spread while the offensive was in progress; by the following March, when the Russian Revolution began, the majority of the troops were no longer prepared to support the old regime. It can therefore be seen that while the Brusilov Offensive did not in itself cause the Revolution, its consequences made it inevitable.

Buena Vista 84

Date: 22–23 February 1847.
Location: 8 miles south of Saltillo in Nuevo Leon province, north-eastern Mexico.
War and campaign: US–Mexican War, 1846–1848: Northern Campaign.
Opposing sides: (a) General Zachary Taylor (b) the Dictator of Mexico, General Antonio Lopez de Santa Anna.
Objective: The Mexicans, aware that the Americans were planning an amphibious landing at Vera Cruz in central Mexico, were attempting to crush the force which had occupied Saltillo (see MONTERREY) before this could take place.
Forces engaged: (a) 5,000; (b) 16,000.
Casualties: (a) 267 killed, 456 wounded, 23 missing and two guns captured; (b) 500 killed and 1,000 wounded.
Result: After a hard-fought battle, in which the Americans came close to defeat on several occasions, Santa Anna withdrew.

This engagement ended the Northern Campaign.

Bulge, The 85

Date: 16 December 1944 to 16 January 1945.
Location: Triangular area extending from Monschau and Echternach on the German frontier to the Meuse at Dinant, Belgium.
War and campaign: Second World War: North-West Europe.
Opposing sides: (a) Field Marshal Gerd von Rundstedt, nominally Commander-in-Chief West; (b) General Dwight D. Eisenhower, Supreme Commander Allied Powers Europe.
Objective: The Germans were attempting to reach Antwerp, hoping thereby to isolate the Allied 21st Army Group and compel the British and American governments to settle for a negotiated peace agreement.
Forces engaged: (a) 6th SS Panzer Army, 5th Panzer Army and 7th Army with a total of nine panzer and fourteen infantry divisions – total some 250,000 men and about 1,000 tanks; (b) US 1st and 3rd Armies, plus elements of British XXX Corps with a total of seven armoured, two airborne and eighteen infantry divisions – total some 400,000 men and about 1,100 tanks.
Casualties: (a) Approximately 100,000 men and 800 tanks; (b) approximately 81,000 Americans, 1,400 British and 800 tanks.
Result: Although it delayed Allied operations in the West for about six weeks, the battle ended in a complete German defeat and the restoration of the American line.

The plan for this German counter-offensive, originally code-named 'Christrose' but later changed to 'Wacht am Rhein', was drafted by Hitler himself. Von Rundstedt, who as

Commander-in-Chief West was responsible for executing the directive, immediately recognized that the concept amounted to little more than a gamble and declined to become personally involved, leaving the day-to-day conduct of the battle to the Führer. Nevertheless, when the offensive opened on 16 December it achieved both tactical and strategic surprise, despite the suspicions of some Allied officers. The German attack succeeded in breaking through a quiet sector of the line known as the Ghost Front and in its early stages captured some 9,000 Americans from divisions which were either inexperienced or resting after spells of combat on more active sectors. The Germans were also lucky in that poor flying weather kept the Allied air forces grounded during the early stages of the battle. On the flanks the German advance was checked but in the centre the 5th Panzer Army made good progress. However, the defence of St Vith by Brigadier-General Hasbrouck's 7th Armored Division, and of the vital communications centre of Bastogne by Brigadier-General McAuliffe's 101st Airborne Division, coupled with the Germans' failure to capture vital fuel dumps on which they were relying, all weighed heavily against the possibility of the counter-offensive succeeding. Moreover, after the first shock, the reaction of Allied commanders was rapid and decisive. Eisenhower appointed Field Marshal Montgomery commander of all forces north of the Bulge and the latter used his American division to construct a hard defensive shoulder, simultaneously moving the British XXX Corps into a blocking position. South of the Bulge, General Omar Bradley, commanding the 12th Army Group, directed Patton's Third Army to advance north into the enemy flank and relieve Bastogne, which it succeeded in doing on 26 December. Meanwhile, on 24 and 25 December, the German spearhead had been defeated and forced to withdraw by the US 2nd Armored and British 11th Armoured Divisions. The weather had now improved sufficiently for Allied air power to intervene and, although heavy fighting continued, by 3 January the Germans had been thrown on to the defensive. By 16 January the Bulge had been eliminated.

Bull Run, First (First Manassas) 86

Date: 21 July 1861.
Location: Near Manassas, Virginia, 26 miles south-west of Washington, D.C. (now Manassas National Battlefield Park, on US Route 29 and Interstate 66).
War and campaign: American Civil War.
Opposing sides: (a) Major-General Irvin McDowell commanding the Federal army; (b) Major-General Joseph E. Johnston and Major-General Pierre Beauregard commanding the Confederate army.
Objective: The Federals marched from Washington to attack a Confederate army based at Manassas Junction, Virginia.
Forces engaged: (a) 39,000; (b) 32,000.
Casualties: (a) 2,896 killed, wounded and missing, plus 27 guns captured; (b) 1,982 killed, wounded and missing.
Result: A Confederate victory which was not exploited. McDowell was replaced by Major-General George B. McClellan as commander of the Army of the Potomac and President Lincoln authorized the enlistment of one million men.

Both armies entered this, the first major battle of the war, with an enthusiasm which was not matched by the standard of their training; nor were their commanders used to handling such large bodies of men. McDowell, unaware that the Confederates were being steadily reinforced by rail from the Shenandoah Valley – the first tactical movement of troops to a battlefield by this means – attempted to turn their left flank and made some progress until his advance was halted by a brigade commanded by Brigadier-General Thomas J. Jackson, on whom the nickname 'Stonewall' was conferred because of his stubborn defence. The Federal right was then enveloped by newly arrived Confederate reinforcements and McDowell's army disintegrated when Beauregard ordered a general advance, its disorderly retreat being covered by a small rearguard of regular units.

Bull Run, Second (Second Manassas)   87

Date: 28–30 August 1862.
Location: Near Manassas, Virginia, 26 miles south-west of Washington, D.C. (now Manassas National Battlefield Park, on US Route 29 and Interstate 66).
War and campaign: American Civil War: Second Bull Run (Manassas) Campaign.
Opposing sides: (a) Major-General John Pope commanding the army of Virginia; (b) General Robert E. Lee commanding the army of Northern Virginia.
Objective: Following CEDAR MOUNTAIN, Lee decided to crush Pope's Federal Army of Virginia before it could effect a junction with McClellan's Army of the Potomac, so placing his own army at a serious numerical disadvantage. He therefore ordered Major-General Thomas ('Stonewall') Jackson's corps to advance north and operate against Pope's rear while he followed with the rest of the army of Northern Virginia. Jackson destroyed the Federal supply depot at Manassas and Pope responded immediately to the threat, to find the Confederates occupying positions on the old battlefield of FIRST BULL RUN.
Forces engaged: (a) 63,000; (b) 55,000.
Casualties: (a) 13,826; (b) 8,353.
Result: Pope was defeated and forced to withdraw; shortly afterwards, he was transferred to an administrative post in the West and his army was disbanded. Lee followed up as far as Chantilly, where an inconclusive action was fought with the Federal rearguard on 31 August, but did not attempt a thrust against the heavily defended approaches to Washington. His victory, however, brought the fortunes of the Confederacy to a high point and opened the way for his first invasion of the North. See HARPER'S FERRY and ANTIETAM (SHARPSBURG).

Pope single-mindedly concentrated his attention on Jackson's corps but failed to reinforce the success of some of his early piecemeal attacks. Thus when Lee reached the battlefield he was able to turn the Federal left, and a counter-attack by Longstreet's corps drove Pope's men back across the old battlefield.

Buna   88

Date: 20 November 1942 to 22 January 1943.
Location: On the northern coast of Papua/New Guinea.
War and campaign: Second World War: Papua/New Guinea Campaign.
Opposing sides: (a) Lieutenant-General Robert L. Eichelberger commanding the US I Corps; (b) Lieutenant-General Hatazo Adachi commanding the Japanese Eighteenth Army, with headquarters in Rabaul.
Objective: The Allied intention was to eliminate the Japanese force which had invaded Papua the previous July.

Forces engaged: (a) Australian 7th and US 32nd Infantry Divisions; (b) elements of various formations totalling about 12,000 men.
Casualties: (a) 6,410 killed and wounded, plus a high proportion incapacitated by tropical diseases; (b) over 7,000 killed, about 1,200 wounded evacuated by sea and 350 wounded prisoners.
Result: The complete destruction of the Japanese forces in the area.

Once their advance on Port Moresby had been halted, the Japanese withdrew along the Kokoda Trail towards Buna, where they were reinforced. Following up, the Australians and Americans found that the entire area had been turned into a formidable jungle fortress. Stuart light tanks were brought forward, and the use of delayed-action fuzes increased the effectiveness of artillery against the enemy's bunkers, although Japanese resistance was fanatical and progress was slow. On 9 December the Australians captured Gona Mission Station on the northern flank of the enemy position, but Buna did not fall until 2 January. The last pocket of resistance, at Sananda some distance to the north, was overrun on 22 January. About 1,000 Japanese survivors escaped through the jungle to Lae. This was an important Allied victory since it proved, for the first time, that the Japanese could be defeated in jungle fighting.

Bunker Hill 89

Date: 17 June 1775.
Location: Breed's Hill, to the north of Charlestown, Boston harbour, Massachusetts.
War and campaign: American War of Independence, 1775–1783: northern theatre of operations (Siege of Boston).
Opposing sides: (a) Major-General Thomas Gage commanding the British garrison; (b) Major-General Artemis Ward commanding the Massachusetts contingent of the besiegers and with limited jurisdiction over the remainder.
Objective: During the night of 16/17 June the Americans, tightening their grip on Boston, had occupied and entrenched Breed's Hill, overlooking the harbour, although their orders specified the fortification of Bunker Hill, which was a little higher. Next day the British counter-attacked.
Forces engaged: (a) Major-General William Howe commanding the 2,200-strong counter-attack force; (b) 1,200 men under Colonel William Prescott.
Casualties: (a) 1,054 killed and wounded; (b) 140 killed, 271 wounded and 30 captured.
Result: The Americans defeated two assaults but their ammunition supply failed during the third and they were driven off the hill. Although the engagement left the local situation unchanged, the fact that the Americans had made so determined a stand against regular troops provided a boost to their morale. In the longer term Howe, who succeeded Gage in October, recognized that it served no purpose to have so many British troops bottled up and evacuated the garrison to Halifax, Nova Scotia, on 17 March 1776.

Both sides displayed exemplary courage during the action, the British sustaining 50 per cent casualties and the Americans 33 per cent, but the latter fought the more intelligent battle, using entrenchments, rail fences and stone walls to good advantage. Howe, normally a sound tactician, underestimated his opponents' tenacity and relied solely on shock action with the bayonet in his first assaults; ordered to advance with unloaded muskets, his men sustained needlessly heavy losses.

Busaco 90

Date: 27 September 1810.
Location: Near Coimbra on the Mondego river, Portugal.
War and campaign: Peninsular War, 1807–1814: French Invasion of Portugal, 1810.
Opposing sides: (a) Lieutenant-General Viscount Wellington commanding the Allied army; (b) Marshal Andre Massena commanding the French Army of Portugal.
Objective: Wellington was fighting a holding action to cover his withdrawal into the Lines of Torres Vedras.
Forces engaged: (a) 50,000, including 24,000 Portuguese; (b) 60,000.
Casualties: (a) 1,250; (b) 4,600.
Result: Having defeated Massena's attacks, Wellington continued his withdrawal to Torres Vedras, occupying the Lines on 10 October. Following up, Massena found not only that the position was too strong to assault but also that the surrounding country had been stripped bare of supplies. The threat of starvation forced him to retreat on 14 November.

Although Wellington's troops occupied a ridge which lay directly across the French line of march, Massena was preoccupied with his mistress and paid little attention to reconnaissance before the battle began. Consequently his attacking columns sustained serious losses and were repulsed after heavy fighting. See also FUENTES DE ONORO.

Bzura, The 91

Date: 9–15 September 1939.
Location: North-Eastern Poland, along the line of the Bzura river.
War and campaign: Second World War: Poland, 1939.
Opposing sides: (a) Colonel-General Walter von Brauchitsch, Commander-in-Chief of the German army; (b) Marshal Edward Smigly-Rydz, Commander-in-Chief of the Polish army.
Objective: The Polish armies were attempting to break out of the double-envelopment which had encircled them.
Forces engaged: (a) Principally the left wing of Army Group South and the right wing of Army Group North; (b) the Pomorz and Poznan Armies.
Casualties: (a) Unknown, but moderate; (b) killed and wounded unknown, but heavy, plus 170,000 captured.
Result: The Polish attempt failed, although the German Army Group South was forced to suspend its drive on Warsaw and redeploy its armour westwards to contain the threat.

Caen

Date: 6 June to 25 July 1944.
Location: Area stretching from Bayeux through Villers Bocage to Caen (including the higher ground to the south-east of the city), Normandy, France.
War and campaign: Second World War: North-West Europe.
Opposing sides: (a) Field Marshal Montgomery commanding the Allied 21st Army Group; (b) Field Marshal Rommel (later, General Hausser) commanding the German Army Group B.
Objective: The Allied intention was to hold the bulk of the German armour on the British sector, thereby assisting the projected American breakout from the Normandy beach-head at the western end of the front.
Forces engaged: (a) The British Second Army with ten infantry, three armoured and one airborne divisions, plus six armoured brigades – total approximately 150,000 men and 1,350 tanks; (b) the German Seventh Army and Panzer Group West with six infantry and seven armoured divisions – total approximately 100,000 men and 670 tanks.
Casualties: (a) About 37,000 killed and wounded; (b) about 117,000 killed, wounded and captured.
Result: The Allied strategy was completely successful.

Montgomery employed the same technique he had used during the SECOND BATTLE OF ALAMEIN, attacking first on one sector and then another to tie down the German armour. His major offensive operations, including 'Epsom', 'Jupiter', 'Charnwood' and 'Goodwood', were at best only limited tactical successes, but the heavy attritional fighting involved achieved his strategic objective. By the time the American First Army mounted its breakout, codenamed 'Cobra', on 25 July, there were seven German armoured divisions plus four heavy Tiger tank battalions in the line opposite the British sector, but only one panzergrenadier and two armoured divisions opposite the Americans. British tank losses were higher than those of the Germans, but were quickly made good, whereas the latter's were not. See also FALAISE.

Cambrai

Date: 20 November to 3 December 1917.
Location: South of Cambrai, between the Canal du Nord and the Canal de l'Escaut.
War and campaign: First World War: Western Front.
Opposing sides: (a) General Sir Douglas Haig, Commander-in-Chief of the British armies in France and Belgium; (b) General Erich Ludendorff, First Quartermaster-General of the German Army.
Objective: Originally conceived as a 'tank raid' in response to a request by the Tank Corps to show what it could achieve over an area of hard going, the plan developed into a more ambitious operation involving a major breakthrough.
Forces engaged: (a) General Sir Julian Byng commanding the British Third Army with nineteen divisions, plus the Tank Corps with 476 tanks (378 in the assault) under the command of Brigadier-General Hugh Elles; (b) General Georg von der Marwitz commanding the German Second Army with six divisions, rising to twenty divisions.

Casualties: (a) Approximately 44,000; (b) approximately 53,000.
Result: Initially a brilliant tactical success which tore a wide gap in the German defence line. Unfortunately, the Cavalry Corps could not be brought forward quickly enough to exploit this and the Germans were able to seal off the penetration. On 30 November they counter-attacked and recovered the lost ground.

The Tank Corps' ideas were vindicated by the ease with which it broke through the German defences. The only check occurred on the Flesquières sector, where the commander of the 51st (Highland) Division, Major-General G. M. Harper, imposed his own plan of attack, with serious consequences. The German counter-attack employed the techniques previously used at RIGA and CAPORETTO. By coincidence, the first battle between British and German tank units also took place on the Cambrai battlefield, on 8 October 1918; the first combat between individual tanks occurred at Villers-Bretonneux on 24 April 1918.

Camden   94

Date: 16 August 1780.
Location: Five miles north of Camden, South Carolina.
War and campaign: American War of Independence, 1775–1783: southern theatre of operations.
Opposing sides: (a) Major-General Lord Charles Cornwallis; (b) Major-Generals Horatio Gates and Baron de Kalb.
Objective: An encounter battle between the British field army in South Carolina and a newly raised American army which had been despatched south to retrieve the situation following the fall of CHARLESTON.
Forces engaged: (a) 2,200; (b) 4,100.
Casualties: (a) 312; (b) 800 killed and wounded, 1,000 prisoners and eight guns captured.
Result: The Americans were routed. Two days later Tarleton's British Legion dispersed Colonel Thomas Sumter's guerrilla force at Fishing Creek and the American cause in South Carolina seemed lost. Cornwallis prepared to invade North Carolina. See KING'S MOUNTAIN.

When the British attacked, the untried Virginia and North Carolina militia, holding the American centre and left, fled without firing a shot. On the right the Continental regulars made a courageous stand but were overwhelmed when charged from the rear by Tarleton's cavalry and de Kalb was mortally wounded. Gates, whose credit for the American victories at SARATOGA was somewhat exaggerated, fled with the militia. Washington replaced him with Major-General Nathanael Greene.

Camerone   95

Date: 30 April 1863.
Location: Farmstead on the road between Vera Cruz and La Puebla, Mexico.
War and campaign: French Intervention in Mexico, 1861–1867.
Opposing sides: (a) Captain Jean Danjou; (b) Colonel Milan.
Objective: The Mexicans' intention was to capture a convoy which included the

French pay chest and heavy guns for the siege of LA PUEBLA, but they became prematurely involved with a Foreign Legion patrol which took cover in some of the farm buildings.
Forces engaged: (a) Three officers and 62 men; (b) between 2,000 and 3,000 men.
Casualties: (a) The entire company was killed, wounded or captured; (b) approximately 300 killed and wounded.
Result: The Mexicans abandoned their attempt to intercept the convoy.

Danjou's company conducted a heroic ten-hour defence which completely demoralized the Mexicans. A month after the action 32 Legion survivors were exchanged. Danjou was killed during the fighting but his artificial hand was recovered from the ruins later and is now the Foreign Legion's most treasured possession. Camerone established the Legion's reputation as one of the world's élite fighting forces.

Cannae 96

Date: 2 August 216 BC.
Location: On the north bank of the Ofanto (Aufidius) river between Canosa and Barletta, Italy.
War and campaign: Second Punic War, 219–202 BC.
Opposing sides: (a) The Consuls Aemilius Paulus and Terentius Varro, alternating daily in command of the Roman army; (b) Hannibal.
Objective: Hannibal, anxious to capitalize on his victory the previous year at LAKE TRASIMENE, wished to bring the Roman army to battle and occupied an important supply depot at Cannae, thereby forcing the Roman Senate to attempt its recovery. Knowing that the impetuous Varro would be in command on 2 August, Hannibal drew up his army provocatively close to the former's camp. Unwisely, Varro accepted the challenge.
Forces engaged: (a) Eight Roman and eight allied legions – total 80,000 infantry and 7,000 cavalry; (b) 40,000 infantry and 10,000 cavalry.
Casualties: (a) Approximately 55,000 killed, including Paulus, 80 senators and 21 tribunes, plus 10,000 captured; (b) 5,700.
Result: The Roman army was annihilated. However, the results of Hannibal's greatest victory proved disappointing, for while some of Rome's allies deserted her and she was shaken to her political and military foundations by the disaster, she remained determined to fight on until a satisfactory conclusion to the war could be reached. Hannibal, lacking a siege train, was unable to attack Rome itself and consolidated his hold on southern Italy.

Varro intended smashing through the Carthaginian army by weight of numbers and doubled the depth of his maniples, the effect being to shorten his front until it corresponded to Hannibal's. The Carthaginian infantry was formed with the Spaniards and Gauls in a convex crescent in the centre, flanked by Hannibal's African troops. Both armies deployed their cavalry on the flanks. The Roman cavalry on both wings was defeated but in the centre the legions were apparently successful, pushing back the Spaniards and Gauls until their convex line had become concave. Gnaius Servilius, commanding the Roman infantry, sensed victory and committed more troops to the struggle. This was exactly what Hannibal hoped he would do and at the critical moment he ordered the hitherto lightly engaged African divisions on both flanks to advance and wheel inwards in a double envelopment. As they did so Hasdrubal's rallied cavalry fell on the Roman rear. The effect was to compress the legionaries so tightly within a pocket that many of them were unable to use their weapons. Perhaps as many as 8,000 managed to fight their way out but the remainder were butchered where they stood. The methods by which Hannibal achieved so complete a victory continue to be applied by commanders to this day, not simply in the tactical battle but also at the operative and strategic levels; in particular, the theme of Cannae was a central pillar in the thinking of Germany's Great General Staff.

Caporetto (The Twelfth Battle of the Isonzo) 97

Date: 24 October to 7 November 1917.
Location: On the border between Italy and Yugoslavia, near the Isonzo river.
War and campaign: First World War: Italian Front.
Opposing sides: (a) The Archduke Eugen, nominal Commander-in-Chief of the Austrian front between the Carnic Alps and the Adriatic; (b) General Luigi Cadorna, Italian Chief of General Staff.
Objective: The intention of the Central Powers was to effect a major breakthrough on the Isonzo front with the ultimate object of driving Italy out of the war.
Forces engaged: (a) General Otto von Below commanding the Austro-German Fourteenth Army, with two Austrian and two German corps, initially with 15 divisions but rising to 35; (b) General Luigi Capello commanding the Italian Second Army, initially with five divisions but rising to 41.
Casualties: (a) Approximately 20,000; (b) 45,000 killed and wounded plus approximately 250,000 prisoners and 2,500 guns captured.
Result: The Italians were routed and driven back to the line of the Piave, where Cadorna managed to stabilize the front. Although the disaster was largely the fault of his subordinates, Cadorna was dismissed and replaced by General Armando Diaz. Nevertheless, while shaken severely, Italy did not sue for peace and the line was stiffened by the rapid despatch of British and French divisions from the Western Front. For the Allies, the most important result of the defeat was the establishment of a Supreme War Council in an attempt to attain unity of command.

Below not only achieved surprise, plus numerical, artillery and air superiority on the sector chosen for his break-in, but also employed the fast-moving infiltration tactics used by von Hutier at RIGA. It was during this battle that Lieutenant Erwin Rommel first attracted the attention of his superiors, capturing 9,000 men and 81 guns in one 48-hour period, a feat which won his promotion to captain and the award of the *Pour le Mérite*.

Carrhae 98

Date: June 53 BC.
Location: Near modern Harran, Turkey, close to the Syrian frontier.
War and campaign: First Parthian War, 55–38 BC.
Opposing sides: (a) Marcus Licinius Crassus; (b) Surenas commanding the Parthians.

Objective: The Parthians were resisting Roman intervention in an internal dynastic dispute.
Forces engaged: (a) 39,000, including 4,000 cavalry and auxiliaries; (b) 1,000 cataphracts (heavy cavalry) and 9,000 horse-archers.
Casualties: (a) Only 5,000 Romans succeeded in reaching safety, 10,000 being captured and enslaved and the remainder, including Crassus, killed; (b) unknown, but light.
Result: The Roman army was destroyed.

Having crossed the Euphrates, Crassus's army entered a wide area of semi-desert. Near Carrhae it was attacked by swarms of galloping horsemen armed with bows specially adapted for use from the saddle. Under an incessant arrow storm the marching legionaries halted to form a square, but this merely provided the mounted archers, circling just beyond reach, with a more concentrated target. As a unit emptied its quivers it retired to replenish them from a camel train brought up by Surenas for the purpose. The Romans' torment was aggravated by intense heat and thirst and at length, in desperation, Crassus decided to counter-attack using a 6,000-strong group consisting of the legionary cavalry, the fittest of the legionaries and some auxiliary archers, under the command of his son Publius. The horse-archers gave way before the group, demonstrating the famous 'Parthian shot' to their rear as they did so, then they and the cataphracts closed round it and slaughtered it to a man. Crassus began to withdraw, abandoning his 4,000 wounded, to whom no mercy was shown. The following day the pattern of the fighting was repeated and when Crassus sought terms he was treacherously killed. The lesson of Carrhae was that in a desert environment infantry are at the mercy of an enemy who combines firepower with mobility unless they possesses comparable firepower and access to water. Compare with HATTIN and ARSUF.

Cassino 99

Date: 17 January to 22 May 1944.
Location: Centred on Monte Cassino in the Rapido valley, south of Rome.
War and campaign: Second World War: Italy.
Opposing sides: (a) Field Marshal Albert Kesselring, Commander-in-Chief South; (b) General Sir Harold Alexander commanding the Allied armies in Italy.
Objective: The German intention was to bring the Allied advance to a complete standstill as it reached the formidable defences of the Gustav Line, in which the key position of Monte Cassino barred all further progress towards Rome.
Forces engaged: (a) General Heinrich von Vietinhoff's German Tenth Army with, initially, four armoured and five infantry divisions (100,000 men), reducing to one panzergrenadier and five infantry divisions (80,000 men); (b) Lieutenant-General Mark Clark's US Fifth Army and Lieutenant-General Sir Oliver Leese's British Eighth Army with, initially, one armoured and six infantry divisions, rising to three armoured and thirteen infantry divisions (300,000 men).
Casualties: (a) Approximately 60,000; (b) approximately 115,000.
Result: After four months of costly fighting the Allies broke through, effecting a junction with the ANZIO beach-head, and went on to capture Rome.

The first Allied attempt to effect a breakthrough, lasting from 17 January until 12 February, was made by the British X Corps, US II Corps and the French Corps. Most of the gains made were lost to counter-attacks. Unjustified suspicions that the monastery on the summit of Monte Cassino was not all it seemed led to the controversial decision to subject it to heavy bombing on 15 February. Immediately afterwards the 4th Indian Division made limited gains north of Monastery Hill and the 2nd New Zealand Division captured Cassino railway station, only to lose it again on 18 February. On 18 March, following a heavy air and artillery bombardment of the town, the New Zealanders recaptured the station and took Castle Hill after three days of fierce fighting against the German 1st Parachute Division. A lull followed, during which the Allies prepared for a major offensive. During the night of 11/12 May the German positions were pounded by 2,000 guns. Monastery Hill was isolated by the Polish II Corps while the British XIII, French and US II Corps crossed the Rapido to the west of the town to penetrate the Liri valley. Complete surprise was achieved, and although the Germans fought hard their defences were overrun. By the morning of 18 May the town of Cassino had been finally cleared and the monastery was in Polish hands. See also ANZIO.

Castillon   100

Date: 17 July 1453.
Location: 30 miles east of Bordeaux.
War and campaign: Hundred Years' War, 1337–1457: French Invasion of Guyenne, 1451–1453.
Opposing sides: (a) The Earl of Shrewsbury; (b) Jean Bureau, Master of the French Artillery.
Objective: An English force attempted to break the French siege of Castillon.
Forces engaged: (a) Approximately 5,000; (b) approximately 8,000, with numerous guns.
Casualties: (a) Heavy, including Shrewsbury killed; (b) light.
Result: The English army was routed. Castillon was the last battle of the war. When Bordeaux fell on 19 October only Calais remained of all the former English possessions in France.

When the French refused to leave the entrenchments of their camp, Shrewsbury launched a concentrated attack on what he believed to be the weakest sector of their lines. This was broken up by Bureau's guns and the French then counter-attacked into the English flank.

Cawnpore   101

Date: 6 December 1857.
Location: Kanpur, Uttar Pradesh, 50 miles south-west of Lucknow.
War and campaign: Indian Mutiny, 1857–1858: Oudh and Rohilkand Campaigns.
Opposing sides: (a) General Sir Colin Campbell; (b) Tantia Topi and Rao Sahib.
Objective: The rebels were attempting to cut the British lines of communication as the latter evacuated LUCKNOW.
Forces engaged: (a) Approximately 5,000 British and Indian troops, plus 20 guns (including eight naval 24prs); (b) 25,000 men and 40 guns.

Casualties: (a) 99 killed and wounded; (b) unknown, but heavy (the pursuit continued for fourteen miles and 32 of the rebels' guns were captured).
Result: After evacuating the civilian refugees and wounded by river to Allahabad, Campbell launched a general attack on the rebels and routed them, employing the same forward artillery tactics that had been used during the Second Relief of LUCKNOW.

After the battle, regarded as a turning point in the history of the Mutiny, it was generally accepted that the British would emerge the ultimate victors, and support for the mutineers declined. See BETWA, THE, and GWALIOR.

Cedar Creek 102

Date: 19 October 1864.
Location: North of Strasburg, Virginia.
War and campaign: American Civil War: Shenandoah Valley Campaign of 1864.
Opposing sides: (a) Major-General Phillip Sheridan commanding the Army of the Shenandoah; (b) Lieutenant-General Jubal A. Early commanding the Army of the Valley.
Objective: In accordance with Grant's philosophy of total war, Sheridan had been devastating the Valley, from which the Confederacy drew much of its supplies. Early decided to launch a surprise attack while the Federals, their task complete, were encamped.
Forces engaged: (a) 32,000; (b) 21,000.
Casualties: (a) 5,672; (b) 2,910.
Result: At first Early's attack was successful, routing VIII Corps and forcing the rest of the Federal army into a fighting retreat. Sheridan, returning from a command conference in Washington, personally restored the situation and mounted a counter-attack which drove the Confederates back, capturing their supply echelon. Since the Valley was now incapable of supporting his army, Early continued his retreat and most of his infantry rejoined Lee at PETERSBURG. The battle effectively marked the end of the Confederate threat from the Valley.

Despite his ultimate defeat, Early's achievements in the Valley had been impressive. His penetration as far as Washington following MONOCACY had caused serious alarm and drawn off so considerable a portion of the Army of the Potomac's strength that Grant was determined to eliminate the menace of the Valley once and for all. Although he was not always successful, winning at Kernstown (24 July) but losing at Opequon Creek (Third Winchester) (19 September) and again at Fisher's Hill (22 September), Early's activities delayed the end of the war in the East by six months.

Cedar Mountain 103

Date: 9 August 1862.
Location: 70 miles south-west of Washington, D.C., between Orange and Culpeper, Virginia.
War and campaign: American Civil War: Second Bull Run (Manassas) Campaign.

Opposing sides: (a) Major-General Nathaniel P. Banks; (b) Major-General Thomas J. ('Stonewall') Jackson.
Objective: An encounter between elements of the Federal Army of Virginia and the Confederate Army of Northern Virginia.
Forces engaged: (a) 12,000; (b) 22,000.
Casualties: (a) 2,500; (b) 1,400.
Result: While inconclusive in itself, the Federal defeat and enforced retreat opened the way for a Confederate advance northwards. See BULL RUN, SECOND).

Banks, commanding the leading Federal corps, launched an impetuous attack against Jackson's position without being fully aware of his opponent's strength. He almost succeeded in turning the Confederate left but Jackson rallied his men and, reinforced, they drove the Federals back towards Culpeper. The battle is said to be the only occasion during the war when Jackson actually drew his sword.

Cerignola 104

Date: 26 April 1503.
Location: Town 20 miles inland from Barletta on the southern Adriatic coast of Italy.
War and campaign: French Sixteenth Century Wars in Italy: Franco–Spanish War in Naples, 1495–1504.
Opposing sides: (a) Hernandez Gonzalo de Cordoba commanding the Spanish army; (b) the Duke of Nemours commanding the French.
Objective: The Spaniards deliberately provoked an action with a stronger French force.
Forces engaged: (a) 6,000; (b) 10,000.
Casualties: (a) Light; (b) uncertain, but heavy (Nemours was killed).
Result: The French were routed and forced to abandon Naples. See also GARIGLIANO.

Cerignola was probably the first battle in which the personal firearm can be said to have been the decisive weapon. Cordoba appreciated that his arquebusiers would perform best behind a ditch and palisade which would not only provide protection but also improve accuracy. The attack of the French cavalry and pikemen was broken up by the arquebusiers' fire and a counter-attack by the Spanish infantry completed the rout.

Cerro Gordo 105

Date: 18 April 1847.
Location: Between Vera Cruz and Puebla, Central Mexico.
War and campaign: US–Mexican War, 1846–1848: Central Mexico Campaign.
Opposing sides: (a) General Winfield Scott; (b) the Dictator of Mexico, General Antonio Lopez de Santa Anna.
Objective: The Americans, advancing on Mexico City from Vera Cruz, found their way barred by a strong defensive position in a mountain defile.

Forces engaged: (a) 8,500; (b) 12,000.	
Casualties: (a) 64 killed and 353 wounded; (b) approximately 700 killed and wounded, 3,041 taken prisoner and some 40 guns captured.	
Result: The discovery of a mountain track helped the Americans to outflank the Mexican position and the pass was forced after hard fighting. Scott continued his advance and on 15 August occupied Puebla, 75 miles from Mexico City. See CONTRERAS-CHURUBUSCO.	

Serving with Scott were a number of junior officers who would achieve prominence during the American Civil War, including Captains Robert E. Lee, George B. McClellan and Joseph E. Johnston and Lieutenants Ulysses S. Grant, Thomas J. Jackson and Pierre Beauregard.

Chaeronea (338 BC) 106

Date: 2 August 338 BC.
Location: Near modern Skripou, Ellas, north-west of Athens.
War and campaign: The Fourth Sacred War, 339–338 BC.
Opposing sides: (a) King Philip; (b) Chares and Theagenes commanding, respectively, the Athenian and Theban contingents.
Objective: Philip of Macedonia's domination of central Greece was challenged by an Athenian-Theban coalition.
Forces engaged: (a) 30,000 infantry and 2,000 cavalry; (b) 35,000.
Casualties: (a) Unknown, but heavy; (b) 6,000 Athenians killed and 2,000 captured, Theban contingent annihilated – total approximately 20,000.
Result: A decisive Macedonian victory which left Philip master of Greece.

Little is known of the course of the battle but it is possible that by feigning a withdrawal of his right wing Philip drew the Athenians forward, thereby extending the allied line until a gap appeared. This was immediately exploited by Philip's 18-year-old son Alexander (later the Great) commanding the Macedonian cavalry, with catastrophic results for the allies. While cavalry was the Macedonian arm of decision, the backbone of the army was its phalanx, which consisted of sixteen ranks instead of the Greek eight-to-twelve and was armed with spears up to 21ft in length, held in both hands. With the spearpoints of its leading five ranks bristling ahead, the phalanx closed with its opponents at a run and in the context of a frontal attack was unstoppable.

Chaeronea (86 BC) 107

Date: 86 BC.
Location: Near modern Skripou, Ellas, north-west of Athens.
War and campaign: First Mithridatic War, 89–84 BC.
Opposing sides: (a) Lucius Cornelius Sulla; (b) Archelaus commanding the Mithridatic army.
Objective: The Romans were contesting possession of Greece with the forces of King Mithridates VI of Pontus, Asia Minor.

Forces engaged: (a) Approximately 15,000 infantry and 1,500 cavalry – total 16,500; (b) approximately 45,000 infantry, 4,500 cavalry and 90 chariots – total 50,000.
Casualties: Unknown, but those of the Mithridatic army were heavy.
Result: Sulla's legions won a complete victory.

Sulla protected his flanks with entrenchments and erected a palisade across his front as a defence against chariots – the first known use of field works during an offensive operation. The legions, deployed in a square, beat off an attack by the Mithridatic cavalry and when Archelaus committed his chariots the horses, maddened by arrow and javelin wounds, bolted through their own phalanx, throwing it into disorder. Sulla immediately ordered his infantry and cavalry to counter-attack and swept the enemy off the field.

Chalgrove Field   108

Date: 18 June 1643.
Location: Near Chalgrove village, 8 miles south-east of Oxford.
War and campaign: First Civil War, 1642–1646.
Opposing sides: (a) Prince Rupert commanding the Royalists; (b) Sir Philip Stapleton commanding the Parliamentarians.
Objective: The Parliamentarians were attempting to intercept a force of Royalist cavalry returning to Oxford after a raid.
Forces engaged: (a) 1,000 cavalry, 350 dragoons and 500 infantry; (b) approximately 1,000.
Casualties: Moderate on both sides, although the Parliamentarians suffered the greater loss, including one of their most important leaders, John Hampden, mortally wounded.
Result: Rupert ambushed his pursuers, then charged and routed them.

Chalons   109

Date: 451.
Location: Two miles west of Méry-sur-Seine, approximately 18 miles north of Troyes.
War and campaign: The Hun Invasion of Gaul.
Opposing sides: (a) Aetius, Roman Master of the Soldiers, and Theodoric, king of the Visigoths; (b) Atilla the Hun.
Objective: The Romans and their allies were attempting to repel the invaders.
Forces engaged: (a) Strength unknown (the Roman army included large contingents of Alans and Visigoths); (b) strength unknown (the Hun army concluded contingents of Ostrogoths and Gepidae but was probably smaller).
Casualties: (a) Unknown, but heavy (Theoderic was among those killed); (b) unknown, but much heavier.
Result: Atilla's army was routed and its remnants withdrew across the Rhine. As a Hun victory would have resulted in the destruction of the last remnants of the

Roman Empire in the West, the battle is regarded as one of the most decisive in European history.

The Huns smashed through the Alans in the centre of the Roman army, then turned on the Visigoths holding the Roman right. However, Aetius' left held firm and a detached body of Visigoth cavalry counter-attacked into the mêlée from the right, driving the Ostrogoths back into their camp. The Huns and Gepidae were forced to conform and at one point Attila, despairing, is said to have had his own funeral pyre constructed. Aetius did not exploit his victory.

Chancellorsville 110

Date: 1–5 May 1863.
Location: West of Fredericksburg, Virginia.
War and campaign: American Civil War.
Opposing sides: (a) Major-General Joseph ('Fighting Joe') Hooker commanding the Army of the Potomac; (b) General Robert E. Lee commanding the Army of Northern Virginia.
Objective: The Federals were attempting to renew the direct advance on Richmond, the Confederate capital, which had failed the previous December at FREDERICKSBURG. Crossing the Rappahannock upstream of the latter, they placed themselves across Lee's lines of communication, provoking an inevitable response.
Forces engaged: (a) 130,000; (b) 60,000.
Casualties: (a) 16,792; (b) 12,754.
Result: Hooker was defeated and forced to retire across the Rappahannock. Lee, having noted the poor morale of the Union troops, decided to mount his Second Invasion of the North.

Despite possessing a numerical superiority of 2:1, Hooker decided to fight a purely defensive battle. On 2 May Lee sent Jackson's II Corps on a wide flanking movement with more than half his available strength and at dusk this began rolling up the Federal line from the right. Meanwhile a 10,000-strong force which Lee had left on Marye's Heights, overlooking Fredericksburg, under the command of Major-General Jubal Early, was being pushed steadily westwards by 40,000 Federals commanded by Major-General John Sedgwick. On 3 May, having satisfied himself that while Hooker was offering stiffer resistance he still presented no threat, Lee reinforced Early and defeated Sedgwick at Salem Church the following day. Hooker withdrew his demoralized army during the night of 5/6 May. Although Lee committed the cardinal sin of dividing his force while still in contact with the enemy, Chancellorsville is regarded by many as his greatest victory; it was, however, marred by the death of 'Stonewall' Jackson, mortally wounded by the fire of his own troops during the twilight of 2 May.

Chapultepec 111

Date: 13 September 1847.
Location: Fortress covering the south-western approach to Mexico City.
War and campaign: US–Mexican War, 1846–1848: Central Mexico Campaign.

Opposing sides: (a) General Winfield Scott; (b) the Dictator of Mexico, General Antonio Lopez de Santa Anna.
Objective: The Americans had to capture the fortress before they could assault Mexico City itself.
Forces engaged: (a) 7,200; (b) 16,000.
Casualties: (a) 130 killed and 703 wounded; (b) estimated at over 2,000.
Result: The fortress was stormed and the pursuit was pressed as far as the city gates. Santa Anna withdrew his army to the north and on 14 September the city's garrison surrendered as the Americans were preparing their final assault.

No major military actions followed the capture of Mexico City. A peace treaty was concluded at Gaudalupe Hidalgo on 2 February 1848, under the terms of which California, Nevada, Utah, most of Arizona and New Mexico and parts of Colorado and Wyoming were ceded by Mexico to the United States; for its part the United States paid Mexico £15 million and withdrew its troops from Mexican territory.

Charasia   112

Date: 6 October 1879.
Location: 10 miles south of Kabul, Afghanistan.
War and campaign: Second Afghan War, 1878–1880.
Opposing sides: (a) Major-General Sir Frederick Roberts; (b) dissident elements opposed to Yakub Khan, the pro-British King of Afghanistan.
Objective: A British punitive expedition, advancing on Kabul to avenge the murder of the British Resident, found its way blocked by an Afghan force.
Forces engaged: (a) 7,500 (of whom only 4,000 engaged); (b) 8,000.
Casualties: (a) 20 killed and 67 wounded; (b) approximately 300 killed and wounded, plus all artillery captured.
Result: The Afghans were routed and Roberts occupied Kabul, although his cantonments were soon surrounded by a large hostile force (see SHERPUR). In the meantime Yakub Khan had sought British protection and abdicated.

Charasia was the first action in which the heliograph was used for communication by the forces engaged.

Charleston, Siege of   113

Date: 13 April to 12 May 1780.
Location: Charleston, South Carolina.
War and campaign: American War of Independence, 1775–1783: southern theatre of operations.
Opposing sides: (a) Lieutenant-General Sir Henry Clinton; (b) Major-General Benjamin Lincoln.
Objective: The British intention was to capture the city.
Forces engaged: (a) 10,000; (b) 5,500.
Casualties: (a) 265 killed and wounded in the siege and in peripheral operations in

the hinterland; (b) approximately 100 killed and wounded and 5,400 prisoners, plus 400 guns and four warships captured.
Result: Following a heavy bombardment, Lincoln surrendered at the request of the civil authorities, who wished to spare the city the horrors of the impending assault.

Clinton returned to New York, leaving Cornwallis with 8,000 men to pacify Georgia and the Carolinas. See WAXHAWS and CAMDEN.

Chateaugay River (Spears) 114

Date: 25 October 1813.
Location: Spears village on the Chateaugay, 15 miles upstream of its confluence with the St Lawrence, Quebec.
War and campaign: War of 1812: Canadian Front.
Opposing sides: (a) Colonel George Macdonell commanding the Canadians; (b) Brigadier-General Wade Hampton commanding the American force.
Objective: An American force had crossed the frontier as part of a general offensive aimed at the capture of Montreal. At the Chateaugay its further progress was blocked by Canadian troops holding an abattis on the north bank.
Forces engaged: (a) Approximately 1,500; (b) approximately 4,000.
Casualties: Light on both sides.
Result: After his attack was repulsed Hampton withdrew across the frontier. On learning of the reverse, the main American invasion force, moving down the St Lawrence, abandoned its offensive – see CHRYSLER'S FARM.

Hampton despatched some 1,500 men to outflank the Canadian position and attack it from the rear while he mounted a frontal assault with the rest of his command. The flanking force lost its way and was itself attacked, and the frontal assault was easily beaten off. By sounding bugle calls from different positions the Canadians not only gave an impression of inflated strength but also caused considerable confusion.

Chateau Thierry/Belleau Wood 115

Date: 30 May to 17 June 1918.
Location: Town on the Marne 50 miles east of Paris.
War and campaign: First World War: Western Front.
Opposing sides: (a) General Denis Duchene commanding the French Sixth Army; (b) General Max von Bohn commanding the German Seventh Army.
Objective: The Allied intention was to halt LUDENDORFF'S THIRD OFFENSIVE.
Forces engaged: (a) US 3rd Division (Major-General J. T. Dickman) at Chateau Thierry under the French XXXVIII Corps and US 2nd Division (Major-General Omar Bundy) at Belleau Wood under the French XXI Corps; (b) leading elements of the German Seventh Army.
Casualties: (a) Chateau Thierry – uncertain; Belleau Wood – 9,777, including 1,811 killed. (b) uncertain at either location, but 1,600 prisoners taken at Belleau Wood.
Result: At Chateau Thierry von Bohn's advance was stemmed by the machine-

gunners of the US 3rd Division which, with rallied French troops, then drove the Germans back across the Marne. At Belleau Wood the US 2nd Division, spearheaded by the 4th Marine Brigade, drove the Germans from their position with six assaults delivered in succession. These tactical victories, together with a third fought by the US 1st Division (Major-General Robert Bullard) at Cantingy on 28/29 May, were won by fresh, aggressive American troops and did much to restore Allied morale.

Chattanooga 116

Date: 24–25 November 1863.
Location: Chattanooga, Tennessee.
War and campaign: American Civil War: western theatre of operations.
Opposing sides: (a) Major-General Ulysses S. Grant, Commander-in-Chief of Union forces in the West; (b) General Braxton Bragg commanding the Confederate Army of Tennessee.
Objective: The Federal intention was to break the Confederate hold on the town, which contained an important railway junction.
Forces engaged: (a) 70,000; (b) 50,000.
Casualties: (a) 752 killed, 4,713 wounded and 350 missing – total 5,815; (b) 361 killed, 2,160 wounded and 3,164 missing – total 6,667.
Result: The siege was raised and Bragg was forced to retreat. The hopes of the Confederacy, which had soared after CHICKAMAUGA, were dashed by the defeat of one of its two major field armies and the way was open for a Federal invasion of Georgia. See KENNESAW MOUNTAIN and ATLANTA.

The Federal concentration for the operation involved troops drawn both from the Mississippi region and from the Army of the Potomac. The action on 24 November is often referred to as Lookout Mountain and that on 25 November as Missionary Ridge.

Chickamauga 117

Date: 18–20 September 1863.
Location: Close to Fort Oglethorpe, Georgia, south of Chattanooga.
War and campaign: American Civil War: western theatre of operations.
Opposing sides: (a) Major-General William S. Rosecrans commanding the Federal Army of the Cumberland; (b) General Braxton Bragg commanding the Confederate Army of Tennessee.
Objective: The Confederates were attempting to recover the important railway junction of Chattanooga, from which they had been manoeuvred earlier in the month.
Forces engaged: (a) 62,000; (b) 65,000.
Casualties: (a) 1,657 killed, 9,756 wounded and 4,757 missing – total 16,170 (b) 2,312 killed, 14,674 wounded and 1,486 missing – total 18,472.
Result: The Confederates won a tactical victory and laid siege to CHATTANOOGA when Rosecrans retired into the town. This in turn resulted in Federal troops being rushed from other theatres of war to restore the situation.

Chilianwallah

Date: 13 January 1849.
Location: Village in north-western Lahore province, south of Jhelum, now in Pakistan.
War and campaign: Second Sikh War, 1848–1849.
Opposing sides: (a) General Lord Gough; (b) Sher Singh.
Objective: The British were attempting to defeat the Sikh army before it could be reinforced.
Forces engaged: (a) 20,000 British and Indian troops; (b) 40,000 Sikhs with 62 guns.
Casualties: (a) 2,746 killed and wounded; (b) 3,894 killed and wounded.
Result: Gough claimed a victory, but other British sources describe the battle variously as a heavy defeat and a ghastly fiasco. The Sikhs were able to disengage and were reinforced.

Gough allowed himself to be provoked into fighting in fading afternoon light and his attack was launched without adequate reconnaissance or artillery preparation; in fact, the British artillery played little part in the action, as the advance of the infantry masked the fire of its guns. On the right flank mistaken orders by one of the East India Company's elderly generals led to the disorderly withdrawal of a cavalry brigade from the field. The fight was resolved by a brutal infantry combat in dense jungle but casualties had been so severe that Gough withdrew to Chilianwallah, enabling the Sikhs to return to the field and recover forty of their guns which had been captured. Despite his victories in the First Sikh War (MUDKI, FEROZESHAH and SOBRAON), Gough's handling of the battle attracted unfavourable comment at home, particularly in relation to the casualties incurred by two Queen's (i.e. British as opposed to Company) regiments, the 24th (South Wales Borderers) and 29th (Worcestershire), whose losses had reduced them to cadre strength. It was decided to replace him with General Sir Charles Napier, but before the orders arrived Gough had fought the decisive battle of GUJERAT, which confirmed that he had absorbed the lessons of Chilianwalla.

Chippewa

Date: 5 July 1814.
Location: On the west bank of the Niagara river, south of the confluence of the Chippewa, Ontario.
War and campaign: War of 1812: Canadian Front.
Opposing sides: (a) Major-General Sir Phineas Riall; (b) Major-General Jacob Brown.
Objective: A British counter-attack against an American force which had invaded Canada.
Forces engaged: (a) Approximately 1,500 regulars; (b) approximately 1,300 regulars.
Casualties: (a) 236 killed, 322 wounded and 46 captured; (b) 61 killed, 255 wounded and 46 captured.

> **Result:** The British attack was repulsed and Riall was forced to withdraw northwards and await the arrival of reinforcements. See LUNDY'S LANE.

The battle, fought between regular troops on even terms, established the prestige of the US Army in the eyes of the American public. The officer responsible was Brigadier-General Winfield Scott, who had trained his brigade thoroughly. His men had recently been issued with new grey uniforms as none of the regulation blue cloth was available. At first, Riall believed that they were militia but, observing their disciplined deployment under fire, is said to exclaimed: 'These are regulars, by God!' The full-dress uniform of the US Military Academy at West Point commemorates the action. Scott was further to distinguish himself during the US–Mexican War and was still active during the early months of the American Civil War.

Chosin Reservoir/Hungnam   120

Date: 27 November to 15 December 1950.
Location: North-eastern Korea.
War and campaign: Korean War, 1950–1953: Chinese Intervention.
Opposing sides: (a) Major-General Oliver Smith commanding the 1st Marine Division; (b) General Sung Shih-lun commanding elements of the Chinese Third Field Army converging on Hungnam.
Objective: The US 1st Marine Division was conforming to the movement of the US X Corps and withdrawing towards its evacuation port of Hungnam to avoid encirclement by numerically superior Chinese forces.
Forces engaged: (a) 1st Marine Division (reinforced) with 41 Royal Marine Commando under command – total approximately 15,000; (b) the Chinese 58th, 59th, 60th, 76th, 77th, 79th and 80th Divisions – total approximately 65,000.
Casualties: (a) 718 killed, 192 missing and 3,508 wounded; (b) 25,000 killed in action, frozen to death or dead from disease, plus approximately 13,000 wounded or captured (the corps-sized formations from which the divisions were drawn – 20th, 26th and 27th Armies – disappeared from the Chinese order of battle).
Result: The Marines succeeded in fighting their way to Hungnam. The Chinese were too exhausted to interfere seriously with X Corps' embarkation. Altogether 105,000 UN and South Korean troops, 98,000 refugees, 17,500 vehicles and 350,000 tons of cargo were taken off.

The 70-mile fighting withdrawal was made through mountainous country in sub-arctic conditions with the temperature sometimes dropping as low as –29 degrees Centigrade. The Chinese employed their greater mobility to mount regular ambushes along the route but the UN air forces possessed total superiority and were able not only to supply the column by air but also to pound the enemy with incessant strikes. As Hungnam was approached heavy naval gunfire support was also available to keep the Chinese at bay. After the embarkation had been completed the port facilities were blown up to deny their use to the Communists.

Chrysler's Farm   121

Date: 11 November 1813.
Location: On the north bank of the St Lawrence near Cornwall, Ontario.

War and campaign: War of 1812: Canadian Front.
Opposing sides: (a) Colonel J. W. Brown commanding the British; (b) Brigadier-General John Boyd commanding the American detachment.
Objective: A 7,000-strong American invasion force commanded by Brigadier-General James Wilkinson was moving down the St Lawrence to attack Montreal. A strong detachment was landed with the intention of dispersing British units which had been harassing the American rear.
Forces engaged: (a) Approximately 800 regulars and Indians; (b) approximately 2,000 regulars.
Casualties: (a) 203 killed and wounded; (b) 249 killed and wounded, plus approximately 100 captured.
Result: Boyd's troops were routed and driven back to their boats. Wilkinson, already disheartened by the defeat of another American invasion force with which he was to co-operate (see CHATEAUGAY RIVER), abandoned his attempt to reach Montreal and went into winter quarters. The following spring he made a half-hearted attempt to renew the offensive but made little progress and was replaced by one of his more capable subordinates, Jacob Brown. See also STONY CREEK, CHIPPEWA and LUNDY'S LANE.

Ciudad Rodrigo, Siege and Storming of   122

Date: 7–19 January 1812.
Location: Fortress city near the Spanish/Portuguese frontier 50 miles west of Salamanca.
War and campaign: Peninsular War, 1807–1814: Campaign of 1812.
Opposing sides: (a) Lieutenant-General Viscount Wellington; (b) Brigadier-General Baron Barrie.
Objective: Wellington, intending to take the offensive, wished to capture the fortress, which covered the northern invasion route from Portugal into Spain.
Forces engaged: (a) Approximately 35,000; (b) 1,890.
Casualties: (a) 710 killed, including Major-General Robert Craufurd, commander of the Light Division, and 580 wounded; (b) 300 killed and wounded and 1,500 prisoners, plus 153 guns captured.
Result: Barrie surrendered once the breaches had been stormed. His troops, however, had inflicted heavy casualties in proportion to their numbers and the attackers subjected the town to a night of drunken plunder. The captured equipment included the entire siege train of the French Army of Portugal. Wellington, created an Earl for his achievement, marched south to besiege BADAJOZ, covering the southern invasion route into Spain.

Cold Harbor   123

Date: 31 May to 3 June 1864.
Location: 15 miles north-east of Richmond, Virginia.
War and campaign: American Civil War: Grant's Virginia Campaign of 1864.
Opposing sides: (a) Lieutenant-General Ulysses S. Grant, the US Army's General-

in-Chief, in the field with Major-General George G. Meade's Army of the Potomac; (b) General Robert E. Lee commanding the Army of Northern Virginia.
Objective: Having slipped past Lee's right at SPOTSYLVANIA COURT HOUSE, and repeated the manoeuvre at the North Anna River, Grant was closing in on Richmond. Believing, incorrectly, that Lee's army was overextended, he decided to split it with an attack against its centre.
Forces engaged: (a) 114,000; (b) 59,000.
Casualties: Approximately 10,000; (b) approximately 4,000.
Result: The Federal assault on Lee's entrenched position was bloodily repulsed. Grant, finding the direct approach to Richmond blocked, resumed his southward march and crossed the James river in the hope that he would be able to capture PETERSBURG, thereby isolating the Confederate capital.

Grant was able to pursue his advance to the south because he knew that Lee would always position the Army of Northern Virginia between him and Richmond. Again, while the Army of the Potomac was now operating deep within hostile territory, it was supplied by river transport and did not have to rely on long and vulnerable lines of communication.

Colenso 124

Date: 15 December 1899.
Location: Town on the Tugela river, south of Ladysmith, Natal, South Africa.
War and campaign: Second Boer War, 1899–1902.
Opposing sides: (a) General Sir Redvers Buller; (b) General Louis Botha.
Objective: A British relief force was attempting to fight its way through to LADYSMITH.
Forces engaged: (a) 21,000 men, five field artillery batteries and fourteen naval guns; (b) 6,000 men and eight guns.
Casualties: (a) 143 killed, 755 wounded, 240 missing and ten guns captured; (b) six killed and 21 wounded.
Result: Buller's attempt to force a passage of the Tugela was decisively repulsed. Colenso was the third of the three defeats in six days, known collectively as 'Black Week', which seriously shook British confidence, the others being STORMBERG and MAGERSFONTEIN. Buller was replaced as Commander-in-Chief South Africa by Field Marshal Lord Frederick Roberts, whose Chief of Staff was General Lord Herbert Kitchener. See also SPION KOP.

Buller's attack was made without adequate reconnaissance or knowledge of either the ground or the Boer positions. He might have been forgiven his heavy casualties, but not the loss of ten guns, although no disgrace attached to those most closely involved in this aspect of the battle. Mohandas (Mahatma) Gandhi was present at Colenso with a contingent of Indian volunteer stretcher bearers.

Constantinople, Siege of 125

Date: 5 April to 29 May 1453.
Location: Now Istanbul.

War and campaign: The Wars of Islam against the Byzantine Empire.
Opposing sides: (a) The Emperor Constantine IX commanding the garrison; (b) Sultan Mahomet II.
Objective: The Turks wished to capture the city, thereby eliminating the last remnant of the Byzantine Empire.
Forces engaged: (a) 8,900; (b) 50,000 (including 15,000 janissaries) with 56 small guns and fourteen heavy cannon, the latter firing stone shot weighing 1,500lb.
Casualties: (a) The entire garrison was either killed or captured and sold into slavery and Constantine died fighting among his troops; (b) uncertain, but undoubtedly heavy.
Result: The city was stormed. The eclipse of the Byzantine Empire exposed the Balkans and eastern Europe to Turkish invasion.

The ancient walls of the city could not withstand Mahomet's heavy cannon, the like of which existed in no other army of the period. The fire of these was focused on the weakest points of the defences to produce the first concentrated artillery bombardment in history. Although the garrison fought gallantly, repelling numerous assaults, it was inevitable that sooner or later it would be overwhelmed. The subsequent sack of the city lasted for three days and resulted in the deaths of 4,000 of its inhabitants and the enslavement of 50,000 more.

Contreras-Churubusco 126

Date: 20 August 1847.
Location: 5–10 miles south of Mexico City.
War and campaign: US–Mexican War, 1846–1848: Central Mexico Campaign.
Opposing sides: (a) General Winfield Scott; (b) the Dictator of Mexico, General Antonio Lopez de Santa Anna.
Objective: The Americans, advancing on Mexico City from Puebla, found the direct route blocked by the fortress of El Penon and Lake Texcuco. Circling Lakes Chalco and Xochimilco to the south, their columns encountered strong Mexican positions at Contreras and Churubusco, covering the roads into the city.
Forces engaged: (a) Approximately 10,000; (b) approximately 30,000.
Casualties: (a) 137 killed, 877 wounded and 38 missing; (b) 4,297 killed and wounded, 2,637 captured and approximately 3,000 missing.
Result: Santa Anna withdrew half of his army within the city walls, leaving the rest to hold the fortress of CHAPULTEPEC and nearby positions.

Corinth 127

Date: 3–4 October 1862.
Location: North-West of Corinth, Mississippi.
War and campaign: American Civil War: western theatre of operations.
Opposing sides: (a) Major-General William S. Rosecrans commanding the Federal Army of the Mississippi; (b) Major-General Earl Van Dorn commanding the Confederate Army of the West.

Objective: The Confederates were attempting to recover the town and its critically important railway junction. See SHILOH.
Forces engaged: (a) 23,000; (b) 22,000.
Casualties: (a) 2,350; (b) 4,800.
Result: After penetrating as far as the town's inner defences, the Confederate assault was decisively repulsed.

Corinth remained in Union hands, as did Memphis on the Mississippi, captured on 6 June. The way was now open for a Federal advance against VICKSBURG.

Corunna 128

Date: 16 January 1809.
Location: On the north-western coast of Spain (the battle was fought to the south of the city).
War and campaign: Peninsular War, 1807–1814: Campaign in Spain, 1808–1809.
Opposing sides: (a) General Sir John Moore; (b) Marshal Nicolas Jean-de-Dieu Soult, Duke of Dalmatia.
Objective: Moore had advanced into Spain to menace the French communications. However, once the French had taken Madrid (4 December), they turned on him in overwhelming strength and forced him into a difficult 250-mile retreat to the coast across the Cantabrian Mountains in the middle of winter. At Corunna he fought a holding action which would gain time for his troops to embark aboard their transports.
Forces engaged: (a) Approximately 15,000; (b) approximately 20,000.
Casualties: (a) Approximately 1,000 killed and wounded (including Moore, mortally wounded) and a number of prisoners; (b) approximately 2,000 killed and wounded.
Result: The French were checked and the British were able to embark in relative safety. In the wider sphere, Moore's advance into northern Spain ensured that the French were unable to re-establish control in the south of the country.

Moore had been appointed commander of the British troops in the Peninsula during the scandal which followed the Convention of Cintra (see VIMEIRO). His previous service in North America had led him to appreciate the value of light infantry, and the training methods he instituted proved their worth throughout the Peninsular War. His foray into Spain was to have been made with the support of up to 125,000 Spanish irregulars, but the latter were of very limited value. Moore's death was a serious blow to the British Army, but fortunately Wellesley was sent back to the Peninsula to assume command.

Cowpens 129

Date: 17 January 1781.
Location: Between the Pacolet and Broad rivers on the North/South Carolina border.
War and campaign: American War of Independence, 1775–1783: southern theatre of operations.

Opposing sides: (a) Lieutenant-Colonel Banastre Tarleton; (b) Brigadier-General Daniel Morgan.	
Objective: A British force had been pursuing an American detachment which had penetrated South Carolina and caught up with it at Cowpens.	
Forces engaged: (a) 1,100; (b) 1,000.	
Casualties: (a) 100 killed, 229 wounded and 525 captured; (b) 12 killed and 60 wounded.	
Result: An American victory which destroyed the myth of Tarleton's invincibility: after Cowpens his hated Legion never achieved quite the same sustained level of success it had formerly enjoyed. Morgan withdrew into North Carolina, pursued by Cornwallis – see GUILFORD COURT HOUSE.	

Morgan seems to have understood that Tarleton tended to repeat his tactics of hard pursuit followed by immediate attack, and planned accordingly. He prepared a defence in depth and advised his inexperienced militia, deployed behind a skirmish line, that they would be permitted to retire behind his regulars after they had fired three volleys; once Tarleton's men were in contact with the latter, they would be counter-attacked on one flank by Colonel William Washington's cavalry, and by the re-formed militia on the other. The plan worked and the British infantry found itself encircled. Ordered to charge and retrieve the situation, the Legion cavalry rode off, save for one small troop of regular light dragoons which accompanied Tarleton in a desperate counter-attack. This achieved nothing and the survivors were lucky to cut their way out. Understandably, the battle has been described as 'an American CANNAE'.

Crater, The 130

Date: 30 July 1864.	
Location: The southern approaches to Petersburg, Virginia.	
War and campaign: American Civil War: Grant's Virginia Campaign of 1864.	
Opposing sides: (a) Major-General George G. Meade commanding the Army of the Potomac; (b) General Robert E. Lee commanding the Army of Northern Virginia.	
Objective: The Federal intention was to explode a large mine beneath the Confederate defences, then use the gap created to storm Petersburg.	
Forces engaged: (a) Major-General Ambrose E. Burnside's Union IX Corps; (b) uncertain.	
Casualties: (a) 3,793; (b) 1,182.	
Result: The mine explosion produced the desired result but the subsequent Federal attack failed. The siege continued with the lines of both sides being extended steadily to the south-west. See FIVE FORKS.	

The operation would have stood a reasonable chance of success had not Meade intervened, ordering Burnside to replace a division of black troops, specially trained to exploit the explosion, with a white division. The latter, whose drunken commander remained in his dugout, believed that its mission was simply to secure the crater itself, and did not exploit towards the town. Having recovered from their initial shock, the Confederates quickly sealed off the penetration, launching a series of vigorous and successful counter-attacks. Burnside, whose heavy casualties at FREDERICKSBURG had never been forgiven, was effectively dismissed.

Crécy

Date: 26 August 1346.
Location: 10 miles north of Abbeville, Picardy, France.
War and campaign: Hundred Years' War, 1337–1457: Normandy-Calais Campaign of 1346.
Opposing sides: (a) Edward III, King of England; (b) Philip IV, King of France.
Objective: The English, retreating northwards to Flanders, turned to give battle to the pursuing French army.
Forces engaged: (a) 5,500 archers, 1,000 Welsh infantry, 2,500 men-at-arms and a few guns – total approximately 9,000; (b) 6,000 professional infantry including Genoese crossbowmen, 10,000 men-at-arms and 14,000 feudal militia – total approximately 30,000.
Casualties: (a) Approximately 100; (b) 1,542 nobles and knights and approximately 10,000 infantry and militia killed.
Result: The French army was destroyed. Edward resumed his march and besieged Calais, which fell the following year.

The English position lay along a shallow ridge between Crécy and Wadicourt, the archers being formed in wedges on the flanks of their men-at-arms. Pot-holes had been dug across the entire front to hinder the French cavalry. The French army was still strung out in line of march as it approached Crécy and Philip was advised to halt, deploy and fight the following morning. However, the hot-headed nobility of his vanguard insisted on attacking at once. The assault was led by the Genoese crossbowmen who were outranged and fled as their ranks were shot to pieces, only to be ridden down by the impatient French knights as they surged forward to attack. Most of the latter were shot down and the few who reached the English line were either cut down or killed by local counter-attacks. As each division of French knights reached the battlefield it, too, attacked over the same ground. Between 18.00 and 22.30 up to fifteen of these unco-ordinated charges were repulsed with heavy loss. Philip withdrew the remnants of his army about midnight. Among those killed was King John of Bohemia. The fact that the chivalry of France had been decimated by a despised infantry army one-third its size sent shock waves through Europe. It signalled the end of centuries of domination of the battlefield by the mounted knight, who had hitherto sustained the feudal system unchallenged save by his own kind on the battlefield. A major factor in the defeat of the French was their failure to understand that they were dealing with disciplined, professional infantry whose weapon handling skills and operational methods had been honed to a pitch of high efficiency; Edward, for example, paid particular attention to maintaining a regular replenishment of arrows for his archers. Yet, for those who chose to read them, the lessons had all been evident in England's fiercely contested wars against the Scots and the Welsh. Edward's guns may have fired a few rounds but they had no influence on the outcome of the battle, although this may have been the first occasion on which gunpowder weapons were deployed on a European battlefield. See also POITIERS and AGINCOURT.

Crete

Date: 20 May to 1 June 1941.
Location: The principal actions took place around Maleme airfield, Galatas, Retimo and Heraklion.

War and campaign: Second World War: Mediterranean theatre of operations.
Opposing sides: (a) Colonel-General Alexander Lohr commanding Fliegerkorps VIII and XI; (b) Major-General Freyberg commanding the Allied forces on the island.
Objective: The Germans sought to capture the island because possession of its airfields would enable them to strike at British shipping in the Eastern Mediterranean as well as targets in Egypt.
Forces engaged: (a) Mainly parachute and air-landed mountain troops, reinforced by sea – total 23,000; (b) about 32,000 British, Australian and New Zealand troops, plus 10,000 Greeks.
Casualties: (a) Some 6,000 killed and wounded, plus 220 aircraft destroyed; (b) approximately 3,600 British and Commonwealth troops killed and wounded and 12,000 captured, plus nine warships lost during the evacuation.
Result: The Germans captured the island, thereby improving the strategic situation of the Axis powers in the Eastern Mediterranean.

The Germans possessed complete air superiority and began bombing the defences of the island daily from 13 May as a prelude to the invasion. Lohr's plan was to secure the airfields with Lieutenant-General Kurt Student's 7th Air Division and use them to air-land Major-General Julius Ringel's 5th Mountain Division. On 20 May paratroops were dropped at Maleme, Cannea, Retimo and Heraklion. In the desperate fighting which followed, they sustained heavy casualties, while at sea during the night the Royal Navy sank or dispersed German reinforcement convoys with heavy loss of life. However, Freyberg's men were critically short of artillery and, 36 hours after their initial drop, the Germans captured Maleme airfield. During the next four days reinforcements were flown in and the Luftwaffe's ground-attack wings continue to batter the defenders. By 28 May Freyberg had decided that the island could not be held and most of his troops retreated to Sfakia on the south coast, although some were also taken off at Heraklion. In total, the Royal Navy evacuated some 18,000 men to Egypt. The German operation, codenamed 'Merkur', was unique in that for the first time air power alone had been used to secure an objective; conversely, the 7th Air Division sustained 50 per cent casualties, and this so shocked Hitler that he refused to sanction further large-scale airborne operations.

Cropredy Bridge 133

Date: 29 June 1644.
Location: Cropedy village on the Cherwell, north of Banbury, Oxfordshire.
War and campaign: First Civil War, 1642–1646.
Opposing sides: (a) Charles I commanding the Royalists; (b) Sir William Waller commanding the Parliamentarians.
Objective: The Parliamentarians were attempting to isolate and destroy the rearguard of the Royalist army.
Forces engaged: (a) 3,500 infantry and 5,000 cavalry; (b) 4,000 infantry and 5,000 cavalry.
Casualties: (a) Light; (b) approximately 700 killed, wounded and desertions, plus all guns lost.
Result: The Parliamentarians were halted by hard fighting, then driven back across the Cherwell when reinforcements arrived from the Royalist main body. The morale

of Waller's troops collapsed and they mutinied; by the middle of July his army had dispersed.

For the Royalists, the success at Cropedy was marred by news of the disaster at MARSTON MOOR.

Ctesiphon 134

Date: 22–25 November 1916.

Location: On the river Tigris, 20 miles south of Baghdad, Iraq.

War and campaign: First World War: Mesopotamia.

Opposing sides: (a) Lieutenant-General Sir John Nixon commanding the British forces in Mesopotamia; (b) Field Marshal Baron Colmar von der Goltz, Commander-in-Chief of Turkish forces in Mesopotamia.

Objective: Having advanced up the Tigris with unexpected ease, the British hoped to capture Baghdad.

Forces engaged: (a) Major-General Sir Charles Townshend commanding the 6th Indian Division (reinforced), with 10,000 infantry, 1,000 cavalry and 29 guns; (b) Nur-ed-Din Pasha commanding the Turkish 35th, 38th, 45th and 51st Divisions – total approximately 13,000 men and 45 guns, plus irregulars.

Casualties: (a) Approximately 4,600; (b) approximately 6,200.

Result: Although Townshend took his tactical objectives and inflicted the greater loss, his division was in no condition to fight fresh Turkish formations emerging from Baghdad and he withdrew to KUT-AL-AMARA. The inadequacy of the British medical services in the aftermath of the battle provoked a national scandal which resulted in dramatic improvements.

Culloden 135

Date: 16 April 1746.

Location: 5 miles east of Inverness.

War and campaign: Forty-Five Rebellion, 1745–1746.

Opposing sides: (a) The Duke of Cumberland commanding the Government army; (b) Prince Charles Edward Stuart commanding the Jacobite army.

Objective: After FALKIRK the Government army had followed the Jacobites as they withdrew into the Highlands. During the night of 15/16 April the latter mounted an abortive night attack on the Government camp, then withdrew to Culloden Moor. The following morning the Government troops advanced with the intention of inflicting a decisive defeat on the enemy.

Forces engaged: (a) Fifteen infantry battalions, four regiments of dragoons, Scottish volunteer units and sixteen guns – total 9,000; (b) 21 infantry battalions, 400 cavalry and twelve guns – total 5,400.

Casualties: (a) 50 killed and 239 wounded; (b) approximately 1,000 killed and 558 prisoners, plus all guns captured.

Result: The complete defeat of the rebel army. At Culloden the Jacobite cause received a mortal blow and the military power of the clans was broken.

The Jacobite army was starving and exhausted after its futile night march. For approximately 30 minutes it withstood the fire of the Government artillery, then launched a series of desperate piecemeal charges. These were defeated largely because Cumberland had spent a considerable time training his men in a bayonet drill specially designed to meet the Highlanders' style of fighting with broadsword and targe. A double-envelopment by the Government cavalry completed the destruction of Prince Charles' army, which was pursued to within a mile of Inverness. Cumberland's savage treatment of his prisoners, coupled with the brutal repressive measures imposed subsequently, earned him the title of 'Butcher', and this has tended to obscure the credit due for so decisive a victory. The romance of a lost cause attracted writers like Sir Walter Scott and Robert Louis Stevenson, who have presented the battle as a Scottish defeat. In fact, Cumberland's army contained a high proportion of Scots, including three regular and two volunteer regiments, while the Jacobite ranks contained French and Irish elements. Culloden was simply the final decisive act in the dynastic struggle between the Houses of Hanover and Stuart.

Cunaxa 136

Date: 401 BC.
Location: North of Babylon between the Tigris and the Euphrates, Iraq.
War and campaign: Persian Civil War of 401 BC.
Opposing sides: (a) Cyrus, with the Spartan general Clearchus commanding the Greek mercenary contingent; (b) Artaxerxes II.
Objective: Cyrus, satrap of Lydia, was attempting to seize the Persian throne from his brother Artaxerxes II.
Forces engaged: (a) Estimated 50,000, including 13,000 Greek mercenaries; (b) estimated 100,000. Both armies contained a large element of chariotry.
Casualties: Unknown, although Cyrus was killed.
Result: The field was virtually cleared by the Greeks but the rest of Cyrus's army fled when he was killed.

The sequel is probably better known than the battle itself. Artaxerxes invited Clearchus and his senior officers to a feast then treacherously murdered them. The junior officers declined to surrender and decided to march their mercenaries to the nearest friendly city, the Greek colony of Trapezus on the Black Sea, over 1,000 miles distant across the mountains of Armenia, living off the country and fighting their way through for most of the journey. The latter, better known as the 'March of the 10,000', lasted five months, at the end of which 6,000 men had reached safety. The story was recorded by Xenophon, a young Athenian officer who played in prominent role, in his *Anabasis*. Alexander the Great was clearly familiar with Xenophon's comment that Persia belonged to the man with the courage to attack it.

Custozza, Second Battle of 137

Date: 24 June 1866.
Location: 12 miles south-west of Verona, northern Italy.
War and campaign: Austro–Prussian (Seven Weeks') War: Campaign in Venetia.

Opposing sides: (a) General Alfonso di La Marmora commanding the Italian army in Lombardy; (b) the Archduke Albert commanding the Austrian army in Venetia.
Objective: The Italians, having allied themselves with Prussia, hoped to drive the Austrians out of Venetia.
Forces engaged: (a) 80,000; (b) 60,000.
Casualties: (a) 3,800 killed and wounded and 4,300 taken prisoner; (b) 4,600 killed and wounded.
Result: The Italian columns, emerging from the hills, were defeated piecemeal before they could deploy and were driven back across the Mincio into Lombardy. Albert was denied the full reward of his victory when, in the aftermath of the Austrian defeat at KÖNIGGRÄTZ, most of his troops were withdrawn for the defence of Vienna.

The peace treaty which ended the war permitted Italy to annex Venetia.

Cynoscephalae 138

Date: 197 BC.
Location: Ridge in south-eastern Thassalia, Greece.
War and campaign: Second Macedonian War, 200–196 BC.
Opposing sides: (a) The Consul Titus Quinctius Flaminius; (b) King Philip V.
Objective: The Romans intended curbing Philip V of Macedonia's empire-building ambitions in Greece. The two armies suddenly became aware of each other's presence on either side of the ridge and a battle ensued.
Forces engaged: Each army numbered approximately 26,000.
Casualties: (a) Unknown, but light; (b) approximately 13,000 killed and wounded.
Result: The Macedonians were routed. Philip paid a large indemnity and renounced his claims on Greece, which Rome declared independent until war broke out again with Macedonia in 172 BC (see PYDNA).

Philip's phalanx drove Flaminius' left down the ridge but on the opposite flank the Macedonians, still deploying, were pushed up the hillside. At this point, acting on his own initiative, a Roman tribune led twenty maniples along the ridge and fell on the rear of the Macedonian centre, which disintegrated in confusion. For the first time, the battle demonstrated the superiority of the Roman legion's flexible organization over the rigid Macedonian phalanx.

Dak To (Hill 875) 139

Date: 19–23 November 1967.
Location: Feature in Kontum Province, approximately 7 miles south-east of the point where the borders of Laos, Cambodia and Vietnam intersect.
War and campaign: Vietnam War, 1956–1975.
Opposing sides: (a) Brigadier-General Leo H. Schweiter commanding the 173rd Airborne Brigade; (b) the commander of the North Vietnamese Army's (NVA) 174th Regiment.

> **Objective:** The Communists provoked an American attack on the hill, planning to ambush the attacking force and so inflict heavy casualties.
>
> **Forces engaged:** (a) Three companies of the II/503rd Infantry, reinforced by three companies of the IV/503rd Infantry, then of the I/12th Infantry; (b) I, II and III Battalions 174th Regiment.
>
> **Casualties:** (a) Heavy, the majority incurred by II/503rd during the opening phase of the battle (for example, the strength of Company A II/503 was reduced from 101 to 28); (b) 719 killed and nine captured, plus an unknown number of wounded.
>
> **Result:** Although the Communists succeeded in springing their ambush, they were driven off the hill and forced to withdraw across the border. In the strategic sense, however, the battle for Hill 875 was one of a series of engagements in the Dak To area, intended by the Communists to distract American attention from South Vietnam's towns and cities in preparation for the Tet Offensive, which was to be mounted in January 1968 – see HUE.

Hill 875 was covered in dense jungle and the summit was protected by numerous strongly constructed bunkers. The Americans believed that it was held in company strength and for this reason committed only three companies to the first assault. When this was stopped short of the summit by II/174th, I and III/174th closed in on the attackers' rear, driving them into a defensive perimeter. The following day IV/503rd broke through to relieve them but, despite heavy artillery support and air strikes, was unable to secure the summit until 23 November, after I/12th Infantry had been committed to the battle.

Dargai 140

> **Date:** 20 October 1897.
>
> **Location:** Village on a precipitous hill feature at the end of Samana Ridge, covering the road to Tirah, Pakistan.
>
> **War and campaign:** North-West Frontier: Tirah, 1897.
>
> **Opposing sides:** (a) Lieutenant-General Sir William Lockhart commanding the Tirah Field Force; (b) an alliance of Afridi and Orakzai tribal leaders.
>
> **Objective:** The advance of a British punitive expedition towards the Tirah Maidan, in the heart of Afridi territory, was being contested by Orakzai tribesmen.
>
> **Forces engaged:** (a) Total available 11,892 British and 22,614 Indian or Gurkha troops with mountain artillery – the largest force ever employed on the Frontier – of which only one brigade (Kempster's) of Major-General Yeatman-Briggs' 2nd Division took part in the action; (b) uncertain, although the Afridis and Orakzais could muster a combined total of over 40,000 fighting men and about 12,000 are believed to have been present at Dargai.
>
> **Casualties:** (a) Heavy in proportion to the size of the force employed (for example, the 1st Gordon Highlanders alone sustained the loss of 36 killed and 159 wounded); (b) unknown, but almost certainly light (the effect of the supporting artillery was reduced by head cover over the sangars and the tribesmen did not await the final shock of the assault).
>
> **Result:** The village was captured and the punitive expedition continued its advance to the Tirah Maidan, which was devastated. The loss of their strongest position in the first action of the campaign was a severe blow to the tribes.

Dargai had been captured at small cost on 18 October but the troops involved had been withdrawn because they lacked the water and supplies necessary for them to defend it against the large force of tribesmen converging on the village. On 20 October the 1st/2nd Goorkhas (*sic*), 1st Dorsets and 2nd Derbys (later the Sherwood Foresters) made repeated attacks on the position for five hours, without success. It was then the turn of the 1st Gordon Highlanders, whose commanding officer, Lieutenant-Colonel Mathias, informed his men of the general's decision that the position must be taken at all costs, and that the Regiment would take it. Mathias, though wounded, continued to lead the assault, which proved unstoppable. This, together with the story of Piper Findlater who, shot through both ankles and lying in an exposed position, continued to play his comrades into battle, caught the public imagination and made Dargai the best known of many score battles along the Frontier.

D-Day 141

Date: 6 June 1944
Location: The coast of Normandy between the Cotentin peninsula and the Orne river.
War and campaign: Second World War: North-West Europe.
Opposing sides: (a) General Dwight D. Eisenhower, Supreme Commander Allied Forces Europe; (b) Field Marshal Gerd von Rundstedt, Commander-in-Chief West.
Objective: The Allies sought to establish a major beach-head on the coast of occupied France, thereby initiating a campaign against the German forces in western Europe.
Forces engaged: (a) General Sir Bernard Montgomery commanding the Allied 21st Army Group (US First and British Second Armies with three airborne and seven infantry divisions and three armoured and two commando brigades – total 175,000); (b) Field Marshal Erwin Rommel commanding Army Group B (Seventh Army on the invasion sector with elements of one armoured and three infantry divisions – total 80,000).
Casualties: (a) 2,500 killed and 8,500 wounded; (b) unknown.
Result: Despite the fact that some of the day's objectives remained untaken, the Allies succeeded in establishing a secure beach-head from which they could not be dislodged.

Involving no fewer than 1,213 warships, 4,126 landing ships and landing craft of various types, 763 ancillary vessels and 864 merchant ships, the whole covered by overwhelming air superiority, the Allied invasion of Normandy, codenamed 'Overlord', was the largest amphibious operation in history. Shortly after midnight the US 82nd and 101st Airborne Divisions were dropped on the western flank of the selected beach-head to secure causeways across flooded ground in the region of the Rivers Merderet and Douve; simultaneously, the British 6th Airborne Division dropped on the eastern flank and captured bridges over the Caen Canal and the Orne river. The seaborne landings began at half-tide, i.e. from 06.30 onwards, when most of the German beach obstacles became visible. The landings were made with the US First Army (General Omar Bradley) on the right and the British Second Army (General Sir Miles Dempsey) on the left. At 'Utah' beach, lying beyond the Vire estuary, the US 4th Division (US VII Corps) landed a mile south of its designated points but advanced inland and by 13.00 was in contact with the American paratroopers. By midnight the 'Utah' beach-head was four miles wide and nine deep. East of the Vire the 2nd US Ranger Battalion captured the coast defence battery at Point du Hoe. At 'Omaha' beach, however, the US 1st and 29th Divisions (US V Corps) were pinned down by unsubdued defences and by midnight had only penetrated a mile and a half inland, having sustained over 3,000 casualties. The British landings had the benefit of a more prolonged naval bombardment and the leading elements included the 79th Armoured Division's teams of armoured assault engineer vehicles which had been specifically designed to overcome the defences of Hitler's Atlantic Wall. The 50th Division (XXX Corps) landed on 'Gold' beach, capturing Arromanches, and by midnight had reached the outskirts of Bayeux. The Canadian 3rd Division (I Corps) landed on 'Juno' beach and by midnight had reached a point seven miles inland. The British 3rd Division (also I Corps) came ashore on 'Sword' beach, effected a junction with the 6th Airborne Division and by midnight had advanced to within sight of CAEN. The German response to the landings was hindered by a complex command structure, poor communications and a belief that they were simply a feint to draw attention away from the area of the Pas de Calais. As a result of this, Hitler declined to commit his armoured reserve until it was too late. During the afternoon the 21st Panzer Division, which was already present in the battle area, launched a counter-attack from Caen into the area between 'Juno' and 'Sword' beaches but was halted and driven back. By midnight 57,000 American and 75,000 British and Canadian troops, plus their equipment, had been put ashore and the process of linking the beach-heads had begun.

Delhi, Siege of   142

Date: 8 June to 20 September 1857.	
Location: The early fighting took place between The Ridge, a feature north of the city where the British had established a fortified encampment, and the city walls. The assault was delivered against the northern defences.	
War and campaign: Indian Mutiny, 1857–1858.	
Opposing sides: (a) Major-General Archdale Wilson commanding the Delhi Field Force; (b) nominally Bahadur Shah, last of the Mogul Emperors.	
Objective: The British were determined to recapture Delhi, which had become the focus of the Mutiny.	
Forces engaged: (a) Approximately 12,000 British and Indian troops; (b) approximately 30,000 mutineers and their supporters.	
Casualties: (a) 1,254 killed and 4,493 wounded; (b) very heavy (the British, avenging the massacre of their women and children at Delhi, Cawnpore and elsewhere, were in no mood to give quarter).	
Result: The city was stormed, its loss being a major blow to the mutineers' hopes of ejecting the British from India. Bahadur Shah was captured and his sons were shot.	

The troops employed in the siege were freed for operations elsewhere. See LUCKNOW, SIEGE OF.

Dessau Bridge   143

Date: 25 April 1626.	
Location: Town on the Elbe 30 miles south-east of Magdeburg.	
War and campaign: Thirty Years' War, 1618–1648: German Campaign of 1626.	
Opposing sides: (a) Count Ernst von Mansfeld commanding the Protestants; (b) General Albrecht von Wallenstein commanding the Imperialists.	

Objective: The Protestant army, invading the bishopric of Magdeburg, was attempting to force its way across the Elbe.
Forces engaged: (a) 12,000; (b) 20,000.
Casualties: (a) 4,000 killed and many captured; (b) uncertain, but light.
Result: Mansfeld's army destroyed itself in attacks against the bridgehead, the approaches to which Wallenstein had turned into a killing ground.

Mansfeld died in mysterious circumstances some months later. See also LUTTER.

Dettingen 144

Date: 27 June 1743.
Location: On the right bank of the Main, between Aschaffenburg and Hanau, Germany.
War and campaign: War of Austrian Succession, 1740–1748: operations in southern Germany, 1743.
Opposing sides: (a) King George II of England commanding the Allied army; (b) Marshal the Duke Adrien de Noailles commanding the French army.
Objective: The Allied army had attempted to separate the French from their Bavarian allies but was outmanoeuvred and forced to give battle.
Forces engaged: (a) Approximately 40,000 British, Hanoverians and Hessians; (b) approximately 30,000.
Casualties: (a) Approximately 2,500; (b) approximately 5,000, including many drowned while trying to escape across the Main.
Result: An Allied victory which led to the French withdrawing across the Rhine. See also FONTENOY.

Although of limited strategic importance, the battle is of interest in that it was the last occasion when a British monarch personally commanded his troops in battle. At one stage George's horse bolted but, dismounting with the comment that he could trust his own legs not to run away with him, he led his infantry in what proved to be the decisive counter-attack.

Diamond Hill 145

Date: 11–12 June 1900.
Location: South-east of Pretoria, Transvaal, South Africa.
War and campaign: Second Boer War, 1899–1902.
Opposing sides: (a) Field Marshal Lord Frederick Roberts; (b) General Louis Botha.
Objective: Roberts, having occupied Pretoria on 5 June, intended to drive the remnants of the Boer field army beyond striking distance of the city.
Forces engaged: (a) 14,000 men and 70 guns; (b) 6,000 men and 22 guns.
Casualties: (a) 162 killed and wounded; (b) approximately 50 killed and wounded.
Result: Roberts succeeded in his aim, but the Boers did not regard their disengagement as a reverse.

The guerrilla phase of the war, which would last until May 1902, had already begun before Diamond Hill, which was one of the last formal encounters between the two sides. See SANNA'S POST.

Dien Bien Phu   146

Date: 20 November 1953 to 7 May 1954.
Location: Fortified base in the Nam Yum valley, north-western Vietnam, close to the Laotian border.
War and campaign: French Indo-China War, 1946–1954.
Opposing sides: (a) Brigadier-General Christian de Castries commanding the garrison; (b) General Vo Nguyen Giap commanding the Viet Minh.
Objective: The French strategy was to establish a fortified base astride the Viet Minh's line of communications with Laos, so provoking the Viet Minh into fighting a decisive battle.
Forces engaged: (a) Initially six, rising to thirteen, battalions (of which seven were parachute battalions), four 155mm guns, 24 105mm guns and ten M24 light tanks – total approximately 16,000; (b) 304th, 308th, 312th, and 316th Divisions, plus 351st Heavy Division and one regular Chinese air-defence regiment, 144 75mm or 105mm field artillery weapons, 48 120mm mortars, 30 75mm recoilless guns, twelve six-barrel multiple rocket launchers and 180 12.7mm and 37mm anti-aircraft weapons – estimated total 50,000.
Casualties: (a) 2,293 killed and 11,000 captured, including 5,143 wounded (only 3,000 of the prisoners survived their captivity) and all equipment destroyed or captured, including 62 aircraft shot down or seriously damaged; (b) estimated minimum 8,000 killed and 15,000 wounded.
Result: The Viet Minh captured the base. Although the losses amounted to no more than 5 per cent of the French troops available in Vietnam, it included the cream of the strategic reserve. The Communist victory therefore placed the Viet Minh delegates at the Geneva Peace Conference in a strong position. In July France agreed that Vietnam, Laos and Cambodia would be granted full independence; that Vietnam would be temporarily partitioned along the 17th Parallel pending national elections; and that in the meantime French and Viet Minh forces would withdraw respectively from north and south Vietnam.

The French intention was that the base would be supplied by air and that its garrison would be supported by air strikes. Unfortunately, Dien Bien Phu lay in a valley ringed by heavily forested hills up to 1,800ft in height (which made flying difficult in the monsoon seasons) and was also 140 miles from the nearest air base; furthermore, the base lay so far from the French-controlled Red River Delta that it could not be relieved by land forces. The possibility that the Viet Minh might deploy heavy weapons in the area was largely discounted, with fatal results. Giap, interpreting the French strategy correctly, mobilized a 75,000-strong labour force which transported his artillery and anti-aircraft guns piecemeal into the area, then emplaced it on the reserve slopes of the surrounding hills. Patrol clashes, followed by harassing artillery fire, began in January 1954, but Giap did not launch his first assault until 13 March. The French artillery was overwhelmed almost immediately. One by one the French strongpoints began to fall, although the horrific casualties incurred during Giap's brutal human-wave assaults brought his men to the point of mutiny at one period. The French High Command continued to reinforce the garrison, and when the airstrip became unusable it resorted to para-dropping supplies, only one-third of which landed within the shrinking perimeter. Despite this, when Giap launched his final assault on 1 May the garrison had only three days' rations in hand, although it held its last remaining positions until the evening of 7 May. Compare with KHE SANH.

Dieppe 147

Date: 19 August 1942.
Location: On the coast of Normandy.
War and campaign: Second World War.
Opposing sides: (a) Major-General H. F. Roberts commanding the Allied ground troops; (b) Lieutenant-General Konrad Haase commanding the German division holding the Dieppe sector of coastline.
Objective: An Allied raid mounted to test the strength of German coastal defences and demonstrate to Stalin that any attempt to open a Second Front in Western Europe at that time was premature.
Forces engaged: (a) 2nd Canadian Division plus Nos 3 and 4 Commandos, including some 50 US Rangers – total about 6,000; (b) German 302nd Division – total about 5,000.
Casualties: (a) Canadians 215 officers and 3,164 men, Commandos 24 officers and 223 men, 28 tanks, Royal Navy 81 officers and 469 men, one destroyer and 33 landing craft lost, Royal Air Force 107 aircraft; (b) 302nd Division 345 killed and 268 wounded, coast defence battery destroyed, Luftwaffe 48 aircraft destroyed plus many more damaged.
Result: Apart from the elimination of a coastal artillery battery on the right flank of the assault, the raid was apparently an expensive tactical failure. This, however, was a superficial impression, as it achieved its political objective and provided many valuable lessons which were put to good use on D-DAY, when casualties were remarkably light on most sectors.

Donauworth (Schellenberg Heights) 148

Date: 2 July 1704.
Location: Village on the Danube between Ulm and Ratisbon (Regensburg), Bavaria.
War and campaign: War of Spanish Succession, 1701–1714: operations in Central Europe, 1704.
Opposing sides: (a) John Churchill, Duke of Marlbrough, commanding the Allied army; (b) the Count d'Arco commanding the Franco-Bavarians.
Objective: To relieve Franco-Bavarian pressure against Vienna (see HOCHSTADT), Marlbrough had marched his army up the Rhine, then moved eastwards to the Danube. Hoping to provoke Elector Maximilian of Bavaria to battle, he burned up to 300 villages and attacked a Franco-Bavarian position on the Schellenberg Heights near Donauworth.
Forces engaged: (a) 52,000, including 10,000 British; (b) 12,000.
Casualties: (a) 5,400; (b) 6,000.
Result: The position was stormed by Marlborough's troops. The Elector, however,

refused to give battle until he had been reinforced by Marshal Tallard's French army, advancing from Strasbourg. See BLENHEIM.

Dorylaeum

Date: 1 July 1097.

Location: Near modern Eskisehir, western Turkey.

War and campaign: The First Crusade, 1096–1099.

Opposing sides: (a) Duke Bohemond of Taranto commanding the northern column and Duke Godfrey de Buillon and Count Raymond of Toulouse commanding the southern column; (b) Kilij Arslan, Sultan of Rum.

Objective: Having captured Nicaea, the Crusaders were continuing their march across Asia Minor towards the Holy Land when the Turks ambushed their northern column.

Forces engaged: (a) Approximately 15,000 in each column – total 30,000; (b) approximately 50,000.

Casualties: (a) 4,000; (b) 3,000.

Result: The Turks were driven off and the Crusaders resumed their advance. See ANTIOCH.

The Turks, mainly mounted archers, drove Bohemond's column back through its camp but were routed when Raymond's troops fell on their rear while they were plundering.

Dresden

Date: 26–27 August 1813.

Location: South and west of the city of Dresden, Germany.

War and campaign: War of the Sixth Coalition, 1812–1814: Campaign in Germany, 1813.

Opposing sides: (a) The Emperor Napoleon I commanding the French army; (b) Marshal Prince Karl von Schwarzenberg commanding the Allied army.

Objective: The Allies attacked Dresden, which they believed was held only by St Cyr's corps. However, Napoleon, aware of the danger, was already arriving with three additional corps.

Forces engaged: (a) 70,000; (b) 158,000.

Casualties: (a) 10,000; (b) 38,000, plus 40 guns captured.

Result: The Allied attack was contained and on the second day Napoleon took the offensive, turning Schwarzenberg's left flank to win a brilliant tactical victory.

This, Napoleon's last victory on German soil, was marred by the onset of one of his periods of lethargy, during which he failed to orchestrate a pursuit of the beaten army. On his own initiative one of his corps commanders, General Dominique Vandamme, attempted to intercept Schwarzenberg as he withdrew across the mountains into Bohemia, but he was not supported and on 29–30 August his 30,000 men were surrounded and overwhelmed at Kulm. See LEIPZIG.

Drumclog

Date: 1 June 1679.
Location: Hamlet 16 miles south of Glasgow.
War and campaign: Covenanter Rising in Scotland, 1679.
Opposing sides: (a) John Graham of Claverhouse (later Viscount Dundee) commanding the Government troops; (b) Robert Hamilton commanding the Covenanters.
Objective: A body of Government cavalry, pursuing the murderers of Archbishop Sharp into the Covenanter south-west of Scotland, attempted to disperse an armed conventicle assembled at Drumclog.
Forces engaged: (a) 150 cavalry, mainly dragoons; (b) four infantry battalions and three cavalry squadrons – total approximately 1,500.
Casualties: (a) Estimated 40 killed; (b) uncertain, but lighter.
Result: The rebels counter-attacked and routed the Government troops.

Encouraged by their success, the rebels attempted to capture Glasgow next day but were beaten off. See also BOTHWELL BRIDGE.

Dunbar

Date: 3 September 1650.
Location: Two miles south-east of the town.
War and campaign: Third Civil War, 1650–1651: operations in Scotland.
Opposing sides: (a) David Leslie commanding the Covenanter/Royalist army; (b) Oliver Cromwell commanding the Parliamentarians.
Objective: The Parliamentary army had been isolated in Dunbar by the Covenanters and was considering an evacuation by sea, at the cost of its guns, baggage and horses. At the critical moment, however, the Covenanters were persuaded by their clergy to abandon their strong position on Doon Hill and give battle.
Forces engaged: (a) 16,000 infantry, 6,000 cavalry and 30 guns; (b) 7,500 infantry, 3,500 cavalry and some guns.
Casualties: (a) 3,000 killed, 10,000 prisoners and all guns captured; (b) undoubtedly greater than the 30 killed suggested by Cromwell.
Result: The Covenanter army was destroyed and Cromwell took Edinburgh. The influence of the Kirk was sharply reduced, although at its behest Charles II was crowned at Scone shortly after the battle. See also WORCESTER.

Responsibility for the disaster does not rest solely on the shoulders of the Covenanters' importunate clerics, unpleasant as some of them undoubtedly were. Leslie was an experienced commander and, knowing that Cromwell's army was short of rations and contained a high proportion of sick, it is unlikely that he would have abandoned his position on Doon Hill unless he believed he could win. Again, he was responsible for ordering the majority of his musketeers to extinguish their matches as an economy measure, so that when Cromwell launched his first-light attack only one in six were ready to fire. Cromwell had detected a weakness in the Covenanter right and it was against this that his main assault was directed while his artillery was concentrated against the enemy left. Outflanked, Leslie's right gave way and the whole Covenanter line was rolled up.

Dunes, The 153

Date: 3 June 1658.	
Location: Four miles east of Dunkirk.	
War and campaign: Franco–Spanish War, 1653–1659: Campaign in Flanders, 1658.	
Opposing sides: (a) Marshal Vicomte Henri de Turenne commanding the Anglo-French army; (b) Don John of Austria and Louis de Bourbon Condé commanding the Spaniards.	
Objective: An Anglo-French army besieging Dunkirk was forced to give battle to a Spanish relief force.	
Forces engaged: (a) 9,000 infantry (including six Cromwellian regiments) and 6,000 cavalry – total 15,000; (b) 6,000 infantry and 8,000 cavalry (including 2,000 English Royalists under the Duke of York, later James II) – total 14,000.	
Casualties: (a) 400 killed and wounded; (b) 1,000 killed and wounded and 5,000 prisoners.	
Result: The Spaniards were defeated. Dunkirk surrendered ten days later, followed by other Spanish fortresses in Flanders.	

Dunkirk was ceded to Cromwell by the French but was sold to Louis XIV by Charles II in 1662.

Dunkirk 154

Date: 26 May to 4 June 1940.	
Location: Coastline stretching from Nieuport, Belgium, westwards through De Panne and across the French frontier through Bray Dunes and Dunkirk to a point approximately 8 miles west of the last.	
War and campaign: Second World War: France, 1940.	
Opposing sides: (a) Field Marshal Lord Gort commanding the BEF, plus French and Belgian troops trapped in the pocket; (b) Generals Gerd von Rundstedt and Fedor von Bock commanding, respectively, Army Groups A and B.	
Objective: The evacuation of the British Expeditionary Force from the coastal pocket in which it had been trapped by the successful German offensive.	
Forces engaged: (a) Nine British and five French divisions – total approximately 400,000; (b) the German Fourth and Eighteenth Armies, employing some nine infantry divisions in the assault – total approximately 200,000.	
Casualties: (a) About 62,000, including 40,000 French (the majority captured during the final stages of the battle); (b) unknown.	
Result: Approximately 338,000 Allied troops, of whom one third were French or Belgian, were evacuated, although all their heavy weapons and equipment had to be left behind. The operation generated an unparalleled sense of unity within the United Kingdom.	

The evacuation of the Dunkirk pocket, codenamed 'Dynamo', was planned by Vice-Admiral Bertram Ramsay, then Flag Officer Dover, and commenced on 26 May. Ramsay assembled over 1,000 vessels, including destroyers and smaller warships, cross-channel ferries, pleasure steamers and other craft as small as cabin cruisers manned by their civilian owners. Added urgency was provided by the capitulation of the Belgian Army, covering the Allied left flank, on 28 May. Throughout, the evacuation area remained under heavy attack by the Luftwaffe and the contracting perimeter of the pocket was under constant pressure by German ground troops. Six British and three French destroyers were sunk and nineteen damaged and 56 other ships and 161 smaller craft were lost. The absence of British aircraft above the embarkation beaches provoked unjustified criticism of the RAF which, flying from bases in England, had actually broken up many of the German air attacks before they reached the target area, destroying over 100 aircraft and sustaining a similar loss. There is no doubt that the scale of the evacuation surprised and disappointed the German High Command, although the Germans were justified in their belief that the troops in the pocket no longer presented a threat and had therefore begun re-deploying their armoured formations against the French armies to the south. The German Navy, having sustained crippling losses during the invasion of Norway, was in no position to interfere. Churchill was quick to point out that Dunkirk was an escape and not a victory, but its effect was inspirational.

Edgehill   155

Date: 23 October 1642.
Location: South of Warwick, between the villages of Radway and Kineton.
War and campaign: First Civil War, 1642–1646.
Opposing sides: (a) Charles I commanding the Royalist army; (b) Robert Devereux, Earl of Essex, commanding the Parliamentarians.
Objective: King Charles, marching on London, was confronted by the Parliamentary army.
Forces engaged: (a) 10,000 infantry, 2,500 cavalry, 1,000 dragoons and twenty guns – total 13,500; (b) 12,000 infantry, 2,150 cavalry, 700 dragoons and fifteen guns – total 13,000.
Casualties: Uncertain – estimates of the total casualties vary between 1,000 and 4,000. The Parliamentarians lost seven guns.
Result: A narrow tactical victory for the Royalists.

Charles continued his march to London but at Turnham Green was opposed by a reinforced Parliamentary army 24,000-strong. After a day-long stand-off the king withdrew to Oxford. Edgehill convinced Parliament that it must improve the quality of its troops, and in particular its cavalry.

Edington (Ethandune)   156

Date: May 878.
Location: Near the village of Edington, 3 miles north-east of Westbury, Wiltshire.
War and campaign: Danish Invasions of England.
Opposing sides: (a) King Alfred the Great; (b) King Guthrum.

Objective: The Anglo-Saxon intention was to recapture Chippenham and eject the Danes from Wessex.
Forces engaged: Unknown, but it is unlikely that either side could field many more than 5,000 men, and the Danish army may have somewhat smaller as a 1,200-strong detachment had recently been destroyed at Countisbury Hill, Devon.
Casualties: Unknown, although those of the Danes were undoubtedly the greater.
Result: The Danes were defeated and fled to Chippenham, surrendering a fortnight later when Alfred laid siege to the town. Guthrum embraced Christianity and withdrew from Wessex, abandoning all Danish conquests south of the Thames and west of Watling Street.

Little is known of the course of the battle except that it was prolonged and hard-fought, although one source specifically states that Alfred's men fought in close order from behind a shield wall (*densa testudine*).

El Obeid 157

Date: 3–5 November 1883.
Location: 220 miles south-west of Khartoum in Kordofan province, Sudan.
War and campaign: Sudan Campaigns: Mahdist Rebellion.
Opposing sides: (a) Hicks Pasha (Colonel William Hicks); (b) the Mahdi Mohammed Ahmed.
Objective: The Egyptians were attempting to put down the revolt.
Forces engaged: (a) 7,000 men, ten mountain guns, four field guns and six Nordenfeldt machine guns: (b) 20,000, with artillery, machine guns and 6,000 modern rifles captured from the garrison of El Obeid.
Casualties: (a) Hicks and all but 500 of his men were killed; (b) unknown.
Result: The Egyptian army, desperately short of water, trapped and surrounded at Shekkan, near El Obeid, was overwhelmed after three days' fighting.

The British and Egyptian governments decided to evacuate the Sudan, but the situation was complicated by Major-General Charles Gordon's refusal to relinquish KHARTOUM.

El Teb, Second Battle of 158

Date: 29 February 1884.
Location: South of Suakin, Sudan.
War and campaign: Sudan Campaigns: Suakin Front.
Opposing sides: (a) Major-General Sir Gerald Graham; (b) Osman Digna, Mahdist Governor of Eastern Sudan.
Objective: The British intention was to destroy the Mahdist army in the area, with the further possibility of opening communications with Berber on the Nile and establishing contact with Gordon at KHARTOUM.
Forces engaged: (a) 4,000 men, four guns and several Gatling and Gardner machine guns; (b) 6,000 men, six guns and one Gatling machine gun.

Casualties: (a) 34 killed and 155 wounded; (b) over 2,100 killed, plus all guns captured.
Result: Osman Digna, despite the severity of his defeat, remained in the vicinity of Suakin and gathered his strength in preparation for the next round. See TAMAI.

The Dervishes had obtained their artillery from a 3,500-strong Egyptian force commanded by Baker Pasha which had been routed near El Teb on 4 February. Many of the modern rifles and much of the ammunition captured on this occasion were also recovered.

Eniwetok Atoll 159

Date: 17–23 February 1944.
Location: Part of the Marshall Islands group, Central Pacific.
War and campaign: Second World War: Central Pacific theatre.
Opposing sides: (a) Brigadier-General Thomas Watson commanding Tactical Group 1; (b) Major-General Yoshima Nishida commanding the 1st Amphibious Brigade.
Objective: Following the unexpectedly rapid capture of KWAJALEIN ATOLL, the islands were to be secured as further bases from which to support the continued American drive across the Central Pacific.
Forces engaged: (a) 22nd Marine and 106th Infantry Regiments; (b) the Japanese garrison of about 2,500 men.
Casualties: (a) 348 killed and 866 wounded; (b) apart from a few prisoners, mainly civilian labourers, the Japanese fought to the death.
Result: The capture of Eniwetok and KWAJALEIN atolls isolated the remaining Japanese garrisons in the Marshall Islands and enabled the Americans to accelerate their drive across the Pacific towards Japan itself.

Eutaw Springs 160

Date: 8 September 1781.
Location: On the south bank of the Santee river, 50 miles north-west of Charleston, North Carolina.
War and campaign: American War of Independence, 1775–1783: southern theatre of operations.
Opposing sides: (a) Lieutenant-Colonel Alexander Stewart; (b) Major-General Nathanael Greene.
Objective: Abandoning his pursuit of Cornwallis (see GUILFORD COURT HOUSE and YORKTOWN, SIEGE OF), Greene marched into South Carolina to continue the campaign against the British garrisons there. Although defeated at Hobkirk's Hill near Camden (25 April) and forced to raise his siege of Fort Ninety-Six (22 May to 19 June), he resumed his offensive in September and attacked the British encampment at Eutaw Springs.
Forces engaged: (a) 2,000; (b) 2,400.
Casualties: (a) 85 killed, 351 wounded and 257 missing; (b) 138 killed, 375 wounded and 41 missing.

Result: The American attack was repulsed.

Inability to replace casualties caused the British to withdraw their outlying garrisons so that, south of Virginia, only Wilmington, Charleston and Savannah remained in their hands. Thus, while Greene had been defeated in every tactical engagement he fought, he had achieved his strategic objective.

Evesham

Date: 4 August 1265.
Location: Green Hill, immediately north of Evesham, Worcestershire.
War and campaign: English Baronial Wars: Simon de Montfort's Campaign, 1264–1265.
Opposing sides: (a) Prince Edward (later Edward I) commanding the royal army; (b) Simon de Montfort, Earl of Leicester, commanding the baronial army.
Objective: The baronial army, trapped in a bend of the river Avon, was forced to accept battle on unfavourable terms.
Forces engaged: (a) 1,000 cavalry and 7,000 infantry – total 8,000; (b) 350 cavalry and 5,000 infantry – total 5,350.
Casualties: (a) Approximately 2,000 killed and wounded; (b) 3,000 barons, knights and infantry killed or captured (Simon was among those killed).
Result: The baronial army was destroyed and the royal authority was re-established.

Eylau (Prussich-Eylau)

Date: 8 February 1807.
Location: On the River Pasmar, 20 miles south of Kaliningrad (Königsberg), Lithuania.
War and campaign: War of the Fourth Coalition, 1806–1807: Campaign in Poland, 1807.
Opposing sides: (a) The Emperor Napoleon I commanding the Grand Army; (b) General Levin Bennigsen commanding the Prusso-Russian army.
Objective: Having defeated the Prussian army at JENA/AUERSTADT, Napoleon entered Berlin then turned his attention to Russia, occupying Warsaw. He also besieged Danzig, which the Russian army was attempting to relieve.
Forces engaged: (a) 53,000 with 200 guns; (b) 72,000 (including 10,000 Prussians) with 400 guns.
Casualties: (a) Approximately 18,000 killed and wounded, plus 1,000 captured; (b) 23,000 killed and wounded, 3,000 prisoners and 23 guns captured.
Result: Despite the heavy losses incurred by both sides, the battle was tactically indecisive and Bennigsen withdrew in good order.

The French did not raise the siege of Danzig, which they captured on 27 April. See also FRIEDLAND.

Falaise Gap

Date: 13–21 August 1944.
Location: South of Falaise, Central Normandy.
War and campaign: Second World War: North-West Europe.
Opposing sides: (a) General Dwight D. Eisenhower, Supreme Commander Allied Forces Europe; (b) Field Marshal Gunther von Kluge, Commander-in-Chief West, followed by Field Marshal Walther Model.
Objective: The Germans were attempting to break out of the trap which was forming around them.
Forces engaged: (a) 12th Army Group (Bradley) with US First and Third Armies and 21st Army Group (Montgomery) with British Second and Canadian First Armies; (b) remnants of the Fifth Panzer Army, Seventh Army and Panzer Group Eberbach – total approximately 80,000.
Casualties: (a) 12th Army Group about 29,000 (for the period commencing with the breakout from the beach-head to the final reduction of the pocket), 21st Army Group somewhat lower; (b) 10,000 killed and 50,000 captured.
Result: The German armies in Normandy were destroyed, although some 20,000 men succeeded in escaping from the pocket.

Having broken out of the Normandy beach-head at Avranches (1 August) and fended off a weak German counter-attack at Mortain (7/9 August), the bulk of the US First and Third Armies swung east to bring pressure on the left of the German line, forcing it back on Argentan. Simultaneously, the British Second and Canadian First Armies advanced south towards Falaise, the effect of the combined movement of the two Allied army groups being to trap the German armies within a pocket from which escape was only possible to the east. The pocket, which began forming on 13 August, was subjected to incessant artillery fire and air attack as it contracted, the escape route to the east being finally closed on 19 August, although fighting continued until the 21st. German equipment captured or destroyed included: 12th Army Group sector – 380 tanks and self-propelled guns, over 700 artillery weapons and 5,000 assorted motor vehicles; 21st Army Group sector – 187 tanks and self-propelled guns, 157 armoured cars and armoured personnel carriers, 252 artillery weapons and 2,500 motor vehicles. Von Kluge, an unwilling conspirator in the 20 July Bomb Plot against Hitler, was dismissed by the latter on 17 August and took his own life; his replacement, Model, was unable to influence the outcome of the battle. See also CAEN.

Falkirk (1298)

Date: 22 July 1298.
Location: 2 miles south of Falkirk, Stirlingshire.
War and campaign: The Anglo–Scottish Wars.
Opposing sides: (a) King Edward I; (b) Sir William Wallace.
Objective: An English army had crossed the border to avenge the defeat of STIRLING BRIDGE. Near Falkirk it found the Scots drawn up and ready to accept battle.
Forces engaged: (a) 2,500 cavalry and 16,000 infantry (including a high proportion of archers) – total 18,500; (b) 200 cavalry and 10,000 infantry – total 12,200.

Casualties: 200 cavalry killed and wounded; (b) 40 cavalry and 5,000 infantry killed and wounded.
Result: An English victory without decisive result as Wallace escaped and the war continued.

The English cavalry drove off the Scottish archers and cavalry but were unable to make any impression on Wallace's pikemen, drawn up in bristling defensive circles known as schiltrons. Edward brought forward his bowmen and when their fire had thinned the ranks of the schiltrons the cavalry were able to break in and complete their destruction. This combination of firepower and shock action had been developed by Edward during his Welsh wars, but Falkirk was the first major battle to be decided by the longbow.

Falkirk (1746)   165

Date: 17 January 1746.
Location: On the ridge to the south-west of Falkirk.
War and campaign: Forty-Five Rebellion, 1745–1746.
Opposing sides: (a) Lieutenant-General Henry Hawley commanding the Government army; (b) Lord George Murray commanding the Jacobites.
Objective: The Government army was attempting to raise the siege of Stirling Castle and inflict a decisive defeat on the rebels.
Forces engaged: Approximately 8,000 on each side.
Casualties: (a) 350 killed and wounded and 600 missing or prisoners, plus seven guns and all baggage captured; (b) 50 killed and 80 wounded.
Result: As at PRESTONPANS, the Government troops were soundly beaten in a short engagement. Hawley retreated to Edinburgh, where the Duke of Cumberland assumed command of the army on 30 January. Falkirk was the Jacobites' last victory, although it availed their cause little, for on 1 February they abandoned the siege of Stirling and retreated into the Highlands. See CULLODEN.

'Hangman' Hawley took his defeat badly, and it was against his own men that he vented his spleen. Thirty-two infantrymen were shot for 'cowardice' and thirty-one cavalry troopers who rejoined after the battle were hanged on the patently absurd charge of 'deserting to the rebels'.

Famagusta, Siege of   166

Date: 18 September 1570 to 6 August 1571.
Location: City on the eastern coast of Cyprus.
War and campaign: War between the Ottoman Empire and Venice over the possession of Cyprus, 1570–1573.
Opposing sides: (a) Lala Mustafa commanding the Turkish army; (b) Marcantonio Bragadino commanding the garrison.
Objective: Having captured NICOSIA, the Turks intended eliminating the last Venetian bastion in Cyprus.
Forces engaged: (a) Estimated 70,000, with artillery siege train; (b) approximately 5,000, including reinforcements which reached the city by sea on 23 January.

Casualties: (a) The quoted figure of 40,000 is probably an exaggeration; (b) the entire garrison and civil population were massacred.	
Result: The city was captured, initiating a period of Turkish rule in Cyprus lasting 207 years. However, Pope Pius V had established the Holy League with the object of initiating a crusade for the relief of Famagusta. Two months after the city had fallen the Ottoman fleet was destroyed at the Battle of Lepanto, effectively curbing further Turkish expansion into the central and western Mediterranean.	

The heroic defence of the city caused the Turks such severe casualties that they offered the garrison the honours of war if they would surrender. Bragadino, his ammunition exhausted and the strength of the garrison reduced to 2,000, was treacherously seized and flayed alive when he entered the Turkish camp to discuss terms. Resistance collapsed and the Turks, furious at the discovery that they had been defied for so long by so weak a garrison, slaughtered everyone within the walls; even Sultan Selim II is said to have been shocked by his men's atrocities.

Ferozeshah 167

Date: 21–22 December 1845.	
Location: Village in the Punjab 15 miles south of Ferozepur.	
War and campaign: First Sikh War, 1845–1846.	
Opposing sides: (a) General Sir Hugh Gough; (b) Lal Singh.	
Objective: Having defeated the Sikhs at MUDKI on 18 December, the British advanced to attack them in their entrenched camp.	
Forces engaged: (a) 17,727 British and Indian troops with 65 guns; (b) 35,000 (including 25,000 regulars) and 88 guns.	
Casualties: (a) 694 killed and 1,721 wounded; (b) 4,590 killed and wounded, plus 78 guns captured.	
Result: The Sikhs were defeated and withdrew beyond the Sutlej river. The battle was the most bitterly contested ever fought by the British in India.	

The assault on the Sikh entrenchments was made in failing light and was bloodily repulsed. It was renewed the following morning and succeeded. Shortly afterwards, Tej Singh reached the battlefield with a fresh Sikh army, 30,000 strong with 70 guns, and attempted to recapture the position. By now Gough's guns had expended their ammunition and, to make matters worse, a staff officer deranged by sunstroke ordered the cavalry to withdraw to Ferozepur, followed by the horse artillery. Fortunately, Tej Singh interpreted this as an aggressive move against his own flank and rear and hastily broke off the action.

Fetterman Massacre, The 168

Date: 21 December 1866.	
Location: Lodge Trail Ridge (now Massacre Ridge) on the Bozeman Trail north of the site of Fort Phil Kearny, Wyoming.	
War and campaign: American Indian Wars.	
Opposing sides: (a) Colonel Henry B. Carrington commanding Fort Phil Kearny; (b) Chief Red Cloud.	

Objective: The Sioux and Cheyenne planned to ambush a major part of the garrison of Fort Phil Kearny.	
Forces engaged: (a) Captain William J. Fetterman with two officers and 78 men; (b) up to 2,000 Sioux and Cheyenne.	
Casualties: (a) Fetterman and his entire force were killed; (b) unknown, but light.	
Result: For a while Fort Phil Kearny was in danger of being overrun, but the Indians did not press their advantage. Carrington was relieved of command. See also WAGON BOX FIGHT, THE.	

The Indian plan was to mount an attack on a party cutting timber for the fort's construction, then ambush the force sent to its relief. On his own initiative Fetterman, a disloyal, disobedient braggart, assumed command of the latter, displacing the officer selected by Carrington. Flagrantly disregarding Carring-ton's specific orders to relieve the wood train and on no account to proceed beyond Lodge Trail Ridge, Fetterman pursued the Indians beyond the crest, with fatal consequences. A curious aspect of the affair was Fetterman's previous boast: 'Give me eighty men and I'll march through the whole Sioux nation!'

Fishguard

Date: 23 February 1797.	
Location: On the headland west of Fishguard, Pembrokeshire, South Wales.	
War and campaign: War of the First Coalition: French attacks on the British Isles. See also BALLINAMUCK.	
Opposing sides: (a) Lord John Cawdor commanding the local yeomanry, militia and naval units; (b) Brigadier-General William Tate, an American in French service, commanding the 2nd French Legion.	
Objective: Originally conceived as a diversion for General Lazare Hoche's aborted expedition to Bantry Bay, Ireland (December 1796), the operation was allowed to proceed by the French authorities despite the failure of the main attack. The small force employed was to act as the focal point of an imagined uprising, and among the absurd objectives it was set was the burning of Bristol, which was to be followed by attacks on Liverpool and Chester. With equally scant regard for geography, the force was set ashore on the remote Pembrokeshire coast on 22 February.	
Forces engaged: (a) 599, including 46 yeomanry cavalry and 153 seamen; (b) 1,229.	
Casualties: (a) Three civilians killed; (b) five killed.	
Result: Tate surrendered shortly after his ships had left. Although there were isolated clashes between local people and French foragers, there was no large-scale fighting. Nevertheless, Fishguard remains the only battle honour awarded for an action in the United Kingdom.	

Given the time factor and distances involved, credit must be given for the speed with which the local forces were mustered to meet the invasion. This apart, the affair had more in common with light opera than with a serious military operation. The majority of Tate's men were former deserters, released criminals or turncoat royalists. Well aware that they were considered expendable, they obtained supplies of drink shortly after landing and were soon out of hand. Documentary evidence confirms that Lord Cawdor asked the local women, in the traditional red shawls and black stove-pipe hats, to align themselves with his troops so that from a distance they resembled infantry and gave the impression that the small British forces was larger than it was. A notable heroine of the day was the formidable Jemima Nicholas, a 47-year-old cobbler who captured a dozen Frenchmen with a pitchfork.

Five Forks   170

Date: 1 April 1865.	
Location: South-west of Petersburg, Virginia.	
War and campaign: American Civil War: Grant's Virginia Campaign of 1865.	
Opposing sides: (a) Lieutenant-General Ulysses S. Grant, the US Army's General-in-Chief, in the field with Major-General George C. Meade's Army of the Potomac; (b) General Robert E. Lee commanding the Army of Northern Virginia.	
Objective: Grant realized that Lee's army, now holding 37 miles of trenches in front of PETERSBURG, was stretched to the limit and ordered Major-General Philip Sheridan to encircle the Confederate right flank with his cavalry, reinforced with additional infantry. Lee reacted by sending Major-General George E. Pickett with two infantry divisions and Major-General Fitzhugh Lee's cavalry to contain the threat.	
Forces engaged: (a) 22,000; (b) 10,600.	
Casualties: (a) 820; (b) 4,444.	
Result: Pickett was decisively defeated and Federal cavalry cut the South Side Railroad, the last Confederate supply route into Petersburg.	

Recognizing that he would have to abandon Petersburg, and Richmond too, Lee set out on his retreat to APPOMATTOX COURT HOUSE.

Fleurus (1690)   171

Date: 1 July 1690.	
Location: 7 miles north of Charleroi, Belgium.	
War and campaign: War of the League of Augsburg, 1688–1697: Netherlands Campaign of 1690.	
Opposing sides: (a) Prince George Frederich of Waldeck commanding the Allied army; (b) Marshal Duke François of Luxembourg commanding the French.	
Objective: The Allies were opposing a French invasion of the Netherlands.	
Forces engaged: (a) 40,000 (British, Spanish and German); (b) 45,000.	
Casualties: (a) 6,000 killed and wounded, 8,000 prisoners and 48 guns captured; (b) 2,500 killed and wounded.	
Result: A French victory which Luxembourg was unable to exploit because of restrictions imposed by Louis XIV. See also NEERWINDEN.	

Luxembourg launched a holding attack with his infantry against the Allied centre, then employed his cavalry in a double envelopment round both flanks.

Fleurus (1794)

Date: 26 June 1794.
Location: Village 7 miles north-east of Charleroi, Belgium.
War and campaign: War of the First Coalition, 1792–1798: Campaign in the Austrian Netherlands, 1794–1795.
Opposing sides: (a) Friedrich Josias, Prince of Saxe-Coburg, commanding the Austro-British-Hanoverian army; (b) General Jean Baptiste Jourdan commanding the French Army of the Sambre and Meuse.
Objective: The Allied army was attempting to relieve Charleroi, unaware that it had fallen to the French the previous day.
Forces engaged: (a) 52,000; (b) 73,000.
Casualties: Uncertain, but the French sustained the heavier losses.
Result: Although the Allied left wing was successful, the centre was held by French counter-attacks and the right, commanded by the Prince of Orange, was driven off the field. The following day Saxe-Coburg commenced a retreat which took him across the Roer into Germany, thereby abandoning Belgium, which Austria would never recover. Jourdan, following up, took Brussels (10 July) and Antwerp (27 July). The British contingent of the Allied army sailed home.

The battle witnessed the first employment of aircraft as an adjunct of land warfare when the French sent up a tethered observation balloon. The balloonist was a Captain Coutelle, who was able to provide complete details of the Allied dispositions. While the idea was ingenious, it was not developed; its principal opponent, in fact, was Napoleon himself, who was critical of the balloon companies' inability to operate at the speed demanded by his operational concepts. The observation balloon was therefore abandoned until the American Civil War.

Flodden

Date: 9 September 1513.
Location: South of Branxton, 2 miles south-east of Coldstream, Northumberland.
War and campaign: The Anglo–Scottish War of 1513–1514.
Opposing sides: (a) The Earl of Surrey commanding the English army; (b) King James IV.
Objective: A pitched battle fought by agreement between the commanders of the invading Scottish army and the English army which had been raised to intercept it.
Forces engaged: (a) 20,000 with 22 light guns; (b) 25,000 (including 5,000 French) with seventeen guns.
Casualties: (a) 4,000 killed; (b) 10,000 killed, including King James, eight earls and thirteen barons; all artillery captured.
Result: A decisive English victory. Almost every Scottish noble family sustained the loss of one or more of its members during the battle.

Surrey had agreed with James that a battle would be fought by Friday 9 September. However, the Scots were holding a strong position on Flodden Edge and Surrey carried out a flank march to the east, so placing his army to the north of James. In response, the Scots abandoned Flodden Edge and advanced north across Branxton Moor to attack. The battle began with an artillery duel. The Scots had the more modern guns but they were not as well served as those of the English and they had the worst of the exchange, their Master Gunner being killed. The Scottish left wing then advanced, defeating its opponents, but stopped to plunder the dead and was routed in turn by the English cavalry reserve under Lord Dacre. The two Scottish divisions in the centre also advanced to engage in a general mêlée, although the right wing was routed by the English left under Sir Edward Stanley, which fell on its flank after approaching under cover of dead ground. With both flanks gone, the Scots in the centre were surrounded, but they continued to fight stubbornly around their king until the majority were killed. In the close-quarter fighting the English had a distinct advantage in that they had adopted the halberd, which could be used to cut as well as thrust, whereas the Scots retained their traditional pike. The pipe lament *Flowers of the Forest*, composed to commemorate Scotland's grievous loss, remains in use with Scottish regiments to this day.

Fontenoy 174

Date: 11 May 1745.
Location: Village 5 miles south-east of Tournai, Belgium.
War and campaign: War of Austrian Succession, 1740–1748: Campaign in Flanders, 1745.
Opposing sides: (a) William, Duke of Cumberland, commanding the Allied army; (b) Marshal Count Maurice de Saxe (accompanied by Louis XV) commanding the French.
Objective: The Allied army was attempting to break the French siege of Tournai.
Forces engaged: (a) British-Dutch-Austrian army of 56 infantry battalions, 87 cavalry squadrons and 80 guns – total 53,000; (b) French army of 66 infantry battalions, 129 cavalry squadrons and 70 guns.
Casualties: (a) 7,500; (b) 7,200.
Result: A hard-won victory for the French, who went on to capture Tournai and other fortresses in the Austrian Netherlands, assisted by the withdrawal of British troops to deal with the Forty-Five Rebellion at home. See also LAFFELDT.

The story that opposing British and French Guards battalions each asked the other to fire first during an exchange of professional compliments is not entirely apocryphal but has been romanticized. Courtesies were exchanged in a spirit of mutual derision and as the French prepared to fire a voice from the British ranks shouted the words of the Grace: 'For what we are about to receive, may the Lord make us truly thankful!' The French fire did little damage but in return the British fired a tremendous volley which shattered the lines opposite. The British and Hanoverian infantry advanced deep into the French position, driving all before them, but to their left the Dutch and Austrians had made no progress in their assaults against, respectively, Fontenoy and Antoing villages, so that Saxe was able to deploy his rallied French and Swiss Guards against the left flank of the British/Hanoverian column while the Irish Brigade, consisting of emigrants in the French service, attacked it from the right. At length the column was halted, then it withdrew slowly and in good order in accordance with Cumberland's instructions.

Ford of the Biscuits, The 175

Date: 7 August 1594.

Location: Ford (now replaced by a bridge) over the river Arney, 5 miles south-west of Enniskillen, Ulster.
War and campaign: Hugh O'Donnell's Revolt, 1594 (a prelude to Tyrone's Rebellion).
Opposing sides: (a) Sir Henry Duke and Sir Edward Herbert commanding the Government troops; (b) Hugh Maguire and Cormac, brother of Tyrone, commanding the rebels.
Objective: The rebels ambushed a Government column marching to the relief of Enniskillen Castle.
Forces engaged: (a) 600 infantry and 46 cavalry; (b) approximately 1,000 infantry.
Casualties: (a) 56 killed and 69 wounded; (b) unknown but minimal.
Result: A tactical success which encouraged the rebels.

The ford was so named because of the Government rations spilled during the fighting. See also YELLOW FORD, THE, and KINSALE.

Formigny 176

Date: 15 April 1450.
Location: 10 miles west of Bayeux, Normandy.
War and campaign: Hundred Years' War, 1337–1457; French Reconquest of Normandy, 1449–1450.
Opposing sides: (a) Sir Thomas Kyriell; (b) the Comte de Clermont.
Objective: An English force, marching to the relief of the besieged garrison of Caen, was opposed by the French.
Forces engaged: (a) 4,000, including 1,500 archers; (b) initially 3,000, reinforced to 5,000 during the battle, plus two culverins.
Casualties: (a) 3,200 killed; (b) estimated between 500 and 1,000 killed.
Result: Kyriell's force was destroyed. The surrender of Caen on 6 July, followed by that of Cherbourg on 12 August, eliminated the English presence in Normandy.

The French deployed their guns on the flanks, beyond the range of the English archers, and opened a galling fire. The archers were provoked into an attack which actually captured the guns but were counter-attacked by the French men-at-arms and driven back. While the mêlée was in progress French reinforcements fell on the English flank and completed the rout. See also CASTILLON.

Fort Donelson 177

Date: 6–16 February 1862.
Location: On the Cumberland river, Tennessee, 28 miles west of Clarksville.
War and campaign: American Civil War: western theatre of operations.
Opposing sides: (a) Brigadier-General Ulysses S. Grant; (b) Brigadier-General John B. Floyd.
Objective: The Federal intention was to capture Fort Donelson and remove the

Confederate threat to Kentucky, which thus far had remained uncommitted to either side.
Forces engaged: (a) 27,000; (b) 21,000.
Casualties: (a) 2,832; (b) approximately 2,000 killed and wounded, plus 15,000 prisoners and 48 artillery weapons captured.
Result: Having failed to break out, the garrison surrendered; only Colonel Nathan Forrest's cavalry and a handful of infantry succeeded in escaping to Nashville. Fort Donelson was the first major Confederate defeat of the war. See SHILOH.

Fort Henry, a parallel Confederate position situated on the Tennessee river 11 miles to the west, had already been abandoned by its garrison after being bombarded by Federal gunboats on 6 February.

Fort Duquesne 178

Date: 24 November 1758.
Location: Pittsburgh, Pennsylvania.
War and campaign: French and Indian War in North America, 1754–1763.
Opposing sides: (a) Brigadier-General John Forbes; (b) the French garrison commander.
Objective: The British intention was to eliminate this French post, thereby removing a threat to the western flank of their strategic offensive against Canada. See also FORT NECESSITY and MONONGAHELA RIVER.
Forces engaged: (a) Estimated 2,000, including one battalion of the newly raised 60th Royal American Regiment; (b) estimated 1,000.
Casualties: Some losses incurred by both sides in skirmishing during Forbes' approach march; none at the fort itself.
Result: The fort was abandoned and blown up by the French, who then withdrew. The strategic initiative in the west passed to the British. See also FORT TICONDEROGA and QUEBEC (1759).

The fort was rebuilt as Fort Pitt and subsequently evolved into Pittsburgh. The concept of light infantry tactics as demonstrated by the Royal Americans was further extended throughout the British army in North America.

Fort Necessity 179

Date: 13 July 1754.
Location: Great Meadows, near modern Uniontown, Pennsylvania.
War and campaign: French and Indian War in North America, 1754–1763.
Opposing sides: (a) Lieutenant-Colonel George Washington; (b) Captain de Villiers.
Objective: Ordered to build a fort at the confluence of the Allegheny and Monongahela rivers, a detachment of colonial militia from Virginia found that the French had already established FORT DUQUESNE on the site. The detachment constructed its own fort some 40 miles to the south, where it was attacked by the French and their Indian allies.

Forces engaged: (a) 150; (b) 600 French and 100 Indians.
Casualties: Unknown.
Result: Washington conducted a vigorous defence but was forced to surrender when his ammunition was exhausted. He was allowed to march out with the honours of war. See also MONONGAHELA RIVER.

Fort Sumter 180

Date: 12–14 April 1861.
Location: In Charleston harbour, South Carolina.
War and campaign: American Civil War.
Opposing sides: (a) Major Robert Anderson commanding the Federal garrison; (b) Brigadier-General Pierre Beauregard commanding the Confederate troops in Charleston.
Objective: The Federal government intended to maintain the fort's garrison as a symbol of its authority; the Confederates demanded its evacuation as a symbol of their independence from Washington and, failing to secure this by other means, opened fire with their batteries around the harbour.
Forces engaged: (a) 84; (b) 5,000.
Casualties: (a) 11, the majority from accidental causes; (b) 4.
Result: Anderson surrendered on 14 April and was permitted to march out with the honours of war; ironically, his garrison was so short of food that, prior to the bombardment by Confederate batteries, he had already undertaken to evacuate the fort on the 15th, but was not believed.

The bombardment made outright hostilities between North and South inevitable. Technically, the first shots of the Civil War were fired on 9 January when the Confederates defeated an attempt by the supply vessel *Star of the West* to revictual Fort Sumter, although the Federal government did not react to the incident.

Fort Ticonderoga 181

Date: 8 July 1758.
Location: At the southern end of Lake Champlain, upper New York state.
War and campaign: French and Indian War in North America, 1754–1763.
Opposing sides: (a) Major-General James Abercromby; (b) Major-General Marquis Louis-Joseph de Montcalm.
Objective: The capture of the fort was the central objective of the three-pronged British strategy against the French. See also FORT DUQUESNE and LOUISBURG.
Forces engaged: (a) 12,000, including 6,000 regulars; (b) 3,000.
Casualties: (a) 493 killed and 1,117 wounded; (b) 400 killed and wounded.
Result: The British assault failed and Abercromby withdrew. He was dismissed and Major-General Jeffrey Amherst was appointed Commander-in-Chief in his place. The following year, after careful preparation, Amherst again advanced against the fort, which was abandoned by the French on his approach on 26 July. See also QUEBEC.

Montcalm held a ridge near the fort, covering his front with an abattis of felled trees. Abercromby, a singularly inept commander, did not attempt to turn the open French flanks, neither did he use his artillery to smash the abattis; instead, his men were committed to a series of costly frontal attacks, all of which failed.

Fort William Henry 182

Date: 9 August 1757.
Location: At the southern end of Lake George, upper New York state.
War and campaign: French and Indian War in North America, 1754–1763.
Opposing sides: (a) Colonel Monro; (b) Major-General Marquis Louis-Joseph de Montcalm.
Objective: The French, marching south from FORT TICONDEROGA, attacked the fort.
Forces engaged: (a) 2,200 regulars and colonials; (b) 4,000 French and 1,000 Indians.
Casualties: (a) 300 killed and wounded, plus a minimum of 50 killed during the subsequent massacre; (b) uncertain, but fewer.
Result: Monro, most of whose guns had been dismounted by the French fire, surrendered when further resistance was impossible and was allowed to march out with the honours of war. The Indians then attacked the disarmed garrison and a massacre ensued before Montcalm restored order. The fort was destroyed and the French withdrew.

The disaster firmed British resolve to eliminate the French presence in North America.

France, Belgium and Holland (1940) 183

Date: 10 May to 25 June 1940.
Location: The decisive battles took place along the Meuse between Dinant and Sedan.
War and campaign: Second World War: France 1940.
Opposing sides: (a) Field Marshal Walter von Brauchitsch, Commander-in-Chief of the German Army; (b) General Maurice Gamelin, Commander-in-Chief of the Allied armies, replaced by General Maxime Weygand on 20 May.
Objective: The German intention was to destroy the French Army and the British Expeditionary Force, simultaneously neutralizing the armies of Holland and Belgium.
Forces engaged: As at 10 May 1940: (a) Army Group B (General von Bock) with 29½ divisions including three armoured, Army Group A (General von Rundstedt) with 45½ divisions including seven armoured, Army Group C (General von Leeb) with nineteen divisions, Reserve 42 divisions, 2,439 tanks (of which 1,478 were in the light category, armed only with machine guns) – total 3,350,000 men; (b) French Army: Second Army Group (General Pretelat) with one British and 43 French divisions, First Army Group (General Billotte) with 22 divisions including two light mechanized, Seventh Army Group (General Giraud) with seven divisions including one light mechanized, General Reserve with 22 divisions including three armoured, approximately 3,000 tanks (many better armed and armoured than the best German vehicles) – total 2,000,000 men. British Expeditionary Force (Field Marshal Lord Gort): nine divisions, 210 light tanks and 100 infantry tanks – total

237,000 men. Belgian Army: eighteen divisions, plus four in reserve – total 375,000 men. Dutch Army: eight divisions with two in reserve – total 250,000 men. Total Allied strength 2,862,000 men.

Casualties: (a) 27,000 killed, 111,000 wounded and 18,000 missing – total German casualties 156,000. (b) French: 90,000 killed, 200,000 wounded and 1,900,000 missing or taken prisoner. Other casualties (killed, wounded and missing): British 68,000, Belgian 23,000, Dutch 10,000. Total Allied casualties 2,292,000.

Result: A complete German victory resulting in the virtual destruction of the French, Belgian and Dutch armies. The majority of the BEF, plus some French and Belgian troops, was evacuated from DUNKIRK, although all their heavy weapons had to be abandoned, and further evacuations were made from Cherbourg.

Gamelin believed that the German offensive would consist of a mechanized version of the Schlieffen Plan of 1914, outflanking the Maginot Line with an advance through neutral Holland and Belgium. In these circumstances he planned to despatch the BEF and the best French armies north to join the Dutch and Belgians, believing that he would then be strong enough to achieve a decisive victory once the Germans had been halted along the line of the river Dyle. While the original German plans had indeed provided for a limited advance into Belgium, these were abandoned when Hitler accepted a more imaginative strategy devised by Lieutenant-General Erich von Manstein, then serving as von Rundstedt's Chief of Staff in Army Group A. This, codenamed 'Sichelschnitt' ('Sickle Cut') envisaged an invasion of Holland and Belgium which was actually intended to draw the BEF and much of the French strength northwards. The bulk of the German armour was then to break through on the weakly held Ardennes sector, cross the Meuse and cut a swathe across northern France to the Channel, the effect being to form a pocket in which the Allied armies to the north would be trapped. The invasion of the Low Countries would be the responsibility of Army Group B; the 'Sichelschnitt' stroke would be delivered by Army Group A, spearheaded by three Panzer Corps; and, at the southern end of the line, Army Group C was to mount holding attacks against the Maginot defences and along the upper reaches of the Rhine. When the offensive opened on 10 May the Luftwaffe quickly attained air superiority. German paratroops and air-landing formations seized strategic locations in Holland while a single armoured division drove west from the frontier to relieve them, simultaneously separating the Dutch Army from French units which were racing north to reinforce it. Following air attacks on Dutch cities, notably Rotterdam, Holland capitulated on 15 May. The lynch-pin of the Belgian defence system, Fort Eben Emael, was also captured by German paratroops on 10 May. In accordance with Gamelin's plan, the BEF and French armies wheeled north-east on to the Dyle line and a major tank battle took place in the Gembloux Gap, each side losing about 100 vehicles. Meanwhile, Army Group A had advanced through the Ardennes and, between 13 and 15 May, secured crossings over the Meuse, shattering the French Ninth Army and severely mauling the Second Army in the process. Breaking out of their bridgeheads, the Panzer Corps cut a 40-mile-wide corridor across northern France between 16 and 21 May, being temporarily checked on the latter date by the British counter-attack at ARRAS. They then swung north into the rear of the Franco-British-Belgian forces in Belgium, which were already engaged with Army Group B. The position of the troops within the pocket was now impossible and the DUNKIRK evacuation began on 26 May, complicated by King Leopold's decision that Belgium would capitulate at midnight the following day. The best of the French armies had been lost, and with them the most powerful of the French armoured formations. Having replaced Gamelin as the Allied Commander-in-Chief on 20 May, Weygand deployed the remainder along a line stretching from the Somme and the Aisne to the Maginot Line. Once they had regrouped, the Germans renewed their offensive on 5 June and, despite fierce resistance, succeeded in breaking through to the south. On 10 June Italy declared war on France and the French government left Paris for Bordeaux, declaring the capital an open city. As the retreat continued General Pretelat's Second Army Group was pinned back against the Maginot Line and forced to surrender on 22 June. Marshal Pétain, who had been appointed President a week earlier, requested an armistice and hostilities ceased on 25 June.

Fredericksburg 184

Date: 13 December 1862.
Location: Fredericksburg, Virginia, 45 miles south of Washington, D.C.
War and campaign: American Civil War.
Opposing sides: (a) Major-General Ambrose E. Burnside commanding the Army of the Potomac; (b) General Robert E. Lee commanding the Army of Northern Virginia.
Objective: The strategic initiative having passed to the Federals at ANTIETAM, their intention was to cross the Rappahannock at Fredericksburg and advance directly against Richmond, the capital of the Confederacy.
Forces engaged: (a) 120,000; (b) 78,000.
Casualties: (a) 12,600; (b) 5,300.
Result: A serious defeat for the Federals, who were forced to postpone their planned advance on Richmond for several months (see CHANCELLORSVILLE). Burnside was replaced in January 1863 by Major-General Joseph ('Fighting Joe') Hooker.

Burnside failed to achieve the surprise he anticipated and was forced to make an opposed crossing of the river on 11/12 December. This enabled Lee to concentrate his army on the high ground to the east with Lieutenant-General Thomas ('Stonewall') Jackson's corps on the right and Lieutenant-General James Longstreet's corps overlooking the town itself. When the Federals advanced on 13 December all their attacks were repulsed; the worst slaughter took place below Marye's Heights, where repeated Union assaults debouched from the town to be cut to pieces by the Confederate artillery and the concentrated fire of riflemen standing six deep in a sunken road behind a stone wall. Many of the wounded froze to death during the night. Burnside was for renewing the assault next day but, dissuaded from doing so by his senior commanders, withdrew his army across the river during the night of 15/16 December.

Freiburg 185

Date: 3–10 August 1644.
Location: Town in Württemberg, 85 miles south-west of Stuttgart.
War and campaign: Thirty Years' War, 1618–1648: German Campaign of 1644.
Opposing sides: (a) Duke Louis d'Enghien and Marshal Vicomte Henri de Turenne commanding the French army; (b) Field Marshal Baron Franz von Mercy commanding the Imperialists.
Objective: The French were attempting to recapture Freiburg from the Imperialists.
Forces engaged: (a) 16,000; (b) 15,000.
Casualties: (a) 8,000 killed and wounded; (b) 5,000 killed and wounded.

> **Result:** Mercy conducted a stubborn defence, but after a series of hard-fought engagements he was outmanoeuvred and forced to withdraw from his positions and abandon Freiburg.

Despite their severe losses, the French continued to reduce Imperial fortresses along the Middle Rhine. See also NÖRDLINGEN, SECOND BATTLE OF.

Frenchtown 186

Date: 22 January 1813.
Location: Now Monroe, on the Raisin river, Michigan.
War and campaign: War of 1812: Canadian Front.
Opposing sides: (a) Colonel Henry Proctor commanding the British; (b) Major-General James Winchester commanding the Americans.
Objective: An American force advancing to recapture Detroit, which had been surrendered without a shot being fired on 16 August 1812, was attacked in its camp by the British garrison.
Forces engaged: (a) Approximately 300 regulars, 300 Canadian militia, 600 Indians and several guns; (b) approximately 300 regulars and 650 militia.
Casualties: (a) Approximately 200 killed and wounded; (b) 197 killed and wounded, plus 737 captured, including Winchester (some prisoners were massacred by the Indians).
Result: The American force was destroyed.

Detroit remained in British hands until the American naval victory on Lake Erie (20 September 1813) rendered it untenable. Proctor then withdrew across the Detroit River into Canada – see THAMES, THE.

Friedland 187

Date: 14 June 1807.
Location: Village on the river Alle 25 miles south-east of Kaliningrad (Königsberg), Lithuania.
War and campaign: War of the Fourth Coalition, 1806–1807: Campaign in Poland, 1807.
Opposing sides: (a) The Emperor Napoleon I commanding the Grand Army; (b) General Levin Bennigsen commanding the Russian army.
Objective: Napoleon seized the opportunity to inflict a decisive defeat on the Russian army, which had unwisely crossed the Alle to attack what it believed, incorrectly, to be an isolated French corps.
Forces engaged: (a) Initially 17,000, rising to 80,000; (b) 46,000, plus 12,000 on the opposite bank of the Alle who played little part in the battle.
Casualties: (a) Approximately 8,000 killed and wounded; (b) approximately 25,000 killed and wounded, plus 80 guns captured.
Result: The Russians were routed and requested an armistice on 19 June. The following month peace terms were concluded at the Treaty of Tilsit between France

on the one hand and Russia and Prussia on the other. The treaty left Napoleon the virtual master of Western and Central Europe.

Lannes' corps, 26,000-strong, fought a holding action for several hours until the rest of the Grand Army arrived. The Russians then found themselves fighting with their backs to the river and with no means of retreat.

Fuentes de Onoro 188

Date: 3–5 May 1811.
Location: Town on the Spanish/Portuguese frontier, 10 miles west of Ciudad Rodrigo.
War and campaign: Peninsular War, 1807–1814: Campaign of 1811.
Opposing sides: (a) Lieutenant-General Viscount Wellington; (b) Marshal Andre Massena, Duke of Rivoli.
Objective: The French were attempting to raise the siege of Almeida; Wellington had taken up a covering position at Fuentes de Onoro.
Forces engaged: (a) 21,450 British and 2,500 Portuguese; (b) 46,000.
Casualties: (a) 1,550; (b) 2,260.
Result: A narrow victory for Wellington. Massena withdrew and was dismissed, his place being taken by Marmont. Almeida was abandoned by the French, although the garrison managed to evade capture.

On 3 May Massena repeated the mistake he had made at BUSACO, mounting abortive attacks without adequate reconnaissance. On 5 May, however, he almost succeeded in turning Wellington's right with a superior force, but the stubborn withdrawal of the British infantry and cavalry, in which each covered the movements of the other by bounds, eventually brought the French advance to a standstill. Wellington had come dangerously close to defeat and commented that had Napoleon been present he would undoubtedly have been beaten. See ALBUERA.

Gallipoli 189

Date: 25 April 1915 to 9 January 1916.
Location: The southern and western coasts of the Gallipoli peninsula.
War and campaign: First World War: Dardanelles.
Opposing sides: (a) General Sir Ian Hamilton commanding the Allied forces on the peninsula, replaced by General Sir Charles Monro on 15 October; (b) General Liman von Sanders commanding the Turkish Fifth Army.
Objective: The Allies hoped to force the Dardanelles and open a supply route to Russia across the Black Sea. This would simultaneously render Constantinople (Istanbul) vulnerable to attack and naval bombardment, inducing a possible Turkish withdrawal from the war.
Forces engaged: (a) Eventually thirteen British and Empire divisions and a French corps – total approximately 490,000; (b) eventually twenty Turkish divisions – total approximately 500,000.
Casualties: Each side sustained approximately 250,000 casualties.

> **Result:** A costly failure culminating in an Allied withdrawal from the peninsula. Russian confidence in the Western Allies in general, and in the Royal Navy in particular, was seriously shaken.

A brilliant concept at the grand strategic level was marred by the inefficiency of its execution. Abortive naval attacks in February and March thoroughly alerted the Turks to their danger, although the attacks came closer to success than the Allies imagined. Thus when the landings eventually took place the Turks had moved troops into the threatened area and prepared defences which were capable of containing them. The first landings were made on 25 April on Cape Helles at the southern tip of the peninsula and at Anzac Cove on the west coast. On 6 August further landings were made at Suvla Bay, north of Anzac Cove, with the objective of outflanking the Turkish defences and establishing control over the neck of the peninsula, but these were not exploited as they should have been. By the autumn it was clear that the entire operation had failed and in December the evacuation began, commencing with the western beach-heads; in contrast to the conduct of operations, the evacuation was a masterpiece of efficiency. The Gallipoli campaign was notable for the courage and endurance shown by both sides, and for this reason, if for nothing else, it holds an honoured place in Australian and New Zealand military tradition. On the Turkish side the aggressive Lieutenant-Colonel Mustafa Kemal demonstrated the drive and energy which, in due course, would lead him to the office of national president.

Garigliano 190

Date: 3 November 1503.
Location: Near the mouth of the Garigliano river on the west coast of Italy.
War and campaign: French Sixteenth Century Wars in Italy: Franco–Spanish War in Naples, 1495–1504.
Opposing sides: (a) Hernandez Gonzalo de Cordoba commanding the Spaniards; (b) Gonzago Marquis of Mantua commanding the Franco-Italian army.
Objective: The Spanish intention was to force a passage of the river and destroy the Franco-Italian army opposite.
Forces engaged: 15,000; (b) 23,000.
Casualties: (a) Light; (b) 4,000 killed, wounded and taken prisoner, plus artillery and baggage captured.
Result: The Franco-Italian army was driven from the river line in confusion to seek refuge in Gaeta; under the terms of what amounted to a capitulation, it was permitted to evacuate by sea. Louis XII of France abandoned his claim to Naples and sued for peace.

Cordoba secretly assembled a pontoon bridge which he used to make a surprise crossing of the swollen river upstream, routing the forces opposite. His deputy, Andrada, then forced a passage of the main bridge and the remains of the Franco-Italian army, caught between the two, broke and fled. See also CERIGNOLA.

Gaza, Third Battle of 191

Date: 28 October to 7 November 1917.
Location: Fortified line between Gaza and Beersheba, Israel.

War and campaign: First World War: Palestine.	

Opposing sides: (a) General Sir Edmund Allenby commanding the British army in Palestine; (b) General Erich von Falkenhayn commanding the Turkish army group in Palestine.

Objective: The British intention was to break through the line and continue the advance into Palestine.

Forces engaged: (a) Desert Mounted Corps (Lieutenant-General Sir Henry Chauvel), XX Corps (Lieutenant-General Sir Philip Chetwode) and XXI Corps (Major-General Edward Bulfin); (b) the Turkish Eighth and Seventh Armies, commanded, respectively, by Colonel Freiherr Friedrich Kress von Kressenstein and Feusi Pasha, each with two corps.

Casualties: To December: (a) 18,000; (b) 25,000, including 12,000 prisoners.

Result: The Turkish line was broken. Turkish prestige, already severely damaged by the loss of the Holy Cities of Mecca and BAGHDAD, was dealt a further serious blow when Jerusalem fell on 9 December. Falkenhayn managed to establish a new defence line north of Jerusalem.

Two attempts to break the Turkish line earlier in the year had both failed. The first (26 March) might have succeeded had not the chain of command broken at the vital moment; the second (17–19 April) failed to penetrate the strengthened defences despite the provision of limited tank support for the first time in a desert environment. Allenby's primary objective during the Third Battle of Gaza was the water supply at Beersheba, without which he felt he would be unable to sustain a further advance. On 31 October the Beersheba wells were captured in a dashing attack by the Desert Mounted Corps, although their capacity was found to be less than had been anticipated. However, on the coastal sector the 54th Division (XII Corps), led by a small but concentrated tank attack, broke clean through the defences on 2 November and, with both flanks turned, the Turks had no option but to withdraw. See MEGIDDO (1918).

Gazala 192

Date: 26 May to 21 June 1942.

Location: 30 miles west of Tobruk, Cyrenaica, Libya.

War and campaign: Second World War: North Africa.

Opposing sides: (a) General Erwin Rommel, nominally subordinate to the Italian Commander-in-Chief North Africa but *de facto* commander of the Axis armies; (b) General Sir Claude Auchinleck, Commander-in-Chief Middle East.

Objective: Both sides intended to take the offensive, but the Axis struck first.

Forces engaged: (a) Italian X and XXI Corps, XX Mechanized Corps, Deutches Afrika Korps – total 113,000 men and 560 tanks; (b) Lieutenant-General Neil Ritchie, commanding the Eighth Army (XII and XXX Corps) – total approximately 125,000 men and 849 tanks.

Casualties: (a) Approximately 60,000; (b) approximately 88,000, including those captured in Tobruk.

Result: The Eighth Army, heavily defeated, was forced to withdraw into Egypt. The capture of Tobruk in the immediate aftermath of the battle was an equally serious blow to British morale.

Rommel opened his offensive during the night of 26/27 May by sweeping round the southern flank of the British line. Despite being caught off balance, the British rallied during the following day and inflicted heavy losses on the Axis armour, so that by evening Rommel had been pushed back against the Eighth Army's minebelt and a defensive box held by 150 Brigade. Desperately short of water, Rommel considered asking Ritchie for terms but the situation eased when the Italian Trieste Division succeeded in opening a corridor through the minefields. Although circumstances now existed in which Rommel's army could have been destroyed, the opportunity was lost because of protracted discussion and delay at the highest levels. While Rommel's position, which became known as 'The Cauldron', remained unmolested, the Axis recovered their strength and on 1 June Rommel overran the 150 Brigade box in his rear. Ritchie mounted unco-ordinated attacks against 'The Cauldron' on 5 June but these were easily repulsed. The next day Rommel returned to the offensive, inflicting serious losses on Ritchie's infantry, then investing the Free French box at Bir Hacheim; during the night of 10/11 June the French succeeded in breaking out and reaching safety. Rommel now repeated the north-easterly thrust with which he had begun the battle. On 12 June XXX Corps' three armoured brigades counter-attacked but were defeated in detail, losing 90 tanks. Next day an Axis attempt to isolate the Knightsbridge Box was foiled, but by evening the Eighth Army had only 70 tanks left and the position was abandoned during the night. Ritchie, recognizing that the battle was lost, initiated the Eighth Army's withdrawal and strengthened the garrison of Tobruk. The latter measure, however, proved of no avail, as Rommel stormed the fortress on 20/21 June. Rommel was awarded his field marshal's baton for the victory at Gazala and the capture of Tobruk, but the overconfidence engendered resulted in his pursuit of the Eighth Army to El Alamein, thereby stretching his supply lines beyond their capacity. See also TOBRUK, ALAM HALFA, FIRST and SECOND BATTLES OF ALAMEIN.

Germantown 193

Date: 4 October 1777.
Location: Hamlet 5 miles north of Philadelphia, Pennsylvania.
War and campaign: American War of Independence, 1775–1783: central theatre of operations.
Opposing sides: (a) Lieutenant-General Sir William Howe; (b) Major-General George Washington.
Objective: Washington's intention was to destroy the British army in its encampment with a series of converging dawn attacks, so recovering Philadelphia.
Forces engaged: (a) 9,000; (b) 11,000.
Casualties: (a) 521 killed and wounded; (b) 673 killed and wounded and 400 captured.
Result: Washington's plan required precise timing and was too complicated for some of his subordinate commanders. The British outposts were driven in but in the confusion of the piecemeal attack some American units fired on each other and a British counter-attack cleared the field.

The capture of Forts Mifflin and Mercer on the Delaware in November opened Howe's seaborne supply route and Washington retired into winter quarters at Valley Forge, intending to renew the contest the following spring. See MONMOUTH.

Gettysburg

Date: 1–3 July 1863.
Location: Gettysburg, Pennsylvania.
War and campaign: American Civil War: Lee's Second Invasion of the North.
Opposing sides: (a) Major-General George C. Meade commanding the Army of the Potomac; (b) General Robert E. Lee commanding the Army of Northern Virginia.
Objective: Lee's aim was to carry the war to the North and inflict a decisive defeat on the Army of the Potomac.
Forces engaged: (a) 95,000; (b) 75,000.
Casualties: (a) 3,155 killed, 14,529 wounded and 5,365 missing; (b) 3,903 killed, 18,735 wounded and 5,425 missing.
Result: Lee was not only defeated but also sustained heavy casualties which neither he nor the limited manpower resources of the South could support. He withdrew in good order after the battle but was never again able to mount a major offensive. Coupled with the surrender of VICKSBURG on 4 July, the battle, while not decisive in itself, marked a turning point in the war following which the fortunes of the Confederacy steadily declined.

Because of the temporary absence of Stuart's cavalry on a raid, Lee was unaware of the approach of the Army of the Potomac until 28 June, when he was also informed that Meade had been appointed its commander following Hooker's resignation the same day after a professional disagreement with Major-General Henry Halleck, the US Army's General-in-Chief. Both armies converged on the important road junction at Gettysburg and on 1 July battle was joined between their advance guards. The Union troops were pushed south through the town but rallied on Culp's Hill and Cemetery Hill and, as more troops arrived during the night, the line was extended southwards along Cemetery Ridge to two hills known as Round Top and Little Round Top; simultaneously, the Confederates developed a parallel line along Seminary Ridge, a little short of a mile to the west. On 2 July Meade came close to losing the battle when Major-General Daniel Sickles pushed his Union III Corps forward to an intermediate ridge, for during the afternoon Lieutenant-General James Longstreet's Confederate I Corps routed it and almost succeeded in turning the Federal left; only prompt action and desperate fighting prevented the fall of Little Round Top, which enfiladed Cemetery Ridge. Elsewhere, Confederate attacks on Culp's Hill during the evening made no progress. On 3 July Lee made the most serious mistake of his career, deciding to mount a frontal assault over open ground against the unshaken enemy on Cemetery Ridge. This was to have been supported by a renewed assault on Culp's Hill and a sweep by Stuart's rejoined cavalry round the Federal right, but neither operation succeeded. At 15.00, following a two-hour bombardment, 12,000 Confederates advanced against the ridge, their ranks torn apart by concentrated artillery and rifle fire. A few reached the lines of the Union II Corps, where they were killed or captured, and the survivors were driven back. The attack, subsequently named Pickett's Charge after Major-General George E. Pickett, one of the divisional commanders involved, incurred 50 per cent casualties and was final act in the battle. Meade, perhaps wisely, chose not to mount a counter-attack – nor did he press Lee's withdrawal.

Gibraltar, Siege of

Date: 24 June 1779 to 7 February 1783.

Location: The peninsula enclosing the eastern side of Algeciras Bay.
War and campaign: American War of Independence, 1775–1783.
Opposing sides: (a) Lieutenant-General George Eliott commanding the garrison; (b) General Alvarez, joined by the Duc de Crillon and Admiral Don Bonaventura Moreno.
Objective: The French and Spanish were attempting to capture the fortress from the British.
Forces engaged: (a) Five British and eight Hanoverian infantry battalions, plus 412 fortress guns – total 5,000, rising to 7,500; (b) initially Spanish only: sixteen infantry battalions, twelve cavalry squadrons and 150 guns – total 14,000. In June 1782 the arrival of French troops (35 infantry battalions and sixteen cavalry squadrons) brought the total number of besiegers to 40,000, with artillery in proportion.
Casualties: (a) 333 killed, 911 wounded and 536 dead from disease; (b) estimated 5,000 killed and wounded.
Result: The garrison conducted a spirited defence, repulsing every attack, and held out for a total of three years, seven months and twelve days until relieved. This did much to sustain British national morale, which would otherwise have been depressed by the news of reverses in the American colonies. Eliott was rewarded with a peerage.

The siege reached its climax on 13 September 1782 when the besiegers supplemented the fire of their land artillery with ten floating batteries designed by the French engineer Michaud d'Arcon. The hulls of these not only had been reinforced to the point at which they were proof against cannon balls but also incorporated layers of sand and cork kept permanently damp as a defence against red hot shot. The latter provision proved inadequate, and when several batteries were set ablaze by concentrated British fire Moreno gave orders for the rest to be abandoned and burned. Some blew up and the remainder sank after burning down to the waterline. The disaster so damaged French and Spanish morale that the final year of the siege amounted to little more than a blockade, which a reinforcement convoy experienced no difficulty in breaking in October 1782.

Golan Heights (1967) 196

Date: 9–10 June 1967.
Location: Plateau on the Israeli/Syrian frontier extending 45 miles southwards from the Mount Hermon massif.
War and campaign: Arab/Israeli War of 1967 ('Six Day War').
Opposing sides: (a) Major-General David Elazar, GOC Northern Command; (b) Major-General Souedan commanding the Golan Front.
Objective: The Israeli intention was to capture the Heights, which had been used by the Syrians to shell settlements in Galilee, and so secure a defensible frontier with Syria.
Forces engaged: (a) Two armoured, one mechanized, one paratroop and three infantry brigades – tank strength 75, rising to 200; (b) two armoured, one mechanized and six infantry brigades – tank strength 450, with 200 in reserve.
Casualties: (a) 115 killed and 306 wounded; (b) estimated 2,500 killed and 5,000 wounded, plus approximately 100 tanks and 200 guns destroyed or captured.

> **Result:** The Israelis, having captured the Heights, accepted a UN ceasefire resolution during the evening of 10 June.

The elimination of the Arab air forces during the early hours of the conflict ensured that the Israeli assault enjoyed total air superiority. This permitted the Israelis to employ helicopter insertions at strategically important points while their mechanized columns fought their way up to the steep tracks of the Golan escarpment, spearheaded by armoured bulldozers. The Israelis were strongly motivated and pressed home their attacks with fierce determination; at first the Syrians resisted stubbornly but their morale suddenly collapsed as one strongpoint after another fell to the Israelis.

Golan Heights (1973) 197

Date: 6–10 October 1973.
Location: Plateau on the Israeli/Syrian frontier extending 45 miles southwards from the Mount Hermon massif.
War and campaign: Arab/Israeli War of 1973 ('Yom Kippur War').
Opposing sides: (a) Major-General Yitzak Hofi, GOC Northern Command; (b) General Hefez al Assad, President of Syria.
Objective: The Syrian intention was to recover the Heights, which had been captured by the Israelis during the Six Day War of 1967.
Forces engaged: (a) Initially 7th and 188th Armoured Brigades with 170 tanks and 60 guns, reinforced by two reserve armoured divisions; (b) 5th, 7th and 9th Infantry Divisions and 1st and 3rd Armoured Divisions with approximately 1,400 tanks and 1,000 guns.
Casualties: (a) 772 killed, 2,453 wounded and 65 captured, plus 250 tanks knocked out (of which 150 were recovered and repaired); (b) 3,500 killed and 370 captured, plus 1,150 tanks knocked out (the Iraqi and Jordanian armies lost, respectively, 100 and 50 tanks in subsequent attempts to intervene in the battle).
Result: The Syrian attack almost succeeded in breaking through into Galilee but was repulsed after heavy fighting. On 22 October both sides accepted a UN ceasefire resolution. See also SUEZ CANAL CROSSING.

To achieve maximum effect, the Syrian offensive was timed to coincide with the Egyptian assault crossing of the Suez Canal. Both sides fought with suicidal bravery, the 7th and 188th Armoured Brigades being all but destroyed where they stood before the Syrians achieved a breakthrough, at a terrible cost in men and equipment, during the evening of 7 October. By then Israel had mobilized her reserve armoured formations and these were rushed to the front, halting the Syrian drive as it approached the Upper Jordan. Further hard fighting was required to stabilize the front but on 10 October the Israelis went over to the offensive, pushing the Syrians back across the frontier and along the road to Damascus. Counter-attacks by Iraqi and Jordanian armour against the Israeli right flank were easily fended off.

Goose Green 198

Date: 27–28 May 1982.
Location: Darwin and Goose Green settlements, on the isthmus between the northern and southern portions of East Falkland.

War and campaign: The Falklands War, 1982.
Opposing sides: (a) Lieutenant-Colonel H. Jones, succeeded by Major C. P. B. Keeble; (b) Air Vice-Commodore Wilson Dosio Pedroza.
Objective: The British intention was eliminate the Argentine garrisons of Darwin and Goose Green, thereby removing the threat to their right flank and rear as they advanced eastwards across the island towards PORT STANLEY.
Forces engaged: (a) 2nd Battalion Parachute Regiment Group, including three 105mm guns and two Blowpipe air defence detachments – total approximately 600; (b) 2nd Airmobile Infantry Regiment, 12th Infantry Regiment, air force personnel, four 105mm howitzers, two 35mm AA guns, six 20mm AA guns and six 120mm mortars – total approximately 1,700.
Casualties: (a) 18 killed (including Jones) and 35 wounded; (b) reported as 250 killed, 150 wounded, approximately 1,000 prisoners and all equipment captured; two Pucará ground-attack aircraft shot down (one by Blowpipe missile, the second by small-arms fire).
Result: The Argentines surrendered after most of their defences had been stormed. The outcome seriously affected Argentine morale for the remainder of the campaign, but of equal importance was the fact that prior to the battle Major-General Mario Menendez, commander-in-chief of the Argentine forces in the Falklands, had reinforced the Goose Green garrison with the greater part of the 12th Regiment, stripping the defences of Mount Kent to do so. By the end of the month this vital feature, overlooking every Argentine position around Port Stanley, was firmly in British hands.

The battle, lasting 15 hours, was the most fiercely contested of the war. The paratroopers were forced to fight their way down the isthmus through defences prepared in depth. At one point the attack came close to stalling but its impetus was restored by the example of Lieutenant-Colonel Jones, who was killed while personally leading an assault on an enemy post – an act which resulted in the posthumous award of the Victoria Cross. His successor, Major Keeble, persevered with the original plan and by nightfall had penned the Argentines in a half-circle around Goose Green settlement. The following morning Air Vice-Commodore Pedroza complied with an ultimatum to surrender or face the consequences.

Gorlice-Tarnow   199

Date: 2 May to 27 June 1915.
Location: 28-mile sector of front overlapping the towns of Gorlice and Tanrow, Austrian Galicia (now southern Poland).
War and campaign: First World War: Eastern Front.
Opposing sides: (a) General Erich von Falkenhayn and Field Marshal Count Conrad von Hotzendorf, Chiefs, respectively, of the German and Austro-Hungarian General Staffs; (b) General Nikolai Ivanov commanding the South-West Front.
Objective: A joint offensive by the Central Powers to recover the territory lost following RAVA RUSSKAYA.
Forces engaged: (a) Army Group Mackensen, including the Austro-Hungarian Third Army, the German Eleventh Army and the Austro-Hungarian Fourth Army; (b) the Russian Third Army (Radko-Dmitriev).

> **Casualties:** (a) Unknown, but heavy (although well below those of the Russians); (b) South-West Front reported 412,000 casualties for May alone.

> **Result:** The battle has been described as a turning point on the Eastern Front. The Russians lost the ground won during their 1914 offensive, the fortress of Przemysl was recaptured on 3 June, Lemberg (Lvov) was recovered on 22 June and the Dniestr was crossed on 23 June.

General August von Mackensen's spearhead was the German Eleventh Army, which achieved its breakthrough by means of a crippling artillery bombardment of the Russians' inadequate trench system. The Russian artillery had far fewer guns and was desperately short of ammunition. Grave deficiencies were revealed in the Russian Army as a result of the battle, particularly in the area of supply. Gorlice-Tanrow was one of the factors which led to Tsar Nicholas II's disastrous decision to dismiss the Grand Duke Nicholas and personally assume the role of Commander-in-Chief with General Mikhail Alexiev as his Chief of Staff.

Gothic Line   200

> **Date:** 30 August to 28 October 1944.

> **Location:** Defence zone 10 miles deep running from the Magra valley, south of La Spezia, through the Apuan Mountains to a chain of strongpoints guarding the Apennine passes, thence to the Foglia valley and a point on the Adriatic between Pesaro and Cattolica.

> **War and campaign:** Second World War: Italy.

> **Opposing sides:** (a) General Sir Harold Alexander, Commander-in-Chief of the Allied armies in Italy; (b) Field Marshal Albrecht Kesselring, Commander-in-Chief South.

> **Objective:** The Allied intention was to mantain steady pressure on the central sectors of the line while a breakthrough was achieved in the east with the objective of unleashing armoured formations into the Po valley.

> **Forces engaged:** (a) US Fifth Army (Clark) and British Eighth Army (Lesse) – total 20 divisions; (b) German Tenth Army (von Vietinghoff) and German Fourteenth Army (Lemelsen) – total 22 divisions.

> **Casualties:** (a) Uncertain, but heavy (by 21 September the Eighth Army had sustained the loss of 14,000 men killed, wounded and missing and the Fifth Army's losses at the beginning of October averaged 550 men per day per division); (b) uncertain, but heavy (on 25 September the Tenth Army recorded that, of its total of 92 infantry battalions, only ten still possessed more than 400 men, while of the rest 38 had fewer than 200 men each).

> **Result:** The Germans bitterly contested every feature, notably the vital Gemmano and Coriano Ridges, and retired so slowly that while the Gothic Line was breached the autumn rains rendered exploitation impossible.

Despite the result, the battle left the Allies in an excellent strategic position from which to mount their successful offensive in the spring of 1945.

Granicus, The   201

> **Date:** May 334 BC.

Location: The river Granicus in north-western Asia Minor.
War and campaign: Conquests of Alexander the Great: Campaign of 334 BC.
Opposing sides: (a) Alexander the Great; (b) the satraps Arsites, Spithridates and Arsames and the Greek mercenary commander Memnon of Rhodes.
Objective: Alexander's army, having crossed the Hellespont into Persian territory, was opposed at the Granicus by the forces of the local satraps.
Forces engaged: (a) 5,100 cavalry, 12,000 heavy infantry and 1,000 light infantry – total 18,100; (b) 10,000 cavalry and 5,000 Greek mercenary infantry – total 15,000.
Casualties: (a) 115 killed; (b) 4,000 killed (including 3,000 Greek mercenaries) and 2,000 Greek mercenaries captured.
Result: The Persian army was destroyed and Alexander overran Asia Minor. See ISSUS.

Alexander permitted the Persian cavalry to push his advance guard back across the river then, when they had been tempted into a disorderly pursuit, counter-attacked in oblique order from the right. The Persians, unable to stand against the long sarissas of the phalanx, broke and fled, leaving the Greek mercenaries isolated. Denied terms, they were surrounded and massacred until the surviving 2,000 surrendered unconditionally.

Granson 202

Date: 2 March 1476.
Location: On the south-western shore of Lake Neuchatel, Switzerland.
War and campaign: Swiss-Burgundian War, 1474–1477.
Opposing sides: (a) The Cantonal leaders of the Swiss army; (b) Charles the Bold, Duke of Burgundy.
Objective: The Burgundians had captured Granson and hanged the entire Swiss garrison the previous month. A Swiss army marched swiftly into the area to exact revenge.
Forces engaged: (a) 18,000 pikemen and halberdiers; (b) 30,000, with ample artillery.
Casualties: (a) 200 killed; (b) approximately 1,000 killed.
Result: The Burgundians were defeated and driven out of Granson. See also MORAT.

The leading Swiss column attacked so quickly that the Burgundians had little chance to use their artillery. Nevertheless, Charles withdrew his centre with the object of enclosing the column in a double envelopment, but his army fled when two more Swiss columns arrived at the critical moment.

Gravelotte-St Privat 203

Date: 18 August 1870.
Location: 6 miles west of Metz, Lorraine, France.
War and campaign: Franco-Prussian War, 1870–1871.
Opposing sides: (a) Field Marshal Count Helmuth von Moltke commanding the

First and Second Armies of the North German Confederation; (b) Marshal François-Achille Bazaine commanding the French Army of the Rhine.

Objective: Having intercepted the French army's retreat to the west at the battle of MARS-LA-TOUR, the Germans now closed in to complete its destruction.

Forces engaged: (a) 210 infantry battalions, 133 cavalry squadrons and 732 guns – total 188,332; (b) 183 infantry battalions, 104 cavalry squadrons and 520 guns – total 112,800.

Casualties: (a) 20,163 killed, wounded and missing; (b) 12,800 killed, wounded and missing.

Result: While the Germans ultimately captured St Privat, albeit at the cost of 8,000 casualties incurred by the Prussian Guard, at the southern end of the line their attacks were thrown back in confusion.

Had Bazaine counter-attacked at the critical period of the battle he would undoubtedly have defeated von Moltke; the war, and history, would then have followed a different course. As it was, he chose to conduct a passive defence and the following day retired into METZ, where his army was besieged.

Grenada 204

Date: 25–27 October 1983.

Location: Southernmost of the Windward Islands, Caribbean Sea.

War and campaign: US intervention made at the request of Sir Paul Scoon, Governor-General of Grenada, and the Organization of Eastern Caribbean States.

Opposing sides: (a) Rear-Admiral Joseph Metcalf commanding the US task force; (b) General Austin Hudson commanding the Grenadian army and Colonel Pedro Tortolo commanding the Cuban contingent.

Objective: The American intention was to overthrow the Communist-supported government which had seized power in a *coup d'état* and was holding American citizens captive.

Forces engaged: (a) I and II/75th Rangers, 22nd Marine Assault Unit and US Navy SEALS, followed by one brigade of the 82nd Airborne Division and token contingents from four Caribbean states – total approximately 7,000; (b) 1,000 Grenadian regulars, 1,000 militia and 784 Cubans, plus advisers from other Communist states – total approximately 3,000.

Casualties: (a) 18 killed and 45 wounded; (b) 60 Grenadians killed and 184 wounded, 24 Cubans killed and 40 wounded.

Result: The Communists were defeated and democracy was restored. The last US troops left the island in December 1983.

Criticism that the size and nature of the American forces employed amounted to 'overkill' were answered by the unexpectedly tough resistance put up by the Communists for several days.

Guadalajara 205

Date: 8–16 March 1937.

Location: Town 34 miles north-east of Madrid.

War and campaign: Spanish Civil War, 1936–1939.
Opposing sides: (a) General Moscarda commanding the Nationalists and General Roatta commanding the Italian contingent; (b) General Pavlov commanding the Soviet counter-attack force.
Objective: The Nationalists were attempting to complete the encirclement of Madrid.
Forces engaged: (a) 22,000 Nationalists and 30,000 Italians; (b) uncertain, but the combined Republic and Soviet strength was comparable.
Casualties: (a) Italian: estimated at 6,000, plus 300 captured; (b) unknown, but lighter.
Result: The Nationalist offensive was defeated.

The Nationalist spearhead consisted of the Italian Black Flames Division under Major-General Coppi, equipped with 50 tankettes and armoured cars. This succeeded in breaking through the Republican lines and penetrating to a depth of 20 miles, although because of atrocious weather the advance was largely road-bound. Pavlov then counter-attacked with air support, using heavier BT and T26 tanks, and drove the Italians back some 25 miles. However, the Soviet armour had outstripped its supporting infantry and was forced to abandon some of its gains. The battle, like others in which tanks were employed during the war, emphasized the need for organic mechanized infantry in armoured formations.

Guadalcanal 206

Date: 7 August 1942 to 7 February 1943.
Location: One of the Solomon Islands.
War and campaign: Second World War: South Pacific.
Opposing sides: (a) Vice-Admiral Robert L. Ghormley (later Vice-Admiral William F. Halsey), Commander-in-Chief South Pacific Area; (b) Admiral Shigeyoshi Inouye, commanding Japanese forces at Rabaul.
Objective: The American intention was to prevent the Japanese from using the island as an air base, and to use it themselves as a springboard for future operations against enemy-occupied territory.
Forces engaged: (a) Major-General Alexander A. Vandergrift's reinforced 1st Marine Division, relieved in December by Major-General Alexander M. Patch's US XIV Corps (2nd Marine, Americal and 25th Divisions); (b) troops rushed to the island, later designated the Seventeenth Army, under the command of Major-General Haruyoshi Hyakutake – total approximately 20,000, plus reinforcements.
Casualties: (a) 1,600 killed, 4,200 wounded and 12,000 incapacitated by disease; (b) 14,000 killed in action, 9,000 dead from disease or starvation, an unknown number of wounded and 1,000 captured.
Result: The first major defeat sustained by the Japanese Army, restoring American morale and improving the Allies' strategic situation.

Confirmation that the Japanese were constructing an airfield on Guadalcanal led directly to the American landings on 7 August. The small Japanese garrison was eliminated and the airfield, subsequently known as Henderson Field, was completed and brought into use on 20 August. The Japanese began pouring reinforcements into the island with a view to recapturing the airfield and began a naval and air offensive against the American beach-head. Between 12 and 14 September major assaults were mounted against the sector of the Marine perimeter later known as Bloody Ridge; these were repulsed with the loss of 600 killed, total American casualties amounting to 143. Further unco-ordinated assaults on the perimeter were repulsed between 23 and 25 October, costing the Japanese a further 2,000 killed. Vandergrift then took the offensive, pushing back the enemy until Henderson Field was no longer within range of his artillery. Following the relief of the 1st Marine Division the pressure was maintained by Patch's corps, driving the starving, disease-ridden Japanese westwards towards Cape Esperance during January. The survivors of Hyakutake's army, about 10,000 men, were evacuated by the Imperial Japanese Navy between 1 and 7 February in a series of night operations. In parallel with the land campaign, a series of fierce naval actions took place, costing each side 24 warships. However, while the American losses could be replaced, those of the Japanese could not, and to these were added some 300,000 tons of merchant shipping sunk. In the sustained air fighting the Japanese also lost heavily.

Guam 207

Date: 21 July to 10 August 1944.
Location: One of the Marianas Islands, Central Pacific.
War and campaign: Second World War: Central Pacific.
Opposing sides: (a) Admiral Chester Nimitz, Commander-in-Chief Central Pacific Theatre; (b) General Hideyoshi Obata commanding the Japanese Thirty-First Army.
Objective: The capture of the Marianas would enable the Americans to mount a bombing offensive against Japan itself and also to sever the enemy's communications with his conquests to the south. In addition, Guam possessed a fine natural harbour which would serve as a base for further operations in the Western Pacific.
Forces engaged: (a) Major-General Roy S. Geiger commanding III Amphibious Corps (3rd Marine Division, 77th Infantry Division and 1st Provisional Marine Brigade); (b) Lieutenant-General Takeshi Takashina commanding the Japanese garrison of eleven infantry battalions, plus supporting arms and naval troops – total about 20,000.
Casualties: (a) 1,023 killed and 6,777 wounded; (b) the majority of the garrison died in the savage fighting, and many of the remainder committed suicide rather than surrender. A few went into hiding in the interior of the island and, of these, the last two survivors did not surrender until 1960.
Result: The fall of Guam concluded the battle for the Marianas.

The loss of the islands, which coincided with their disastrous naval defeat at the Battle of the Philippine Sea (19–21 June), convinced the Japanese that they had finally lost the strategic initiative and resulted in the resignation of the Tojo cabinet on 18 July. See also SAIPAN and TINIAN.

Guilford Court House 208

Date: 15 March 1781.
Location: Between the headwaters of the Deep and Cape Fear rivers, North Carolina.
War and campaign: American War of Independence, 1775–1783: southern theatre of operations.

Opposing sides: (a) Major-General Lord Charles Cornwallis; (b) Major-General Nathanael Greene.
Objective: Following their victory at COWPENS, Brigadier-General Morgan's troops retreated across North Carolina into Virginia, rejoining the main American army on the way. Cornwallis, in pursuit, was unable to cross the swollen Dan river because the boats had been removed and, critically short of supplies, he decided to withdraw to Wilmington on the North Carolina coast. The Americans followed, forcing Cornwallis to fight a holding battle at Guilford.
Forces engaged: (a) 1,900; (b) 4,400.
Casualties: (a) Approximately 500 killed, wounded and missing; (b) approximately 1,300 killed, wounded and missing, plus four guns captured.
Result: Greene was defeated and Cornwallis continued his withdrawal to Wilmington.

Like Morgan at COWPENS, Greene had prepared a defence in depth consisting of three lines. However, as much of the battlefield consisted of woodland and his various elements were deployed too far apart to provide mutual support, Cornwallis' troops were able to fight their way through each in turn. Nevertheless, Greene understood that, win or lose, the British could not replace their casualties, whereas his own army was not so seriously handicapped. See EUTAW SPRINGS.

Guise

Date: 29 August 1914.
Location: Area between St Quentin and Guise, northern France.
War and campaign: First World War: Western Front.
Opposing sides: (a) General Charles Lanrezac commanding the French Fifth Army; (b) General Karl von Bulow commanding the German Second Army.
Objective: General Joseph Joffre, Commander-in-Chief of the French Army, had ordered a local counter-attack against the flank of von Kluck's German First Army to relieve pressure on the British Expeditionary Force as it retreated from LE CATEAU.
Forces engaged: (a) I, III, X and XVIII Corps; (b) Guard, VII, X and X Reserve Corps, plus half of IX Corps from the First Army.
Casualties: (a) Approximately 3,500; (b) over 6,000.
Result: Although the Fifth Army was compelled to withdraw the following day to avoid encirclement, its counter-attack not only succeeded in its objective but also had far-reaching effects on the conduct of the campaign. The blow actually fell on Bulow's troops and he requested assistance from Kluck. The latter, still believing that he had destroyed the BEF at LE CATEAU and refusing to accept that Joffre was forming a fresh army (Manoury's Sixth) to the north-west of Paris, assumed that Lanrezac now held the extreme left of the Allied line. He therefore began wheeling prematurely to the east to threaten his flank and rear, but in so doing he exposed his own flank to counter-attacks by Manoury and the BEF. See MARNE, FIRST BATTLE OF THE.

Despite having won an undoubted victory, Lanrezac had already fallen foul of Joffre before the battle and was dismissed on 3 September. His successor was General Franchet d'Esperey who, mounted on his charger, had led his I Corps and went into battle behind its colours and with its bands playing, so providing one of the last echoes of a vanished era. In German histories the battle is referred to as St Quentin.

Gujerat 210

Date: 21 February 1849.
Location: 68 miles north of Lahore city, Punjab (now in Pakistan).
War and campaign: Second Sikh War, 1848–1849.
Opposing sides: (a) General Lord Gough; (b) Sher Singh.
Objective: After CHILIANWALLAH the reinforced British army followed up the Sikhs and brought them to battle at Gujerat.
Forces engaged: (a) 25,000 British and Indian troops with 90 guns; (b) 60,000 Sikhs and Afghans with 60 guns.
Casualties: (a) 92 killed and 682 wounded; (b) over 2,000 killed and wounded.
Result: The Sikhs were decisively defeated and the Punjab was annexed.

Gough had learned the lessons of Chilianwallah, opening the battle in the morning with a two-and-a-half hour bombardment by his artillery. When the infantry assault was delivered the Sikhs broke and all their artillery was captured. Dost Muhammed, King of Afghanistan, still smarting from the First Afghan War (see JUGDULLUCK and JELLALABAD), had sent a contingent to support the Sikhs and this was pursued by Gough's cavalry through the Khyber Pass as far as Fort Jumrud.

Gumbinnen 211

Date: 20 August 1914.
Location: 55 miles east of Königsberg, East Prussia (now Kaliningrad, Lithuania).
War and campaign: First World War: Eastern Front.
Opposing sides: (a) General Helmuth von Moltke, Chief of the German General Staff; (b) Grand Duke Nicholas, Commander-in-Chief of the Russian Army.
Objective: The Germans were opposing the Russian advance on Königsberg.
Forces engaged: (a) General Max von Prittwitz und Gaffron commanding the German Eighth Army (nine divisions); (b) General Pavel Rennenkampf commanding the Russian First Army (twelve divisions).
Casualties: (a) Unknown, but heavy; (b) approximately 16,000.
Result: A German reverse.

Prittwitz, depressed, was further unsettled by reports that the Russian Second Army was advancing from the south against his right-rear and suggested a withdrawal to the line of the Vistula. Moltke replaced him with General Paul von Hindenburg, to whom General Erich Ludendorff was attached as Chief of Staff. See TANNENBERG (1914).

Gwalior 212

Date: 17–20 June 1858.

Location: Central India, 150 miles south of Delhi.
War and campaign: Indian Mutiny 1857–1858: Central India Campaign.
Opposing sides: (a) Major-General Sir Hugh Rose; (b) Tantia Topi, the Rani of Jhansi and Rao Sahib.
Objective: The army of Maharaja Sindhia had deserted to the rebels, who seized Gwalior. The British advanced to disperse them.
Forces engaged: (a) The Central India Field Force consisting of British and Indian troops, reinforced by a contingent from Hyderabad – numbers uncertain but inferior to those of the rebels; (b) estimated 7,000 infantry, 5,500 cavalry and twenty guns.
Casualties: (a) Uncertain; (b) unknown, but far heavier than those of the British (the Rani of Jhansi was killed during an engagement at Kotah-ke-Serai on 17 June).
Result: The rebels were decisively defeated and the fortress of Gwalior was captured. Tantia Topi and Rao Sahib fled but were subsequently betrayed and hanged.

Gwalior was the last major battle of the Mutiny, although pacification continued until December.

Habbaniya 213

Date: 30 April to 5 May 1941.
Location: 55 miles west of Baghdad on the Euphrates, Iraq.
War and campaign: Second World War: Rebellion in Iraq.
Opposing sides: (a) Air Vice-Marshal H. G. Smart commanding Habbaniya air base; (b) Rashid Ali (an Iraqi politician with pro-German sympathies).
Objective: The rebels were attempting to capture Habbaniya air base.
Forces engaged: (a) 1,000 airmen, 300 men of the King's Own Royal Regiment and 1,200 Assyrian and Kurdish levies under the overall command of Colonel O. L. Roberts, supported by eighteen RAF armoured cars and two ancient ornamental howitzers (the base also contained 88 aircraft, mostly obsolete or training types); (b) a division-sized force of regular Iraqi troops, some 10–15,000 men, with supporting artillery.
Casualties: (a) Light; (b) unknown, but heavier.
Result: The siege was broken by the garrison's own aircraft and the rebels were pursued to Fallujah by the armoured cars.

The base was relieved by a flying column from Transjordan on 18 May.

Halidon Hill 214

Date: 19 July 1333.
Location: 3 miles north-west of Berwick-upon-Tweed.
War and campaign: Anglo–Scottish Wars.
Opposing sides: (a) Edward III; (b) Archibald Douglas, Regent of Scotland.
Objective: The Scottish army was attempting to relieve Berwick, besieged by the English who were supporting Edward Balliol's claim to the Scottish throne.

Forces engaged: (a) Estimated 10,000; (b) 1,155 cavalry and 13,500 infantry – total 14,655.
Casualties: (a) One knight, one esquire and twelve infantrymen; (b) approximately 4,000 killed, including Douglas and most of the nobles present.
Result: The Scottish army was routed, Berwick surrendered and Edward III placed Balliol on the throne.

The Scottish schiltrons advanced uphill into the teeth of the English archers' fire; the few pikemen who reached the summit were easily dealt with by the men-at-arms, whose counter-attack routed the survivors.

Harper's Ferry 215

Date: 13–15 September 1862.
Location: Harper's Ferry (now a National Historical Park), West Virginia.
War and campaign: American Civil War: Lee's First Invasion of the North.
Opposing sides: (a) Colonel Dixon S. Miles commanding the Federal garrison; (b) Major-General Thomas ('Stonewall') Jackson.
Objective: While Lee advanced north into Maryland after his victory at SECOND BULL RUN, he ordered Jackson's corps to eliminate the Federal garrison at Harper's Ferry, which presented a threat to his lines of communication.
Forces engaged: (a) 14,000; (b) 22,000.
Casualties: (a) 219 killed and wounded and 12,500 taken prisoner, plus 73 guns, 11,000 small arms and 200 wagons captured; (b) 286 killed and wounded.
Result: After two days of fighting Miles, surrounded and dominated by the Confederate guns, surrendered when his artillery ammunition was exhausted.

This was the largest Federal capitulation of the war. See ANTIETAM (SHARPSBURG).

Hastings 216

Date: 14 October 1066.
Location: To the south of the town of Battle, East Sussex.
War and campaign: Norman Conquest of England.
Opposing sides: (a) King Harold; (b) Duke William of Normandy.
Objective: (a) King Harold was attempting to defeat the Norman invasion; (b) Duke William was determined to secure the crown of England.
Forces engaged: (a) 2,000 huscarls (regular troops) and 5,550 fyrd (militia) – total 7,500 infantry; (b) 2,000 cavalry and 5,000 infantry – total 7,000.
Casualties: Unknown, although each side is believed to have sustained in excess of 2,000. The English losses included Harold and his brothers Leofwine and Gyrth killed.
Result: The English army was defeated and William quickly consolidated his hold on the country, being crowned on Christmas Day. Superficially, Hastings was a small engagement which resolved a struggle for the throne of a kingdom occupying only part of the British Isles, but in the wider context it is acknowledged to have been one of the most decisive battles in history. In the words of Major-General J. F. C. Fuller,

'In the place of a loosely knit and undisciplined country was substituted a unified and compact kingdom under a firm and hereditary central authority.' The American historians Ernest and Trevor Dupuy express a broader, long term view of the consequences, describing the battle as 'The initiation of a series of events which would lead a revitalized Anglo-Saxon-Norman people to a world leadership more extensive even than that of ancient Rome.'

Hurrying south after his victory at STAMFORD BRIDGE, Harold sought battle at the earliest possible moment; whether he would have been well advised to wait until he had recovered his strength remains a matter for debate. The speed of the English march suggests that part, at least, of Harold's army was mounted, although it fought a defensive infantry battle from a good position behind its traditional shield wall. The first Norman attacks were thrown back with serious losses. The Bretons forming William's left wing broke but were rallied and turned on a portion of the English army which had pursued, destroying it. At about this time a report that William had been killed brought the Norman army to the verge of collapse, but the Duke, removing his helmet, was able to restore order. A series of mounted attacks against the shield wall met incredibly stubborn resistance and failed until a feigned retreat attracted pursuit by another portion of the English army, which was also destroyed. Yet, despite the thinning of its ranks, the shield wall held. William resorted to a combination of firepower and shock action, alternating high-angle fire by his archers with further mounted attacks. As dusk closed in after an eight-hour struggle, Harold is said to have been struck in the eye by an arrow. Shortly afterwards, the Normans broke through by sheer weight of numbers and the English king was killed in a mêlée around his standards. The English were driven off their position and into the forest behind, although even at this stage a group of knights who rashly attempted pursuit in the twilight were trapped and slaughtered by rallied huscarls in a ravine subsequently known as the Malfosse.

Hattin 217

Date: 4 July 1187.
Location: The Horns of Hattin, west of Tiberias on the Sea of Galilee.
War and campaign: Wars of the Crusader States.
Opposing sides: (a) King Guy of Jerusalem; (b) Salah-al-din Yusuf ibn-Ayub (Saladin).
Objective: The Crusader army was marching to the relief of Tiberias, which was being besieged by the Saracens.
Forces engaged: (a) 1,200 knights and 18,000 men-at-arms – total 19,200; (b) 12,000 regular troops and approximately 6,000 levies – total about 18,000.
Casualties: (a) Of the entire Crusader army only a handful escaped, the remainder being either killed or captured and sold into slavery – 200 captured Knights Templar and Knights of St John (Hospitallers) were beheaded on the spot; (b) unknown, but probably heavy.
Result: Guy's army was annihilated, although Saladin spared his life. The Saracens went on to capture the major Crusader strongholds. Jerusalem itself fell on 2 October, thus provoking the Third Crusade – see ARSUF. After Hattin the Crusader States were thrown on to the strategic defensive for the remainder of their history and the battle therefore marks a turning point in the fortunes of Outremer.

Rejecting the wisest counsels, Guy chose to advance across an arid region at the hottest time of the year. His column was harassed continuously by the Saracens' mounted archers and was approaching a source of water beyond the twin peaks of the Horns of Hattin when it found its way blocked by Saladin's army. Saladin immediately sent out his two wings to encircle the Crusaders and deny them access to a second source of water at Turun, to their rear. The Saracens then set fire to the scrub surrounding the Crusader camp, aggravating their torment. Next morning the Crusaders attempted to break through to the springs at Hattin but were repulsed and fled up one of the Horns when they were counter-attacked from the rear. Following the failure of several attempted break-outs by what had degenerated into a thirst-crazed mob, Saladin launched a decisive attack in the late afternoon and resistance collapsed. Compare with CARRHAE.

Hexham 218

Date: 15 May 1464.
Location: 2 miles south-east of Hexham, Northumberland.
War and campaign: Wars of the Roses, 1455–1485.
Opposing sides: (a) John Neville, Marquess of Montagu, commanding the Yorkists; (b) the Duke of Somerset commanding the Lancastrians.
Objective: The Yorkists were putting down a Lancastrian rising in Northumbria.
Forces engaged: (a) Probably less than 10,000 (Montagu's force is said by one source to have outnumbered its opponents by 8:1 but this is almost certainly an exaggeration); (b) perhaps 5,000.
Casualties: (a) Light; (b) the entire Lancastrian force was killed, captured or dispersed and Somerset and other captured Lancastrian leaders were executed.
Result: Montagu routed the Lancastrians with a surprise attack on their camp, crushing the rising.

Queen Margaret and Edward Prince of Wales fled to France; Henry VI went into hiding in a monastery in northern England but was discovered a year later and imprisoned in the Tower. For the moment the crown remained firmly in Edward IV's hands.

Hindenburg Line 219

Date: 27 September to 17 October 1918.
Location: Major German defensive line on the Western Front. The sector attacked stretched from Arras in the north to Soissons in the south.
War and campaign: First World War: Western Front.
Opposing sides: (a) Marshal Ferdinand Foch, Allied Supreme Commander; (b) General Erich Ludendorff, First Quartermaster-General of the German Army.
Objective: The Allied intention was to break the Hindenburg Line, with the further object of capturing the railway junction of Aulnoye. The offensive was mounted in parallel with the MEUSE-ARGONNE operations.
Forces engaged: The French Tenth (Mangin), Third (Humbert) and First (Debeney) Armies and the British Fourth (Rawlinson), Third (Byng) and First (Horne) Armies, with tank support; (b) the German Seventeenth (von Below), Second (von der Marwitz), Eighteenth (von Hutier) and Ninth (von Eben) Armies.
Casualties: (a) Approximately 350,000; (b) approximately 500,000, including a

high proportion of prisoners (the remaining German artillery was reduced by one-third).
Result: Once the Hindenburg Line had been breached the German armies had no alternative other than to embark on a fighting withdrawal along the front. Within Germany itself moves towards the request for an armistice were well advanced before the battle ended.

The principal burden of the offensive fell on the British armies. Both Haig and Ludendorff ascribed the tank as being a major element in the Allied success. While tanks were used regularly in assaults on the Hindenburg defences, after AMIENS there were only sufficient available to support local attacks and their effect, on both sides, though critically important, was largely moral.

Hochkirch 220

Date: 14 October 1758.
Location: Village near Bautzen, 40 miles east of Dresden, Saxony, Germany.
War and campaign: Seven Years' War, 1756–1763: Central European Campaign of 1758.
Opposing sides: (a) Frederick the Great; (b) Marshal Leopold von Daun.
Objective: Frederick II of Prussia had marched south after his costly victory at ZORNDORF. The much larger Austrian army surrounded his camp at Hochkirch during the night of 13/14 October and attacked at dawn.
Forces engaged: (a) 30,000; (b) 78,000.
Casualties: (a) 9,500 killed, wounded and taken prisoner, plus 101 guns captured; (b) 7,500 killed and wounded.
Result: Frederick fought his way out at the cost of most of his artillery and retreated. Instead of following up, Daun besieged Dresden but, learning that Frederick had received reinforcements and was again advancing, he withdrew into fortified winter quarters at Pirna.

Despite his reverse at Hochkirch, Frederick ended the 1758 campaign in possession of Silesia and Saxony.

Höchst 221

Date: 20 June 1622.
Location: Village on the Main between Frankfurt and Mainz.
War and campaign: Thirty Years' War, 1618–1648: German Campaign of 1622.
Opposing sides: (a) Duke Christian of Brunswick commanding the Protestants; (b) Count John Tzerklaes de Tilly and Gonzales de Cordoba commanding the Imperialist/Bavarian/Spanish Catholic army.
Objective: The Catholic army was attempting to prevent one Protestant force crossing the Mainz and joining forces with another under Count Ernst von Mansfeld in Alsace.
Forces engaged: (a) Maximum 15,000, with three guns (only one of which was serviceable); (b) approximately 30,000.

Casualties: (a) Over 2,000 killed, drowned, wounded and taken prisoner and much baggage and all guns lost; (b) fewer than those of the Protestants.
Result: The Catholics claimed a victory but the fact remains that, despite a five-hour struggle around the bridgehead, the bulk of Christian's army did succeed in crossing the bridge and joining Mansfeld, producing a combined strength of 25,000.

Hochstadt 222

Date: 30 September 1703.
Location: Village on the Danube between Ingolstadt and Ulm, Württemberg, Germany.
War and campaign: War of Spanish Succession, 1701–1714: operations in Central Europe, 1703.
Opposing sides: (a) Count Hermann Styrum commanding the Austrians; (b) Marshal Claude de Villars commanding the combined Franco-Bavarian army.
Objective: The Austrians were opposing the advance of a Franco-Bavarian army towards Vienna.
Forces engaged: (a) 20,000; (b) 35,000.
Casualties: (a) 11,000; (b) 1,000.
Result: The Austrians were defeated and the road to Vienna lay open.

When Maximilian, Elector of Bavaria, rejected Villars' recommendation to take advantage of the situation, the latter resigned and was replaced by Marshal Count Ferdinand de Marsin. See DONAUWORTH and BLENHEIM.

Hohenfriedberg 223

Date: 4 June 1745.
Location: Near Strzegom (Striegau), 35 miles south-west of Wroclaw (Breslau), Poland.
War and campaign: War of Austrian Succession, 1740–1748: Central European Campaign of 1745.
Opposing sides: (a) Frederick the Great; (b) Prince Charles of Lorraine.
Objective: Frederick II of Prussia launched a surprise attack on an Austro-Saxon army which had invaded Silesia.
Forces engaged: (a) Approximately 65,000; (b) approximately 85,000.
Casualties: (a) 2,000 killed and wounded; (b) 11,000 killed, wounded and taken prisoner, plus 65 guns captured.
Result: The Austro-Saxon army was defeated and pursued into Bohemia. See also SOHR (SOOR).

Hohenlinden 224

Date: 3 December 1800.
Location: Town and forest 20 miles east of Munich, Germany.

War and campaign: War of the Second Coalition, 1798–1800: Campaign in Germany.
Opposing sides: (a) General Jean Moreau commanding the French Army of the Rhine; (b) the Archduke John commanding the combined Austrian and Bavarian army.
Objective: Following the defeat of the Austrians in Italy at MARENGO, the French intention was to inflict a similar reverse on the Austrian army in Germany, then advance on Vienna and dictate peace.
Forces engaged: (a) 45 infantry battalions, 100 cavalry squadrons and 100 guns – total approximately 60,000; (b) 50 infantry battalions, 140 cavalry squadrons and 150 guns – total approximately 70,000.
Casualties: (a) 5,000 killed and wounded; (b) 6,000 killed and wounded, 11,000 prisoners and 87 guns captured.
Result: Moreau succeeded in provoking the Archduke to attack him. However, the complicated Austrian plan broke down when the advancing columns were separated in close country, and these were defeated in detail by the French.

The battle was decisive and Austria sued for peace shortly afterwards.

Hue 225

Date: 31 January to 25 February 1968.
Location: City on the Perfume (Huong) river near the coast of Annam, central Vietnam.
War and campaign: Vietnam War, 1956–1975: Tet Offensive.
Opposing sides: (a) Brigadier-General Ngo Quang Truong commanding the 1st South Vietnamese (ARVN) Division and Brigadier-General Foster LaHue commanding Task Force X-Ray; (b) overall command uncertain – the largest North Vietnamese (NVA) unit involved was the 6th Regiment of three battalions, commanded by Lieutenant-Colonel Nguyen Trong Dan.
Objective: The recapture of the city, which had been seized by Communist troops in a surprise attack on 30/31 January.
Forces engaged: (a) Eleven ARVN battalions, three US Marine battalions and three US Army battalions; (b) four NVA and six Viet Cong battalions.
Casualties: (a) 384 ARVN killed and 1,800 wounded and 119 Americans killed and 961 wounded; (b) 5,113 killed and 89 captured.
Result: The city was recaptured after heavy fighting.

Hue was the former Annamese Imperial capital and, because it contained numerous buildings of historic and cultural importance, the Allies were inhibited in their use of artillery; consequently, the task of clearing the city took longer than it would normally have done and involved protracted street fighting. The modern area south of the Perfume river was cleared first, followed by the fortifications of the ancient Citadel to the north. After the battle it was discovered that during their occupation the Communists had massacred several thousand innocent civilians, including foreign nationals, whom they believed to be unsympathetic to their cause. During their Tet Offensive the Communists launched attacks on five major cities, 36 provincial capitals and 23 Allied bases (see KHE SANH). All were defeated and the major rising predicted by the Viet Cong did not take place. Allied casualties amounted to 4,324 killed, 16,063 wounded and 598 wounded.

Estimates of Communist dead varied between 30,000 and 50,000; 6,991 members of the NVA or Viet Cong were captured. After Tet, the Viet Cong were a spent force, a fact which Hanoi did not unduly regret since it had no intention of sharing power with the southerners.

Hydaspes, The 226

Date: June 326 BC.
Location: Near Jalalpur on the Jhelum (formerly Hydaspes) river, Pakistan.
War and campaign: Conquests of Alexander the Great: Invasion of India, 328–327 BC.
Opposing sides: (a) Alexander the Great; (b) King Porus.
Objective: An Indian army was attempting to prevent Alexander crossing the river.
Forces engaged: (a) 5,300 cavalry and 14,000 infantry from an approximate total of 25,000; (b) 35,000, including 3,000 cavalry, 300 chariots and 100 elephants.
Casualties: (a) 930 killed; (b) 12,000 killed and 9,000 captured (including Porus), plus 80 elephants captured.
Result: Alexander won a brilliant tactical victory. Shortly afterwards, however, his Macedonian troops, now weary and further from home than any of them could once have imagined, refused to go any further. He returned to Persia, dying at Babylon in 323.

Leaving part of his army behind to demonstrate, Alexander marched upstream and secured a crossing under cover of a thunderstorm. He then advanced down the opposite bank while Porus deployed to meet him. Aware that his cavalry would not face the Indian elephants, Alexander used the bulk of it to threaten Porus's left-wing cavalry, causing him to extend his flank and reinforce it with troops down from his right. The remainder of the Macedonian cavalry, sent on a wide march round the Indian right, rode across the enemy rear to assail Porus's cavalry, thus enclosed within a tactical trap, from behind. It was now the turn of the phalanx to advance. The Indian elephants, pushed steadily back by the bristling sarissas, began to rampage through the ranks of their own infantry, which soon broke. The pursuit was taken up by the hitherto disengaged portion of Alexander's army which had swarmed across the river.

Ia Drang Valley (Pleiku) 227

Date: 19 October to 26 November 1965.
Location: In the Central Highlands of southern Vietnam, south-west of Pleiku.
War and campaign: Vietnam War, 1956–1975.
Opposing sides: (a) Major-General Harry Kinnard commanding the 1st Cavalry Division; (b) Brigadier-General Chu Huy Man commanding the Western Highlands Field Front.
Objective: An abortive Communist attack on the Special Forces Camp at Plei Mei (19 October) led to the movement of the US 1st Cavalry Division (Airmobile) into the area. Search operations by this in the area of the Chu Pong massif, south of the Ia Drang, provoked a major battle when the Communist concentration area was penetrated.

Forces engaged: (a) 1st Cavalry Division; (b) 32nd, 33rd and 66th Regiments, North Vietnamese Army, plus several Viet Cong battalions.
Casualties: (a) 304 killed and 524 wounded; (b) 1,519 counted dead (plus an unknown number removed from the battlefield), approximately 1,000 wounded and 157 prisoners.
Result: The Communists sustained crippling losses and withdrew from the area. The failure of their first division-sized operation in South Vietnam resulted in their abandoning plans to dominate the Central Highlands. For the Americans, the battle vindicated the concept of large airmobile formations.

The most critical action took place from 14 to 16 November in and around Landing Zone X-Ray, north-east of Chu Pong, and involved I/7th, II/7th and II/5th Cavalry. Some Communist attacks reached the perimeter and were only contained by savage hand-to-hand fighting, but most were stopped by sustained and accurate artillery fire from nearby fire support bases, supplemented by air strikes by helicopter gunships and fixed-wing aircraft. B-52 heavy bombers, flying for the first time in the tactical support role, pounded Chu Pong itself with hundreds of tons of bombs. By first light on 16 November the Communists had broken contact. American casualties on this sector amounted to 79 killed and 121 wounded; 634 NVA and Viet Cong dead were counted and others, together with the numerous wounded, had obviously been dragged away.

Imjin River   228

Date: 22–30 April 1951.
Location: On the line of the Imjin river north of Seoul, South Korea.
War and campaign: Korean War, 1950–1953: Phase I of the Second 1951 Communist Offensive.
Opposing sides: (a) Lieutenant-General James Van Fleet commanding the US Eighth Army, Lieutenant-General Frank Milburn commanding the US I Corps, Major-General Robert Soule commanding the US 3rd Division and Brigadier Tom Brodie commanding the British 29th Independent Brigade Group; (b) General Peng Teh-huai, *de facto* commander-in-chief of the Communist armies in Korea.
Objective: The Communist intentions were (i) to isolate part of the US I Corps by cutting its main supply route and (ii) to capture Seoul.
Forces engaged: (a) British 29th Brigade Group and elements of the US 3rd Division; (b) Chinese 63rd Army (187th, 188th and 189th Divisions, each about 9,000 strong).
Casualties: (a) Approximately 1,000 killed, wounded and missing; (b) estimated 11,000, including a high proportion killed.
Result: The Communists were unable either to isolate part of US I Corps or to capture Seoul. The 63rd Army sustained 40 per cent casualties and orders for its withdrawal to China were issued on 25 April. The Communists' April offensive failed with the loss of 70,000 casualties overall.

The British 29th Brigade Group – consisting of a composite Belgian infantry battalion, the First Battalions of the Royal Northumberland Fusiliers, the Gloucestershire Regiment and the Royal Ulster Rifles, 45 Field Regiment Royal Artillery, 170 Independent Mortar Battery RA, 11 Light AA Battery RA, 55 Field Squadron Royal Engineers and C Squadron 8th Hussars – lay squarely in the path of the 63rd Army's offensive. The

Belgian battalion, north of the river line, held its ground until a counter-attack by the US 65th Regiment Combat Team enabled it to be withdrawn temporarily into brigade reserve. On the left the Glosters were quickly isolated but fought a magnificent defensive battle during which two Victoria Crosses (Lt-Colonel J. P. Carne and Lieutenant P. K. E. Curtis) were won, together with a US Presidential Unit Citation; in the morning of 25 April the battalion, having exhausted its ammunition, food and water, broke out but only 63 men succeeded in reaching safety. On the right flank the Fusiliers, Rifles and Belgians fought an equally bitter battle culminating in a fighting withdrawal covered by the Hussars' Centurion tanks. The effect of the brigade group's dogged resistance was to throw the Communist timetable completely out of phase and inflict such horrific casualties on the 63rd Army, brought south specifically for the capture of Seoul, that it was no longer capable of performing its function.

Imphal 229

Date: 29 March to 22 June 1944.
Location: The Imphal Plain, Manipur, Assam.
War and campaign: Second World War: Burma.
Opposing sides: (a) Lieutenant-General Masakuzu Kawabe commanding the Japanese Burma Area Army; (b) Lieutenant-General Sir William Slim commanding the British Fourteenth Army.
Objective: The Japanese sought to secure an impregnable defence line along the line of the Naga Hills, which would contain the British within India and prevent their resuming operations in Burma.
Forces engaged: (a) Lieutenant-General Renya Mutaguchi's Fifteenth Army, consisting of the 15th, 31st and 33rd Divisions; (b) Lieutenant-General G. A. P. Scoones' IV Corps, consisting of the 17th, 20th and 23rd Divisions plus two regiments of 254 Indian Tank Brigade, reinforced by the 5th Indian Division.
Casualties: (a) 53,000 dead from all causes, including starvation and tropical disease, plus the loss of all heavy equipment; (b) 17,000 casualties, including 13,000 wounded evacuated by air.
Result: A catastrophic Japanese defeat which marked a major turning point in the Burma campaign.

Kawabe's intention was to isolate IV Corps on the Imphal Plain by using the 31st Division to cut the road behind it at KOHIMA; the 33rd Division was then to converge on the plain from the south and west while the 15th Division would attack from the north and east. Slim, aware of the enemy plan, instructed Scoones to concentrate his corps on the plain, where it could be supplied by air and the British armour could be used to best advantage; once the Japanese had exhausted themselves in attacks on defensive boxes, IV Corps would take the offensive. On 10 April the Japanese almost succeeded in capturing the vital hill feature of Nunshigum, which overlooked the principal airstrips, but were driven off after hard fighting. Thereafter the battle took the form Slim had predicted. The Japanese divisions, prevented by distance from co-ordinating their operations, began to exhaust their supplies while, far behind the lines, Chindit columns preyed on the enemy's communications, tying down troops which could otherwise have been used in Kawabe's offensive. The attrition imposed by British air superiority and armour eroded Mutaguchi's strength and further progress was impeded by bitter quarrels between the Japanese generals. At the end of May Lieutenant-General Montagu Stopford's British XXXIII Corps broke through the 31st Division's road-block at KOHIMA and on 22 June effected a junction with IV Corps north of Imphal. By then, the remnants of the Japanese army had already begun their withdrawal to the Chindwin.

Inchon

Date: 15–25 September 1950.
Location: Port on the west coast of South Korea.
War and campaign: Korean War, 1950–1953.
Opposing sides: (a) General Douglas MacArthur in overall command of the UN forces, Major-General Edward M. Almond commanding the US X Corps; (b) Marshal Choe Yong Gun in overall command of the North Korean forces.
Objective: The capture of the port by a UN amphibious task force was to be followed by the liberation of Seoul, the South Korean capital, with the result that the North Korean forces grouped around the PUSAN PERIMETER to the south would be isolated.
Forces engaged: (a) US X Corps (1st Marine and 7th Infantry Divisions, reinforced); (b) estimated 2,000 men in the general area of Inchon and a further 5,000 in Seoul.
Casualties: (a) Light; (b) 125,000 prisoners captured, together with most of their equipment (in the overall context, the North Korean Army ceased to exist as a direct result of the landing).
Result: The landing succeeded and the capture of Seoul severed the supply artery of the Communist troops in the south. Simultaneously, the US Eighth Army broke out from the Pusan perimeter and Choe's army disintegrated. MacArthur pursued its remnants deep into North Korea – see CHOSIN RESERVOIR/HUNGNAM.

A tidal rise of 32ft, making the landing beaches accessible for only six hours in twenty-four, made Inchon an extremely difficult objective for an amphibious landing, and for this reason the Communist high command discounted the prospect. In the event, the beach-head was secured without difficulty although stiffer resistance was encountered around Seoul. The landing was one of the greatest strategic master-strokes in military history and can be compared to Slim's capture of Meiktila during the battle for MANDALAY.

Indus, The

Date: 1221.
Location: On the river in the northern Punjab, precise location uncertain.
War and campaign: Mongol war against the Kwarezmian Empire, 1218–1224.
Opposing sides: (a) Genghis Khan; (b) Jallalladin, Shah of the Kwarezmian Empire.
Objective: Following the fall of SAMARKAND, the Kwarezmians had raised a fresh army which defeated a Mongol force near Ghazni. Genghis Khan acted swiftly to avenge the reverse, following up the Kwarezmian retreat into the Punjab.
Forces engaged: (a) 50,000; (b) 30,000.

Casualties: (a) 8,000; (b) 19,000 killed or drowned.
Result: Although Jallalladin escaped, his army was routed and driven into the river.

The Mongols ravaged the Punjab but, rather than overextend themselves in India, withdrew to consolidate their gains.

Inkerman 232

Date: 5 November 1854.
Location: South-eastern outskirts of Sevastopol, Crimea.
War and campaign: Crimean War.
Opposing sides: (a) Field Marshal Lord Raglan; (b) General Prince Alexander Menshikov.
Objective: The Russians were attempting to break the SIEGE OF SEVASTOPOL with a combined sortie by the garrison and an attack by their field army in the Crimea.
Forces engaged: (a) Approximately 20,000; (b) 55,000.
Casualties: (a) 2,573 British and 1,743 French; (b) 11,959, including 4,400 killed.
Result: Both Russian attacks were defeated and the siege of Sevastopol continued.

Heavy mist assisted the Russians in achieving surprise but also prevented them from appreciating how few troops were confronting them during the early stages of the action; it also hindered commanders attempting to exercise control, so that the fighting resolved itself into a fiercely contested, hand-to-hand 'soldiers' battle'. The weight of the attack fell on the British sector but the arrival of a French division finally tipped the scales.

Inonu, First and Second 233

Date: 10–11 January and 28–30 March 1921.
Location: Town 20 miles west of Eskisehir, north-western Turkey.
War and campaign: Graeco–Turkish War, 1920–1922.
Opposing sides: (a) General Papoulas; (b) Ismet Pasha (known later as Ismet Inonu).
Objective: Following the collapse of the Ottoman Empire, Greek expansion into Anatolia was resisted by Turkish Nationalists. The Greek advance was directed at Ankara, the Nationalist capital, along the axes Smyrna–Afionkarahisar and Bursa–Eskisehir.
Forces engaged: (a) Four infantry divisions – total approximately 18,000; (b) approximately 23,000.
Casualties: Heavy on both sides.
Result: The Greek advance on Eskisehir was halted on both occasions.

On their southern axis of advance the Greeks, under the personal command of King Constantine, took Afionkarahisar in July and swung north to outflank Eskisehir. Ismet withdrew to the Nationalists' final defence line on the SAKARIA RIVER.

Inverlochy

Date: 2 February 1645.

Location: North of Fort William at the head of Loch Linnhe in the Western Highlands.

War and campaign: First Civil War, 1642–1646: operations in Scotland.

Opposing sides: (a) John Graham, Marquis of Montrose; (b) Archibald Campbell, Marquis of Argyll.

Objective: Having occupied Perth and Aberdeen after its victory at TIPPERMUIR, Montrose's Royalist army marched west to Inverlochy, where it was opposed by a larger force of Campbells and Lowland Covenanters.

Forces engaged: (a) 1,500; (b) 3,000.

Casualties: (a) Uncertain but moderate; (b) approximately 1,700 killed and wounded.

Result: Argyll's army was routed.

The loss of so great a proportion of its manpower curbed the power of Clan Campbell for many years and the Highland taunt "Tis a far cry to Loch Awe!' is a reference to the battle and the flight of the fugitives from Inverlochy to the heart of Campbell territory. See also KILSYTH.

Isandhlwana

Date: 22 January 1879.

Location: Prominent hill in western Zululand, 10 miles east of Rorke's Drift on the Buffalo river.

War and campaign: Zulu War, 1879.

Opposing sides: (a) Lieutenant-General Lord Chelmsford, Commander-in-Chief of the British troops in Zululand; (b) Tshingwayo and Mavumengwana commanding the Zulu army.

Objective: A British camp below the hill was attacked by the Zulu army.

Forces engaged: (a) Approximately 1,500 British and native troops with two guns; (b) approximately 20,000.

Casualties: (a) 1,329 killed, including 21 officers and 578 other ranks belonging to the 24th Regiment (South Wales Borderers), and two guns captured; (b) between 2,000 and 3,000 killed plus a comparable number wounded.

Result: The camp was overrun and Chelmsford was forced to retire and revise his plans for the invasion of Zululand. However, the heavy casualties they had incurred, both at Isandhlwana and at RORKE'S DRIFT that night, destroyed the Zulus' confidence in their ability to win the war.

Chelmsford, with a large part of the column which had established the camp, was absent when the attack took place. It is possible that the defence might have held had not the ammunition supply failed at the critical moment. About 350 managed to escape the massacre, among them Lieutenant Horace Smith-Dorrien, who was to become an army commander during the First World War.

Isly

Date: 14 August 1844.
Location: On the Isly river, eastern Morocco.
War and campaign: French Conquest of Algeria, 1830–1847.
Opposing sides: (a) Marshal Thomas Bugeaud; (b) Abd-el-Kader, Emir of Mascara.
Objective: The Algerian army had been driven westwards into Morocco and the French, crossing the frontier in pursuit, attacked its camp.
Forces engaged: (a) 6,000 infantry, 1,500 cavalry and some artillery; (b) appoximately 45,000, mainly cavalry.
Casualties: (a) 250 killed and wounded; (b) 800 killed, plus an unknown number of wounded.
Result: A decisive French victory. Abd-el-Kader remained actively hostile to the French but surrendered in December 1847; by then Bugeaud had initiated his successful policy of pacification.

The French attack was delivered in a formation devised by Bugeaud to combine the weight of the assault column with the defensive strength of the square. Known as the Boar's Head, this consisted of a blunted wedge with battalions deployed in echelon to the rear, the 'tusks' being cavalry counter-attacks delivered from the base of the wedge. The wild charges of Abd-el-Kader's irregular horsemen were easily dispersed by the disciplined musketry of Bugeaud's infantry, then the French cavalry counter-charged and drove the Algerians back through their camp. Isly was fought in a temperature of 140°F.

Isonzo, Eleven Battles of the

Date: 1. 23 June to 7 July 1915; 2. 18 July to 3 August 1915; 3. 18 October to 4 November 1915; 4. 10 November to 2 December 1915; 5. 11–29 March 1916; 6. 6–17 August 1916; 7. 14–26 September 1916; 8. 10–12 October 1916; 9. 1–14 November 1916; 10. 12 May to 8 June 1917; 11. 18 August to 15 September 1917.
Location: On the Italian-Yugoslav border, along the line of the river Isonzo.
War and campaign: First World War: Italian Front.
Opposing sides: (a) General Count Luigi Cadorna, Chief of the Italian General Staff; (b) Field Marshal Conrad von Hotzendorff, Chief of the Austro-Hungarian General Staff.
Objective: The Italians were hoping to acquire Austro-Hungarian territory, notably Trieste and the surrounding area.
Forces engaged: (a) Italian Second and Third Armies; (b) Austro-Hungarian Fifth Army, later First and Second Isonzo Armies.
Casualties: Continuously heavy on both sides. For example, during the Sixth, Seventh, Eighth and Ninth Battles the Italians sustained a total of 126,000 casualties and the Austrians 103,000; during the Tenth Battle Italian casualties were 157,000 and Austrian 75,000.
Result: The Italians advanced a few miles but were unable to break through. While the constant attrition affected the morale of both sides, by the end of the Eleventh Battle the Austrians were close to collapse and requested German assistance. See also CAPORETTO (THE TWELFTH BATTLE OF THE ISONZO).

Issus

Date: October 333 BC.
Location: On the river Payas near Iskenderun, south-eastern Turkey.
War and campaign: Conquests of Alexander the Great: Campaign of 333 BC.
Opposing sides: (a) Alexander the Great; (b) Darius III, King of Persia.
Objective: The Persian king had placed his army across Alexander's lines of communication, forcing the latter to give battle.
Forces engaged: (a) 35,000; (b) possibly 90,000, including 30,000 Greek mercenaries and an equal number of Perisan infantry similarly armed.
Casualties: (a) 450 killed; (b) estimates vary from 15,000 to 50,000 killed, wounded and captured.
Result: The Persian army was destroyed. Alexander completed the conquest of Syria and occupied Egypt before advancing into the Persian heartland. See ARBELA.

The battle was fought on a comparatively narrow plain between the sea and the mountains. Thus Darius was only able to deploy a fraction of his total strength, estimated by some authorities at 500,000, the greater part of which remained spectators to the fighting. On the flanks, Alexander's cavalry and light troops quickly defeated offensive moves by their immediate opponents then went over to the attack, wheeling inwards against the Persian innner centre. The Macedonian phalanx, advancing in echelon from the right across the river, beame engaged in a bitter struggle with Darius' Greek mercenaries, but the Persian 'hoplites' had already given way and the Greeks were compelled to withdraw when their left flank was enveloped. The entire Persian army disintegrated in panic, pursued by Alexander with only 1,000 cavalry. Among those captured were Darius's queen and family.

Ivry

Date: 14 March 1590.
Location: Ivry-la-Bataille on the Eure river, 40 miles west of Paris.
War and campaign: French Wars of Religion, 1560–1598: Campaign of 1590.
Opposing sides: (a) King Henry IV (Henry of Navarre) commanding the Royalist/Huguenot army; (b) Duke Charles de Mayenne commanding the army of the Catholic League.
Objective: A deliberate pitched battle sought by both armies.
Forces engaged: (a) 8,000 infantry, 3,000 cavalry and five guns: (b) 15,000 infantry and 4,000 cavalry.
Casualties: (a) 500 killed and wounded; (b) 4,000 killed, wounded and captured.
Result: After a hard fight the Catholic army was routed and put to flight.

Several years of inconclusive warfare followed, but Ivry was the last major engagement of the French Wars of Religion. In 1593 Henry was formally reconciled with the Catholic faith and five years later he issued the Edict of Nantes, granting religious freedom to the Huguenots.

Iwo Jima

Date: 19 February to 16 March 1945.
Location: One of the Bonin Islands.
War and campaign: Second World War: Central Pacific.
Opposing sides: (a) Major-General Harry Schmidt commanding the US V Amphibious Corps; (b) Major-General Todomichi Kuribyashi commanding the Japanese garrison.
Objective: The Americans' intention was to capture the island and use its airfields for the strategic bombing offensive against Japan.
Forces engaged: (a) 4th and 5th Marine Divisions, with the 3rd Marine Division initially held in corps reserve; (b) 22,000 men manning heavily fortified defensive positions.
Casualties: (a) 6,891 killed and 18,700 wounded; (b) except for 212 Japanese who chose to surrender, the entire garrison fought to the death.
Result: An American victory.

Jassy-Kishinev

Date: 20–30 August 1944.
Location: Soviet and Romanian Moldavia.
War and campaign: Second World War: Russian Front.
Opposing sides: (a) Marshal Rodion Malinovsky commanding the 2nd Ukrainian Front and Marshal F. I. Tolbukhin commanding the 3rd Ukrainian Front; (b) Colonel-General Johannes Freissner commanding Army Group South Ukraine.
Objective: The Soviet intention was to inflict a severe defeat on the German army group holding the southern sector of the front, with a view to detaching Romania from the Axis alliance.
Forces engaged: (a) 2nd Ukrainian Front – 6th tank Army, 7th Guards Army, 27th, 52nd and 53rd Armies, Cavalry Mechanized Group Gorshkhov; 3rd Ukrainian Front – 37th, 57th and 46th Armies, Cavalry Mechanized Group Pliyev. (b) Romanian 3rd and 4th Armies, German 6th Army.
Casualties: (a) Unknown, but light; (b) unknown, but the Romanian 3rd and 4th Armies disintegrated and part of the German 6th Army was trapped.
Result: Army Group South Ukraine was effectively destroyed. Romania changed sides on 25 August and Bulgaria, at war with Great Britain and the United States but not the Soviet Union, declared war on Germany on 8 September.

The two Soviet Fronts achieved complete surprise, smashing through the Romanian armies to execute a double envelopment which isolated the German 6th Army. The speed with which the Russians exploited their victory led to the defection of Romania and Bulgaria from the Axis cause. By October the Soviet advance had reached Yugoslavia and overrun half of Hungary.

Jellalabad, Siege of

Date: 14 November 1841 to 16 April 1842.

Location: Fortified town on the Kabul river, Afghanistan, west of the Khyber Pass.
War and campaign: First Afghan War, 1839–1842.
Opposing sides: (a) Brigadier-General Sir George Sale; (b) Akbar Khan, son of Dost Muhammed, the dethroned king of Afghanistan.
Objective: The garrison had been under intermittent attack since November but in February the Afghans, having just massacred a British column at JUGDULLUCK, closed in and laid siege to the town.
Forces engaged: (a) 13th Regiment (later Somerset Light Infantry), 35th Bengal Native Infantry, one squadron 5th Bengal Light Cavalry, one troop Afghan irregular horse, artillerymen and engineers – total approximately 2,000; (b) unknown, but present in far greater numbers.
Casualties: (a) Unknown, but comparatively light; (b) unknown, but heavier.
Result: Hale conducted a vigorous defence, mounting regular attacks against the Afghan seige works and capturing livestock and supplies. On 7 April most of the garrison took part in a sortie which captured Akbar's artillery, burned his camp and drove off his army.

General Sir George Pollock's relief force arrived on 16 April.

Jemmingen   243

Date: 21 July 1568.
Location: Village in north-eastern Holland.
War and campaign: Eighty Years' War (War of Dutch Independence), 1568–1648: Campaign of 1568.
Opposing sides: (a) Louis of Nassau commanding the rebels; (b) Duke Fernando of Alva.
Objective: The Spanish intention was to crush the rebel Dutch army.
Forces engaged: (a) 15,000; (b) 15,000.
Casualties: (a) 7,000 killed and wounded; (b) 100 killed and wounded.
Result: A crushing Spanish victory which destroyed the rebellion locally for several years.

Elsewhere in the Netherlands, despite Alva's deliberate policy of terror, the rebel cause survived. See ALKMAAR, SIEGE OF.

Jena/Auerstadt   244

Date: 14 October 1806.
Location: Jena lies at the confluence of the Saale and Muhlbach rivers, 13 miles east of Weimar, Germany; Auerstadt is some 13 miles north of Jena.
War and campaign: War of the Fourth Coalition, 1806–1807: Campaign in Germany, 1806.
Opposing sides: At Jena: (a) The Emperor Napoleon I; (b) Prince Friedrich Hohenlohe. At Auerstadt: (a) Marshal Louis Nicolas Davout; (b) Karl Wilhelm, Duke of Brunswick.

Objective: Napoleon, having concentrated his army in southern Germany, was marching north and intended to sever the Prussian army's communications with Berlin. The Prussians, aware of the danger, turned about to engage the French and two tactically separate though strategically interrelated battles were fought on the same day.
Forces engaged: At Jena: (a) rising from 46,000 to 54,000 with 70 guns; (b) rising to 55,000 with 120 guns. At Auerstadt: (a) 26,000 with 44 guns; (b) 50,000 with 230 guns.
Casualties: At Jena: (a) 4,000 killed and wounded; (b) 25,000 killed, wounded and captured. At Auerstadt: (a) 7,000 killed and wounded; (b) 10,000 killed, wounded and captured. Brunswick was killed during the fighting and the Prussian king, Frederick William III, assumed personal command. A total of 200 Prussian guns were captured in both engagements.
Result: French victories, the combined effect of which was to eliminate the Prussian army. King Frederick William III fled to Russia. Berlin was occupied on 24 October and the French hold over Germany was complete.

At Jena Napoleon took the initiative and drove Hohenlohe's detachment off the field. At Auerstadt, however, Davout's corps was confronted by the main body of the Prussian army and, although outnumbered by two to one, held it in check for three hours before taking the offensive and routing it.

Jerusalem, Siege of 245

Date: 9 June to 18 July 1099.
Location: The northern and western walls of the Old City, the Gate of the Column, the al-Aqsa mosque and the Tower of David.
War and campaign: The First Crusade, 1096–1099.
Opposing sides: (a) Duke Godfrey de Bouillon; (b) the Emir Iftikhar.
Objective: The Crusaders' intention was to secure possession of Jerusalem and the Holy Places.
Forces engaged: (a) 1,250 knights and 10,000 infantry; (b) estimated 20,000.
Casualties: (a) Approximately 1,500; (b) only Iftikhar and a few retainers were allowed to leave, after they had handed over their treasure, the survivors of the garrison, together with every Moslem and Jew in the city, being massacred (total number killed approximately 70,000).
Result: The city was stormed using two siege towers supported by escalade.

Godfrey was elected Guardian of Jersualem; on his death the following year he was succeeded by his brother Baldwin, who assumed the title King of Jerusalem. See also ASCALON.

Jugdulluck (Gandamack) 246

Date: 6–13 January 1842.
Location: On the Kabul–Jellalabad road, Afghanistan.
War and campaign: First Afghan War, 1839–1842.

Opposing sides: (a) Major-General William Elphinstone; (b) Akbar Khan, son of Dost Muhammed, the dethroned King of Afghanistan.
Objective: A small British force at Kabul, having been promised safe conduct during its march back to India, was treacherously ambushed and massacred by the Afghans over a period of days. The last stand of the survivors took place at Gandamack.
Forces engaged: (a) Initially 4,500 British and Indian troops, encumbered by 12,000 camp followers; at Gandamack, less than 50 men remained, the majority belonging to the 44th (Essex) Regiment. (b) unknown, but present in overwhelming strength.
Casualties: (a) The entire column was wiped out, although some officers, women and children were captured as hostages (only one European, a Dr Brydon, and a few sepoys reached Jellalabad safely); (b) unknown.
Result: A punitive expedition commanded by General Sir George Pollock relieved JELLALABAD (16 April) and fought its way through to Kabul where most of the hostages were rescued (15 September). It then destroyed the citadel and Grand Bazaar as a reprisal before withdrawing to India. Dost Muhammed was permitted to resume the throne.

'Junction City,' Operation 247

Date: 22 February–14 May 1967.
Location: 30- by 50-mile area of Tay Ninh province on the South Vietnamese border with Cambodia, approximately 65 miles north of Phann Bo Ho Chi Minh (formerly Saigon).
War and campaign: Vietnam War, 1956–1975.
Opposing sides: (a) General William C. Westmoreland, Head of the US Military Assistance Command; (b) COSVN.
Objective: US/South Vietnamese (ARVN) search-and-destroy operation in War Zone C with the primary object of locating the Communist field headquarters (the Central Office of South Vietnam, or COSVN).
Forces engaged: (a) US 1st and 25th Infantry Division, 173rd Airborne Brigade and 11th Armored Cavalry Regiment, plus four ARVN battalions – total 27,000; (b) uncertain.
Casualties: (a) 282 killed and 1,576 wounded, plus three tanks, five howitzers and 21 APCs destroyed; (b) 2,700 killed and 200 prisoners, plus 500 weapons, a large quantity of ammunition, 850 tons of rations and 500,000 pages of documents captured.
Result: War Zone C was cleared and COSVN was forced to withdraw into Cambodia. COSVN's morale was so severely affected that, to save face, it informed Hanoi that no fewer than 13,000 Americans had been killed during the operation. This encouraged the Communist leadership so much that, believing South Vietnam to be on the verge of collapse, it launched its disastrous Tet Offensive the following January – see HUE and KHE SANH, SIEGE OF.

'Junction City' was the second corps-sized operation mounted by Westmoreland to overrun a Communist-dominated area, the first being Operation 'Cedar Falls' (8–26 January 1967), which cleared the Iron Triangle, somewhat closer to Saigon. Westmoreland believed that he could impose a rate of attrition on the Communists which the latter would find unacceptable; unfortunately, casualty figures were deliberately withheld from the North Vietnamese public and General Vo Nguyen Giap, the Communist commander-in-chief, was not-oriously indifferent to such considerations.

Kadesh 248

Date: 1294 BC.
Location: South-east of Qadesh on the Orontes river, Syria.
War and campaign: War between Egypt and the Hittite Empire for control of Syria.
Opposing sides: (a) Pharaoh Rameses II; (b) the Hittite King Muwatalis.
Objective: The Egyptians, having been deliberately misled into believing that the Hittite army had withdrawn, were advancing north with the object of capturing Kadesh. The Hittites were, in fact, waiting in ambush east of the town.
Forces engaged: (a) Infantry and chariotry – total 20,000; (b) infantry 8,500, chariotry 10,500 (3,500 chariots).
Casualties: (a) Estimated 5,000 killed and wounded; (b) estimated 3,000 killed and wounded.
Result: Although the Hittite ambush failed at some cost, the Egyptian army was severely mauled. Rameses was unable to capture Kadesh and eventually made peace.

The Egyptian army was advancing in four brigades, plus a strong flank guard to the west, strung out over many miles of country. Rameses, with the Amun brigade, was in the lead and established a fortified camp near Kadesh. As the second brigade, the Re, approached the camp it was suddenly assailed in flank by the Hittite chariotry and routed, its survivors fleeing northwards towards the camp. Rameses counter-attacked with the Amun, hoping to fight his way through to the Ptah brigade, which was approaching from the south, but was soon encircled. Many of the Hittites began plundering the abandoned Egyptian camp. At this stage the Ptah brigade began entering the battle and the Egyptian flank guard arrived from the west, with the result that the Hittites were driven off. One Egyptian brigade, the Seth, and the Hittite infantry took no part in the fighting, the latter remaining on the eastern bank of the river. Rameses recorded the details of the action, one of the great chariot battles of ancient times, on the walls of the many temples he built. The Egyptian chariot was superior to the Hittite vehicle and its crews used the long-range composite bow, which gave them a decided advantage over their opponents, who used short-range bows, javelins and spears during the missile phase of an engagement. Conversely, when it came to hand-strokes it was the Hittites who held the technical advantage, as they had begun to use iron weapons while the Egyptians were still using bronze.

Kalka River 249

Date: 1223.
Location: Southern Ukraine, near the mouth of the Dniepr.
War and campaign: Mongol invasion of Russia, 1221–1224.
Opposing sides: (a) Subotai and Chepe commanding the Mongols; (b) Prince Mstislav of Kiev.

Objective: The Russians and their Cuman allies had assembled an army to expel the invaders.	
Forces engaged: (a) 40,000; (b) 80,000.	
Casualties: Unknown, although the Russians sustained severe losses.	
Result: The Russian army was routed.	

The Mongols continued to raid north into the heart of the country until recalled by Genghis Khan, who regarded the invasion simply as a reconnaissance in force.

Kambula 250

Date: 29 March 1879.
Location: Northern Zululand, near the Transvaal border, 15 miles south of Luneberg.
War and campaign: Zulu War, 1879.
Opposing sides: (a) Colonel Evelyn Wood; (b) Tshingwayo.
Objective: Having repulsed a raid on Inhlobane Mountain the previous day, the Zulus attacked the British camp.
Forces engaged: (a) 2,086 men, including colonial mounted units, and eight guns; (b) 22,000 men.
Casualties: (a) 29 killed and 55 wounded; (b) estimated 2,000 killed and as many wounded.
Result: The attack was decisively repulsed. See ULUNDI.

Kamenets-Podolsk 251

Date: 25 March to 16 April 1944.
Location: Area north of the Dniestr between Kamenets-Podolsk and Buczacz, Western Ukraine.
War and campaign: Second World War: Russian Front.
Opposing sides: (a) Field Marshal Erich von Manstein commanding Army Group South; (b) Marshal Georgi Zhukov commanding the 1st Ukrainian Front and General Ivan Konev commanding the 2nd Ukrainian Front.
Objective: The trapped First Panzer Army was attempting to fight its way back to its own lines.
Forces engaged: (a) General Hans Hube commanding the First Panzer Army with nine under-strength panzer divisions, one panzergrenadier division, ten infantry division, one heavy tank regiment and several smaller formations; (b) elements of the 1st and 2nd Ukrainian Fronts (strength variable from day to day).
Casualties: (a) Uncertain, but known to be heavy; (b) uncertain, but heavy (the Germans claimed the destruction of 357 Soviet tanks and 42 self-propelled guns).
Result: The Russians were unable to prevent the First Panzer Army from fighting its way through to the new German line. Hube, promoted Colonel-General and awarded the Diamonds to his Knight's Cross in recognition of his feat, was killed in an air crash on his way to receive the decoration.

During the last weeks of the Soviet winter offensive a double-envelopment by the 1st and 2nd Ukrainian Fronts succeeded in isolating the First Panzer Army on 25 March. The Russians believed that Hube would attempt to break out to the south, using a bridgehead over the Dniestr which remained in his possession, as this provided good going and would enable his army to reach Romania. Hube, however, chose to break out to the west, although this involved crossing the rivers Sbrucz, Sereth and Strypa, partly because such a course would seem unattractive to the enemy and partly because of the possibility of effecting a junction with a relief force. The breakout began during the night of 27/28 March and slow but steady progress was maintained for the next fortnight. On 15 April the leading elements of the army crossed the Strypa and the following day made contact with II SS Panzer Corps, leading the relief force, near Buczacz.

Kandahar 252

Date: 1 September 1880.
Location: Fortified city in southern Afghanistan.
War and campaign: Second Afghan War, 1878–1880.
Opposing sides: (a) Lieutenant-General Sir Frederick Roberts; (b) Ayub Khan.
Objective: Having relieved their besieged garrison at Kandahar, the British intended to destroy the dissident Afghan army.
Forces engaged: (a) 14,000 with 36 guns (including one heavy battery of 40pdr guns); (b) 15,000 (including 5,000 regulars) with 32 guns.
Casualties: (a) 35 killed and 213 wounded; (b) approximately 1,200 killed and wounded, plus all artillery captured (including two guns lost by E/B Battery Royal Horse Artillery at MAIWAND).
Result: Ayub Khan's army was defeated and dispersed. Abdur Rahman Khan, who was acceptable to both the Afghans and the British, assumed the throne, having undertaken to curtail Russian influence in the country, and the British withdrew to India.

Roberts' remarkable self-sufficient march from Kabul to Kandahar covered 313 miles in 21 days, traversing mountain and desert terrain in which the temperature soared by day to 110° and dropped to freezing point by night. On 27 August the column established heliograph contact with the Kandahar garrison, which was relieved four days later. Ayub Khan abandoned the siege on learning of Roberts' approach but offered battle from a strong position north of the city.

Kandurchka 253

Date: 1391.
Location: East of the Volga and south of the Kama rivers, Russia (precise location unknown).
War and campaign: Second war between the Mongol Jagatai and Kipchak khanates, 1388–1395.
Opposing sides: (a) Tamerlane (Timur the Lame), Khan of the Jagatai Mongols; (b) Toktamish, Khan of the Kipchak Mongols and commander of the Golden Horde.
Objective: The Jagatai army had invaded Russia with the object of forcing a decisive battle on its opponents.

Forces engaged: (a) 100,000; (b) estimated 130,000.

Casualties: (a) 30,000; (b) 70,000.

Result: Toktamish was defeated but escaped. Tamerlane, unable to pursue immediately because of a rebellion in Persia, finally crushed him at the Battle of the Terek (1395). The Golden Horde never recovered and ceased to be a menace to Europe. See also PANIPAT.

Kars 254

Date: 17–18 November 1877.

Location: Fortified city in Turkish Armenia, close to the frontier with the former USSR.

War and campaign: Russo–Turkish War, 1877–1878: Trans-Caucasian Campaign.

Opposing sides: (a) General Loris Melikoff; (b) Hussein Pasha.

Objective: Having defeated the Turks at the Battle of Aladja Dagh on 15 Ocober, the Russians invested the fortress.

Forces engaged: (a) Approximately 65,000; (b) 24,000.

Casualties: (a) 2,273 killed and wounded; (b) 2,500 killed, 4,500 wounded and 17,000 taken prisoner, plus 303 guns captured.

Result: The Russians stormed the fortress in a surprise night attack. Compare with PLEVNA, SIEGE OF.

Kasserine Pass 255

Date: 14–22 February 1943.

Location: About 120 miles south-west of Tunis.

War and campaign: Second World War: North Africa (Tunisia).

Opposing sides: (a) Field Marshal Erwin Rommel commanding the Deutsches Afrika Korps and Colonel-General Hans-Jurgen von Arnim commanding the Fifth Panzer Army; (b) Lieutenant-General Dwight D. Eisenhower, Allied Supreme Commander North-West Africa, and Lieutenant-General Kenneth Anderson, commanding the First Army.

Objective: The German intention was to mount a spoiling attack which would temporarily blunt the offensive capacity of the Anglo-American First Army, so enabling the Axis armies to consolidate their hold on Tunisia.

Forces engaged: (a) 10th and 21st Panzer Divisions, plus elements of the Deutsches Afrika Korps; (b) US II Corps (Major-General Lloyd R. Fredendall), later reinforced by the British 6th Armoured Division and other formations.

Casualties: (a) About 2,000; (b) US II Corps – 2,816 killed and wounded, 2,459 missing or captured and much equipment lost; British – comparatively few personnel casualties but some equipment losses.

Result: While American self-confidence was briefly shaken, the German thrust was contained. In the longer term the battle benefited the career of Major-General George S. Patton, who replaced Fredendall as commander of the US II Corps.

On 14 February the Fifth Panzer Army broke through the positions of the inexperienced US II Corps at Sidi Bou Zid, isolating one combat command of Major-General Orlando

Ward's 1st Armored Division and badly mauling two more when they counter-attacked next day. Simultaneously the DAK broke through at Gafsa and Thelepte and advanced to Kasserine, where it was joined by the 10th Panzer Division before storming the pass. Fredendall failed to take effective control of the battle but Anderson, supported by General Sir Harold Alexander, Eisenhower's Deputy Supreme Commander, quickly moved Allied reinforcements into blocking positions on the Thala and Sbiba roads, where they halted further thrusts by the 10th and 21st Panzer Divisions. Elsewhere, the rallied 1st Armored Division checked further progress by the DAK east of Tebessa. Having inflicted serious damage on II Corps, Rommel withdrew during the night of 22 February and began preparing for a similar spoiling attack against the British Eighth Army on the MARETH sector of the front.

Kennesaw Mountain 256

Date: 27 June 1864.
Location: Near Marietta, north-west of Atlanta, Georgia.
War and campaign: American Civil War: Sherman's Campaign in Georgia.
Opposing sides: (a) Major-General William T. Sherman commanding an army group consisting of Major-General George H. Thomas's Army of the Cumberland, Major-General James B. McPherson's Army of the Tennessee and Major-General John M. Schofield's Army of the Ohio; (b) General Joseph E. Jonnston commanding the reinforced Army of Tennessee.
Objective: Sherman's intention was to destroy the Confederate army and break through to Atlanta.
Forces engaged: (a) 110,000; (b) 65,000.
Casualties: (a) 3,000; (b) 1,000.
Result: The Federal frontal assaults were repulsed. On 2 July Sherman sent the Army of the Tennessee and a strong force of cavalry to outflank the Confederate left. Johnston withdrew to the Chattahoochie river, where he was again outflanked by Sherman on 9 July; having fought a remarkable series of delaying actions against odds during the preceding months, he was somewhat unfairly replaced by General John Hood on 18 July. See ATLANTA.

Khalkin-Gol 257

Date: 20–31 August 1939.
Location: On the Khalkin river near the Manchurian/Outer Mongolian border.
War and campaign: Border dispute between the Soviet Union and Japan.
Opposing sides: (a) General Georgi Zhukov; (b) the commander of the Japanese Sixth Army.
Objective: The Russian intention was to expel the Japanese from their territory.
Forces engaged: (a) 35 infantry battalions, twenty cavalry squadrons and 500 tanks; (b) 25 infantry battalions, seventeen cavalry squadrons and 180 tanks.
Casualties: (a) 9,800; (b) 18,000.
Result: The Japanese were defeated and withdrew across the border.

Zhukov mounted holding attacks along the Japanese front but used an independent armoured brigade to execute a double envelopment of the enemy's flanks and establish a blocking position beyond. While supporting aircraft prevented Japanese reinforcements from entering the battle, the Russians stormed the enemy's main position on Namon-Han-Burd-Obo Hill with an all-arms attack which annihilated the defenders. Zhukov's tactics at Khalkin-Gol echoed the ideas of the late Marshal Tukhachevsky, the first victim of Stalin's Great Purge, and were therefore unpopular with the Kremlin, which decreed that the correct role for tanks was infantry support rather than employment in independent formations. The success of the German panzer divisions during the campaigns of 1939 and 1940 led to a radical alteration of views within the Soviet establishment, but this came too late to prevent the Red Army sustaining a series of crushing defeats in 1941 – see BRODY-DUBNO, KIEV and SMOLENSK.

Kharkov (1942)   258

Date: 12–22 May 1942.
Location: North-Eastern Ukraine.
War and campaign: Second World War: Russian Front.
Opposing sides: (a) Marshal Semyon Timoshenko commanding the South-West Front; (b) Colonel-General Ewald von Kleist commanding Army Group von Kleist.
Objective: The Russian intention was to recapture Kharkov, the third most important city in the Soviet Union.
Forces engaged: (a) Soviet 6th, 9th and 57th Armies with 640,000 men and 1,200 tanks; (b) 1st Panzer Army and 6th and 17th Armies.
Casualties: (a) Every Soviet armoured formation in the pocket was wiped out and over 250,000 prisoners were taken; (b) unknown, but moderate.
Result: A major defeat which seriously damaged the morale of the Soviet Army.

Timoshenko's plan was to recapture Kharkov by striking north-west from the Izyum Salient, a bulge in the German lines 60 miles deep and the same distance across. His initial progress was encouraging, but on 17 May the German 1st Panzer and 17th Armies smashed through the southern wall of the salient, achieving a local superiority of 4.4:1 in tanks, 1.3:1 in infantry and 1.7:1 in artillery. Realizing that he had driven into a trap, Timoshenko requested permission to withdraw, but by the time Stalin agreed the German 6th Army (von Paulus) had broken through the northern wall of the salient and sealed the exit from the pocket which had been formed.

Kharkov (1943)   259

Date: 16 February to 15 March 1943.
Location: North-Eastern Ukraine.
War and campaign: Second World War: Russian Front.
Opposing sides: (a) Colonel-General Filipp Golikov commanding the Voronezh Front and General Nikolay Vatutin commanding the South-West Front; (b) Field Marshal Erich von Manstein commanding Army Group South.
Objective: The Russian strategic intentions were first to liberate Kharkov, then isolate the German Army Group South with a drive to the Black Sea coast.
Forces engaged: (a) Both Soviet Fronts; (b) First and Fourth Panzer Armies.

Casualties: (a) Voronezh Front – 40,000 men, 600 tanks and 500 guns; South-West Front – 23,000 dead, 9,000 prisoners, 615 tanks and 400 guns; (b) unknown, but moderate.
Result: A disastrous reverse which dispelled the euphoria generated by the Soviet Army's great victory at STALINGRAD; conversely, the German Army recovered its confidence, although this was to be its last major strategic success on the Russian Front. The position of the lines when Manstein's counter-stroke had run its course directly influenced Hitler's decision to mount his next offensive against the KURSK salient.

Although Army Group South possessed only 350 tanks, these enjoyed a 7:1 numerical superiority at the point of contact. On 16 February Manstein permitted Golikov to capture Kharkov, but four days later he counter-attacked into the southern flank of both Soviet Fronts, which had already begun to outrun their fuel supplies, inflicting crippling losses and forcing them to retire behind the Donets. On 15 March Kharkov once again passed into German hands. The Lucy spy ring, which had penetrated OKW, the highest level of the German command structure, was unable to provide the Soviets with advance warning of the counter-stroke, the details of which were decided in Manstein's own headquarters.

Khartoum, Siege of   260

Date: 12 March 1884 to 26 January 1885.
Location: At the junction of the Blue and White Niles, Sudan.
War and campaign: Sudan Campaigns: Mahdist Rebellion.
Opposing sides: (a) Major-General Charles Gordon; (b) the Mahdi Mohammed Ahmed.
Objective: The city was besieged by the Mahdists.
Forces engaged: (a) 7,000 Egyptians and handful of British officers; (b) estimated 60,000.
Casualties: (a) The entire garrison was massacred; (b) unknown.
Result: Following the fall of the city Anglo-Egyptian forces withdrew from the Sudan, with the exception of Suskin on the Red Sea.

Gordon's orders were supervise the withdrawal of the Egyptian garrisons from the Sudan in the aftermath of the disaster at EL OBEID, but he obstinately refused to abandon Khartoum and its population to the Mahdists and conducted a vigorous defence. The British public supported him and, reluctantly, Prime Minister William Gladstone despatched a relief expedition up the Nile. It was the approach of this (see ABU KLEA and ABU KRU) that led the Mahdi to storm the city. See also OMDURMAN.

Khe Sanh, Siege of   261

Date: 21 January to 14 April 1968.
Location: American base on a plateau overlooking the Quang Tri valley, central Vietnam.
War and campaign: Vietnam War, 1956–1975: Tet Offensive.
Opposing sides: (a) Colonel David Lownds commanding the garrison; (b) a Front

Headquarters established to control NVA divisional operations in Quang Tri province.
Objective: The Communists wished to eliminate the base, which was used for operations against their supply lines. The Americans, fearing another DIEN BIEN PHU, were determined to hold it at all costs.
Forces engaged: (a) 26th Marine Regiment, I/9th Marines, ARVN 37th Ranger Battalion and supporting arms – total approximately 6,000; (b) NVA 304 and 325C Divisions and supporting artillery – total approximately 20,000; 320 and 324 Divisions were also located within 16 miles and could be committed to the battle very quickly.
Casualties: (a) 199 killed and 1,600 wounded; (b) the lowest estimate puts the NVA's loss at 9,800, of whom one-third were killed.
Result: On 6 April the base was relieved by Operation 'Pegasus', involving the 1st Cavalry Division and the 1st Marine Regiment in a joint airmobile/ground assault along Route 9 from the east.

A comparison with Dien Bien Phu is tempting, and indeed influenced American opinion at the time, but is not appropriate. For example, the garrison's artillery, consisting of three batteries of 105mm howitzers and one of 155mm howitzers, had additional support from four US Army batteries of 175mm guns, firing from bases to the north and east; the total American artillery expenditure during the siege amounted to 159,000 rounds. Again, air strikes around the base, including some delivered by B-52 heavy bombers, dropped no less than 96,000 tons of bombs. Furthermore, the Communists never succeeded in interdicting Lownds' air supply line. It is not possible, therefore, to equate the situation of those holding Khe Sanh with that of de Castries' doomed garrison at Dien Bien Phu. The battle nevertheless continues to be the subject of controversial discussion, not least regarding the intentions of General Vo Nguyen Giap, the NVA's commander-in-chief. Later, Giap was to deny that he had ever intended repeating the triumph of Dien Bien Phu at Khe Sanh, but if he regarded the base as holding a lower priority why was such a high proportion of his strength concentrated in the area? Quite probably, the fall of Khe Sanh was intended to crown the other achievements of the Tet Offensive, so demonstrating that the Americans could be defeated as easily in the field as the French. Tet, however, was itself defeated and Giap was faced with a radically altered perspective. A failed assault on Khe Sanh would merely add to the catastrophic losses sustained in Tet and undermine his prestige. It was possible, if unlikely, that a successful assault might induce the US administration to withdraw from Vietnam, but it was also possible that the loss of 6,000 Marines would provoke an angry reaction from the American public, who would demand revenge, and this would almost certainly destroy the American peace movement, the efforts of which were so valuable to the Communist cause. A long-term strategist by instinct, Giap was unwilling to take the risk. Thus, while Communist artillery fire continued to hit Khe Sanh, causing considerable damage in the process, and determined probing attacks were directed against the perimeter and outposts, the base was never in any real danger.

Kiev   262

Date: 9–26 September 1941.
Location: Capital city of the Ukraine, situated on the Dniepr.
War and campaign: Second World War: Russian Front.
Opposing sides: (a) Field Marshal Gerd von Rundstedt commanding Army Group

South and Field Marshal Fedor von Bock commanding Army Group Centre; (b) Marshal Semen Budenny, Commander-in-Chief of the Soviet armies in the Ukraine.

Objective: The encirclement and destruction of the Soviet armies concentrated around Kiev.

Forces engaged: (a) Mainly Panzer Groups 1 and 2, commanded by, respectively, von Kleist and Guderian, supported by mechanized and infantry divisions – total approximately 300,000; (b) the South-West Front, commanded by Colonel-General Mikhail Kirponos, including elements of the Soviet 5th, 21st, 26th and 37th Armies – total approximately 50 divisions with 676,000 men.

Casualties: (a) About 100,000; (b) approximately 665,000, the majority of whom were captured, plus 900 tanks and 3,719 guns.

Result: A crushing German victory which, in the long term, was counter-productive. The loss of time involved in the reduction of the Kiev pocket ensured that the strategic objective of MOSCOW could not be reached before the onset of the Russian winter. Ultimately, therefore, Hitler's decision to divert so much of the German effort to Kiev can be regarded as an important factor in the failure of Operation 'Barbarossa', his grand design for the destruction of the USSR.

Following his defeat at BRODY-DUBNO, Kirponos withdrew the South-West Front towards Kiev, which Stalin insisted must be held at all costs. In the meantime, Hitler had begun meddling with the conduct of the campaign and, contrary to professional advice, insisted that Guderian's Panzer Group 2 should be detached from Army Group Centre and sent south to assist Army Group South in its conquest of the Ukraine. On 16 September Guderian's advance units, driving south from SMOLENSK, met those of von Kleist's Panzer Group 1 at a village named Lokhvitsa some 100 miles east of Kiev, thereby trapping most of the South-West Front within a huge pocket. By the time the Russians awoke to their danger, Rundstedt's infantry divisions and artillery had them held tight within an iron ring. Kirponos was killed leading one of several attempts to break out of the trap. Resistance within the pocket finally ended on 26 September.

Killiecrankie 263

Date: 27 July 1689.

Location: At the northern end of the Pass of Killiecrankie, 7 miles north-west of Pitlochry, Perthshire.

War and campaign: War of the League of Augsburg, 1688–1697: Jacobite Rebellion in Scotland, 1689.

Opposing sides: (a) Major-General Hugh Mackay commanding the Government army; (b) John Graham of Claverhouse, Viscount Dundee, commanding the rebels.

Objective: An encounter provoked by the need for each side to hold Blair Atholl on the strategically important road between the Highlands and the Lowlands.

Forces engaged: (a) 4,000 with three guns; (b) 2,500.

Casualties: (a) 2,000 killed and wounded, 500 prisoners and all guns captured; (b) 600 killed and wounded, including Dundee killed.

Result: The Government army was destroyed but the death of 'Bonny Dundee' proved disastrous to the Jacobite cause in Scotland.

Mackay's deployment fatally weakened the strength of his battle line when he opted for extended length rather than depth, for the impetus of the Highlanders' charge, delivered down a steep hillside, smashed through his ranks. Under Dundee's leadership the clans had submerged their separate interests, but after Killiecrankie the cohesion of the Jacobite army began to suffer. On 21 August the army, now 5,000 strong, attacked Dunkeld and was repulsed after a bitter four-hour struggle with the 1,200 men of the Earl of Angus's Regiment (later The Cameronians), sustaining 300 casualties to the defenders' 45. After this the clans dispersed to their homes and the rebellion collapsed.

Kilsyth   264

Date: 15 August 1645.
Location: 10 miles north-east of Glasgow.
War and campaign: First Civil War, 1642–1645: Operations in Scotland.
Opposing sides: (a) James Graham, Marquis of Montrose; (b) Major-General William Baillie and Archibald Campbell, Marquis of Argyll.
Objective: Following its victories at INVERLOCHY (2 February), Auldearn (9 May) and Alford (2 July), Montrose's Royalist army advanced south until it was within striking distance of Glasgow. At Kilsyth it was opposed by a Covenanter army.
Forces engaged: (a) Approximately 2,000; (b) 6,000.
Casualties: (a) Unknown, but moderate; (b) entire force killed, wounded or captured.
Result: Montrose's victory left the Royalists temporarily supreme in Scotland. Although he had succeeded in his strategic objective of drawing Scottish troops out of England, the decisive battle of NASEBY had already been fought on 14 June and his tiny army now stood alone. See also PHILIPHAUGH.

Kimberley   265

Date: 15 October 1899 to 15 February 1900.
Location: Cape Colony, close to the border of the Orange Free State (now part of the Republic of South Africa).
War and campaign: Second Boer War, 1899–1902.
Opposing sides: (a) Lieutenant-Colonel Robert Kekewich commanding the garrison; (b) Commandant Wessels, then Commandant J. S. Ferreira, responsible for conducting the siege, under General Piet Cronje, overall commander of the Western Front.
Objective: The Boers were besieging the town and its diamond workings.
Forces engaged: (a) 596 regulars, 352 Cape Police and 3,658 volunteers, six field guns, one 'home made' heavy gun and six machine guns; (b) 4–5,000 with a dozen or so guns, including one Creusot 155mm heavy gun (Long Tom).
Casualties: (a) Moderate; (b) moderate.
Result: The siege was broken by Major-General (later Field Marshal Lord) John French's cavalry division, reinforced with mounted infantry.

Kimberley was the focus of fighting on the Western Front – see MODDER RIVER and MAGERSFONTEIN. The siege itself was not pressed and most of the action consisted of artillery exchanges; in this context De Beers' workshops produced not only artillery shells but also a 28pdr heavy gun named Long Cecil after the company's chairman, Cecil

Rhodes, who remained in the town. French's approach march outflanked the Boers' blocking position at Magersfontein and Cronje, failing to appreciate its significance, delayed his withdrawal too long and was run down at PAARDEBERG. Ferreira and some of the besiegers managed to disengage and retire north from Kimberley.

King's Mountain 266

Date: 7 October 1780.
Location: 35 miles south-west of Charlotte, North Carolina.
War and campaign: American War of Independence, 1775–1783: southern theatre of operations.
Opposing sides: (a) Major Patrick Ferguson; (b) Colonels John Sevier, Isaac Shelby and Richard Campbell.
Objective: A column of loyalists, covering the left flank of Cornwallis' invasion of North Carolina, was surrounded on King's Mountain by a concentration of local frontiersmen under the command of American militia officers.
Forces engaged: (a) Approximately 1,000; (b) approximately 900.
Casualties: (a) 157 killed, 163 seriously wounded and 689 captured; (b) 28 killed and 62 wounded.
Result: Ferguson's column was destroyed and Cornwallis was forced to postpone his advance into North Carolina.

With the exception of Ferguson, all the participants in this action were Americans. Ferguson had personally designed an excellent breech-loading rifle, although the idea was not accepted by the British Army; it was ironic, therefore, that he should die in a battle in which he and his men attemped to fight their way out with the bayonet when many of their opponents employed rifles fired from cover. The disgraceful behaviour of the victors (some loyalists were shot after they had surrendered while others, seriously wounded, were left to die on the field, and nine prisoners were hanged) can be seen as direct revenge for loyalist savagery at WAXHAWS and is indicative of the bitterness which divided Americans in the southern states.

Kinsale 267

Date: 26 December 1601.
Location: 2 miles east of Kinsale, County Cork, Eire.
War and campaign: Tyrone's Rebellion, 1598–1603.
Opposing sides: (a) The Lord Deputy, Lord Charles Mountjoy, commanding the Government forces; (b) the Earl of Tyrone commanding the rebels.
Objective: The rebels were attempting to relieve a Spanish force besieged in Kinsale by Government troops.
Forces engaged: (a) 1,000 infantry and 500 cavalry; (b) 200 Spaniards and 6,300 rebels, including cavalry.
Casualties: (a) Minimal – perhaps 20 killed and wounded; (b) 2,500 killed and wounded.
Result: A decisive Government victory which led to the eventual collapse of the

rebellion. The Spanish garrison of Kinsale surrendered and were permitted to sail home.

Tyrone gave himself up in March 1603. See also FORD OF THE BISCUITS, THE, and YELLOW FORD, THE.

Kohima

268

Date: 5 April to 30 May 1944.
Location: Manipur, Assam.
War and campaign: Second World War: Burma.
Opposing sides: (a) Lieutenant-Gernal Renya Mutaguchi commanding the Japanese Fifteenth Army; (b) Lieutenant-General Sir William Slim commanding the British Fourteenth Army.
Objective: The Japanese intention was to establish an impregnable road-block at Kohima, thereby isolating the British IV Corps at IMPHAL.
Forces engaged: (a) The Japanese 31st Division commanded by Major-General Sato; (b) the British XXXIII Corps commanded by Lieutenant-General Montagu Stopford.
Casualties: Included in figures for IMPHAL.
Result: The Japanese 31st Division was virtually destroyed in some of the bitterest fighting of the war. The British XXXIII Corps broke through to relieve IV Corps at IMPHAL on 22 June.

Sato's first attack on Kohima was made on 5 April. The garrison consisted of 161 Indian Infantry Brigade with the 4th Queen's Own Royal West Kent Regiment in Kohima itself and 1/1st Punjabis and 4/7th Rajputs holding a defensive box at Jotsoma, two miles along the Dimapur road, which was in turn isolated on 7 April. Repeated Japanese attacks were thrown back until, on 14 April, the 2nd British Division broke through to the Jotsoma box, the exhausted West Kents at Kohima being relieved four days later. The Japanese were now forced on to the defensive, but they held excellent positions which they defended tenaciously until the end of May when, starving and diseased, the remnants began withdrawing towards the Chindwin, pursued by the 7th Indian Division. Towards the end of the battle the complete failure of the 31st Division's logistic support provoked Sato into despatching a series of insubordinate signals to Mutaguchi, bitterly criticizing the latter's conduct of operations. Neither commanded troops in the field again.

Kolin

269

Date: 18 June 1757.
Location: Town 27 miles east of Prague, Czechoslovakia.
War and campaign: Seven Years' War, 1756–1763: Central European Campaign of 1757.
Opposing sides: (a) Frederick the Geat; (b) Marshal Leopold von Daun commanding the Austrian army.
Objective: Frederick II of Prussia, gathering all the troops he could spare from his

siege lines at PRAGUE, confronted an Austrian army which was marching to the city's relief.

Forces engaged: (a) 32 infantry battalions, 116 cavalry squadrons and 50 guns – total 32,000; (b) 42 infantry battalions, seventeen cavalry squadrons and 145 guns – total 40,000.

Casualties: (a) 13,768 killed, wounded and missing, plus 45 guns captured; (b) approximately 9,000 killed and wounded.

Result: Frederick's planned attack on Daun's right flank was mishandled and degenerated into a frontal assault; when this was repulsed with heavy loss his infantry broke.

Frederick was compelled to raise the siege of Prague and retire from Bohemia. Simultaneously, Austrian, French, Russian and Swedish armies all converged on Prussian territory – see ROSSBACH.

Königgrätz (Sadowa) 270

Date: 3 July 1866.

Location: 65 miles east of Prague and 5 miles north-west of Hradec Kralove (Königgrätz), Czechoslovakia.

War and campaign: Austro–Prussian (Seven Weeks') War: Bohemian Campaign.

Opposing sides: (a) Field Marshal Count Helmuth von Moltke co-ordinating the advance of the Prussian armies – the First (Prince Friedrich Karl), the Second (Crown Prince Friedrich Wilhelm) and the Army of the Elbe (General Herwarth von Bittenfeld); (b) Field Marshal Ludwig von Benedek commanding the Austrian army in Bohemia.

Objective: The Prussian intention was to destroy the Austrians within a double-envelopment formed by three armies.

Forces engaged: (a) Eight corps and three cavalry divisions – total 278,000 men; (b) one Saxon and seven Austrian corps and four cavalry divisions – total 271,000 men.

Casualties: (a) 1,935 killed and 7,237 wounded; (b) 13,000 killed, 18,393 wounded, 13,000 prisoners and 174 guns captured.

Result: The Austrians sustained a critical defeat but managed to withdraw the bulk of their army. In the wider context, the battle decided that Prussia and not the Austro-Hungarian Empire would be the dominant power in Central Europe. See also LANGENSALZA.

Moltke's plan envisaged the Austrians' being crushed between the Army of the Elbe in the south, the First Army in the centre and the Second Army in the north. However, during the morning a premature attack by a Prussian division developed into a hard-fought general engagement at a time when Moltke had lost contact with the Crown Prince's army, 15 miles to the north, and this did not start bringing decisive pressure to bear on the Austrian right flank until mid-afternoon. Self-sacrificial actions by his cavalry and artillery enabled Benedek to disengage and withdraw south of the Upper Labe (Elbe). The Prussian infantry's breech-loading Dreyse 'needle gun' had a higher rate of fire than the Austrian muzzle-loading rifle, but the Austrian artillery was superior to the Prussian, which was re-equipped as a result of the battle and proved to be a major contributory factor in the German victories of the Franco-Prussian War four years later. See WÖRTH.

Korsun (Cherkassy)

Date: 6–17 February 1944.

Location: West of Cherkassy, Ukraine.

War and campaign: Second World War: Russian Front.

Opposing sides: (a) General Ivan Konev, commanding the 2nd Ukrainian Front; (b) Lieutenant-General Stemmermann, commanding the German troops.

Objective: (a) The Russians were attempting to eliminate the German troops trapped in the pocket at Korsun, formed by converging thrusts of the 1st and 2nd Ukrainian Fronts; (b) the Germans were attempting to break out of the pocket.

Forces engaged: (a) Major elements of the 2nd Ukrainian Front; (b) XI and XLII Corps, 5th SS Panzer Division Wiking and SS Brigade Wallonien (known collectively as Group Stemmermann) – total about 50,000 men.

Casualties: (a) Unknown. (b) German accounts admit to having to abandon the wounded within the pocket but claim that 30,000 men of the 35,000 who took part in the breakout reached safety; Soviet claims of having inflicted 55,000 casualties and taken 18,000 prisoners are exaggerated.

Result: Both German corps and the 5th SS Panzer Division managed to escape but required complete re-equipment and were unfit for action for several months; SS Brigade Wallonien was virtually wiped out. Konev was promoted to Marshal of the Soviet Union.

Having rejected a call to surrender on 9 February, Stemmermann decided to break out to the south-west while units of the First Panzer Army attempted to create an escape corridor from the outside. The breakout commenced during the night of 16/17 February and although Group Stemmermann lost its remaining tanks and transport vehicles contact was established with the First Panzer Army the following afternoon. Stemmermann himself was killed while fighting among his rearguard.

Kunersdorf

Date: 12 August 1759.

Location: Village 4 miles east of Frankfurt on Oder, Germany.

War and campaign: Seven Years' War, 1756–1763: Central European Campaign of 1759.

Opposing sides: (a) Frederick the Great; (b) Lieutenant-General Gideon von Laudon and Count Peter Soltikov commanding, respectively, the Austrian and Russian contingents.

Objective: Frederick II of Prussia attacked a combined Austro-Russian army which had invaded his territory.

Forces engaged: (a) 43,000; (b) 90,000.

Casualties: (a) 20,000 killed, wounded and missing, plus 178 guns captured; (b) 15,700 killed and wounded.

Result: Frederick's attempted double-envelopment of the Austro-Russian army became disorganized in broken, wooded country and was decisively repulsed. It was his worst defeat and, in despair, he considered abdication.

Had the allies exploited their victory they might have ended the war, but the Russians had exhausted their supplies and withdrew eastwards. Frederick was thus allowed time to recover and rebuild his army.

Kursk

Date: 5–17 July 1943.
Location: City 100 miles north of Kharkov, USSR.
War and campaign: Second World War: Russian Front.
Opposing sides: (a) Field Marshal Erich von Manstein commanding Army Group South and Field Marshal Gunther von Kluge commanding Army Group Centre; (b) Marshal Georgi Zhukov co-ordinating the defence of the salient, which was held by Rokossovsky's Central Front (northern sector), Vatutin's Voronezh Front (southern sector) and Konev's Reserve or Steppe Front (in immediate reserve).
Objective: The German intention was to eliminate the huge salient which had been formed around Kursk as a result of the fighting at KHARKOV earlier in the year.
Forces engaged: (a) 2,380 tanks and assault guns, 10,000 artillery weapons, 2,500 aircraft and 900,000 men; (b) 3,330 tanks and assault guns, 20,000 artillery weapons, 2,650 aircraft and 1,337,000 men.
Casualties: (a) Approximately 120,000 men and 1,500 tanks; (b) approximately 100,000 men and 1,500 tanks (many of the latter being recovered from the battlefield).
Result: Following the failure of this last great German offensive in the east, the strategic initiative along the entire Russian Front passed to the Soviet Army, which retained it for the remainder of the war. Kursk remains the largest tank battle in history.

When the spring thaw halted von Manstein's counter-offensive in the KHARKOV area, a Soviet salient 100 miles across by 70 miles deep, centred on Kursk, remained in the German lines. Hitler believed that this could be eliminated by directing converging thrusts through its flanks, thereby weakening the Soviet Army to such an extent that Stalin would be prepared to open peace negotiations. The detailed planning of the operation, codenamed 'Zitadelle' (Citadel), was undertaken by General Zeitzler, Chief of Army General Staff, but many Germany senior officers had serious reservations about the undertaking. Kept fully informed of German intentions by the Lucy spy ring, the Soviets fortified the salient to a depth of 25 miles with three concentric defensive belts incorporating minefields with a density of 2,500 anti-personnel and 2,200 anti-tank mines per mile of front, covered by artillery and anti-tank guns. Zhukov's strategy was to write down the Germans' strength as they fought their way through the defences, then counter-attack. The battle began on 5 July and was, from the outset, one of attrition. In the north, the Germans penetrated to a depth of ten miles and were then fought to a standstill. In the south, however, they almost succeeded in achieving a breakthrough, and on 12 July the battle reached its climax on this sector when the 700 tanks of Hoth's Fourth Panzer Army met the 850 tanks of Rotmistrov's Fifth Guards Tank Army in a fierce but inconclusive mêlée near the village of Prokhorovka. The following day, in the wake of the Allied landings in Sicily on 10 July, Hitler informed his senior officers that the Russian Front would have to be stripped of troops to form fresh armies in Italy. Simultaneously, the Soviets launched a counter-offensive into the Orel salient – a mirror image of the Kursk salient situated immediately to the north – using Sokolovsky's West Front and Popov's Bryansk Front. The Second Panzer Army was badly mauled and

Manstein was forced to transfer several of his armoured divisions to Kluge. On 17 July Hitler formally announced that 'Zitadelle' was at an end.

Kut-al-Amara, Siege of 274

Date: 8 December 1915 to 29 April 1916.
Location: On the river Tigris, approximately half-way between Baghdad and Basra, Iraq.
War and campaign: First World War: Mesopotamia.
Opposing sides: (a) Lieutenant-General Sir John Nixon commanding the British forces in Mesopotamia (replaced by Lieutenant-General Sir Percy Lake in late December); (b) Field Marshal Baron Colmar von der Goltz, Commander-in-Chief of the Turkish forces in Mesopotamia (succeeded on his death in April 1916 by Khalil Pasha).
Objective: Having retreated from CTESIPHON, Townshend needlessly allowed his division to be besieged by the Turks in Kut; the remainder of the British army in Mesopotamia was attempting to relieve him.
Forces engaged: (a) Major-General Sir Charles Townshend commanding the 6th Indian Division in Kut (about 12,500 men) and Lieutenant-General Sir Fenton Aylmer commanding the Tigris Corps (relief force), replaced by Lieutenant-General Sir George Gorringe in April (about 40,000 men); (b) Khalil Pasha commanding the Turkish troops besieging Kut and holding the blocking position downstream of the town – total about 35,000 men.
Casualties: (a) The Kut garrison was starved into surrender, 7,000 of its men dying in captivity (mainly from starvation and disease) and the Tigris Corps sustained 23,000 casualties in repeated attempts to break through; (b) approximately 10,000.
Result: The surrender of Kut-al-Amara damaged British prestige throughout the Middle East; its effect at home was comparable to that of the fall of SINGAPORE in 1942. The disaster forced the War Office to take a more realistic view of the campaign in Mesopotamia. See BAGHDAD.

Townshend deliberately engineered the siege, hoping to repeat an earlier triumph when he had successfully held Chitral Fort in 1895. Once casualties among the relief force had risen to almost twice the strength of the garrison, Kitchener signalled Lake that further effort would not be justified. This was the first occasion when attempts were made to supply a besieged garrison by air; from 15 April provisions totalling 16,800lb were flown in, but this fell far short of the 5,000lb daily requirement.

Kutna Hora (Nebovidy) 275

Date: 6 January 1422.
Location: Village near Kolin, 45 miles south-east of Prague, Czechoslovakia.
War and campaign: Hussite Wars, 1419–1436.
Opposing sides: (a) Jan Ziska commanding the Hussites; (b) Sigismund, Holy Roman Emperor, commanding the Catholic army.
Objective: The Hussites had mounted a counter-offensive against the Catholic army which had occupied Kutna Hora, provoking it into attacking their *wagenburg*.
Forces engaged: (a) 25,000; (b) 50,000.

Casualties: (a) Light; (b) uncertain, but heavy.	
Result: The Catholic assault was repulsed.	

Sigismund was forced to abandon Kutna Hora and retreat. See NEMECKY BROD, PRAGUE (1419).

Kuwait (Operation 'Desert Sabre')   276

Date: 24–28 February 1991.
Location: Kuwait and south-eastern Iraq.
War and campaign: Gulf War, 1990–1991.
Opposing sides: (a) General Norman Schwarzkopf commanding the Coalition army; (b) President Saddam Hussein, commander-in-chief of the Iraqi armed forces.
Objective: The liberation of Kuwait which, in defiance of UN resolutions, had been occupied by Iraq since 2 August 1990.
Forces engaged: (a) 17,000-strong US Marine Corps amphibious landing force plus (ashore) 2nd Marine Division, Egyptian 4th Armoured Division, Syrian, Saudi Arabian, Kuwaiti and other Arab contingents, US VII Corps (British 1st Armoured Division, US 1st and 3rd Armored Divisions, US 1st Infantry Division and US 2nd Armored Cavalry Regiment) and US XVIII Corps (French 6th Light Armoured Division, US 82nd and 101st Airborne Divisions and US 24th Mechanized Infantry Division) – total approximately 665,000; (b) 43 divisions with approximately 350,000 men, 4,000 tanks and 3,000 artillery weapons.
Casualties: (a) Total less than 500; (b) uncertain, but total losses, including those inflicted during the protracted Allied air offensive, have been estimated at 60,000 killed with 175,000 prisoners, plus 3,700 tanks, 2,400 APCs and 2,600 artillery weapons destroyed or captured.
Result: The Iraqi army in Kuwait was destroyed. Unfortunately, when Saddam Hussein indicated his willingness to comply with UN resolutions regarding Kuwait, President Bush imposed a ceasefire. This proved to be premature since it left those Iraqi formations which had not been involved in the débâcle, including a substantial part of the Republican Guard, free to deal with revolts by the Shi'ites and Kurds in, respectively, southern and northern Iraq. These revolts were ruthlessly put down, leaving Saddam's political power-base intact.

Although the well-equipped Iraqi Army was the fourth largest in the world, its ability to fight a modern high-technology war was overestimated. Nevertheless, it possessed the capacity to inflict heavy casualties on any troops attempting to fight their way through its extensively fortified defensive zone in Kuwait. Because of this General Schwarzkopf initiated a major air offensive, codenamed 'Desert Storm', on 15 January. Over a period of weeks, this succeeded in its aims of destroying the command network, logistic infrastructure, equipment and morale of the Iraqi field army; little opposition was offered by the Iraqi Air Force, part of which was neutralized on the ground while the rest fled abroad. By the time 'Desert Sabre' was launched, many Iraqi divisions were 50 per cent below strength and others had incurred losses in excess of 25 per cent; little evidence of their will to fight remained. Because of the threat of an amphibious landing, the Iraqis had concentrated the bulk of their strength within Kuwait itself, leaving their own territory to the west largely undefended. Schwarzkopf took advantage of this by mounting holding attacks against southern Kuwait while his XVIII Corps, with airmobile and light armoured formations, struck deep into Iraq itself, capturing Al Nasiriyah on the

Euphrates, with the result that the Iraqi army in Kuwait was isolated. On the right of XVIII Corps, VII Corps, with the bulk of the armour, also advanced into Iraq, then swung east to defeat counter-attacks by armoured formations of Saddam's much vaunted Republic Guard, the performance of which was unimpressive. In the event, even the holding attacks broke through and developed into a rapid advance on Kuwait City. By the time the ceasefire was imposed, a total of 42 Iraqi divisions had been destroyed as fighting formations. Although, for the first time, the outcome of a campaign had been decided by air power, it was still necessary for the *coup de grâce* to be administered by ground troops. The execution of 'Desert Sabre' was a textbook example of the 'Blitzkrieg' technique applied to a desert environment.

Kwajalein Atoll 277

Date: 1–4 February 1944.
Location: Part of the Marshall Islands group, Central Pacific.
War and campaign: Second World War: Central Pacific theatre.
Opposing sides: (a) Major-General Holland M. Smith commanding the US V Amphibious Corps; (b) Rear-Admiral Akiyama commanding the Japanese garrison.
Objective: The islands were to be secured as bases for the continued American drive across the Central Pacific.
Forces engaged: (a) 4th Marine and 7th Infantry Divisions; (b) approximately 8,000 (mainly Naval Infantry).
Casualties: (a) 486 killed and 1,295 wounded; (b) except for a handful of prisoners (mostly Korean labourers), the garrison fought to the death.
Result: The unexpectedly rapid capture of the atoll enabled the Americans to bring forward their plan for the capture of ENIWETOK ATOLL.

Ladysmith 278

Date: 2 November 1899 to 28 February 1900.
Location: Town and railway junction in western Natal, South Africa.
War and campaign: Second Boer War, 1899–1902.
Opposing sides: (a) Lieutenant-General Sir George White; (b) General Piet Joubert.
Objective: After fighting actions at Talana Hill, Elandslaagte and Nicholson's Nek, the British army in Natal retired to the town and was besieged by the Boers.
Forces engaged: (a) 13,745, plus 50 guns (including two 4.7in naval guns); (b) initially 20,000, plus 40 guns (including two Creusot 155mm heavy guns).
Casualties: (a) 894 killed and wounded; (b) estimated approximately 1,600 killed and wounded.
Result: General Sir Redvers Buller finally broke through the Boers' blocking position on the Tugela river and relieved the town.

Ladysmith was the focus of operations on the eastern front. See also COLENSO and SPION KOP.

Laffeldt (Lauffeld)

Date: 2 July 1747.
Location: On the Dutch/Belgian border to the south-west of Maastricht.
War and campaign: War of Austrian Succession, 1740–1748: Campaign in the Netherlands, 1746–1748.
Opposing sides: (a) William, Duke of Cumberland, commanding the Allied army; (b) Marshal Count Maurice de Saxe commanding the French army.
Objective: Cumberland had almost succeeded in isolating a detached French corps near Maastricht when Saxe arrived with the remainder of the French army, making a general engagement inevitable.
Forces engaged: (a) Approximately 90,000; (b) approximately 120,000.
Casualties: (a) 6,000; (b) 14,000.
Result: A hard-fought battle in which Laffeldt village changed hands three times and ending with a costly French victory.

The French remained in secure possession of their conquests in the Netherlands until peace was concluded the following year. See also FONTENOY.

Laing's Nek

Date: 28 January 1881.
Location: Pass in the foothills of the Drakensberg mountains on the Newcastle–Standerton road, Natal, South Africa.
War and campaign: First Boer War, 1880–1881.
Opposing sides: (a) Major-General Sir George Colley; (b) P. J. Joubert commanding the Boer commandos.
Objective: The British were attempting to fight their way through the Drakensberg range to relieve their besieged garrisons in the Transvaal.
Forces engaged: (a) Approximately 1,160, including 150 cavalry, plus four guns; (b) approximately 2,000.
Casualties: (a) 198 killed and wounded; (b) 14 killed and 27 wounded.
Result: Having repulsed a cavalry charge, the Boers inflicted serious losses on Colley's infantry as it advanced in close order. Colley was forced to abandon his assault on the Nek.

See also MAJUBA HILL.

Lake Narotch

Date: 18 March to 14 April 1916.
Location: East of Vilna (Vilnius), mainly on the isthmus between Lakes Narotch and Vishniev.
War and campaign: First World War: Eastern Front.
Opposing sides: (a) General Paul von Hindenburg, responsible as Head of *Oberost*

for operations on the northern sector of the Eastern Front; (b) General Alexei Kuropatkin commanding the North Front.

Objective: Offensive mounted in response to requests received from France for Russia to relieve German pressure on VERDUN. The particular objective was the railway junction at Vilna.

Forces engaged: (a) The German Tenth Army (Eichhorn); (b) the Russian Second Army (Ragosa) with approximately 350,000 men and 1,000 guns.

Casualties: (a) Approximately 20,000; (b) approximately 100,000.

Result: Despite numerical superiority and what was believed to be adequate artillery support, the Russian offensive failed, partly because of the mud induced by the spring thaw. The greatest penetration of the German lines was a mere 2,000yds deep on a 4,000yd front, lost in a single day when the Germans counter-attacked.

The disaster destroyed Russian self-confidence and belief in victory.

Lake Trasimene 282

Date: 21 June 217 BC.

Location: Along the north-eastern shore of Lago Trasimeno, west of Perugia, central Italy.

War and campaign: The Second Punic War, 219–202 BC.

Opposing sides: (a) Gaius Flaminius; (b) Hannibal.

Objective: Hannibal, advancing south towards Rome after his victory at the battle of THE TREBBIA, ambushed a Roman army which was pursuing him.

Forces engaged: (a) 40,000; (b) 35,000.

Casualties: (a) 15,000 killed, including Flaminius, and 15,000 captured; (b) 2,500.

Result: The Roman army was destroyed and Hannibal resumed his march. Now seriously alarmed, the Senate granted Quintus Fabius Maximus dictatorial powers and his tactics of delay and harassment temporarily stabilized the situation until the catastrophe of CANNAE.

Hannibal used a blocking force of infantry to halt the Roman column, then launched the bulk of his troops, hidden by mist on the hills to the left of the Romans, in a flank attack, simultaneously closing the rear of the trap with his cavalry. The ambush achieved complete surprise and Flaminius' legions, caught between the hills and the lake, were cut to pieces before they could deploy.

Langensalza 283

Date: 27–29 June 1866.

Location: 19 miles north-west of Erfurt, Germany.

War and campaign: Austro–Prussian (Seven Weeks') War: Central German Campaign.

Opposing sides: (a) General Vogel von Falkenstein commanding the Prussian army; (b) King George V of Hanover with General Alexander von Arentschildt as his Chief of Staff.

Objective: The Prussians had invaded Hanover, which had allied itself with Austria.	
Forces engaged: (a) 50,000; (b) 12,000.	
Casualties: (a) Approximately 2,000; (b) approximately 1,400.	
Result: After Falkenstein's leading corps had been mauled on 27 June, the Prussians concentrated in overwhelming strength, forcing the King to surrender. See also KÖNIGGRÄTZ.	

As the Hanoverian constitution did not permit a female monarch, the country had been separated from the British crown when Queen Victoria ascended the throne in 1837. Langensalza was the last battle fought by an independent Hanoverian army; subsequently the state was absorbed into the German Empire.

La Puebla, Siege of 284

Date: 4–17 May 1863.
Location: Fortified city on the route between Vera Cruz and Mexico City.
War and campaign: French Intervention in Mexico, 1861–1867.
Opposing sides: (a) General Elie-Frédéric Forey; (b) General Ignacio Zaragoza.
Objective: The French intention was to create a puppet empire in Mexico under Archduke Maximilian of Austria, but their advance on Mexico City had been seriously checked at La Puebla on 5 May 1862. Now, reinforced, they laid siege to the city.
Forces engaged: (a) 25,000; (b) 12,000;
Casualties: Uncertain, but heavy on both sides.
Result: Too weak to invest the city completely, Forey reduced its defences by stages. On 8 May a Mexican relief column was defeated by General Achille Bazaine. Zaragoza surrendered on 17 May.

The French resumed their advance on Mexico City, where Maximilian was crowned Emperor of Mexico the following month. See also CAMERONE.

Laswari 285

Date: 1 November 1803.
Location: Village near Alwar, 85 miles south-west of Delhi.
War and campaign: Second Maratha War, 1803–1805: Hindustan Campaign.
Opposing sides: (a) General Gerard Lake; (b) Surwar Khan.
Objective: Lake's intention was to destroy the Maratha power in northern India. Having already stormed the fortress of Aligarh (4 September), defeated the enemy field army near Delhi (16 September) and captured Agra, he now sought a decisive battle.
Forces engaged: (a) Approximately 6,000 British and Indian troops; (b) approximately 14,000.
Casualties: (a) 834 killed and wounded; (b) approximately 7,000 killed and wounded, plus 2,000 captured together with 74 guns.

> **Result:** A decisive victory which, coupled with that won by Wellesley at ASSAYE, forced the dissident Maratha chief Dowlut Rao Scindia to sue for terms.

Lake, like the majority of British generals who served in India, believed that attacking troops enjoyed a moral superiority over those who were attacked, however great the odds in favour of the latter. The Marathas had formed ranks behind a line of guns which had been chained together. This blunted Lake's first cavalry charge but his infantry renewed the attack and the enemy was routed in less than two hours' fighting.

Laupen 286

Date: 21 June 1339.
Location: Town 10 miles south-west of Berne.
War and campaign: Swiss Wars of Independence.
Opposing sides: (a) Rudolph von Erlach commanding the Swiss cantonal contingents; (b) Count Gerard de Vallangin commanding the Burgundians.
Objective: The Swiss intention was to break the Burgundian siege of Laupen.
Forces engaged: (a) 5,000 pikemen and halberdiers; (b) 12,000 infantry and 3,000 cavalry.
Casualties: (a) Light; (b) approximately 4,000 killed.
Result: The Burgundians were defeated and Laupen was relieved.

Two of the three Swiss divisions quickly defeated their infantry opponents then wheeled against the flank and rear of the Burgundian cavalry, which was attacking the defensive hedgehog formed by the third, cutting it to pieces. Like CRÉCY, Laupen demonstrated that the mounted knight was no longer invincible when confronted with suitably equipped, disciplined infantry.

Le Cateau 287

Date: 26 August 1914.
Location: Along the line of the main highway between Cambrai and Le Cateau, then east to the Forest of Mormal, northern France.
War and campaign: First World War: Western Front.
Opposing sides: (a) Field Marshal Sir John French commanding the BEF; (b) General Alexander von Kluck commanding the German First Army.
Objective: The German Army was attempting to turn the Allied left flank and was following up the withdrawal of the British Expeditionary Force from MONS.
Forces engaged: (a) General Sir Horace Smith-Dorrien commanding the British II Corps – total approximately 40,000; (b) the German IV, IV Reserve and part of III Corps – total approximately 140,000.
Casualties: (a) 7,812, plus 38 guns lost; (b) unknown, but personnel casualties were heavier.
Result: Smith-Dorrien succeeded in fighting his way out of a double-envelopment and disengaging, simultaneously inflicting a more serious check on Kluck than that at MONS.

Although it was soon to be dwarfed in size, Le Cateau was the largest battle fought by the British Army since Waterloo. In his report Kluck paid an unwitting tribute to the quality of the BEF by stating that he had been engaged with no fewer than nine divisions when only three were present. Kluck also made a serious error of judgement in believing that he had finally defeated the BEF and that it was retreating south-west towards the Channel Ports; in fact, it was withdrawing to the south, conforming to the general Allied movement, and its I Corps had not yet been seriously engaged. As a young officer, Smith-Dorrien had been one of the very few to survive the Battle of ISANDHLWANA. See also GUISE and MARNE, FIRST BATTLE OF THE .

Leipzig ('The Battle of the Nations')   288

Date: 16–18 October 1813.
Location: The city and suburbs of Leipzig, Germany.
War and campaign: War of the Sixth Coalition, 1812–1814: Campaign in Germany, 1813.
Opposing sides: (a) The Emperor Napoleon I commanding the French army; (b) Marshal Prince Karl von Schwarzenberg, Prince Gerhard von Blücher and Crown Prince Charles-Jean of Sweden (formerly Marshal Jean-Baptiste Bernadotte) commanding the Allied armies.
Objective: Following a series of military reverses and the desertion of his Saxon and Bavarian allies, Napoleon concentrated his army at Leipzig. The three armies of the Confederation converged on the area with the intention of isolating and destroying it.
Forces engaged: (a) Approximately 185,000, with 600 guns; (b) approximately 300,000 Austrians, Prussians, Russians and Swedes, with 1,400 guns (the Swedish contingent contained a British rocket troop).
Casualties: (a) 70,000, including 30,000 prisoners, plus 150 guns lost; (b) approximately 54,000 killed and wounded.
Result: In three days of heaving fighting the French were driven back through Leipzig. Their losses would have been smaller had not a bridge across the Elster been prematurely blown, leaving 20,000 men trapped in the city.

Following this serious defeat, Napoleon retired across the Rhine, fending off a Bavarian attempt to cut his line of retreat at Hanau on 30–31 October. See also PARIS.

Leningrad   289

Date: 1 September 1941 to 27 January 1944.
Location: Now (and formerly) St Petersburg, a city on the river Neva at the head of the Baltic.
War and campaign: Second World War: Russian Front.
Opposing sides: (a) Successively, Field Marshals Wilhelm Ritter von Leeb, Ernst Busch and Georg von Kuchler commanding Army Group North; (b) Marshals Klimenti Voroshilov and Georgi Zhukov, initially responsible for the defence of the city, followed by General L. A. Govorov commanding the Leningrad Front.
Objective: Hitler, contrary to his generals' advice, wished to starve the city into surrender by means of a protracted siege.

Forces engaged: (a) The German Sixteenth and Eighteenth Armies and the Finnish Karelian Army – total approximately 350,000; (b) the Soviet 42nd, 55th and 67th Armies, 2nd Shock Army and units supplied by the Baltic Fleet – total approximately 250,000.
Casualties: (a) About 200,000 Germans and Finns; (b) about 1,800,000 Russian soldiers and civilians.
Result: The city was finally relieved after a horrific siege lasting 900 days.

By 8 September 1941 Leningrad had been completely encircled and the following month the population began to die of starvation. Although supply routes into the city were opened across the frozen Lake Ladoga, for many the scant rations arrived too late. Throughout the siege further casualties were caused by constant air and artillery bombardment. Several Soviet attempts to relieve the city were defeated, as were a smaller number of German attempts to capture it. Not until January 1944 was the deadlock broken, when a major Soviet offensive in the north enabled General Kiril Meretskov's Volkhov Front to effect a junction with Golikov's garrison and drive the German forces beyond artillery range.

Leuctra 290

Date: July 371 BC.
Location: 10 miles west of Thivai (Thebes), Voiotia, Greece.
War and campaign: Wars of the Greek City-States.
Opposing sides: (a) Epaminondas commanding the Theban army; (b) Cleombrotus, King of Sparta.
Objective: The Thebans were opposing a Spartan invasion of their territory.
Forces engaged: (a) 6,000; (b) 11,000.
Casualties: (a) Neglible; (b) 2,000 killed, including Cleombrotus.
Result: A Theban victory which destroyed the military prestige of Sparta.

Epaminondas abandoned the contemporary Greek convention of placing the best troops on the right of the line and instead formed them on the left in a column 80 wide and 50 deep, with the rest of his army echeloned back to the right, so providing the first recorded instances of a columnar attack and a refused flank. The Spartans, who had deployed in the traditional manner, were unable to respond to these novel tactics and their right was quickly overwhelmed. As the rest of his army closed up, Epaminondas wheeled his phalanx to the right and the Spartans broke.

Leuthen 291

Date: 5 December 1757.
Location: Village 10 miles west of Wroclaw (Breslau), Poland.
War and campaign: Seven Years' War, 1756–1763: Central European Campaign of 1757.
Opposing sides: (a) Frederick the Great commanding the Prussians; (b) Prince Charles of Lorraine and Marshal Leopold von Daun commanding the Austrians.

Objective: Following his victory at ROSSBACH, Frederick marched into Silesia to engage the invading Austrian army.
Forces engaged: (a) 48 infantry battalions, 129 cavalry squadrons and 71 guns – total 35,000; (b) 84 infantry battalions, 144 cavalry squadrons and 65 guns – total 60,000.
Casualties: (a) 6,400 killed and wounded; (b) 6,750 killed and wounded, 12,000 prisoners and many guns captured.
Result: The Austrian army was destroyed and its remnants withdrew to Bohemia.

The Austrian position extended for five miles from Nypern in the north to the Schweidnitz river in the south, both flanks being partially protected by marshland. Frederick, advancing from Neumarkt, first drove in his opponents' cavalry outposts, leaving the Austrians blind, then feinted towards their right; Charles, responding, moved his reserves to Nypern. Frederick, however, wheeled the remainder of his army to the right and marched it south across the Austrian front, screened from view by a range of low hills. When his columns overlapped the enemy's left wing they faced left and attacked in echelon from the right, covered by fire from the massed Prussian artillery. The Austrians, outnumbered at the point of contact, began to give way. Charles struggled to establish a new line to meet the threat and counter-attacked with the cavalry of his right wing, but neither measure was successful and his army disintegrated as the Prussians fought their way across his former position. Leuthen provides a perfect example of the oblique order of attack and was described by Napoleon as 'a masterpiece of movements, maneouvres and resolution. Alone it is sufficient to immortalize Frederick and place him in the ranks of the greatest generals.'

Lewes 292

Date: 14 May 1264.
Location: Offham Hill north of Lewes, Sussex.
War and campaign: English Baronial Wars: Simon de Montfort's Campaign, 1264–1265.
Opposing sides: (a) King Henry III; (b) Simon de Montfort, Earl of Leicester.
Objective: A pitched battle forced on the royal army by the barons.
Forces engaged: (a) 1,500 cavalry and 8,500 infantry – total 10,000; (b) 600 cavalry and 4,400 infantry – total 5,000.
Casualties: Total 2,800, the royal army incurring the heavier share.
Result: Henry's right was victorious but his centre and left were repulsed and driven down the hill into Lewes in some confusion.

Henry was captured and, for a while, Simon became the effective ruler of England. See also EVESHAM.

Lexington and Concord 293

Date: 19 April 1775.
Location: On the road between Boston and Concord, Massachusetts.

War and campaign: American War of Independence, 1775–1783: northern theatre of operations.
Opposing sides: (a) Overall – Lieutenant-Colonel Francis Smith, then Brigadier-General Hugh Percy during the final stages of the march; at Lexington – Major John Pitcairn; at Concord – Lieutenant-Colonel Francis Smith. (b) No overall American commander; at Lexington – Captain John Parker; at Concord – Colonel James Barrett.
Objective: A battalion-sized British force was despatched from Boston to seize arms and munitions at Concord. At Lexington, Concord and on the way back to Boston it was opposed by local militia units.
Forces engaged: (a) Approximately 800, rising to 1,800 during the final stages; (b) approximately 3,500.
Casualties: (a) 73 killed, 174 wounded and 26 missing – total 273; (b) 95 killed and wounded.
Result: The British accomplished their mission, albeit at prohibitive cost. In the wider context the use of force by both sides escalated the political dispute between the colonists and the government of the mother country into open warfare. The British garrison in Boston was besieged – see BUNKER HILL.

Forewarned by Paul Revere, William Dawes and Dr Samuel Prescott, local militia units were assembling even before Smith's column left Boston. Already alarmed by the disturbed state of the countryside, Smith prudently sent back a messenger requesting reinforcements. At Lexington his advance guard, com-manded by Major Pitcairn, encountered the local militia company. Tempers were running high and someone fired a shot, the responsibility for which has never been established. The engagement quickly became general and the militia were brushed aside. Stiffer opposition was encountered at Concord but the column completed its task and set off on its return march. Throughout this it was harassed continually by American snipers and sustained serious losses; the probability is that, had it not met Percy's relief column at Lexington, it would not have reached Boston. Near Cambridge the Americans discontinued their attacks.

Leyte 294

Date: 20 October to 25 December 1944.
Location: Island in the centre of the Philippine archipelago.
War and campaign: Second World War: Liberation of the Philippines.
Opposing sides: (a) General Douglas MacArthur and Admiral Chester W. Nimitz commanding the American forces; (b) General Tomoyuki Yamashita and Admiral Jisaburo Ozawa commanding the Japanese.
Objective: The American landing on the island was the opening move in the re-conquest of the Philippines.
Forces engaged: (a) General Walter Krueger commanding the US Sixth Army, with X Corps (Major-General Franklin Sibert) and XXIV Corps (Lieutenant-General John Hodge) – total approximately 150,000; (b) Lieutenant-General Sosaku Suzuki commanding the Japanese Thirty-Fifth Army, of which initially only the 16th Division (16,000 men) was engaged on Leyte.
Casualties: (a) 15,584 killed, wounded and missing; (b) about 74,000, the majority killed.

> **Result:** Leyte was captured and, in the process, the strength of Yamashita's ground troops in the Philippines was seriously weakened. See also MANILA.

The opening phase of the operation coincided with the Battle of Leyte Gulf, the greatest naval battle in history, which destroyed the offensive capacity of the Imperial Japanese Navy. On Leyte itself, Suzuki's troops, heavily reinforced by Yamashita, fought hard to contain the American advance but were outflanked by a further amphibious landing to the south and eventually encircled and destroyed by a double-envelopment.

Liaoyang 295

Date: 25 August to 3 September 1904.	

Location: On the Mukden–Port Arthur railway, south of the confluence of the Taitzu and Liao rivers, Manchuria.

War and campaign: Russo–Japanese War, 1904–1905.

Opposing sides: (a) General Alexei Kuropatkin, Commander-in-Chief of the Russian army in Manchuria; (b) Field Marshal Marquis Iwao Oyama, Commander-in-Chief of the Japanese armies in Manchuria.

Objective: Each side was attempting to inflict a decisive defeat on the other.

Forces engaged: (a) 150,000; (b) the Japanese First (Kuroki), Second (Oku) and Fourth (Nodzu) Armies – total 125,000.

Casualties: (a) 17,900; (b) 23,615.

Result: After a hard-fought action, Kuropatkin believed that he had been beaten and withdrew towards Mukden. See SHA-HO.

Liegnitz (Wahlstatt) (1241) 296

Date: 9 April 1241.

Location: Near the town of Legnica, 30 miles west of Wroclaw (Breslau), Poland.

War and campaign: Mongol Invasion of Europe, 1237–1242.

Opposing sides: (a) Kaidu, grandson of Genghis Khan; (b) Henry II, Duke of Silesia.

Objective: Having defeated King Boleslaw V of Poland at Cracow (3 March), the Mongols advanced westward to find themselves opposed by an army consisting of Germans, Poles and Teutonic Knights. Aware that this would be reinforced two days later by a further 50,000 men under King Wenceslas of Bohemia, the Mongols attacked at once.

Forces engaged: (a) 20,000; (b) 40,000.

Casualties: (a) Unknown; (b) heavy.

Result: The European army was routed.

Wenceslas retreated and Kaidu turned south to rejoin the main Mongol horde in Hungary – see MOHI (SAJO RIVER).

Liegnitz (1760)

Date: 15 August 1760.

Location: Legnica, 35 miles west of Wroclaw (Breslau), Poland.

War and campaign: Seven Years' War, 1756–1763: Central European Campaign of 1760.

Opposing sides: (a) Frederick the Great; (b) Lieutenant-General Gideon von Laudon.

Objective: Frederick II of Prussia, finding himself almost surrounded by a concentration of Austrian and Russian armies in Silesia, had decided to withdraw during the previous night but in the darkness his troops encountered an Austrian force which was marching to complete his encirclement and an encounter battle followed.

Forces engaged: (a) 30,000; (b) 30,000 (overall allied strength 90,000).

Casualties: (a) Approximately 1,000; (b) 4,000 killed and wounded, 6,000 prisoners and 82 guns captured.

Result: Having fought his way out of the trap, Frederick resumed his war of manoeuvre against the main Austrian army.

Frederick was unable to prevent an Austro-Russian force occupying and partially burning Berlin in October – see TORGAU.

Ligny

Date: 16 June 1815.

Location: Village 10 miles north-west of Namur, Belgium.

War and campaign: Napoleon's Hundred Days: Campaign in Belgium.

Opposing sides: (a) The Emperor Napoleon I commanding the Army of the North; (b) Field Marshal Prince Blücher commanding the Prussian army.

Objective: Having crossed the Belgian frontier, Napoleon sought to defeat the Prussian and Anglo-Netherlands armies in separate engagements. Ordering Ney to engage the latter at QUATRE BRAS, he attacked the Prussians at Ligny with the centre and right wing of his army.

Forces engaged: (a) 77,000, with 218 guns; (b) 84,000, with 224 guns.

Casualties: (a) 11,500; (b) 16,000 killed, wounded and captured, plus 8,000 deserters.

Result: Although the Prussians were defeated and forced to withdraw, Napoleon had only won a partial victory, for Blücher's army not only remained in being but also was still capable of co-operating with Wellington's Anglo-Netherlands army to the west.

The inexperienced Prussians fought doggedly until their centre was broken by the Imperial Guard during the evening. Blücher had been injured and command evolved temporarily to General Count August von Gneisenau, who decided to withdraw northwards on Wavre rather than eastwards along his line of communications towards Namur. While this may have been primarily motivated by self-interest, it nevertheless enabled the Prussians to maintain contact with Wellington's army and, having recovered sufficiently to resume command, Blücher promised Wellington that he would join him at

WATERLOO. In the meantime, the second important consequence of Gneisenau's decision had become apparent. In the morning after the battle, Napoleon detached Marshal Emmanuel de Grouchy with 33,000 men to pursue the Prussians, but Grouchy, encouraged by the flood of deserters streaming towards Namur, set off in the wrong direction and did not regain contact until late on 17 June. Consequently, he never succeeded in engaging more than the Prussian rearguard, which covered the rest of Blücher's army as it advanced on WATERLOO. For this, somewhat unfairly, he has been reviled by his countrymen ever since.

Little Big Horn 299

Date: 25–26 June 1876.
Location: In the lower valley of the Little Big Horn river, Montana.
War and campaign: American Indian Wars.
Opposing sides: (a) Major-General Alfred H. Terry; (b) Chiefs Sitting Bull, Crazy Horse and others.
Objective: The Army was attempting to drive the Sioux and Cheyenne back to their reservations.
Forces engaged: (a) Lieutenant-Colonel (Brevet Major-General) George Armstrong Custer commanding the 7th Cavalry, plus scouts – total approximately 600; (b) 1,500–2,000 Sioux and Cheyenne.
Casualties: (a) Over 250 killed, about 50 wounded and several missing; (b) some 50 killed outright, plus a larger number who subsequently died as a result of wounds.
Result: Custer was killed and the 7th Cavalry was so severely mauled that Terry was forced to abandon his campaign. Nevertheless, the disaster marked a turning point in the history of the Indian Wars. The Army's response was such that never again did the tribes take the warpath in such numbers, and never again were they able to win such a victory.

Terry's plan of campaign envisaged a converging advance against the enemy with his own columns from the north and a column commanded by Brigadier-General George Crook from the south. Unfortunately, the distances involved were such that liaison was impossible and, unknown to Terry, Crook had been defeated even before he commenced his own operations against the tribes encamped along the Little Big Horn. Custer's part in the latter was to advance up the Rosebud then cross the watershed and drive down the Little Big Horn while Terry penetrated the valley from the north. However, Custer's personal fortunes were at a low ebb and, hoping to retrieve these with a dashing action, he disobeyed orders and launched a premature attack, rashly dividing his regiment in the process. Of the five troops which rode with him into an Indian ambush, there were no survivors; the remainder of the regiment also sustained serious casualties but managed to consolidate a defensive position and hold out until relieved. About one-third of the Indians possessed firearms, but these included some 200 Winchester and Henry repeating rifles which alone were capable of a higher volume of fire than all the single-shot carbines of Custer's men.

Lobositz 300

Date: 1 October 1756.

Location: Lovocice village in the Erzgebirge, 35 miles north-west of Prague, Czechoslovakia.	
War and campaign: Seven Years' War, 1756–1763.	
Opposing sides: (a) Frederick the Great; (b) Marshal Maximilian von Browne.	
Objective: The Prussians intercepted an Austrian army marching to the relief of a Saxon force which they were besieging in a fortified camp at Pirna on the Elbe.	
Forces engaged: Approximately 30,000 on each side.	
Casualties: Approximately 3,000 on each side.	
Result: The Austrians were repulsed.	

The Saxons at Pirna surrendered and were promptly impressed into the Prussian army, together with their 80 guns. See PRAGUE (1757).

Lodi   301

Date: 10 May 1796.
Location: Village on the Adda river, 20 miles south-east of Milan.
War and campaign: War of the First Coalition, 1792–1798: Campaign in Italy, 1796–1797.
Opposing sides: (a) General Napoleon Bonaparte commanding the Army of Italy; (b) General Jean Pierre Beaulieu commanding the Austrian army.
Objective: Having been defeated by the French at Monenotte (12 April) and Dego (14–15) April, the Austrians were retiring from north-western Italy towards the Tyrol. At Lodi the French caught up with the Austrian rearguard, which contested the passage of the bridge.
Forces engaged: (a) Approximately 6,000; (b) 10,000.
Casualties: (a) 2,000 killed and wounded, including 400 on the bridge itself; (b) 2,000 killed and wounded.
Result: Under Napoleon's personal leadership the French stormed the bridge and forced the Austrian rearguard to retire.

Napoleon entered Milan on 15 May and went on to besiege Mantua, the major Austrian garrison town in northern Italy. See BASSANO, ARCOLA and RIVOLI.

Long Island   302

Date: 26–29 August 1776.
Location: Area stretching from line Gowanus Road–Flatbush–Bedford Pass–Jamaica Pass north-east to Brooklyn Heights, Long Island, New York.
War and campaign: American War of Independence, 1775–1783: central theatre of operations.
Opposing sides: (a) Major-General William Howe; (b) Major-General Israel Putnam.

Objective: The British intention was to capture New York by securing Brooklyn Heights, possession of which would render the city untenable.
Forces engaged: (a) 15,000; (b) 5,000 rising to 9,500.
Casualties: (a) 392 killed and wounded; (b) 1,102, including approximately 800 prisoners, and six guns captured.
Result: Howe's landing force quickly established control over southern Long Island and confined the Americans to their entrenchments on Brooklyn Heights. Following his experience at BUNKER HILL Howe was reluctant to assault these, but on 29 August Washington ordered the evacuation of the position, then, when Howe crossed the East River to effect a landing at Kip's Bay in his rear, he abandoned New York and withdrew up the Manhattan peninsula to Harlem Heights. See WHITE PLAINS.

While holding attacks were mounted against the American right at Gowanus Road, during the night of 26 August Howe directed a flank march round Putnam's left through Jamaica Pass. The Americans were forced to retire into the Brooklyn position, but those at Gowanus Road were cut off and surrendered.

Long Tan 303

Date: 18 August 1966.
Location: Rubber plantation east of Nui Dat in Phouc Tuy province, south-east of Phann Bo Ho Chi Minh (formerly Saigon), Vietnam.
War and campaign: Vietnam War, 1956–1975.
Opposing sides: (a) Brigadier O. D. Jackson commanding the 1st Australian Task Force; (b) the commander of the Viet Cong 5th Division.
Objective: An encounter between a strong Australian patrol and a large Viet Cong force closing in on the Australian base at Nui Dat.
Forces engaged: (a) A and D Companies 6th Royal Australian Regiment, 1st Field Regiment Royal Australian Artillery with 103, 105 and 162 (New Zealand) Batteries (105mm howitzers) and Battery A II/35 US Artillery (155mm SP howitzers) under command, and 3 Troop 1st APC Squadron; (b) D445 Provisional Mobile Battalion and 275 Regiment, VC Main Force.
Casualties: (a) 17 killed and 24 wounded; (b) the official figure of 245 killed does not take into account many bodies discovered after the formal count had been completed – and the VC must have sustained a similar if not larger number of wounded, although all but three were removed from the battle area.
Result: The Viet Cong sustained a serious defeat and withdrew. 1 ATF consolidated its hold on the province.

Following a mortar attack on Nui Dat the previous Day, D Company 6 RAR was patrolling Long Tan rubber plantation when it ran into a much stronger Communist force. The Viet Cong promptly counter-attacked and the company was forced into a defensive perimeter which, with sustained artillery support, it held until a relief force consisting of M113s of 3 Troop 1st APC Squadron with A Company 6 RAR broke through from Nui Dat. The Viet Cong then broke contact. Artillery ammunition expenditure amounted to 2,639 rounds of 105mm and 155 rounds of 155mm. D Company was awarded a US Presidential Unit Citation.

Loos

Date: 25 September to 8 October 1915.

Location: Village in Artois between Lens and La Bassée.

War and campaign: First World War: Western Front.

Opposing sides: (a) Field Marshal Sir John French commanding the British armies in France and Belgium; (b) General Erich von Falkenhayn, Chief of the German General Staff.

Objective: Part of the Allied offensive to pinch out the German salient in Artois and Champagne.

Forces engaged: (a) General Sir Douglas Haig commanding the British First Army; (b) Crown Prince Rupprecht of Bavaria commanding the German Sixth Army.

Casualties: (a) Approximately 60,000; (b) approximately 30,000.

Result: Small gains were made by the British at disproportionate cost.

The first occasion on which the British Army employed gas to support an offensive; much · of it drifted back on to the attacking troops. As a result of the recriminations following the battle, notably the handling of reserves, Haig replaced French as the British Commander-in-Chief in December. On Haig's right, a parallel attack by the French Tenth Army against Vimy Ridge produced smaller gains at even higher cost. The two operations together are sometimes referred to as the Third Battle of Artois.

Lorraine

Date: 14–22 August 1914.

Location: East of the Moselle, between Sarrebourg and Metz.

War and campaign: First World War: Western Front.

Opposing sides: (a) General Joseph Joffre, Commander-in-Chief of the French Army; (b) General Helmuth von Moltke, Chief of the German General Staff.

Objective: Part of the French Plan XVII, which required an offensive into German territory on the outbreak of war.

Forces engaged: (a) General Auguste Dubail and General Noel de Castelnau commanding, respectively, the French First and Second Armies; (b) Crown Prince Rupprecht of Bavaria and General Josias von Heeringen commanding, respectively, the German Sixth and Seventh Armies.

Casualties: (a) French losses in this, the most important element of Plan XVII, coupled with smaller offensive in the Ardennes and on the Sambre (known collectively as The Battle of the Frontiers), amounted to some 300,000 incurred over an eleven-day period; (b) German losses, while heavy, were not as severe.

Result: A disastrous French defeat, the importance of which was, however, overestimated by von Moltke, who reinforced his left wing armies at the expense of those on his right and ordered them to take the offensive, simultaneously despatching two corps from the right wing to the Eastern Front. See MONS, LE CATEAU, GUISE and MARNE, FIRST BATTLE OF THE.

French reliance on the offensive spirit was no match for modern firepower. After making planned withdrawals, both German armies counter-attacked and drove the French back to the hills above Nancy.

Lostwithiel

Date: 21 August and 2 September 1644.
Location: Approximately midway between Liskeard and St Austell, Cornwall.
War and campaign: First Civil War, 1642–1646.
Opposing sides: (a) Charles I commanding the Royalists; (b) the Earl of Essex commanding the Parliamentarians.
Objective: A Parliamentary army, having penetrated the hostile country of Cornwall, was surrounded and trapped as the Royalists converged on the area.
Forces engaged: (a) 16,400; (b) initially 10,000.
Casualties: (a) Light; (b) killed and wounded uncertain, but 6,000 men plus artillery and baggage captured.
Result: During the first action the Royalists captured Beacon Hill, confining the Parliamentarians within a beach-head with their backs to the sea. On 31 August Essex's cavalry broke out but during a second engagement the Parliamentary perimeter was further compressed. Essex escaped by boat and the remainder of his army surrendered on 2 September.

Louisburg, Siege of

Date: 3 June to 20 July 1758.
Location: On the east coast of Cape Breton Island, Canada.
War and campaign: French and Indian War in North America, 1754–1763.
Opposing sides: (a) Major-General Jeffrey Amherst; (b) the Chevalier de Drucour.
Objective: The British intention was to capture the fortress, which was then the strongest in North America.
Forces engaged: (a) 11,600; (b) approximately 6,800, including 3,800 regulars.
Casualties: (a) Uncertain, though probably less than 1,000 from all causes; (b) 1,200 killed and wounded, 5,600 prisoners and 239 guns captured, plus twelve warships destroyed or captured in the harbour.
Result: The French surrendered after their defences crumbled under a sustained bombardment.

The St Lawrence was now open as an invasion route to the interior of Canada (see QUEBEC), although an advance along this axis was delayed until the following year because of the British defeat at FORT TICONDEROGA.

Lucknow, Siege of

Date: 1 July to 19 November 1857.
Location: Principal city of Oudh (Uttar Pradesh), northern India.
War and campaign: Indian Mutiny, 1857–1858: Oudh and Rohilkand Campaigns.
Opposing sides: (a) Sir Henry Lawrence, Chief Commissioner of Oudh, until killed on 4 July, then Brigadier-General John Inglis until the First Relief (25 September), then Major-General Sir James Outram; (b) various leaders with differing interests, notably Ahmadullah Shah (also known as the Maulvie of Faizabad) and Hazrat

Mahal, a minor wife of the former King of Oudh, acting on behalf of her son, Birjis Qadr.
Objective: The small British and Indian garrison, together with many civilians, was besieged by mutineers in the Residency.
Forces engaged: (a) Initially 1,729, plus 750 civilians, reinforced by approximately 1,500 combatants during the First Relief; (b) estimated between 50,000 and 100,000.
Casualties: (a) Approximately 2,500, including relief forces; (b) unknown, but many times greater – during the Second Relief over 2,000 were killed in the assault of the Secondrabagh alone.
Result: On 16 November the garrison was finally relieved by a force commanded by General Sir Colin Campbell and then evacuated. In March 1858 the city was recaptured from the rebels.

Had the rebel leadership possessed any ability, or been less concerned with the pursuit of its sectional interests, the British defences would have been overwhelmed. The first relief force sustained such serious casualties in breaking through that it could merely reinforce the garrison. Forward artillery tactics were employed by the second relief force, the walls of objectives such as the Secondrabagh and Sha Najaf being battered into breaches at point-blank range before the infantry assault was delivered. Lucknow, like DELHI, was a focus of rebel activity. It was also a wealthy city and was officially looted following its recapture in 1858. The Prize Agents estimated plunder to the value of £1.5 million, of which a private soldier's share amounted to Rs.17.8 (£1). Unofficial loot founded family fortunes and served to redeem a number of mortgaged estates.

Ludendorff's Offensives (1): 'Michael' (The Kaiserschlacht) 309

Date: 21 March to 5 April 1918.
Location: Along a 60-mile stretch of front between La Fère on the Oise and the Scarpe east of Arras, extending westwards in a deep salient towards Amiens.
War and campaign: First World War: Western Front.
Opposing sides: (a) Field Marshal Sir Douglas Haig, Commander-in-Chief of the British armies in France and Belgium; (b) General Erich Ludendorff, First Quartermaster-General of the German Army.
Objective: The German intention was to employ the resources released by the collapse of Russia in a series of major offensives against the British and French, before American troops could reach France in any numbers. The object of 'Michael' was to separate the British and French armies by driving a wedge through to the Somme estuary.
Forces engaged: (a) General Sir Hubert Gough and General Sir Julian Byng commanding, respectively, the British Fifth and Third Armies, with a total of 33 infantry and three cavalry divisions, 1,710 field artillery weapons and 976 medium and heavy guns, reinforced by twelve French divisions; (b) General Otto von Below, General Georg von der Marwitz and General Oskar von Hutier commanding, respectively, the German Seventeenth, Second and Eighteenth Armies with a total of 67 infantry divisions, 4,010 field artillery weapons and 2,588 medium and heavy guns.

Casualties: (a) 255,000 (178,000 British and 77,000 French), including over 90,000 prisoners and 1,100 guns captured; (b) approximately 250,000.

Result: The Germans made a spectacular advance of 40 miles but failed to reach the Somme estuary and incurred heavier losses than had been anticipated, particularly among the élite storm troop battalions. On 26 March Marshal Ferdinand Foch was appointed co-ordinater of the Allied response and on 3 April he became Allied Supreme Commander. Unfairly, Gough was made a scapegoat for the disaster, the remnants of his Fifth Army being transferred to the newly formed Fourth Army commanded by General Sir Henry Rawlinson.

The hallmark of the Ludendorff offensives was saturation bombardment with high-explosive and gas shells, coupled with fast-moving infiltration by highly trained storm troop battalions who had perfected their techniques at RIGA, CAPORETTO and CAMBRAI; in places, the Germans also used tanks to lead their assault.

Ludendorff's Offensives (2): 'Georgette' (The Battle of the Lys) 310

Date: 9–30 April 1918.

Location: A twelve-mile sector of the Western Front, extending from the Ypres salient southwards to La Bassée Canal.

War and campaign: First World War: Western Front.

Opposing sides: (a) Marshal Ferdinand Foch, Allied Supreme Commander; (b) General Erich Ludendorff, First Quartermaster-General of the German Army.

Objective: Ludendorff believed that if the British were defeated the French would seek an armistice and, following the success of 'MICHAEL' (see above), his next offensive was intended to unhinge the British left flank, mainly by capturing the strategic railway junction of Hazebrouck.

Forces engaged: (a) General Sir Henry Horne and General Sir Herbert Plumer commanding, respectively, the British First Army (sixteen divisions) and Second Army (thirteen divisions), subsequently reinforced by Foch with French divisions; (b) General Sixt von Arnim and General Ferdinand von Quast commanding, respectively, the German Fourth Army (33 divisions) and Sixth Army (28 divisions) (of the total of 61 divisions, only 35 were available for the assault).

Casualties: (a) 82,000; (b) 98,000.

Result: Although the British were forced to abandon the gains made during the THIRD BATTLE OF YPRES and the Germans captured MESSINES RIDGE, the offensive failed.

The principal effect of 'Georgette' was further to deplete the ranks of Ludendorff's storm troop battalions, which were of far higher quality than the rest of the German Army.

Ludendorff's Offensives (3): 'Blücher' (The Third Battle of the Aisne) 311

Date: 27 May to 6 June 1918.

Location: A 30-mile sector of the Western Front stretching from Noyon eastwards

along the Chemin des Dames to Rheims, extending south-westwards in a deep salient to the Marne.
War and campaign: First World War: Western Front.
Opposing sides: (a) Marshal Ferdinand Foch, Allied Supreme Commander; (b) General Erich Ludendorff, First Quatermaster-General of the German Army.
Objective: The German intention was to force the French to withdraw their reserves from Flanders prior to launching a final and decisive offensive against the British.
Forces engaged: (a) General Jacques Duchêne commanding the French Sixth Army with seventeen divisions, of which four were British, joined on 2 June by General Micheler's Fifth Army on the right and General Maistre's Tenth Army on the left as the salient developed; (b) General Baron von Bohn and General Fritz von Below commanding, respectively, the German Seventh and First Armies.
Casualties: Heavy on both sides and comparable to the two earlier offensives. The Germans claimed the capture of 55,000 prisoners and 650 guns.
Result: Although the Germans won a great tactical victory which took them across the Aisne and on to the Marne, the effects of this were counter-productive.

Ludendorff allowed himself to be diverted from his original objective by the prospect on a drive on Paris, and too few troops were available to man the extended line formed by the new salient.

Ludendorff's Offensives (4): 'Gneisenau' (The Battle of Noyon-Montdidier)   312

Date: 9–13 June 1918.
Location: 25-mile stretch of front between Noyon and Montdidier, north of Compiègne.
War and campaign: First World War: Western Front.
Opposing sides: (a) Marshal Ferdinand Foch, Allied Supreme Commander; (b) General Erich Ludendorff, First Quartermaster-General of the German Army.
Objective: Intended to shorten the line between the salients gained in 'BLÜCHER' and 'MICHAEL' and to secure the railway system leading through Compiègne to Paris.
Forces engaged: (a) General Charles Mangin and General Georges Humbert commanding, respectively, the French Tenth and Third Armies, with 165 tanks in support; (b) General Oskar von Hutier and General Max von Bohn commanding, respectively, the German Eighteenth and Seventh Armies.
Casualties: (a) 35,000 and 70 tanks; (b) approximately 35,000.
Result: In practical terms, the offensive achieved nothing. Some of the ground gained during the early hours of the offensive was lost to French counter-attacks.

The Allies were now familiar with the new German method of attack and had begun to evolve methods of dealing with it. See MARNE, SECOND BATTLE OF THE .

Lundy's Lane   313

Date: 25 July 1814.

Location: The site now occupied by the town of Niagara, Ontario, Canada.
War and campaign: War of 1812: Canadian Front.
Opposing sides: (a) General Sir Gordon Drummond; (b) Major-General Jacob Brown.
Objective: Having been defeated at CHIPPEWA by the invading American army, the British withdrew to await reinforcements and then advanced again. The two armies clashed at Lundy's Lane.
Forces engaged: (a) 1,000, rising to 3,000; (b) 1,000, rising to 2,600.
Casualties: (a) 84 killed, 559 wounded and 235 missing or captured; (b) 171 killed, 572 wounded and 110 missing or captured.
Result: The British had marginally the better of the most bitterly contested action of the war. Brown withdrew to Fort Erie, which he successfully held against Drummond, but on 5 November he abandoned the fort. No further attempts were made to invade Canada.

The battle, much of it fought out in darkness at close quarters, lasted for five hours. Scott's brigade, which had distinguished itself at CHIPPEWA and was the best in the American army, lost over half its remaining strength. Casualties among senior officers were high on both sides: Drummond, Brown and Scott were wounded and Riall, who had commanded the British at Chippewa, was wounded and captured.

Lutter 314

Date: 27 August 1626.
Location: Close by Lutter Castle, near Wolfenbüttel, south-west of Brunswick.
War and campaign: Thirty Years' War, 1618–1648: Danish Intervention, 1625–1629.
Opposing sides: (a) King Christian IV of Denmark commanding the Danish/North German Protestant army; (b) Count John Tzerklaes de Tilly commanding the Imperialist/Catholic army.
Objective: The Protestant army, withdrawing towards Brunswick, turned to make a stand against its pursuers.
Forces engaged: (a) 15,000; (b) 26,000.
Casualties: (a) 6,500 killed, wounded and captured, plus 22 guns captured; (b) uncertain, but moderate.
Result: Christian's army was overrun and destroyed. The defeat, following that at DESSAU, brought the fortunes of the Protestant cause to a low ebb and many anti-Imperialist princes made peace. Denmark, thrown on to the defensive, sustained further reverses and in 1629 she withdrew from the war. These Imperialist successes so alarmed the French Cardinal Richelieu that he supported the intervention of Sweden's King Gustavus Adolphus in the German war – see BREITENFELD, FIRST BATTLE OF.

Lützen (1632) 315

Date: 16 November 1632.
Location: 15 miles south-west of Leipzig.

War and campaign: Thirty Years' War, 1618–1648: German Campaign of 1632.
Opposing sides: (a) Gustavus Adolphus commanding the Swedish army; (b) General Albrecht von Wallenstein commanding the Imperialists.
Objective: The Imperialist-Catholic army, attempting to sever Swedish communications with the Baltic, was pursued and brought to battle.
Forces engaged: (a) 200 infantry companies, 178 cavalry squadrons and 20 guns – total 19,000; (b) 102 infantry companies, 203 cavalry squadrons and 30 guns – total 19,200, joined by a further 8,000 cavalry under Pappenheim during the course of the action.
Casualties: (a) 5,000 killed and wounded, including Gustavus Adolphus mortally wounded; (b) 6,000 killed and wounded and all guns lost.
Result: A hard-won Swedish victory which destroyed the Imperialist strategy.

The death of Gustavus Adolphus deprived the Protestant cause of a great champion.

Lützen (1813) 316

Date: 2 May 1813.
Location: Town 13 miles south-west of Leipzig, Germany.
War and campaign: War of the Sixth Coalition, 1812–1814: Campaign in Germany, 1813.
Opposing sides: (a) The Emperor Napoleon I commanding the French army; (b) General Ludwig Wittgenstein and Prince Gerhard von Blücher commanding the Allied army.
Objective: A combined Russo-Prussian army had surprised Ney's corps and Napoleon, quickly concentrating the rest of his army, mounted a counter-attack.
Forces engaged: (a) 100,000; (b) 73,000.
Casualties: (a) 22,000; (b) 20,000.
Result: The Allies withdrew after their centre had been broken by concentrated artillery fire followed by an infantry attack.

Napoleon went on to capture Dresden on 9 May. See BAUTZEN.

Mafeking 317

Date: 13 October 1899 to 17 May 1900.
Location: Town on the Transvaal/Bechuanaland border, situated on the Cape Colony–Southern Rhodesia railway, 250 miles north of Kimberley.
War and campaign: Second Boer War, 1899–1902.
Opposing sides: (a) Colonel Robert Baden-Powell commanding the garrison; (b) General Piet Cronje commanding the Boer commandos in the area until mid-November, then General J. P. Snyman.
Objective: The Boers were besieging the town.
Forces engaged: (a) 745 plus 450 irregulars, four ancient muzzle-loading 7pdr cannon and two 'home made' guns, seven medium and two heavy machine guns and one 'home made' armoured train; (b) initially 10,000 (reduced to 4,000 after

Cronje's departure for KIMBERLEY), ten Krupp 12pdr field guns (reduced to four after Cronje's departure) and one Creusot heavy gun.
Casualties: (a) 212 killed and wounded; (b) over 500 killed, plus an unknown number of wounded.
Result: The garrison was relieved by the combined mounted columns of Colonel Bryan Mahon and Lieutenant-Colonel (later Field Marshal Lord) Herbert Plumer.

Although Mafeking possessed no strategic significance, its possession became a point of honour to both sides. Baden-Powell's real achievement lay in tying down so many Boers at a critical period of the war, but his energetic and imaginative defence, involving such features as dummy minefields, made him a national hero and later assisted him when he founded the Scout movement. The news that Mafeking had been relieved was greeted with such wild enthusiasm in the United Kingdom that for many years afterwards the term 'maffick', meaning to exult riotously, remained in popular use and can still be found in numerous dictionaries.

Magdeburg, Siege of   318

Date: November 1630 to 20 May 1631.
Location: Fortified city on the Elbe, 70 miles south-west of Berlin.
War and campaign: Thirty Years' War, 1618–1648.
Opposing sides: (a) Dietrich von Falkenberg commanding the Protestant garrison; (b) Count Gottfried zu Pappenheim, succeeded by Count John Tzerlkaes de Tilly, commanding the besiegers.
Objective: The Imperial/Catholic army wished to secure the city as its principal base in northern Germany.
Forces engaged: (a) Uncertain; (b) 22,000.
Casualties: (a) Only 5,000 of the original population of 30,000 survived the sack and subseqent holocaust; (b) uncertain, but heavy.
Result: The approach of a relieving army under Gustavus Adolphus led to the defences' being stormed after three days' fighting.

The city was given over to three days of massacre, rape and looting, at the end of which it was completely destroyed by fire, the causes of which have never been ascertained. This in itself deprived Tilly of the base he sought, but the episode, savage even by the standards of the Thirty Years' War, was counter-productive in that it caused widespread revulsion throughout Europe and actually brought Saxony and the Netherlands into the Protestant camp. For years afterwards Imperialist soldiers requesting mercy were given 'Magdeburg quarter' and killed on the spot; both Tilly and Pappenheim met their deaths the following year, the former at the Battle of the Lech (15/16 April) and the latter at LÜTZEN (16 November). See also BREITENFELD, FIRST BATTLE OF.

Magenta   319

Date: 4 June 1859.
Location: 14 miles west of Milan, Lombardy, Italy.

War and campaign: Italian Wars of Independence.
Opposing sides: (a) Marshal Edme-Patrice-Maurice MacMahon commanding the Franco-Piedmontese Army; (b) General Count Eduard von Clam-Gallas commanding the Austrian army.
Objective: An encounter battle, provoked when the Franco-Piedmontese army invaded Lombardy.
Forces engaged: (a) 49,517 French and Italians; (b) 53,183 Austrians.
Casualties: (a) 4,000 killed and wounded and 600 missing; (b) 5,700 killed and wounded and 4,500 missing.
Result: The Austrians were defeated and forced to retreat.

Napoleon III and King Victor Emmanuel entered Milan in triumph. See also SOLFERINO.

Magersfontein 320

Date: 10–11 December 1899.
Location: 14 miles south of Kimberley, Cape Colony, South Africa.
War and campaign: Second Boer War, 1899–1902.
Opposing sides: (a) Lieutenant-General Lord Methuen; (b) Generals Piet Cronje and Jacobus De La Rey.
Objective: Having achieved a limited success at the MODDER RIVER, a British relief force was attempting to fight its way through to KIMBERLEY.
Forces engaged: (a) 14,000 men and 27 guns; (b) 7,000 men, five guns and three heavy machine guns.
Casualties: (a) 120 killed and 690 wounded; (b) 87 killed and 213 wounded.
Result: Methuen was defeated and the attempt to relieve Kimberley was temporarily abandoned.

Magersfontein was the second of the three reverses in six days, collectively known as 'Black Week', which seriously shook British confidence, the others being STORMBERG and COLENSO.

Maida 321

Date: 4 July 1806.
Location: Village 12 miles west of Catanzaro, Calabria, southern Italy.
War and campaign: War of the Third Coalition: Mediterranean theatre of war.
Opposing sides: (a) General Sir John Stuart; (b) General Jean Reynier.
Objective: A British amphibious raid intended to support guerrillas opposed to Joseph Bonaparte, recently installed as King of Naples.
Forces engaged: (a) 5,000; (b) 6,440.
Casualties: (a) 387; (b) 1,785.
Result: A British victory which temporarily cleared Lower Calabria of the French.

The French soon began concentrating troops in the area and Stuart withdrew his force to Sicily. Maida Vale in London takes its name from the battle.

Maiwand   322

Date: 27 July 1880.	
Location: 45 miles west of Kandahar, southern Afghanistan.	
War and campaign: Second Afghan War, 1878–1880.	
Opposing sides: (a) Brigadier-General G. R. S. Burrowes; (b) Ayub Khan.	
Objective: Ayub Khan claimed the throne of Afghanistan and had provoked a rising in the west of the country. A British brigade was despatched from Kandahar to support government troops in halting his advance on the city, but the latter deserted and the brigade commander unwisely decided to attempt the task alone.	
Forces engaged: (a) 2,700 and twelve guns; (b) 25,000 (including 10,000 regulars) and 30 guns.	
Casualties: (a) 971 killed and 168 wounded, plus eight guns captured or abandoned; (b) unknown, but personnel casualties may have been comparable.	
Result: Outflanked and subjected to overwhelming firepower, the British brigade was effectively destroyed.	

Thanks largely to a self-sacrificial stand by the 66th (Royal Berkshire) Regiment and the fire of E/B Battery Royal Horse Artillery's remaining guns, the remnants of Burrowes' command reached KANDAHAR, which was promptly besieged by Ayub Khan. A relief column, commanded by Lieutenant-General Sir Frederick Roberts, was despatched from Kabul on 8 August.

Majuba Hill   323

Date: 27 February 1881.	
Location: On the edge of the Drakensberg mountains, four miles west of the Newcastle–Standerton road, Natal.	
War and campaign: First Boer War, 1880–1881.	
Opposing sides: (a) Major-General Sir George Colley; (b) P. J. Joubert, commanding the Boer commandos.	
Objective: Colley's motive in occupying the hill remains obscure. The Boers believed, perhaps correctly, that he was attempting to outflank their position at Laing's Nek and were determined to recapture the feature.	
Forces engaged: (a) Total engaged approximately 650, of whom some 400 held the summit of the hill; (b) less than 2,000.	
Casualties: (a) 90 killed (including Colley), 133 wounded, 58 captured and two missing; (b) one killed and five wounded.	
Result: The British force was driven off the hill.	

Following the defeats at LAING'S NEK and Majuba Hill, an armistice was concluded with the Boers and the Transvaal was granted self-government in April 1881. Unfortunately, the sharp lessons taught by Boer marksmanship, tactical flexibility and use of ground had largely been forgotten when war broke out again in 1899.

Maldon

Date: 11 August 991.
Location: South-east of Maldon, Essex, beside the river Blackwater.
War and campaign: Danish Raids on England.
Opposing sides: (a) Ealdorman Brihtnoth commanding the English army; (b) Olaf Tryggvason.
Objective: The Danes occupied Northey Island in the river, connected to the mainland by a tidal causeway. They requested, and were granted, permission to cross the causeway and form up for a pitched battle, which both sides desired.
Forces engaged: (a) Brihtnoth's hearth-guard and the local fyrd – total probably not more than 2,500; (b) about the same.
Casualties: (a) Unknown, but heavy (Brihtnoth was killed); (b) unknown, but heavy.
Result: The English were defeated. The weak Aethelred the Unready made the first payment of Danegeld demanded by the victors (£10,000), in return for their departure. Thus encouraged, the Danes returned regularly in greater numbers. See ASHINGDON.

Brihtnoth has been criticized for permitting the Danes to cross the causeway, but he was an experienced commander and his decision can be justified on two counts. First, the Danes had their ships with them and could simply have gone elsewhere, although this might have involved Olaf in some loss of face; second, he wished to engage the elusive raiders in a decisive battle while the opportunity existed. Standing 6ft 9in tall, Brihtnoth exercised a commanding presence over his men and, despite being 65 years of age, played a vigorous part in the fighting. When he was killed much of the English army melted away but his hearth-guard made an epic stand around his body until they were overwhelmed by weight of numbers. The Danes, baldy mauled and exhausted, did not attempt a pursuit.

Maloyaroslavets

Date: 24 October 1812.
Location: Town 70 miles south-west of Moscow, Russia.
War and campaign: War of the Sixth Coalition: Napoleon's Invasion of Russia, 1812.
Opposing sides: (a) Prince Eugene de Beauharnais; (b) General Dmitri Docturov.
Objective: Following BORODINO, Napoleon entered Moscow, which was burned by the Russians themselves. After waiting in vain for Tsar Alexander to acknowledge his peace overtures, he decided to withdraw on 19 October, selecting a south-westerly axis which would enable the Grand Army to renew its supplies of food and fodder in the Kaluga region. Near Maloyaroslavets, however, his advanced guard found a Russian force blocking the route forward.
Forces engaged: (a) 15,000; (b) 20,000.
Casualties: (a) 5,000; (b) 6,000.
Result: Tactically a drawn battle.

The strategic consequences of the battle were extremely important. Napoleon abandoned his attempt to reach Kaluga and decided instead to retreat via Smolensk, along an axis which had already been stripped bare by his own troops and laid waste by the Russians as part of their scorched-earth policy. With the onset of winter imminent, the results of this decision were catastrophic. See BEREZINA RIVER.

Malplaquet 326

Date: 11 September 1709.
Location: Village 10 miles south of Mons on the Franco-Belgian border.
War and campaign: War of Spanish Succession, 1701–1714: Netherlands Campaign of 1709.
Opposing sides: (a) The Duke of Marlborough and Prince Eugene of Savoy commanding the Allied army; (b) Marshals the Dukes Claude de Villars and Louis de Boufflers commanding the French.
Objective: Following their victory at OUDENARDE, the Allies intended to capture Mons, destroy the French army which had marched to its relief and then advance on Paris.
Forces engaged: (a) 128 infantry battalions, 253 cavalry squadrons and 100 guns – total 110,000; (b) 96 infantry battalions, 180 cavalry squadrons and 60 guns – total 80,000.
Casualties: (a) 6,500 killed and 14,000 wounded, including Prince Eugene; (b) 4,500 killed and 8,000 wounded, including Villars.
Result: The French were forced out of their carefully prepared defences after seven hours of severe fighting.

The cost to the Allies was such that, while they captured Mons on 26 October, they abandoned the idea of advancing on Paris and went into winter quarters. In the long term, French morale was restored by the battle. Malplaquet was Marlborough's last and most expensive victory. His enemies at court did not hesitate to use the heavy casualty figures to weaken his position and by 1711 this had been so severely undermined that he was recalled.

Malta, The Great Siege of 327

Date: 19 May to 11 September 1565.
Location: Around Grand Harbour, centred on Fort St Elmo and the Birgu and Senglea peninsulas.
War and campaign: Turkish Wars of the Sixteenth Century.
Opposing sides: (a) Jean de la Valette, Grand Master of the Knights of St John; (b) Mustapha Pasha and Admiral Piali in joint command of the besiegers.
Objective: The Turkish intention was to capture the island and so deprive the Knights of St John of their base in the Mediterranean.
Forces engaged: (a) 700 knights, 8,500 men-at-arms and 80 guns – total 9,200; (b) 32,000 (including 6,000 janissaries) and 100 guns, reinforced regularly during the siege.
Casualties: (a) 250 knights and 3,000 men-at-arms killed, 400 knights and 5,000

men-at-arms wounded; (b) a minimum estimate of 20,000 dead from battle casualties and disease.

Result: The arrival of a small Spanish relief army under Garcia de Toledo led the demoralized survivors of the Turkish army to abandon the siege and sail home. Malta's stand halted the westward advance of Islam in the Mediterranean. See also MOHACS (1526).

Both sides fought with the utmost ferocity and determination. The capture of Fort St Elmo, for example, cost the Turks no fewer than 8,000 casualties, and lives were spent as freely in desperate attempts to carry the remaining fortifications. By the end of the siege only 600 of the garrison were capable of manning the defences, this figure including a high proportion of walking wounded.

Manchuria 328

Date: 9–17 August 1945.

Location: All of Manchuria, with action focused on the cities of Harbin and Mukden (Shenyang), extending southwards into northern Korea.

War and campaign: Second World War: China and Eastern Asia.

Opposing sides: (a) Marshal Alexandr Vasilevsky, Commander-in-Chief of Soviet forces in the Far East; (b) General Yamada Otozo commanding the Japanese Kwantung Army Group.

Objective: Stalin, having declared war against Japan on 8 August 1945, was determined to occupy Japanese-held Manchuria (then known as Manchukuo), thereby enabling the USSR to claim its share of the spoils arising from the inevitable Allied victory in the Far East.

Forces engaged: (a) Trans-Baikal Front (Malinovsky), 1st Far Eastern Front (Meretskov) and 2nd Far Eastern Front (Purkeyev), 5,550 tanks, 28,000 artillery weapons and 4,370 aircraft – total 1,600,000; (b) Kwantung Army Group, 1,155 tanks, 5,360 artillery weapons and 1,800 aircraft – total 1,040,000.

Casualties: (a) 8,219 killed and 22,264 wounded; (b) estimated 84,000 killed and 594,000 captured.

Result: The Japanese, untrained for mechanized war, were quickly routed by the converging thrusts of the Soviet Fronts.

In the long term, the imposition of Communist rule in North Korea led to the Korean War, 1950–1953.

Mandalay/Meiktila 329

Date: 14 January to 21 March 1945.

Location: Central Burma, on the plains east of the Irrawaddy and south of Mandalay.

War and campaign: Second World War: Burma.

Opposing sides: (a) General Sir William Slim commanding the British Fourteenth Army; (b) General Hoyotaro Kimura commanding the Burma Area Army.

Objective: The British intention was to destroy the Japanese Burma Area Army, thus ensuring the rapid reconquest of Burma and the re-opening of the road link between Burma and China.
Forces engaged: (a) IV Corps (Lieutenant-General F. W. Messervy) and XXXIII Corps (Lieutenant-General Montagu Stopford), each with one armoured brigade; (b) the Japanese Fifteenth Army (Lieutenant-General Katamura) with four divisions, plus reinforcements and one tank regiment.
Casualties: (a) Approximately 35,000, the majority wounded; (b) approximately 45,000, the majority killed.
Result: The complete defeat of Kimura's army group, followed by the pursuit of its remnants to Rangoon.

Following his victories in the defensive battles at IMPHAL and KOHIMA, Slim took the offensive and, having noted Kimura's dispositions along the Irrawaddy, planned a series of operations which would lead to the destruction of the Japanese armies in Burma. In January–February 1945 XXXIII Corps established bridgeheads across the Irrawaddy on either side of Mandalay, deliberately attracting repeated counter-attacks. Meanwhile, in great secrecy, IV Corps had moved down through the Kabaw and Gangaw valleys and on 13 February crossed the Irrawaddy at Pakokku, 100 miles downstream from Mandalay. The enemy's communications centre at Meiktila was then captured by a fast-moving armoured column. The effect of this was to isolate not only the Fifteenth Army, grouped around Mandalay, but also the Thirty-Third Army confronting Lieutenant-General Dan Sultan's Chinese/American troops to the north, and it was described by the Japanese themselves as the master-stroke of the entire campaign. All attempts to recapture Meiktila failed and both Japanese fronts collapsed, Mandalay itself falling on 21 March. Slim then directed both corps to execute a parallel dash southwards to Rangoon before the monsoon broke; in fact, the city fell to XV Corps on 2 May in the last of a series of amphibious landings by which it had advanced along the Arakan coast. The combined effect of these operations was to isolate the Japanese Twenty-Eighth Army in the Arakan, and this was destroyed as it attempted to escape from Burma into Thailand.

Manila 330

Date: 3 February to 4 March 1945.
Location: Capital city of the Philippine Islands, located on Luzon.
War and campaign: Second World War: Liberation of the Philippines.
Opposing sides: (a) General Walter Krueger commanding the US Sixth Army; (b) General Tomoyuki Yamashita commanding the Japanese Fourteenth Area Army.
Objective: Contrary to the wishes of the Japanese army commander, the naval troops of the Manila garrison were determined to make a last stand.
Forces engaged: (a) Lieutenant-General Oscar Griswold commanding the US XIV Corps, supplemented by elements of the 11th Airborne Division; (b) Rear-Admiral Sanji Iwabuchi commanding the Manila garrison – total approximately 17,000 (mainly naval troops).
Casualties: (a) 1,000 killed and 5,500 wounded; (b) 16,665 killed.
Result: The Japanese gesture merely resulted in needless loss of life and the destruction of most of the city.

Mannerheim Line

Date: 30 November 1939 to 13 February 1940.
Location: A fortified zone stretching across the Karelian isthmus from the Gulf of Finland to Lake Ladoga (in 1939 part of Finland; now within Russia).
War and campaign: Second World War: Winter War between the USSR and Finland, 1939–1940.
Opposing sides: (a) Marshal Semyon Timoshenko commanding the Soviet armies in Finland; (b) Marshal Carl Gustav von Mannerheim, Commander-in-Chief of Finland's armed forces.
Objective: The Soviet armies were attempting to break through the defences and invade southern Finland.
Forces engaged: (a) The Soviet Seventh and Thirteenth Armies; (b) the Finnish II and III Corps under the command of Lieutenant-General Hugo Ostermann.
Casualties: (a) Never officially published, but believed to be approximately 200,000 killed and 400,000 wounded; (b) about 20,000 killed and 40,000 wounded.
Result: Timoshenko, disregarding the horrific losses inflicted on his troops, finally breached the defences on 13 February 1940. The Finns, lacking the manpower to hold a longer line, were forced to sue for peace.

The poor showing made by the Soviet Army in Finland convinced Hitler that it was no match for his own and was a major factor in his decision to invade the USSR. See also SUOMOSSALMI.

Mansfield (Sabine Crossroads)

Date: 8–9 April 1864.
Location: 4 miles south of Mansfield, Louisiana.
War and campaign: American Civil War: Red River Expedition.
Opposing sides: (a) Major-General Nathaniel P. Banks commanding the Federal army; (b) Major-General Richard Taylor commanding the Confederates.
Objective: The expedition was mounted with the strategic objectives of, first, destroying the Confederate forces beyond the Mississippi and, second, penetrating Texas via the Red River as a means of discouraging potential French intervention from Mexico. Near Mansfield the retreating Confederates decided to make a stand.
Forces engaged: (a) 7,000; (b) 8,800.
Casualties: (a) 113 killed, 581 wounded and 1,541 missing, plus twenty guns, 150 wagons and 1,000 horses captured; (b) approximately 1,000 killed, wounded and missing.
Result: The Federal vanguard was overwhelmed and Banks ordered a general withdrawal. Taylor followed up some 20 miles to Pleasant Hill, where a drawn battle was fought. Despite this, Banks's nerve was broken and the entire expedition was abandoned.

Overall, the consequences were that the Confederates were able to release some 15,000 troops from the Gulf states for service in Georgia while Sherman was forced to detach an entire corps which he planned to use in his advance on ATLANTA. See also KENNESAW MOUNTAIN.

Mansura

Date: 8–11 February 1250.

Location: On the Bahr-es-Seghir canal near Mansura, north of Cairo.

War and campaign: The Seventh Crusade, 1248–1254.

Opposing sides: (a) Louis IX, King of France; (b) the Emir Fakr-ed-Din, succeeded by Baibars Bundukdari.

Objective: The Crusaders, having landed at Damietta the previous year, had marched on Cairo but found their advance blocked on the line of the canal. The discovery of a ford enabled them to cross and attack the Egyptians.

Forces engaged: (a) 20,000 cavalry and 40,000 infantry – total 60,000 (mostly French); (b) 70,000, including 10,000 Mamelukes.

Casualties: (a) Ultimately most of the Crusader army were killed, died of disease or captured and sold into slavery though Louis and a handful were held to ransom; (b) initially heavy, including Fakr-ed-Din killed.

Result: The Crusader army was destroyed and the Crusade collapsed. The loss of men affected France for a generation.

The Crusader vanguard, commanded by Robert of Artois and including the Knights Templar and an English contingent, succeeded in crossing the canal and driving the Egyptians from their camp. Disobeying orders which required him to wait until the king crossed with the main body, Robert then charged into Mansura, where the vanguard was trapped and overwhelmed. For a while, the main body maintained itself in the bridgehead under heavy attack. However, decimated by disease and with its communications threatened, it attempted to withdraw to Damietta but was overwhelmed at Fariskur.

Marathon

Date: 490 BC.

Location: Beside the Bay of Marathon, 26 miles north-east of Athens.

War and campaign: The Graeco–Persian Wars, 499–448 BC: Persian expedition against Athens, 490 BC.

Opposing sides: (a) Callimachus and Miltiades commanding the Athenians and their Plataean allies; (b) the Persian generals Datis and Artaphernes.

Objective: The Persians had landed part of their army at Marathon, drawing the Athenians away from the city while the fleet, carrying the remainder, sailed round Attica with the intention of attacking Athens itself. The Athenians, however, interpreted the Persian plan correctly and decided to force a battle on the landing force at Marathon.

Forces engaged: (a) 10,000 Athenian hoplites and light troops, plus 1,000 Plataeans – total 11,000; (b) approximately 20,000.

Casualties: (a) 192 killed, including Callimachus; (b) 6,400 killed.

Result: The Persian landing force was driven back aboard its ships with heavy losses. The return of the victorious army to Athens forestalled the landing of the second Persian force, which sailed away. The victory encouraged the Greek states to resist further Persian invasions – see THERMOPYLAE and PLATAEA.

Before launching their attack, the Greeks waited until the Persian cavalry was absent from the battlefield, watering its horses at springs to the north – a decision based on information supplied by a deserter. Militiades, elected commander, extended his line to equal that of the Persians by thinning his centre but maintaining a twelve-deep phalanx on either flank. In the centre the Greeks were repulsed, but on both flanks the phalangites were victorious and when they swung inwards in a double envelopment the Persians broke and fled to their ships. Militiades despatched news of the victory to Athens by the famed runner Pheidippedes – an event still commemorated in the athletic event named after the battle – while the rest of the army followed by forced march.

Marengo   335

Date: 14 June 1800.
Location: Village 45 miles north of Genoa and 3 miles south-west of Alessandria, Italy.
War and campaign: War of the Second Coalition, 1798–1800: Italian Campaign.
Opposing sides: (a) Napoleon Bonaparte, First Consul of France, commanding the French Army of the Reserve; (b) General Baron Michael Melas commanding the Austrian Army of Italy.
Objective: The Austrians, having just taken Genoa, discovered that Bonaparte's march across the Great St Bernard Pass had placed his army across their lines of communication and had concentrated to deal with the threat.
Forces engaged: (a) 25,500 infantry, 2,000 cavalry and fifteen guns – total 28,000; (b) 26,000 infantry, 5,000 cavalry and 100 guns – total 31,000.
Casualties: (a) Approximately 6,000 killed and wounded; (b) 9,400 killed and wounded, 8,000 prisoners and 40 guns captured.
Result: After coming dangerously close to defeat, Bonaparte won a crushing victory. The following day Melas agreed to evacuate the whole of northern Italy west of the Mincio, ending the Italian Campaign.

Bonaparte, unaware that the Austrians had concentrated in the area of Alessandria, conducted a negligent advance with his corps widely dispersed. Thus he had only 18,000 men with which to meet Melas' attack and was driven back four miles. Melas, believing the battle won, failed to follow up his success, apparently unaware that the remaining French corps were converging on the battlefield. During the late afternoon General Louis Desaix's corps initiated counter-attacks against the Austrian front and flank and Melas' army was routed. Marengo was undoubtedly Desaix's victory, but he was killed in the fighting and, despite his own defeat during the early part of the action, Bonaparte was quick to claim the credit.

Mareth Line   336

Date: 20–27 March 1943.
Location: Defence line based on the Wadi Zigzaou, running from the Gulf of Gabes some 30 miles inland to the Matmata Hills, located within the Tunisian frontier with Libya.
War and campaign: Second World War: North Africa.
Opposing sides: (a) General Sir Bernard Montgomery commanding the British Eighth Army; (b) General Giovanni Messe commanding the Italian First Army.

> **Objective:** The British intention was to force the Axis to abandon the Mareth defences by a combination of direct assault and a threat to their inland flank.
>
> **Forces engaged:** (a) New Zealand Corps (Freyberg), plus elements of the British X Corps (Horrocks) and XXX Corps (Leese); (b) Italian XX Corps (Orlando) and XXI Corps (Berardi), plus elements of Panzergruppe Afrika.
>
> **Casualties:** (a) Unknown, but moderate; (b) unknown, but heavier than those of the British because of sustained low-level tactical support by the RAF.
>
> **Result:** Messe was forced to abandon the Mareth Line and retire to the line of the Wadi Akarit.

Having defeated Rommel's counter-attack at MEDENINE, Montgomery closed up to the Mareth Line and on 20 March the 50th Division (XXX Corps) established a bridgehead across the Wadi Zigzaou while the New Zealand Corps began a wide turning movement across the southern Matmata Hills. When determined counter-attacks halted further progress by the 50th Division, Montgomery switched the emphasis of his attack to the outflanking force and despatched the 1st Armoured Division (X Corps) along the same axis into the Tebaga Gap, breaking through the enemy's hastily formed defences there on 26 March. Only a rearguard action by the 21st Panzer Division enabled Messe to extract the defenders of the Mareth Line.

Marignano 337

> **Date:** 13–14 September 1515.
>
> **Location:** South of Milan near Melegnano and San Giuliano (precise site uncertain).
>
> **War and campaign:** French Sixteenth Century Wars in Italy: French Reconquest of the Duchy of Milan, 1515.
>
> **Opposing sides:** (a) King Francis I commanding the Franco-Venetian army; (b) Arnold von Winkelried commanding the Swiss.
>
> **Objective:** The Swiss marched out of Milan to engage the Franco-Venetian army which had interposed between them and their Spanish/Papal allies.
>
> **Forces engaged:** (a) 20,000 pikemen, 10,000 arquebusiers, 2,500 cavalry and 70 guns – total 32,500; (b) 22,000 infantry, 200 cavalry and eight guns – total 22,200.
>
> **Casualties:** (a) 6,000 killed and wounded; (b) 12,000 killed and wounded.
>
> **Result:** A decisive French victory which destroyed the myth of Swiss invincibility.

Francis occupied Milan and the anti-French alliance collapsed.

Marne, First Battle of the 338

> **Date:** 5–10 September 1914.
>
> **Location:** East of Paris and south of the Marne along the line of the Grand and Petit Morins as far east as Fère Champenois.
>
> **War and campaign:** First World War: Western Front.
>
> **Opposing sides:** (a) General Joseph Joffre, Commander-in-Chief of the French Army; (b) General Helmuth von Moltke, Chief of the German General Staff.

Objective: Initially an Allied spoiling counter-attack into the flank of the German First Army as it wheeled to the east.
Forces engaged: (a) The French Ninth Army (Foch) and Fifth Army (Franchet d'Esperey), the British Expeditionary Force (French) and the French Sixth Army (Manoury); (b) the German First Army (von Kluck), Second Army (von Bulow) and Third Army (von Hausen).
Casualties: Difficult to determine as the battle comprised more a series of manoeuvres than one of engagements. It did, however, mark the end of the first phase of fighting on the Western Front and it has been estimated that during this period, lasting three weeks, each side sustained in excess of half a million casualties.
Result: A clear-cut Allied victory which destroyed Moltke's plan of campaign in the West and induced a general retreat by the German armies.

Although Hausen's Third Army continued to make progress against Foch's Ninth, to the west Manoury's counter-stroke against Kluck's flank caused the latter to re-deploy and meet the threat. This opened a gap between the German First and Second Armies and, while this was penetrated by the BEF, Franchet d'Esperey took the offensive against Bulow. On 9 September, with the entire German right wing in danger, Moltke's personal emissary to the front, Lieutenant-Colonel Richard Hentsch, sanctioned Bulow's plan to withdraw and ordered Kluck to conform. Moltke ordered a general withdrawal to the line Noyon–Verdun; he was relieved by General Erich von Falkenhayn on 14 September. See AISNE, THE.

Marne, Second Battle of the (first phase also known as the Fourth Battle of Champagne) 339

Date: 15 July to 7 August 1918.
Location: From Chalons in the east to Soissons in the west.
War and campaign: First World War: Western Front.
Opposing sides: (a) Marshal Ferdinand Foch, Allied Supreme Commander; (b) General Erich Ludendorff, First Quartermaster-General of the German Army.
Objective: Commenced as Ludendorff's Fifth Offensive under the codename 'Marneschutz-Rheims', the object of which was to cross the Marne and achieve the isolation of Rheims by converging thrusts to the east and west of the city, and developed into a French strategic counter-offensive into the flank of the Marne salient, intended to remove the danger to Paris.
Forces engaged: (a) French Fourth (General Henri Gouraud), Fifth (General Henri Berthelot), Sixth (General Jean Degoutte), Ninth (General M. A. H. de Mitry and Tenth (General Charles Mangin) Armies, including strong American, British and Italian elements, plus 746 tanks (mainly light Renault FTs); (b) German Ninth (General von Eben), Seventh (General von Bohn), First (General von Mudra) and Third (General Karl von Einem) Armies, plus a small number of tanks (including captured British vehicles).
Casualties: Total German losses in Ludendorff's five offensives now exceeded half a million men, plus huge quantities of equipment; Allied losses were comparable.
Result: The Germans were halted and forced to retreat. The battle marked the point

of balance in the 1918 fighting on the Western Front. The Allies regained the strategic initiative and held it for the rest of the war.

Ludendorff made the mistake of describing the battle as the *Friedensturm*, implying a decisive victory that would bring peace. When it did not, the morale of his men was seriously affected while that of the Allies rose in proportion. Had he succeeded, Ludendorff intended resuming the offensive against the British under the codename 'Hagen', and he was actually engaged in planning this when the French counter-attack began. The German numerical superiority, achieved by the release of divisions from the Eastern Front following the collapse of Russia, had now evaporated, and as American troops were reaching France in large numbers the only alternative remaining to Ludendorff was to remain on the defensive. See AMIENS.

Mars-la-Tour (Vionville)   340

Date: 16 August 1870.
Location: 10 miles west of Metz, Lorraine, France.
War and campaign: Franco–Prussian War, 1870–1871.
Opposing sides: (a) Prince Friedrich Karl commanding the Second Army of the North German Confederation; (b) Marshal François-Achille Bazaine commanding the French Army of the Rhine.
Objective: The French, following their defeat at SPICHEREN, were attempting to withdraw from Metz towards Verdun but found that the Germans had cut their line of retreat.
Forces engaged: (a) Initially only III Corps (von Alvensleben), later joined by X Corps (Voigts-Rhetz) – total approximately 80,000; (b) approximately 127,000.
Casualties: (a) 15,780 killed and wounded; (b) 13,761 killed, wounded and missing.
Result: Tactically a drawn battle ending with both sides still in position. However, Bazaine was now more concerned with maintaining his communications with Metz than with breaking out towards Verdun and the west, and the following day he withdrew his army into a stronger defensive position along the line GRAVELOTTE–ST PRIVAT.

The battle witnessed the last great cavalry mêlée in Western European history. For the next forty years the successful but self-destructive 'death ride' of Major-General von Bredow's cavalry brigade was quoted as an argument for the retention of cavalry.

Marston Moor   341

Date: 2 July 1644.
Location: 6 miles west of York.
War and campaign: First Civil War, 1642–1646.
Opposing sides: (a) Prince Rupert commanding the Royalists; (b) a Council-of-War including Lord Ferdinando Fairfax and the Earls of Manchester and Leven commanding a concentration of the Parliamentary West Yorkshire, Eastern Association and Scottish armies.
Objective: Having relieved York, the Royalists unwisely offered battle to the larger Parliamentary army.

Forces engaged: (a) 11,000 infantry, 6,500 cavalry and sixteen guns – total 17,500; (b) 18,000 infantry, 9,000 cavalry and 25 guns – total 27,000.
Casualties: No accurate figures exist, although estimates place the Royalist and Parliamentary killed at 3,000 and 2,000 respectively; the number of wounded and desertions is unkown.
Result: A decisive Parliamentary victory which destroyed the Royalist cause in the north.

Although initially successful on its left, the Royalist cavalry on both flanks was contained by counter-attacks. A Parliamentary general advance then overwhelmed the outnumbered Royalist infantry in the centre after a bitter struggle. The remnants of Rupert's army disintegrated, leaving him with only 6,000 men with which he withdrew into Lancashire. When York surrendered on 16 July the Royalist presence in the north was reduced to a handful of beleaguered garrisons. Marston Moor was the largest battle of the war.

Masada, Siege of 342

Date: AD 73.
Location: Fortified mountain on the western shore of the Dead Sea, Israel.
War and campaign: Mopping-up operations following the Jewish Rebellion against Rome, AD 66–70.
Opposing sides: (a) Flavius Silva commanding the besiegers; (b) Eleazer, leader of the Zealots.
Objective: The Romans intended eliminating the last centre of resistance to their rule in Palestine.
Forces engaged: (a) The X Legion and auxiliaries – total perhaps 7,000; (b) initially more than 1,000, including families.
Casualties: (a) Unknown, but light; (b) with the exception of two women and five children who concealed themselves, all of those who survived the earlier fighting, 960 in number, committed suicide when it was apparent that the fortress was about to fall.
Result: The Romans took possession of the fortress.

The situation of Masada, set on a towering rock, made it impregnable, and as the garrison had ample supplies of food and water it could not be starved into submission. Silva therefore resorted to military engineering to solve his problem, constructing a 300ft high ramp, topped with a stone platform 75ft high on which an armoured siege tower was constructed, adding a further 90ft to the height of the siege works. Catapults drove the defenders from this sector of the walls, part of which was brought down with a ram. The Zealots reacted by building a timber and earth rampart to seal off the breach, but when the Romans set fire to this Eleazar exhorted all those present to take their own lives rather than submit. The modern Israeli saying 'Masada shall not fall again' shows the depths to which the story has inspired the Jewish people for 2,000 years.

Masurian Lakes 343

Date: 9–14 September 1914.

Location: South-east of Königsberg (Kaliningrad) along a front stretching south from Allenburg (Druzhba) to the Masurian Lakes, East Prussia (now in Russia and Poland).
War and campaign: First World War: Eastern Front.
Opposing sides: (a) General Helmuth von Moltke, Chief of the German General Staff; (b) General Yakov Zhilinsky commanding the North-West Front.
Objective: Following TANNENBERG (1914), the German Eighth Army re-deployed eastwards against the Russian First Army, the defeat of which would remove the remaining threat to East Prussia.
Forces engaged: (a) Colonel-General Paul von Hindenburg commanding the German Eighth Army (thirteen divisions); (b) General Pavel Rennenkampf commanding the Russian First Army (twelve divisions).
Casualties: (a) Approximately 10,000; (b) 45,000, including numerous prisoners, and 150 guns captured.
Result: The First Army was badly mauled although Rennenkampf managed to extract it from a double-envelopment and retreat into Russia.

Zhilinsky was dismissed and Allied confidence in the Russian Army was severely shaken.

Medenine 344

Date: 6 March 1943.
Location: Approximately 15 miles south-east of the MARETH LINE, Tunisia.
War and campaign: Second World War: North Africa.
Opposing sides: (a) Field Marshal Erwin Rommel commanding the Axis forces in southern Tunisia; (b) General Sir Bernard Montgomery commanding the British Eighth Army.
Objective: Having mounted a successful spoiling attack against the US II Corps in the area of the KASSERINE PASS, Rommel turned about with the intention of inflicting a similar check on the British Eighth Army as it approached the MARETH LINE.
Forces engaged: (a) 10th, 15th and 21st Panzer Divisions, 90th Light Division and the Italian Spezia Division; (b) reinforced XXX Corps (Leese).
Casualties: (a) Over 600 (two-thirds German) and about 50 tanks; (b) negligible.
Result: The Axis attack was repulsed by a text-book defence incorporating artillery concentrations and anti-tank guns which only opened fire at point-blank range.

After Medenine, Rommel, tired and ill, handed over command to von Arnim and returned to Germany.

Medway, The 345

Date: AD 43.
Location: Near Rochester, Kent.
War and campaign: Roman Conquest of Britain.
Opposing sides: (a) Aulus Plautius; (b) Caratacus and Togodumnus.

Objective: The Britons were attempting to prevent the Romans crossing the river.
Forces engaged: (a) Four legions (II Augusta, IX Hispana, XIV Gemina and XX Valeria) plus auxiliaries – total approximately 40,000; (b) estimates varying between 60,000 and 80,000 must be treated with caution, given the size of the population (nevertheless, the tribes has set aside their differences for the moment and an army of at least 40,000 is not improbable; in addition, the Britons deployed a large number of chariots which they employed in what would later be described as the mounted infantry role).
Casualties: (a) Unknown, but obviously acceptable; (b) unknown, but probably heavy (Togodumnus may have been mortally wounded during the fighting).
Result: The Romans won a decisive victory. They went on to secure a crossing of the Thames and capture Camulodunum (Colchester), Caratacus's capital. Many tribes sued for peace but Caratacus continued to fight a guerrilla war. This did not prevent the legions fanning out to the north and west so that by AD 47 Roman control was complete east of a line stretching from the Humber to the coast of Dorset.

During the first day's fighting the auxiliaries on the Roman right flank swam the river and mounted a diversionary attack. While the Britons were engaged in containing this, II Augusta, using boats and rafts for the crossing, secured a bridgehead on the left. As the remaining legions crossed, this was expanded and consolidated. The following day the Britons mounted fierce but abortive attacks against the bridgehead. The Roman strength increased steadily until the legions were able to break out of their perimeter and at this point the Britons, realizing that their defence of the river line had failed, disengaged.

Meeanee 346

Date: 17 February 1843.
Location: Village on the river Indus approximately 40 miles upstream from Hyderabad, Pakistan.
War and campaign: The British Conquest of Sind, 1843.
Opposing sides: (a) General Sir Charles Napier; (b) the Amirs of Sind.
Objective: The hostility of the Amirs of Sind to the East India Company had resulted in their besieging the British residency at Hyderabad (not to be confused with the city of the same name in southern India). A British relief column encountered the Amirs' army at Meeanee.
Forces engaged: (a) 2,600 British and Indian troops; (b) approximately 20,000 Baluchis.
Casualties: (a) 256 killed and wounded; (b) approximately 5,000 killed and wounded, plus several guns captured.
Result: The Amirs were defeated.

Napier was a veteran of the Peninsula War and, despite his 61 years, personally led his men into action with a musket and bayonet. At Meeanee he had only one British unit, the 22nd (Cheshire) Regiment (500 strong), at his disposal and, believing that a defensive stance would unsettle his native regiments, he attacked at once. Napier also won a second victory at Hyderabad on 24 March and relieved the residency. By August he had brought the campaign to a successful conclusion, advising the Governor General of the fact with his famous Latin cryptogram *Peccavi* ('I have sinned'). The conquest of

Sind, coupled with the First and Second Sikh Wars (1845–1846 and 1848–1849), extended the Company's rule beyond the Indus and established the North-West Frontier.

Megiddo (1469 BC)   347

Date: 1469 BC.
Location: Fortified city close to the Plain of Esdraelon, Israel.
War and campaign: Rebellion by the Kings of Megiddo and Kadesh against the authority of Egypt.
Opposing sides: (a) Pharaoh Thutmosis III commanding the Egyptian army; (b) the King of Megiddo commanding the rebel army.
Objective: The Egyptian intention was to destroy the rebel army and capture Megiddo.
Forces engaged: Unknown, although a full mobilization of the Egyptian army seems to have taken place, suggesting that the size of the rebel army was also considerable.
Casualties: Unknown, but those of the rebel army were the greater.
Result: The rebel army was routed and fled into the city, which surrendered after a siege of three weeks. The rebellion was crushed, although the Kings of Megiddo and Kadesh seem to have escaped.

Megiddo is the first recorded battle in history. Thutmosis achieved surprise by personally leading his troops through a narrow defile in the hills south of the city, probably by night. Mounting a holding action against one flank of the rebel army, he then turned the other with his main assault, which he again led personally. Believing that Megiddo could have been taken in the immediate aftermath of the battle, he was angry with his troops when they interrupted their pursuit to plunder the enemy camp.

Megiddo (1918)   348

Date: 18 September to 31 October 1918.
Location: From a line extending eastwards from Arsuf on the Mediterranean coast to beyond the river Jordan, and the area north of this to the Sea of Galilee, Israel.
War and campaign: First World War: Palestine.
Opposing sides: (a) General Sir Edmund Allenby commanding the British army in Palestine; (b) General Liman von Sanders commanding the Turkish army group in Palestine.
Objective: The British intention was to strike a decisive blow against the Turkish armies in Palestine.
Forces engaged: (a) XX Corps (Lt-General Sir Philip Chetwode), XXI Corps including a small French contingent (Lt-General Sir Edward Bulfin) and the Desert Mounted Corps (Lt-General Sir Harry Chauvel) – total 57,000 infantry, 12,000 cavalry and 400 guns; (b) the Turkish Eighth Army including the German Asia Corps (total 10,000 men and 157 guns), Seventh Army (7,000 men and 111 guns) and Fourth Army including one German regiment (total 8,000 men and 74 guns) commanded by, respectively, Djevad Pasha, Mustafa Kemal and Djemal Kucuk, plus, in army group reserve, 3,000 men and 30 guns.
Casualties: (a) 782 killed, 4,179 wounded and 382 missing; (b) killed and wounded

unknown, but 76,000 captured including 4,000 Germans and Austrians, plus 360 guns and much other material.
Result: One of the most complete victories in the history of warfare. The three Turkish armies were destroyed and Allenby had advanced 350 miles before Turkey requested an armistice on 31 October.

Required to send troops to France to contain the LUDENDORFF OFFENSIVES, Allenby had to wait until his strength was restored before striking the decisive blow. The preparatory phase of the battle included an elaborate deception plan which convinced Sanders that the main blow would fall in the Jordan valley rather than on the coastal sector as Allenby intended. Once a breach had been made in the enemy defences, the Desert Mounted Corps passed through and wheeled north-eastwards across the rear of the Turkish armies, blocking their withdrawal and capturing Sanders' headquarters in Nazareth; beyond the Jordan, Lawrence's Arab irregulars harried Kucuk's Fourth Army without mercy. Latterly the spearhead element of the British advance consisted of armoured car units. During the battle itself the Palestine squadrons of the newly formed Royal Air Force provided the closest possible tactical support, beginning with the destruction of Sanders' command telephone network. At dawn on 21 September the airmen discovered Kemal's Seventh Army attempting to escape through the Wadi Far'a and strafed it continuously for four hours, so providing the first instance of unaided air power completing the destruction of an army.

Messines Ridge 349

Date: 7–14 June 1917.
Location: South of the Ypres salient, Belgium.
War and campaign: First World War: Western Front.
Opposing sides: (a) Field Marshal Sir Douglas Haig commanding the British armies in France and Belgium; (b) General Erich Ludendorff, First Quartermaster-General of the German Army.
Objective: The British needed to capture the dominant ridge prior to opening the THIRD BATTLE OF YPRES.
Forces engaged: (a) General Sir Herbert Plumer, commanding the British Second Army; (b) General Sixt von Arnim and General Otto von Below commanding, respectively, the German Fourth and Sixth Armies.
Casualties: (a) 17,000; (b) 25,000, including 7,500 prisoners.
Result: The capture of the ridge during an advance of 2½ miles on a 10-mile front during the first day.

Plumer's well-planned operation involved tunnelling beneath the German front line and the explosion of nineteen mines containing over a million pounds of ammonal just before the main assault, with the result that the enemy's forward defences were blown out of existence. The best known of these mines was located beneath Hill 60 at the northern end of the ridge.

Metaurus, The 350

Date: 207 BC.

Location: South of the Metaurus near the modern village of Sant' Angelo, 4 miles south of Fano on the Adriatic coast of Italy.
War and campaign: Second Punic War, 219–202 BC.
Opposing sides: (a) The Consuls Marcus Livius and Claudius Nero; (b) Hasdrubal commanding a Carthaginian army.
Objective: In 208 BC Hannibal had ordered his brother Hasdrubal to join him in Italy and the latter had marched from Spain and spent the winter in southern France before crossing the Alps in the spring. The Romans intercepted correspondence between the brothers and decided to destroy Hasrdubal's army before the two could combine their resources.
Forces engaged: (a) 50,000; (b) 50,000, plus an unknown number of war elephants.
Casualties: (a) 2,000; (b) 10,000 including Hasdrubal killed.
Result: Hasdrubal's army was defeated and its remnants dispersed. The victory not only restored the morale of the Roman army but also recovered the strategic initiative from the Carthaginians. See ZAMA.

Nero commanded an army which was watching Hannibal in the south, but on learning of Hasdrubal's approach he detached 6,000 infantry and 1,000 cavalry and embarked on a forced march of 250 miles in seven days to reinforce Livius. Hasdrubal's troops were deployed with the Spaniards on the right, the Ligurians in the centre and the Gauls on the left. The last were separated by a steep ravine from Nero's troops on the Roman right and, as this made engagement impossible, Nero used the dead ground to his rear to lead several cohorts south, where they fell on the flank and rear of the unsuspecting Spaniards, rolling up the Carthaginian line. The Ligurians, whose ranks had become disordered when their elephants, after some success in the first shock of battle, took fright and became unmanageable, also gave way when they saw the rout of the Spaniards. Hasdrubal, seeing the battle lost, deliberately rode into a Roman cohort and was killed fighting.

Metz 351

Date: 19 August to 27 October 1870.
Location: City and fortress on the Moselle, northern Lorraine, France.
War and campaign: Franco–Prussian War, 1870–1871.
Opposing sides: (a) Prince Friedrich Karl commanding the First and Second Armies of the North German Confederation; (b) Marshal François-Achille Bazaine commanding the French Army of the Rhine.
Objective: The Germans were besieging the fortress, which contained the better part of the French army.
Forces engaged: (a) 197,000 men and 658 field and siege guns; (b) 173,000 men, 622 field guns and 876 pieces of fortress artillery.
Casualties: (a) Approximately 47,000 from all causes (including sickness); (b) the entire garrison, which had incurred 38,000 casualties from all causes (including sickness), surrendered with all its artillery, 72 *mitrailleuses*, 300,000 rifles and 56 eagles.
Result: By tamely permitting his army to be besieged in Metz, Bazaine also created the situation which led to the disaster at SEDAN.

Bazaine's surrender released two German armies for use elsewhere in France. After the war he was court-martialled, found guilty of treason and sentenced to twenty years' imprisonment.

Meuse-Argonne 352

Date: 26 September to 11 November 1918.
Location: 35-mile stretch of front west of Verdun, extending northwards from the Argonne Forest to Sedan.
War and campaign: First World War: Western Front.
Opposing sides: (a) Marshal Ferdinand Foch, Allied Supreme Commander; (b) General Erich Ludendorff, First Quartermaster-General of the German Army, replaced by General Wilhelm Groener on 27 October.
Objective: Part of the general Allied advance on the Western Front. The specific objective of this operation was the German rail and supply centre of Mezières near Sedan.
Forces engaged: (a) General John J. Pershing commanding the US First Army (until 12 October, then Major-General Hunter Liggett), General H. J. E. Gouraud commanding the French Fourth Army and Major-General Robert Bullard commanding the US Second Army (formed on 12 October) – total 22 American and six French divisions (approximately 500,000 men), plus tank support; (b) Colonel-General Karl von Einem and General Max von Gallwitz commanding, respectively, the German Third and Fifth Armies – total 43 divisions (approximately 470,000 men).
Casualties: (a) 117,000; (b) approximately 126,000.
Result: The Allied advance had reached Sedan by the time the Armistice came into force on 11 November. See also HINDENBURG LINE.

Minden 353

Date: 1 August 1759.
Location: 4 miles north-west of Minden, Westphalia, Germany.
War and campaign: Seven Years' War, 1756–1763: West German Campaign of 1759.
Opposing sides: (a) Duke Ferdinand of Brunswick commanding the Allied army consisting of British, Hanoverian, Hessian and Prussian elements; (b) Marshal the Marquis Louis de Contades commanding the French army.
Objective: The Allied army was attempting to reopen its communications with Hanover.
Forces engaged: (a) 46 infantry battalions, 61 cavalry squadrons and 187 guns – total 42,500; (b) 80 infantry battalions, 61 cavalry squadrons and 170 guns – total 54,000.
Casualties: (a) 2,762, including 1,330 British; (b) 7,086 killed, wounded and prisoners and 43 guns captured.
Result: An Allied victory which removed the French threat to Hanover.

Following the receipt of an ambiguously worded order, six British and three Hanoverian infantry battalions advanced *in line* against the mass of cavalry in the centre of Contades' army, contrary to all the usual practices. In an astonishing display of discipline, courage and aggression, they repulsed three cavalry charges in succession, then went on to break the French infantry in the centre. The six British units were later known, respectively, as the Suffolk Regiment, the Lancashire Fusiliers, the Royal Welch Fusiliers, the King's Own Scottish Borderers, the Royal Hampshire Regiment and the King's Own Yorkshire Light Infantry; they, and their successors, celebrate the achievement annually on what is known to them as Minden Day. A charge by the British cavalry would have turned the French defeat into a rout, but its commander, Lord George Sackville, refused to obey three specific orders to attack. The cavalry was to recover its honour at WARBURG, but Sackville was court-martialled and dismissed from the service. However, he became a favourite of George III, and as Lord George Germain, Secretary of State for America, he was to make a major contribution to the loss of the American colonies (he was, *inter alia*, in favour of the operations in Virginia which culminated in the British surrender at YORKTOWN).

Modder River   354

Date: 28 November 1899.
Location: 20 miles south of Kimberley, Cape Colony (now South Africa).
War and campaign: Second Boer War, 1899–1902.
Opposing sides: (a) Lieutenant-General Lord Methuen; (b) Generals Piet Cronje and Jacobus De La Rey.
Objective: A British relief force was attempting to fight its way through to KIMBERLEY.
Forces engaged: (a) 10,000 men and twenty guns; (b) 6,000 men, six guns and three heavy machine guns.
Casualties: (a) 72 killed and 396 wounded; (b) 80 killed and wounded.
Result: After a 10-hour firefight the Boers withdrew several miles from the river line.

As his troops were exhausted, Methuen decided to await the arrival of reinforcements before resuming his march on Kimberley. See MAGERSFONTEIN.

Mohacs (1526)   355

Date: 29 August 1526.
Location: Town on the Danube near the southern frontier of Hungary.
War and campaign: Turkish Wars of the Sixteenth Century: Invasion of Hungary, 1526.
Opposing sides: (a) King Louis II of Hungary; (b) Sultan Suleiman the Magnificent.
Objective: The Hungarian army had concentrated for a decisive battle against the Turkish invaders.
Forces engaged: (a) 13,000 infantry, 12,000 cavalry and twenty guns; (b) total approximately 80,000, including janissaries, spahis and timariots, with 300 guns.
Casualties: (a) 15,000 killed, including Louis, seven bishops and over 500 nobles

(prisoners were beheaded by the Turks); (b) unknown, but at least as heavy – it took Suleiman three days to reorganize his army on the battlefield.
Result: The Hungarian army was destroyed and Budapest was occupied. Hungarian independence was lost for more than a century. Suleiman's victory enabled him to threaten Austria and central Europe. See VIENNA (1529).

The Hungarians were at first successful, defeating successive elements of the Turkish army. They were, however, unable to overrun the Turkish guns, which were chained together, and began to suffer serious casualties. At this point Suleiman launched a counter-attack with his janissaries and spahis, the best troops in his army, and these swept the outnumbered and exhausted Hungarians off the field.

Mohacs (1687) (Berge Harson, Magyharsany or Harkany) 356

Date: 12 August 1687.
Location: 15 miles south-west of Mohacs, southern Hungary.
War and campaign: Great Turkish War, 1683–1699: Habsburg Conquest of Hungary, 1683–1688.
Opposing sides: (a) Duke Charles of Lorraine and the Elector Max Emanuel of Bavaria commanding the Christian army; (b) the Ottoman Grand Vizier commanding the Turks.
Objective: After their victory at VIENNA, the Christian army had followed up the Turkish withdrawal into Hungary, over which it gradually extended its control. The battle resulted from Turkish attempts to stabilize the situation.
Forces engaged: (a) 60,000, including 45,000 Austrians, 8,500 Bavarians and 6,000 Croats and Hungarians; (b) uncertain, but larger.
Casualties: (a) Perhaps 1,000 killed and wounded; (b) over 10,000 killed and wounded, the majority during the pursuit.
Result: The Turks were decisively defeated and ejected from Hungary, upon which the Habsburgs were imposed as hereditary rulers.

The Christian army advanced into Slovenia and Transylvania. Disaffected Turkish elements deposed Sultan Mohammed IV in favour of Suleiman II. See also ZENTA.

Mohi (Sajo River) 357

Date: 11 April 1241.
Location: Near Miskolc, 90 miles north-east of Budapest.
War and campaign: Mongol Invasion of Europe, 1237–1242.
Opposing sides: (a) Sabutai; (b) Bela IV, King of Hungary.
Objective: The Hungarians were attempting to repel the invaders.
Forces engaged: (a) 90,000; (b) 100,000.
Casualties: (a) Unknown; (b) estimates of killed vary between 40,000 and 70,000.
Result: The Hungarian army was destroyed. The Mongol victory, following that at

LIEGNITZ, brought all of eastern Europe from the Baltic to the Danube under Sabutai's control.

The Mongols first overwhelmed a bridgehead which Bela had seized over the Sajo, then fought their way across the bridge. Bela, mistakenly believing that this was the Mongols' main effort, concentrated his army against it. However, Sabutai forded the river to the south of the battle with 30,000 men and fell on the Hungarian flank and rear. Bela's troops were forced back into their fortified camp, which was overwhelmed after several hours of severe fighting. Most of those who attempted to escape were cut down by a fresh Mongol pursuit force. The attacks on the bridgehead and camp were supported by catapults and ballistae hurling stones, bolts and blazing naphtha ('Greek Fire'), accompanied by 'thundrous noise and flashes of fire'. Gunpowder is believed to have originated in China and the Mongols would have been familiar with some of its properties if not its application as an artillery propellant, and the possibility is that their missiles were accompanied by large firecrackers, the explosion of which would induce terror and confusion among those unfamiliar with them. Had the Mongol advance continued, it is doubtful whether the disunited feudal armies of western Europe could have withstood the shock, since they were inferior in the fields of command and control, organization, training, discipline, equipment, communications, deception, intelligence and, above all, strategic perception. Luckily for Europe, Ogati Khan died in 1242 and, obedient to the law of his father Genghis Khan, the horde returned to Mongolia to elect a successor, never to penetrate so far west again.

Molino del Rey   358

Date: 8 September 1847.
Location: 3 miles south-west of Mexico City.
War and campaign: US–Mexican War, 1846–1848: Central Mexico Campaign.
Opposing sides: (a) General Winfield Scott; (b) the Dictator of Mexico, General Antonio Lopez de Santa Anna.
Objective: The Americans were clearing advanced Mexican positions so that they could assault the fortress of CHAPULTEPEC, covering the final approach to Mexico City.
Forces engaged: (a) 3,450; (b) approximately 12,000.
Casualties: (a) 116 killed and 665 wounded; (b) approximately 2,000 killed and wounded and 700 captured.
Result: The operation succeeded, but at heavier cost than had been anticipated.

Mollwitz   359

Date: 10 April 1741.
Location: Village 25 miles south of Wroclaw (Breslau), Poland.
War and campaign: War of Austrian Succession, 1740–1748: Campaign in Silesia, 1740–1742.
Opposing sides: (a) Frederick the Great; (b) Marshal Count Adam von Neipperg.
Objective: Frederick II of Prussia had invaded Silesia the previous December. In

March the Austrians mounted a counter-offensive which cut the Prussian lines of communication and the two armies met at Mollwitz.
Forces engaged: (a) Approximately 22,000, with 60 guns; (b) approximately 19,000, with eighteen guns.
Casualties: (a) Approximately 2,500; (b) approximately 5,000.
Result: The Austrians were defeated. Sensing her military weakness, France, Bavaria, Savoy and Saxony all declared war on Austria.

When the cavalry forming his right wing was beaten, Frederick was persuaded to leave the field, but the battle was won for him by the discipline and rapid fire of his infantry.

Monmouth 360

Date: 28 June 1778.
Location: Monmouth Court House, Monmouth County, New Jersey.
War and campaign: American War of Independence, 1775–1783: central theatre of operations.
Opposing sides: (a) Lieutenant-General Sir Henry Clinton; (b) Major-General George Washington.
Objective: In view of the now global nature of the war, British strategy in America had become defensive. Clinton was ordered to withdraw from Philadelphia to New York so that troops could be made available for the defence of the financially important sugar islands in the West Indies. As his ships were needed to evacuate some 3,000 loyalists who did not wish to remain, the troops retreated overland through New Jersey. Washington followed up and near Monmouth Court House the advance and rear guards of the two armies clashed, provoking a general engagement.
Forces engaged: (a) 7,000; (b) 12,000.
Casualties: (a) Approximately 350 on either side.
Result: The battle itself was indecisive but Clinton was able to resume his withdrawal to New York.

Although several minor operations took place, Monmouth was the last major action to be fought between field armies until CAMDEN in August 1780. By the end of 1778 the emphasis of the war had begun to shift to the south. See SAVANNAH, SIEGE OF.

Monocacy, The 361

Date: 9 July 1864.
Location: 3 miles south of Frederick, Maryland.
War and campaign: American Civil War: Shenandoah Valley Campaign of 1864.
Opposing sides: (a) Major-General Lewis Wallace; (b) Lieutenant-General Jubal A. Early.
Objective: Lee, hoping to reduce Federal pressure on the PETERSBURG sector, had ordered Early to clear the Valley of Union troops and menace Washington. At the Monocacy Early found his route to the capital barred by a scratch force.

Forces engaged: (a) 5,800; (b) 14,000.
Casualties: (a) 1,968; (b) 900.
Result: Wallace was defeated after an unexpectedly hard fight. Two days later Early penetrated the outskirts of Washington, creating a panic, but withdrew in the face of a build-up of Federal reinforcements (VI Corps followed by XIX Corps) hurriedly sent north by Grant from the Army of the Potomac.

Lew Wallace is best remembered for his book *Ben Hur*, on which several films were based. Although some, at least, of his superiors did not hold him in high regard, it is possible that had his stand not imposed a 24-hour delay on Early, the latter might have fought his way into Washington on 10 July, with incalculable political consequences.

Monongahela River   362

Date: 9 July 1755.
Location: On the Monongahela river near FORT DUQUENSE (now Pittsburgh), Pennsylvania.
War and campaign: French and Indian War in North America, 1754–1763.
Opposing sides: (a) Major-General Edward Braddock; (b) identity of senior French officer uncertain.
Objective: A British and colonial force, marching to attack Fort Duquesne, was ambushed in close country by the French and their Indian allies.
Forces engaged: (a) 1,400 regulars and 450 colonials; (b) 900 French and Indians.
Casualties: (a) 777 killed and wounded, including Braddock mortally wounded; (b) approximately 60 killed and wounded.
Result: The British column was destroyed. The survivors were led back to Virginia by Colonel George Washington.

Braddock was criticized for maintaining rigid linear formation during the engagement, but the two regular regiments present contained a high proportion of raw recruits who could not be handled in any other way; the wonder is that they stood their ground as long as they did. Be that as it may, a specialist light infantry unit, the 60th Royal American Regiment (subsequently the King's Royal Rifle Corps, now part of the Royal Green Jackets) was formed at New York shortly after the Monongahela disaster, and soon light infantry tactics were adopted by all British troops serving in North America. The famous colonial unit known as Rogers' Rangers was formed at about the same time, specifically for service in the wilderness, its role and methods placing it within the category of Special Forces.

Mons   363

Date: 23 August 1914.
Location: Mainly along the line of the Mons–Conde canal to the west and north of Mons, Belgium.
War and campaign: First World War: Western Front.
Opposing sides: (a) Field Marshal Sir John French commanding the British

Expeditionary Force; (b) General Alexander von Kluck commanding the German First Army.

Objective: The German Army was attempting to turn the Allied left flank.

Forces engaged: (a) General Sir Horace Smith-Dorrien commanding the British II Corps; (b) the German IV, III and IX Corps.

Casualties: (a) 1,600; (b) approximately 3,000.

Result: The German advance was temporarily checked but not halted. The BEF withdrew that night to conform to the movements of the French Fifth Army on its right. See also LE CATEAU.

A feature of the battle was the rapid and accurate British rifle fire which led the Germans to believe that they were opposed by many more machine guns than was the case.

Mons Graupius 364

Date: AD 84.

Location: Possibly Bennachie, near Inverurie, north-west of Aberdeen.

War and campaign: Roman Conquest of Britain.

Opposing sides: (a) Gnaius Julius Agricola; (b) Calgacus commanding the tribal army.

Objective: The Roman intention was to subdue the Caledonian tribes.

Forces engaged: (a) Two legions (IX Hispana and XX Valeria), 8,000 Batavian and Tungrian auxiliary infantry and 5,000 auxiliary cavalry – total approximately 22,000; (b) approximately 30,000, including charioteers.

Casualties: (a) 367 auxiliaries; (b) 10,000 killed.

Result: Agricola won a victory which broke the power of the Caledonian tribes for a generation. In terms of military economics, however, the permanent occupation of Caledonia made little sense and, once they had recovered, the tribes remained a continual threat to the northern provinces of Roman Britain.

One unusual feature of the battle was that the legions were not committed during the fighting, which was done solely by the auxiliaries. Another was the extensive use made by Agricola of his cavalry, which first defeated the enemy's charioteers, then attacked the Caledonian rear and finally carried out a ruthless pursuit.

Monterrey 365

Date: 20–24 September 1846.

Location: Fortified city in Nuevo Leon province, north-eastern Mexico.

War and campaign: US–Mexican War, 1846–1848: Northern Campaign.

Opposing sides: (a) General Zachary Taylor; (b) General Pedro de Ampudia.

Objective: The capture of the city was necessary for the continued American advance south into Mexico.

Forces engaged: (a) 6,000; (b) 10,000.

Casualties: (a) 120 killed and 368 wounded; (b) 367 killed and wounded.

Result: Ampudia surrendered when his defences were stormed and was allowed to march out with the honours of war. Taylor granted a Mexican request for an eight-week armistice, but this was repudiated by President James Polk and, having advised the Mexicans of the fact, Taylor advanced to Saltillo. See BUENA VISTA.

Morat (Murten) 366

Date: 22 June 1476.

Location: South of the town of Morat on the shores of the Murtensee, 17 miles west of Berne.

War and campaign: Swiss–Burgundian War, 1474–1477.

Opposing sides: (a) The Cantonal commanders and the Duke of Lorraine commanding the army of the Swiss Confederation; (b) Charles the Bold, Duke of Burgundy.

Objective: The Swiss intention was to break the siege of Morat, which the reorganized Burgundian army had invested following its defeat at GRANSON.

Forces engaged: (a) 23,200 infantry, 1,800 cavalry and some guns; (b) 23,000 with ample artillery.

Casualties: (a) 410 killed; (b) 8,000 killed.

Result: The Swiss launched a surprise attack on the Burgundians, driving them through their entrenchments and camp into the lake. Morat was relieved and the Confederation gained Louis XI of France as an ally, a combination which led to the defeat of Burgundy the following year.

Morgarten 367

Date: 15 November 1315.

Location: Pass at the southern end of Lake Ageri, 10 miles south-east of Zug, Switzerland.

War and campaign: Swiss Wars of Independence.

Opposing sides: (a) The Cantonal leaders of Unterwalden, Schwyz and Uri; (b) Duke Leopold of Austria.

Objective: The Swiss ambushed an invading Austrian army.

Forces engaged: (a) Approximately 1,500 pikemen and halberdiers; (b) 5,000 infantry and 3,000 cavalry.

Casualties: (a) Light; (b) 4,500 killed.

Result: Most of the Austrian army was destroyed and the rest fled from the trap.

The Swiss first halted the Austrian column by attacking its head with a force of pikemen, then rolled boulders and tree trunks down the steep slopes into the packed ranks. Finally, a flank attack drove the remnants of Leopold's army into the lake. See also LAUPEN.

Mortimer's Cross 368

Date: 2 February 1461.

Location: 5 miles north-west of Leominster, Herefordshire.
War and campaign: Wars of the Roses, 1455–1485.
Opposing sides: (a) The Earls of Pembroke and Wiltshire commanding the Lancastrians; (b) Edward Duke of York (later Edward IV) commanding the Yorkists.
Objective: Following the battle of WAKEFIELD, two Lancastrian armies planned to march on London and rescue King Henry VI. The Yorkists moved first against the recently raised Lancastrian army on the Welsh borders.
Forces engaged: (a) Estimated 6,000; (b) estimated 8,000.
Casualties: (a) Over 3,000, including a number of captured Lancastrian nobles executed on the spot; (b) light.
Result: The western Lancastrian army was destroyed, although elsewhere Yorkist fortunes were temporarily reversed at the SECOND BATTLE OF ST ALBANS.

Moscow 369

Date: 8 October 1941 to 30 April 1942.
Location: An arc stretching north, west and south of the Russian capital.
War and campaign: Second World War: Russian Front.
Opposing sides: (a) Field Marshal Walter von Brauchitsch, Commander-in-Chief of the German Army until 16 December 1941, then Adolf Hitler; (b) Iosef Stalin in overall command of Soviet forces.
Objective: Hitler believed that by capturing Moscow he would induce Stalin's fall and the collapse of the Soviet Union.
Forces engaged: (a) Field Marshal Fedor von Bock (later Field Marshal Gunther von Kluge) commanding Army Group Centre – total 60 divisions with 750,000 men; (b) Marshal Semyon Timoshenko (until 6 December, then Marshal Georgi Zhukov) commanding the West Front – total 100 divisions with 1,000,000 men.
Casualties: (a) Approximately 340,000; (b) approximately 680,000.
Result: The failure to capture Moscow, followed by the successful Soviet counter-offensive, meant that Germany was committed to a prolonged war and that, in due course, when the Western Allies returned to Europe, this would have to be fought on a minimum of two fronts. The battle for Moscow can therefore be seen as one of the most significant turning points in the Second World War.

Following the great victory at KIEV, Hitler ordered the resumption of the drive on Moscow. However, priceless time had been lost and the deep mud induced by autumn rains slowed the rate of advance to a crawl. The first frosts hardened the ground sufficiently for progress to be resumed for a while, but the combination of winter snows, fuel shortages, a reduction in tank strength and fierce Russian resistance denied the Germans the sort of success they had enjoyed during the early days of Operation 'Barbarossa'. Nevertheless, by the end of November it began to look as though Moscow would be encircled by a double-envelopment and German infantry actually penetrated the suburbs of the city, only to be driven out by workers' militia. On 5 December Hitler, having accepted that further progress was impossible, decided to abandon the operation until the following spring, simultaneously initiating a purge of those senior commanders whom he believed to be responsible for the failure. Almost immediately, Zhukov initiated a counter-offensive, using fresh Siberian troops properly equipped for the winter. As this became general along the line, the Kalinin Front and the Bryansk Front assisted the West Front in pinching out the German salients to the north and south of Moscow and von Kluge was forced to withdraw approximately 100 miles to Viazma. Here the momentum of the Soviet offensive ran down, partly from natural causes and partly because Hitler strictly forbade any further withdrawals. As the winter was unduly severe, the Germans recognized that in any event their survival depended upon retaining possession of the villages, but Hitler drew the wrong conclusions and in subsequent operations issued similar 'no withdrawal' orders which lacked the same practical application and were disastrous in their result.

Mount Badon (Mons Badonicus)   370

Date: c.490–500.
Location: Uncertain. Possible sites include Badbury in Wiltshire, Badbury Rings in Dorset and one of the hills overlooking Bath.
War and campaign: Anglo-Saxon Settlement in England, 450–600.
Opposing sides: (a) Arthur, military leader of the Britons; (b) Cerdic, leader of the West Saxons.
Objective: The Britons were attempting to stem further Saxon expansions to the west.
Forces engaged: The army of the Britons included a cavalry element under Arthur's personal command; the Saxons fought on foot. The numbers engaged on either side are unknown.
Casualties: Unknown, although those of the Saxons were clearly crippling. The *Historia Brittonum*, though compiled four centuries later, suggests that the majority of these were caused by Arthur's cavalry.
Result: The Britons won a decisive victory which halted Saxon expansion for at least a generation.

There is little doubt that the Britons possessed in Arthur a military leader of outstanding ability who is credited with having fought and won twelve battles, of which Mount Badon was the last. It was probably Arthur who recognized the value of mounted shock action against a primarily infantry enemy such as the Saxons. Whether he was ever a king remains a subject for discussion, but it seems more probable that he was appointed *Dux Bellorum* of the combined contingents supplied by minor British kingdoms in recognition of the threat posed to them all by the Saxons and others. In this context his position could best be described as first among equals, the concept being romanticized into the Round Table during the Middle Ages. Not the least of his achievements must have been the ability to hold together these disparate elements in the common cause.

Mudki   371

Date: 18 December 1845.
Location: Village in the Punjab, 30 miles south of Ferozepur.
War and campaign: First Sikh War, 1845–1846.
Opposing sides: (a) General Sir Hugh Gough; (b) Lal Singh.

Objective: The British were opposing a Sikh invasion of their territory.
Forces engaged: (a) 11,000 British and Indian troops with 42 guns; (b) 20,000 with 22 guns.
Casualties: (a) 215 killed and 655 wounded; (b) approximately 3,000, plus fifteen guns captured.
Result: The Sikhs were defeated after a hard-fought battle and withdrew to FEROZESHAH.

Mukden 372

Date: 21 February to 10 March 1905.
Location: Along an approximate 90-mile front to the south of Mukden (Shen-yang), Manchuria.
War and campaign: Russo–Japanese War, 1904–1905
Opposing sides: (a) General Alexei Kuropatkin, Commander-in-Chief of the Russian armies in Manchuria; (b) Field Marshal Marquis Iwao Oyama, Commander-in-Chief of the Japanese armies in Manchuria.
Objective: A Japanese attempt to inflict a decisive defeat on the Russians.
Forces engaged: (a) Third Manchurian Army (Kaulbars), Second Manchurian Army (Bilderling) and First Manchurian Army (Linievich) – total approximately 276,000 men, 1,200 guns and 54 machine guns; (b) the Japanese Fifth (Kawamura), First (Kuroki), Fourth (Nodzu), Second (Oku) and Third (Nogi) Armies – total approximately 207,000 men, 1,000 guns and 254 machine guns.
Casualties: (a) Estimated 59,800, plus 60–70 guns and a large quantity of material; (b) estimated 53,500. Other estimates show a wide variation in these figures with the Russians losing as many as 156,000 men and the Japanese 70,000. It is, however, certain that the Japanese sustained the higher loss in killed and wounded while the Russians lost the greater number of prisoners.
Result: Kuropatkin, his right flank almost turned, executed a difficult disengagement and withdrew north to Tieling and Harbin. Mukden was the last major land battle of the war.

Kuropatkin was handicapped not only by having to fight at the end of the tenuous 5,000-mile supply route provided by the Trans-Siberian Railway but also by Russian inefficiency and intrigue. He was a conscientious commander although he tended to lose control both at Mukden and in the previous series of battles, LIAOYANG, SHA-HO RIVER and SANDEPU/HEIKOUTAI. After Mukden, which together with Liaoyang indicated the nature of industrialized warfare, the Tsar dismissed him from the post of Commander-in-Chief and he changed places with Linievich. For his part, while Oyama had won the battle, it was not the crushing victory he had sought and Japan was coming to the end of her manpower reserves. The Russian armies were still in the field and, despite spreading internal unrest, Russia still possessed enormous resources. Both sides were becoming war-weary and a peace treaty was concluded after the Russian Baltic Fleet, having circumnavigated the globe, was destroyed at the Battle of Tsushima on 27 May. As a result of this, Russia evacuated Manchuria and ceded other territory to Japan. Japan emerged from the war as one of the world's powers and in this context it is possible to regard Mukden as one of the decisive encounters of the twentieth century, despite the fact that the result was less complete than Oyama had hoped.

Mulhouse (Mülhausen)

Date: August/September 58 BC.	
Location: Between Belfort and Mulhouse on the Upper Rhine, France.	
War and campaign: Caesar's Gallic War	
Opposing sides: (a) Julius Caesar; (b) Ariovistus leading an alliance of Germanic tribes.	
Objective: Caesar was repelling a Germanic invasion of Gaul.	
Forces engaged: (a) Six legions and a contingent of Gallic cavalry – total possibly 35,000; (b) possibly 75,000.	
Casualties: Unknown. Those of the Germans were immense and included a large number drowned while escaping across the Rhine.	
Result: The invaders were routed and driven out of Gaul.	

The right wings of both armies were successful during the initial mêlée. The Germans broke when the third line of cohorts was committed to the fight.

Munda

Date: 17 March 45 BC.	
Location: Uncertain, but probably near the modern village of Montilla, 20 miles south of Cordoba, southern Spain.	
War and campaign: Wars of the First Triumvirate.	
Opposing sides: (a) Julius Caesar; (b) Gnaius and Sextus Pompey, sons of the late Pompey the Great.	
Objective: Caesar's intention was to destroy the last remaining Pompeian army.	
Forces engaged: (a) Approximately 40,000; (b) approximately 60,000.	
Casualties: (a) 1,000 killed and 5,000 wounded; (b) 30,000, including Gnaius captured and executed.	
Result: Caesar was victorious.	

Munda was Caesar's last, and hardest fought, battle; he was assassinated a year later. See PHILIPPI, FIRST AND SECOND BATTLES OF.

Nanshan

Date: 25 May 1904.	
Location: Defence line across the narrowest part of the Liaotung peninsula, covering the approaches to Port Arthur (Lu-shun), Manchuria.	
War and campaign: Russo–Japanese War, 1904–1905.	
Opposing sides: (a) General Alexei Kuropatkin, Commander-in-Chief of the Russian army in Manchuria; (b) Field Marshal Marquis Iwao Oyoma, Commander-in-Chief of the Japanese armies in Manchuria.	
Objective: The Japanese intention was to break through and lay siege to Port Arthur.	

Forces engaged: (a) Major-General Baron Anatoli Stoessel commanding the Port Arthur garrison, of which about 3,000 men were engaged; (b) General Yasukata Oju commanding the Japanese Second Army, of which about 30,000 men were engaged.

Casualties: (a) Approximately 1,400; (b) approximately 4,500.

Result: The Japanese stormed the position, opening the way to Port Arthur.

Narva 376

Date: 20 November 1700.

Location: Fortified city on Narva river, north-eastern Estonia.

War and campaign: Great Northern War, 1700–1721: Baltic Campaign of 1700.

Opposing sides: (a) Charles XII of Sweden; (b) General Prince Dolgorouky commanding the Russians.

Objective: The Swedish intention was to relieve the garrison of Narva, which was being besieged by the Russians.

Forces engaged: (a) 10,000; (b) 40,000.

Casualties: (a) Approximately 600 killed and wounded; (b) approximately 10,000 killed, wounded and captured.

Result: The three-hour battle, fought in a blizzard, ended in a complete victory for the seventeen-year-old Charles.

Following the reverse, Tsar Peter the Great reorganized his army.

Naseby 377

Date: 14 June 1645.

Location: Between the villages of Naseby and Sibbertoft, Northamptonshire, 8 miles south-west of Market Harborough.

War and campaign: First Civil War, 1642–1646.

Opposing sides: (a) Charles I commanding the Royalist army; (b) Sir Thomas Fairfax and Oliver Cromwell commanding the Parliamentarians.

Objective: Following the Royalist capture of Leicester, the Parliamentarians were determined to force a decisive action on the King's army.

Forces engaged: (a) 4,000 infantry, 5,000 cavalry and twelve guns – total 9,000; (b) 7,000 infantry, 6,000 cavalry and thirteen guns – total 13,000.

Casualties: (a) 6,000 killed, wounded and prisoners, plus all guns captured; (b) estimated less than 1,000 killed and wounded.

Result: A Parliamentary victory which destroyed the Royalist cause in the Midlands. As the north had been lost to the Crown the previous year at MARSTON MOOR, the few troops remaining to the King were confined to the south and west and these were unable to stem the Parliamentary tide of victory. Naseby was the decisive battle of the war.

Both armies were drawn up with their infantry in the centre and their cavalry on the flanks, with a small reserve behind; in addition, the Parliamentarians also deployed a regiment of dragoons under Colonel John Okey along the hedges to the west of the battlefield, covering the approach to their position. The battle began with successful cavalry charges by the right wings of both armies, but while Prince Rupert's troopers pursued their opponents as far as the Parliamentary wagon lines, where they were beaten off by musketeers, Cromwell exercised tighter control and after he had driven off Sir Marmaduke Langdale's Northern Horse he led his second line in an attack on Lord Astley's Royalist infantry which, despite, its inferior numbers, was pushing back the Parliamentarian centre. At this point Charles could have launched his reserve and Langdale's rallied cavalry in a decisive counter-attack into Cromwell's flank, but one of his supporters, mistakenly believing that the battle was lost, attempted to lead the King away. In the ensuing confusion the reserve was not committed and the moment passed. Okey's dragoons mounted their horses and joined in the attack on the Royalist infantry which, heavily outnumbered and beset simultaneously from three sides, surrendered, although at least one regiment fought on to the bitter end. After this, the remainder of the Royalist army broke and fled, abandoning its guns and baggage.

Nashville 378

Date: 15–16 December 1864.
Location: Nashville, Tennessee.
War and campaign: American Civil War: Tennessee Campaign of 1864.
Opposing sides: (a) Major-General George H. Thomas commanding the Federal Army of the Cumberland; (b) General John B. Hood commanding the reinforced Confederate Army of Tennessee.
Objective: While Sherman was making his march from ATLANTA to SAVANNAH, the Confederates, seeking to distract him, mounted a counter-offensive into Tennessee in the hope provoking the Federal troops there into fighting a decisive battle.
Forces engaged: (a) 49,773; (b) 31,000.
Casualties: (a) 499 killed and 2,562 wounded; (b) 1,500 killed or wounded and 4,462 captured.
Result: The outflanked Confederate line collapsed under the weight of Federal attacks and Hood's army disintegrated.

This battle is regarded as the most conclusive tactical engagement of the war.

Neerwinden (Landen) 379

Date: 29 July 1693.
Location: 7 miles south-west of St Truiden, Belgium.
War and campaign: War of the League of Augsburg, 1688–1697: Netherlands Campaign of 1693.
Opposing sides: (a) William III of England and Holland commanding the Allied army; (b) Marshal Duke François of Luxembourg commanding the French.
Objective: The Allies had detached a substantial part of their army for operations near Liège and the French, taking advantage of this, attacked their now overextended position.
Forces engaged: (a) 50,000; (b) 80,000.

Casualties: (a) 18,000 killed, wounded and prisoners, plus 104 guns captured; (b) 9,000 killed and wounded.
Result: A complete French victory which, like FLEURUS, was not exploited.

Nemecky Brod (Deutschbrod)   380

Date: 10 January 1422.
Location: 40 miles north-east of Brno, Czechoslovakia.
War and campaign: Hussite Wars, 1419–1436.
Opposing sides: (a) Jan Ziska commanding the Hussites; (b) Sigismund, Holy Roman Emperor, commanding the Catholic army.
Objective: The Hussites, exploiting their victory at KUTNA HORA, pursued and caught the retreating Catholic army.
Forces engaged: (a) 10,000; (b) 23,000.
Casualties: (a) Light; (b) estimated 10,000, including 500 knights drowned attempting to escape across a frozen river.
Result: The Catholic army was destroyed.

Unfortunately for the Hussites, Ziska died in 1424 and doctrinal disputes resulted in a civil war between the factions. Nevertheless, by 1436 they had secured a measure of religious toleration. Subsequently, Ziska's revolutionary tactics fell into disuse.

Neville's Cross   381

Date: 17 October 1346.
Location: 1 mile to the west of Durham.
War and campaign: Anglo–Scottish Wars.
Opposing sides: (a) Ralph Neville, Henry Percy and Sir Thomas Rokeby commanding the English army; (b) David II.
Objective: In response to a request from the French king, Philip VI, who had recently been defeated at CRÉCY, David II of Scotland launched a destructive raid into England. The northern shires quickly raised an army which intercepted the Scots near Durham.
Forces engaged: (a) 15,000; (b) 20,000.
Casualties: (a) Unknown, but moderate; (b) uncertain, but heavy – a quoted figure of 15,000 (i.e. 75 per cent of those engaged) seems improbably high (David was captured and imprisoned in the Tower until 1357, when the last instalment of his 100,000-mark ransom was paid).
Result: The Scottish army was routed.

As at HALIDON HILL, the Scots advanced into a blizzard of English archery. The right wing, finding its way forward barred by a ravine, crowded in on the centre and the assault broke down as casualties and confusion mounted. The left wing succeeded in reaching the English line but was driven off by a cavalry counter-attack. This exposed the centre to flank attacks and finally this too was overwhelmed.

New Orleans 382

Date: 8 January 1815.
Location: On both banks of the Mississippi, 5 miles downstream from New Orleans, Louisiana.
War and campaign: War of 1812: southern theatre of operations.
Opposing sides: (a) Major-General Sir Edward Pakenham; (b) Major-General Andrew Jackson.
Objective: A British landing force was attempting to capture New Orleans but found its passage barred by American field works.
Forces engaged: (a) Approximately 7,000; (b) approximately 3,500.
Casualties: (a) 2,100 killed and wounded, including Pakenham killed; (b) seven killed and 70 wounded.
Result: Pakenham's assault was decisively repulsed and the British withdrew to their ships; Jackson did not pursue. Neither side was aware that Great Britain and the United States had concluded a peace treaty at Ghent on 24 December.

The main American position was located on the left bank of the river. Downstream on the right bank was a smaller work, the guns of which enfiladed the British approach to the main position opposite. Obviously, Pakenham should not have launched his assault before the right bank defences were in his hands, but he chose to do so, with disastrous consequences. The small force detailed to capture the left bank defences, although delayed by various causes, actually did so, but only after the main assault had failed. Whether the British assault would have succeeded if the correct priorities had been followed is a matter for debate, as other factors were at work in Pakenham's army; had it succeeded, the probability is that casualties would still have been unacceptably heavy. Andrew Jackson became President of the United States in 1828.

Nicosia, Siege of 383

Date: 25 July to 9 September 1570.
Location: City in the central plain of Cyprus.
War and campaign: War between the Ottoman Empire and Venice over possession of Cyprus, 1570–1573.
Opposing sides: (a) Lala Mustafa commanding the Turkish army; (b) Nicolo Dandolo commanding the garrison.
Objective: The Turks intended capturing the island's capital.
Forces engaged: (a) Estimated 52,000, reinforced by a further 20,000 in September, plus an artillery siege train; (b) 3,000 regulars and 5,000 militia.
Casualties: (a) Unknown, but heavy; (b) the entire garrison was massacred, as was the civil population except for 2,000 who were enslaved.

> **Result:** The city was stormed and Lala Mustafa marched on FAMAGUSTA, the last remaining Venetian bastion in Cyprus.

Dandolo possessed adequate artillery but little powder or ammunition. Nevertheless, he conducted a vigorous defence, including a destructive sortie on 15 August. Significantly, the effect of the Turkish artillery on the earth banks of the main defences was disappointing, confirming that earthworks provided more lasting protection against gunfire than masonry walls.

Nivelle Offensive, The (Second Battle of the Aisne or Third Battle of Champagne)   384

Date: 16–29 April 1917.
Location: Along a 25-mile sector of the front stretching from Rheims westwards to Soissons.
War and campaign: First World War: Western Front.
Opposing sides: (a) General Robert Nivelle, Commander-in-Chief of the French armies; (b) General Erich Ludendorff, First Quartermaster-General of the German Army.
Objective: Nivelle promised a breakthrough that would lead to victory in the West.
Forces engaged: (a) French Fifth Army (General Oliver Mazel), Tenth Army (General Denis Duchene) and Sixth Army (General Charles Mangin); (b) German Seventh Army (General Max von Boehn) and First Army (General Fritz von Below).
Casualties: (a) 134,000 (including 30,000 killed and 4,000 captured), of which 80 per cent occurred during the first day's fighting; (b) much lighter (although they included over 15,000 men taken prisoner).
Result: Limited French gains, notably on the Chemin des Dames sector. The terrible losses incurred induced an outbreak of mutiny in the French armies. Nivelle was replaced by General Henri Philippe Pétain on 15 May.

The Germans were aware of the details of the French offensive and achieved air superiority over the battlefield before it began. They also knew that the French would be employing tanks for the first time and widened their trenches to prevent their crossing. Altogether, the French committed 128 tanks of which the majority were destroyed by the German artillery. For its part, the French artillery's rolling barrage moved too quickly for the advancing infantry, who were left exposed to German fire and counter-attacks. Nivelle promised that the methods he had used during the last phase of the Battle of VERDUN would produce victory, and when they failed to do so the disillusion among his war-weary troops led to mutinies in 68 of the French Army's 112 divisions; in general, these took the form of a short-lived refusal to return to the line. Incredibly, the full extent of the mutiny was kept secret from the Germans until 30 June, when the worst of the danger had passed. A total of 2,873 men were convicted by courts martial but there were comparatively few executions as Pétain was anxious to restore the Army's morale. A further consequence of the mutinies was that Haig agreed to maintain pressure on the British sector of the Western Front. See also ARRAS/VIMY RIDGE.

Date: 5/6 September 1634.	
Location: The village of Holheim to the south of Nördlingen, approximately 45 miles east of Stuttgart.	
War and campaign: Thirty Years' War, 1618–1648: German Campaign of 1634.	
Opposing sides: (a) Duke Bernard of Saxe-Weimar and Field Marshal Count Gustaf Horn commanding the Protestant forces; (b) King Ferdinand of Hungary, the Cardinal Infante Ferdinand of Spain and Duke Charles IV of Lorraine commanding the Imperialist, Spanish and Catholic League army.	
Objective: The Swedes and their Protestant allies were marching to the relief of the garrison in Nördlingen, which was besieged by the Imperialists.	
Forces engaged: (a) 16,000 infantry, 9,000 cavalry and 55 guns; (b) approximately 40,000.	
Casualties: (a) 10,000 killed and wounded, plus 4,000 prisoners and all guns lost; (b) approximately 2,500 killed and wounded.	
Result: A crushing Imperialist victory which eliminated the Swedish military presence in southern Germany. The Protestant cause was in serious danger of collapsing, but from this point onward the purely religious aspect of the conflict was overshadowed by the rivalry between the Hapsburg and Bourbon families, as a result of which France, opposed to the expansion of Imperial and Spanish influence, openly entered the war. In the long term, therefore, the Catholic victory at Nördlingen was counter-productive.	

Poor co-ordination, a failure to appreciate the odds he faced and the inability to seize and hold the vital Allbuch hill, occupied by well-disciplined Spanish infantry, all contributed to Horn's repulse. When he attempted to withdraw behind Bernhard's position the Imperialists counter-attacked in strength and the result was a rout in which the Swedish infantry was all but annihilated.

Nördlingen, Second Battle of (Allerheim) 386

Date: 3 August 1645.	
Location: Centred on the village of Allerheim, south-east of Nördlingen, approximately 45 miles east of Stuttgart.	
War and campaign: Thirty Years' War, 1618–1648: German Campaign of 1645.	
Opposing sides: (a) Prince Louis de Bourbon Condé (the Great Condé) commanding the French/German Protestant army; (b) Field Marshal Baron Franz von Mercy commanding the Imperialist/Bavarian army.	
Objective: A French army invading Bavaria was opposed by Imperialist troops holding a partially entrenched position near Nördlingen.	
Forces engaged: (a) 6,000 infantry, 11,000 cavalry and eleven guns; (b) 5,000 infantry, 9,000 cavalry and 23 guns.	
Casualties: (a) 4,000 killed and wounded; (b) 5,000 killed and wounded (including von Mercy killed), plus fifteen guns captured.	
Result: Condé's tenancity won him a costly victory.	

After years of devastation the German countryside would no longer support the operations of large armies and, despite its comparatively small scale, the Second Battle of Nördlingen was the last major engagement of the war.

Northampton

Date: 18 July 1460.
Location: South of the town beside the river Nene.
War and campaign: Wars of the Roses, 1455–1485.
Opposing sides: (a) Edward, Earl of March (younger son of Richard Duke of York and later Edward IV) and Richard Neville, Earl of Warwick, commanding the Yorkists; (b) the Duke of Buckingham commanding the Lancastrians.
Objective: The Yorkists, advancing north from London, were opposed by the entrenched Lancastrian army.
Forces engaged: (a) 7,000; (b) 5,000, with several guns.
Casualties: (a) Light; (b) uncertain, but Buckingham and most of the Lancastrian nobility were killed and Henry VI, freed by political manoeuvre after the FIRST BATTLE OF ST ALBANS, was captured by the Yorkists again.
Result: The Lancastrians were routed, partly because their gunpowder was drenched by a rainstorm but mainly because of the treachery of Lord Edmund Grey, who permitted the Yorkists to penetrate the entrenchments.

See also MORTIMER'S CROSS.

Okinawa

Date: 1 April to 22 June 1945.
Location: Largest island in the Ryukyu group, midway between Formosa and the Japanese home islands.
War and campaign: Second World War: Central Pacific.
Opposing sides: (a) Admiral Chester Nimitz, Commander-in-Chief Central Pacific Theatre; (b) Lieutenant-General Mitsuru Ushijima commanding the Japanese garrison.
Objective: The capture of the island by the Americans as a preliminary to the projected invasion of Japan, partly because it possessed a number of air bases and partly because its possession would sever the enemy's sea communications with his troops in southern China.
Forces engaged: (a) Lieutenant-General Simon Buckner commanding the US Tenth Army, with III Amphibious Corps (Major-General R. S. Geiger) and XXIV Corps (Major-General J. R. Hodge) – total 180,000 men; (b) the Japanese Thirty-Second Army and attached units – total 130,000 men.
Casualties: (a) 7,374 killed and 32,056 wounded, excluding naval casualties (Buckner was killed by artillery fire on 18 June); (b) 107,500 known dead and an unknown number sealed within their fortified caves during the fighting, plus 7,400 captured (Ushijima committed suicide on 22 June).
Result: A clear American victory.

The casualties inflicted by the Japanese in the tenacious defence of their own soil convinced President Truman that, to preserve Allied lives, it would be necessary to use atomic weapons against Japan as a means of hastening the end of the war.

Omdurman 389

Date: 2 September 1898.
Location: 7 miles downstream from Omdurman, lying at the confluence of the Blue and White Niles, opposite Khartoum, Sudan.
War and campaign: Sudan Campaigns: Reconquest of the Sudan.
Opposing sides: (a) General Sir Herbert Kitchener (the Sirdar); (b) the Khalifa Abdullah.
Objective: Following its victory at ATBARA RIVER, the Anglo-Egyptian army resumed its advance on Omdurman, where the Mahdists also intended fighting the decisive battle of the war.
Forces engaged: (a) 25,800 men (8,200 British and 17,600 Egyptians), with 44 guns and twenty Maxim machine guns, plus ten gunboats in support with 36 guns and 24 Maxim machine guns; (b) 60,000.
Casualties: (a) 43 killed and 428 wounded; (b) 9,700 killed, up to 16,000 wounded and 5,000 prisoners.
Result: The dervish army was destroyed and with it the power of the Mahdists. The Khalifa escaped but was later hunted down and killed. The Sudan was pacified.

Following the repulse of the dervish attack on his zariba at El Egeiga, Kitchener gave the order for a general advance. As a large body of the enemy still lay on his right flank, such a move was premature and might have resulted in serious consequences had the situation not been relieved by the prompt action of Colonel H. A. MacDonald's 1st Egyptian Brigade, which contained the threat until reinforcements arrived. Omdurman itself was captured with little difficulty. One of the best remembered episodes in the battle was the charge of the 21st Lancers, in which Lieutenant Winston Churchill took part.

Orléans, Siege of 390

Date: 12 October 1428 to 7 May 1429.
Location: The decisive action took place on the south bank of the Loire.
War and campaign: Hundred Years' War, 1337–1457: Campaign of 1428–1429.
Opposing sides: (a) The Earl of Salisbury until wounded by cannon fire on 24 October, succeeded by the Earl of Suffolk; (b) the Sire de Goncourt and the Comte de Dunois commanding the garrison, the Duke of Alençon and Joan of Arc commanding the relief force.
Objective: The English intention was to capture the city, the French intention to relieve it.
Forces engaged: (a) 4,500 with 50 guns; (b) garrison – 2,400 soldiers and 3,000 armed citizens with 72 guns; relief force – 4,000.
Casualties: Unknown, although the French loss was probably the heavier. During the battle for the forts of Les Augustins and Les Tourelles on 6/7 May the English losses were 300 killed and 200 captured.
Result: The city was relieved and the siege was abandoned. The event marked a

The English lacked the numbers to enforce anything more than a loose blockade and
established themselves in a series of pallisaded forts to the west of the city and across the
river to the south, plus the isolated Fort St Loup to the east. After the relief force
marched in, St Loup was captured by a sortie on 3 May. The French then crossed the
river to assault the works covering the bridgehead, including a barbican named Les
Tourelles and the fort of Les Augustins, assisted by a sortie across the bridge itself. The
outnumbered garrisons were overwhelmed and the English withdrew from their
remaining positions on 8 May. During the fight for the southern forts, Joan was wounded
by an arrow in the shoulder. When she returned to the fray, both sides, believing that she
had been killed, credited her with supernatural powers. In May 1430 she was captured by
the Burgundians and handed over to the English, who tried and burned her as a witch the
following year – an act both savage and counter-productive, since her memory continued
to inspire the French.

Ostend, Siege of 391

Date: 5 July 1601 to 14 September 1604.	
Location: Fortified port on the Flanders coast, Belgium.	
War and campaign: Eighty Years' War (War of Dutch Independence), 1568–1648.	
Opposing sides: (a) The Dutch garrison; (b) Archduke Albert of Austria, succeeded by the Marquis Ambrogio de Spinola during the closing stages.	
Objective: The Spaniards were attempting to recapture this important harbour from the Dutch, whose use of sea power was a continual thorn in their side.	
Forces engaged: Numbers uncertain, although both sides committed as many men as possible to the siege. The Dutch were reinforced and supplied by sea.	
Casualties: (a) 30,000; (b) 60,000. Both figures include deaths from disease.	
Result: The prohibitive cost of holding Ostend, coupled with Spinola's increased pressure, led the Dutch States General to instruct the garrison to surrender after a siege lasting over three years.	

The success, while dearly bought, enabled the Spaniards to consolidate their hold over
the southern Netherlands.

Otterburn 392

Date: 19 August 1388.	
Location: West of Otterburn village, Redesdale, Northumberland.	
War and campaign: The Anglo–Scottish Wars.	
Opposing sides: (a) Sir Henry Percy (also known as Hotspur); (b) James, Earl of Douglas, commanding the Scots.	
Objective: The English, pursuing a Scottish raiding force, made a dusk attack on its encampment.	
Forces engaged: (a) 8,000; (b) 7,000.	

Casualties: (a) 2,000, including Percy captured; (b) fewer, although Douglas was killed; 200 were captured during a rash pursuit.	
Result: The English were defeated and the raiders resumed their march northwards with their plunder.	

The Scots continued to ravage the borderlands until the Percys defeated Archibald Douglas at Homidon Hill on 14 September 1402.

Oudenarde 393

Date: 11 July 1708.
Location: Town on the Scheldt, 19 miles south of Ghent, Belgium.
War and campaign: War of Spanish Succession, 1701–1714: Netherlands Campaign of 1708.
Opposing sides: (a) The Duke of Marlborough and Prince Eugene of Savoy commanding the Allied army; (b) Marshal Duke Louis Joseph de Vendôme and the Duke of Burgundy commanding the French army.
Objective: Marlborough's intention was to force a battle on the French with a view to recovering the Allied territorial losses of the previous two years.
Forces engaged: (a) 85 infantry battalions and 150 cavalry squadrons – total 80,000; (b) 90 infantry battalions and 170 cavalry squadrons – total 85,000.
Casualties: (a) 2,000 killed and 5,000 wounded; (b) 4,000 killed, 2,000 wounded, 9,000 prisoners and 3,000 desertions.
Result: The French army was almost trapped and destroyed by a double-envelopment, although many of its troops managed to escape during the night.

Marlborough's victory restored the strategic initiative to the Allies, who eventually recovered Ghent and Bruges as well as capturing the French city of Lille. See also MALPLAQUET.

Paardeberg 394

Date: 18–27 February 1900.
Location: 4 miles upstream from Paardeberg Hill on the Modder river, east of Kimberley, South Africa.
War and campaign: Second Boer War, 1899–1902.
Opposing sides: (a) Field Marshal Lord Frederick Roberts; (b) General Piet Cronje.
Objective: Following the relief of KIMBERLEY, the Boer army on the western front was encircled by the British as it withdrew into the Orange Free State.
Forces engaged: (a) 30,000; (b) 5,000.
Casualties: (a) 1,535 killed and wounded; (b) 1,000 killed and wounded, 4,000 captured.
Result: Cronje was forced to surrender. The destruction of his army enabled Roberts to capture Bloemfontein, capital of the Orange Free State, on 13 March, then march north into the Transvaal.

Cronje's capitulation, coupled with the relief of LADYSMITH the following day, made the eventual defeat of the Boer republics inevitable. Cronje might well have succeeded in breaking out, but he declined to abandon his wounded and his men's families. The majority of the British casualties were incurred needlessly when Kitchener, in temporary command at the beginning of the siege, launched a frontal attack on the Boer laager, which was bombarded and starved into surrender.

Palo Alto/Resaca de la Palma 395

Date: 8–9 May 1846.	
Location: Near Brownsville, Texas.	
War and campaign: US–Mexican War, 1846–1848: Northern Campaign.	
Opposing sides: (a) General Zachary Taylor; (b) General Mariano Arista.	
Objective: The Americans were marching to the relief of Camp Texas, which had been invested by the Mexicans on 3 May.	
Forces engaged: (a) 2,200; (b) 4,500.	
Casualties: (a) 170 killed and wounded; (b) approximately 1,100.	
Result: Camp Texas was relieved and the Mexicans retired across the Rio Grande.	

The United States formally declared war on 13 May. See MONTERREY.

Panipat 396

Date: 17 December 1399.	
Location: 60 miles north of Delhi.	
War and campaign: Mongol Invasion of India, 1398–1399.	
Opposing sides: (a) Tamerlane (Timur the Lame); (b) Mahmud Tughluk, Sultan of Delhi.	
Objective: The invaders simply wished to plunder Delhi of it riches.	
Forces engaged: (a) Approximately 90,000; (b) probably in excess of 100,000, with 120 armoured elephants.	
Casualties: (a) Unknown; (b) crippling, estimates of prisoners massacred varying between 50,000 and 80,000.	
Result: The Sultan's army was routed. Tamerlane entered Delhi in triumph, was paid a ransom, then allowed his troops to rape and pillage for ten days. Finally, he burned the city and returned to Samarkand burdened with captured treasure, cutting a swathe of devastation across northern India.	

The Sultan's attack was spearheaded by his war elephants, which were unable to penetrate beyond obstacles which included a belt of caltrops, a line of wagons and tethered buffaloes. Injured by the caltrops and stung by a hail of arrows, the elephants turned back into their own ranks, opening the way for a decisive Mongol counter-attack.

Paris 397

Date: 30 March 1814.	

Location: The suburbs of Vincennes, Belleville and Monmartre.
War and campaign: War of the Sixth Coalition, 1812–1814: Campaign in France, 1814.
Opposing sides: (a) Marshals Auguste Marmont and Edouard Mortier commanding the French army; (b) Marshal Prince Karl von Schwarzenberg commanding the Allied army.
Objective: Despite having fought a brilliant campaign on interior lines, Napoleon was forced back on Paris and the Allies closed in to administer the *coup de grâce*.
Forces engaged: (a) Approximately 22,000; (b) approximately 110,000.
Casualties: (a) 4,000; (b) 8,000.
Result: The French were defeated and Marmont agreed to an armistice, surrendering Paris the following day – an act for which he was never to be forgiven, either by Napoleon or by his countrymen.

Convinced by his marshals that all was now lost, Napoleon abdicated unconditionally on 11 April and Louis XVIII was restored to the throne of France. See also TOULOUSE.

Paris, Siege of

Date: 20 September 1870 to 28 January 1871.
Location: All round the environs of the city.
War and campaign: Franco–Prussian War, 1870–1871.
Opposing sides: (a) Field Marshal Count Helmuth von Moltke commanding the Third and Meuse Armies of the North German Confederation; (b) General Louis Trochu, Military Governor of Paris.
Objective: Having neutralized or destroyed the best of the French field armies at, respectively, METZ and SEDAN, the Germans intended capturing Paris in the hope that this would bring the war to an end.
Forces engaged: (a) 206,000 infantry and 34,000 cavalry, with 898 field and 240 seige guns – total 240,000; (b) 355,000 infantry (including naval and National Guard units), 5,000 cavalry and 1,964 guns – total 400,000.
Casualties: (a) 10,000 killed and wounded, 2,000 missing; (b) 16,000 killed and wounded, 8,000 missing.
Result: The city was starved into surrender and its capitulation ended the war. See BELFORT.

Although the garrison of Paris outnumbered the besiegers, the majority of Trochu's men were poorly trained, undisciplined, unreliable and politically motivated National Guardsmen. The Germans experienced no difficulty in containing sorties at Champigny (30 November to 2 December) and Buzenval (2 January), nor in defeating attempts by the inexperienced Army of the Loire to relieve the city. Throughout the siege the garrison's only communication with the outside world was by means of hot air balloons which maintained an ingenious micro-photographic postal system. The German Empire was proclaimed at Versailles on 18 January. Most of the Paris National Guard units supported the Commune Uprising of March 1871 and in May some 300,000 Government troops, mainly released prisoners of war commanded by Marshal MacMahon, stormed the city with heavy loss of life and damage to property.

Pavia

Date: 25 February 1525.
Location: Fortified city in northern Italy, south of Milan.
War and campaign: French Sixteenth Century Wars in Italy: First War between Francis I and Emperor Charles V, 1521–1526.
Opposing sides: (a) The Marquis of Pescara commanding the Imperialist relief army; (b) Francis I.
Objective: The Imperialists were attempting to break the French siege of the city.
Forces engaged: (a) 12,000 German pikemen, 6,500 Spanish-Italian infantry, 800 men-at-arms, 1,500 light cavalry and seventeen guns – total 23,000 (excluding the 6,000-strong garrison of Pavia); (b) 9,000 French and Swiss pikeman, 9,000 French and Italian infantry and arquebusiers, 1,200 men-at-arms, 2,000 light cavalry and 53 guns – total 22,000.
Casualties: (a) 500 killed and wounded; (b) 13,000 killed and wounded, 5,000 captured (including Francis) and all guns lost.
Result: The destruction of the French army and the relief of Pavia inaugurated a period of Spanish control in Italy (Charles was also King of Spain).

At the end of January the Imperialist army approached Pavia to find its path barred by strong entrenchments. Both sides bombarded each other across an unfordable stream. During the night of 24/25 February Pescara broke the deadlock by marching north to cross the stream under cover of a storm and artillery fire, leaving a few men in his trenches to create the illusion that they were fully manned. He then penetrated a walled enclosure on the French left, achieving complete surprise. Francis led a counter-attack with his cavalry while his army ponderously changed front, but the French horsemen were routed when a force of Spanish arquebusiers and pikemen fell on their rear while they were engaged with the Imperialist cavalry to their front. The French infantry was destroyed piecemeal as it entered the fray and its artillery played little part in the battle as the fire of the guns was masked by the unexpected redeployment. At this point the garrison of Pavia made a sortie to complete the destruction of Francis's army.

Peking

Date: 20 June to 14 August 1900.
Location: The Legation Quarter and the Pei T'ang Cathedral.
War and campaign: Boxer Rebellion.
Opposing sides: (a) Sir Claude MacDonald, British Minister and senior member of the Peking diplomatic corps; (b) uncertain – Prince Tuan, head of the Chinese Foreign Office, was a noted pro-Boxer, and the Dowager Empress Tzu Hsi was in sympathy with the movement.
Objective: The intention of the Boxers (members of a patriotic but violent secret organization known as the Society of Righteous Harmony Fists) was to eliminate the foreign presence in Peking.
Forces engaged: (a) Legation guards: American – 56; Austro-Hungarian – 35; British – 82; French – 48; German – 51; Italian – 29; Japanese – 25; Russian – 81; total regular troops – 407. Civilian volunteers with previous military experience – 75. Civilian volunteers without military experience – 50. One old 9pdr gun recovered from a ditch and four machine guns. (b) Unknown, but the thousands of

Boxers present also had the active support of Imperial Chinese troops and their artillery.

Casualties: (a) 64 regulars and civilian volunteers killed and 156 wounded, plus up to 1,000 civilians killed or wounded, the great majority being Chinese Christian refugees; (b) unknown, but undoubtedly heavy.

Result: The siege was broken by an international relief expedition which, having already captured the Taku Forts and relieved the International Settlement at Tientsin, fought its way to Peking. Numerous punitive expeditions were then mounted against the remaining rebel strongholds. China was forced to pay an indemnity of £67 million and the Boxer Society was abolished; Russia occupied Manchuria, thereby setting herself on a collision course with Japan.

Pelelieu-Anguar 401

Date: 15 September to 25 November 1944.

Location: Islands in Palau Group, Caroline Islands, Central Pacific.

War and campaign: Second World War: Central Pacific.

Opposing sides: (a) Admiral Chester Nimitz, Commander-in-Chief Central Pacific Theatre; (b) Major-General Sadai Inoue commanding the Japanese garrison.

Objective: The capture of the islands by the Americans as a preliminary move to their landing on LEYTE, Philippine Islands.

Forces engaged: (a) Major-General R. S. Geiger commanding III Amphibious Corps (1st Marine and 81st Infantry Divisions); (b) about 10,000 men on Pelelieu and 1,400 on Anguar, plus 2,600 reinforcements from other islands.

Casualties: (a) 1,460 killed and 6,459 wounded and missing (the highest casualty rate of any American amphibious operation); (b) 13,600 killed and 400 captured.

Result: Anguar fell after three days' fighting but the entrenched Japanese garrison on Pelelieu fought a determined battle of attrition before its remnants were finally overwhelmed on 25 November.

In the opinion of some American historians the operation was unnecessary.

Perryville 402

Date: 8 October 1862.

Location: Perryville, Kentucky, 35 miles south-west of Lexington.

War and campaign: American Civil War: western theatre of operations.

Opposing sides: (a) Major-General Don Carlos Buell commanding the Federal Army of the Ohio; (b) General Braxton Bragg commanding the Confederate Army of the Mississippi.

Objective: The Federals were attempting to eject the Confederates from Kentucky, which the latter had invaded in the hope of attracting support for the Southern cause.

Forces engaged: (a) 36,940; (b) 16,000.

Casualties: (a) 3,696; (b) 3,145.

Result: Although the battle was drawn, Bragg had sustained proportionally the heavier casualties and, recognizing that thus far he had only been engaged by a part of Buell's army, he withdrew through the Cumberland Gap into Tennessee. Buell, who had exercised little tactical control during the battle, did not pursue.

President Lincoln, dissatisfied with Buell, replaced him with Major-General William S. Rosecrans – see STONES RIVER. Kentucky remained within the Union.

Petersburg 403

Date: 15–18 June 1864.	
Location: Petersburg, 25 miles south of Richmond, Virginia.	
War and campaign: American Civil War: Grant's Virginia Campaign of 1864.	
Opposing sides: (a) Lieutenant-General Ulysses S. Grant, the US Army's General-in-Chief, in the field with Major-General George G. Meade's Army of the Potomac and Major-General Benjamin F. Butler commanding the Army of the James; (b) General Robert E. Lee commanding the Army of Northern Virginia and Lieutenant-General Pierre Beauregard commanding the Confederate troops south of the James river.	
Objective: Following his rebuff at COLD HARBOR, Grant was attempting to sever communications between Richmond and the rest of the Confederacy by capturing Petersburg and cutting the surrounding rail routes.	
Forces engaged: (a) Up to 14,000 on 15 June, rising to 65,000 on 18 June; (b) about 2,500 on 15 June, rising to 38,000 on 18 June.	
Casualties: (a) 8,150; (b) 4,752.	
Result: The failure to capture Petersburg spelled the end of mobile operations in this theatre of war. Both sides entrenched for what amounted to a virtual siege lasting for the next 9½ months. See CRATER, THE.	

Grant ordered Butler, whose army in the Bermuda Hundred was closer to Petersburg, to detach Major-General W. F. ('Baldy') Smith's corps and use it to capture the virtually undefended town from the west, while the Army of the Potomac marched to join him. Smith neither pressed his attack nor exploited such success as he achieved. Beauregard was forced to strip his lines opposite the Bermuda Hundred to meet the assault, but Butler declined to take advantage of the fact, either to threaten Petersburg from the north or to interfere with Lee's hurried march southward into the battle area. As the Army of the Potomac's corps arrived, they were committed against a progressively stronger defence and were unable to make further progress. The chance of ending the war in 1864 was therefore lost. Smith was dismissed; Butler, who possessed great political clout but scant military ability, kept his job.

Pharsalia 404

Date: 9 August 48 BC.	
Location: Uncertain, but probably beside the Enipeus river below Mount Dogantzis, Thessaly, Greece.	
War and campaign: Wars of the First Triumvirate.	
Opposing sides: (a) Julius Caesar; (b) Gnaius Pompeius (Pompey the Great).	
Objective: Having unsuccessfully besieged Pompey at Dyrrachium (modern Durres,	

Albania), Caesar retreated across the mountains into Greece. Pompey followed with a much superior force and both sides accepted the need for a decisive pitched battle.

Forces engaged: (a) 22,000 infantry and 1,000 cavalry – total 23,000; (b) 45,000 infantry and 7,000 cavalry – total 52,000.
Casualties: (a) 230 killed and probably 700 wounded; (b) 15,000 killed and wounded, plus 24,000 prisoners.
Result: Pompey's army was routed. Pompey fled to Egypt where he was murdered. His sons attempted to continue the struggle (see MUNDA) but Pharsalia left Caesar the victor in the civil war and master of the Roman world.

Caesar guessed that Pompey would use his cavalry to turn his exposed right flank and created a reserve consisting of his own cavalry and six cohorts to meet the threat. The counter-attack by this reserve put the Pompeian cavalry to flight and Pompey himself left the field. Caesar then ordered a general advance which overran the Pompeian position.

Philiphaugh 405

Date: 13 September 1645.
Location: 2 miles west of Selkirk.
War and campaign: First Civil War, 1642–1646: operations in Scotland.
Opposing sides: (a) James Graham, Marquis of Montrose, commanding the Royalists; (b) Major-General David Leslie.
Objective: The Covenanters launched a surprise dawn attack on the Royalist camp.
Forces engaged: (a) 1,500; (b) approximately 6,000 (mainly cavalry).
Casualties: (a) All but a few were killed, wounded or captured; (b) light.
Result: Montrose's troops were overrun and cut to pieces. Montrose escaped but the Royalist cause in Scotland had sustained a mortal blow and he fled abroad.

Philippi, First and Second Battles of 406

Date: 26 October and 16 November 42 BC.
Location: 9 miles north-west of modern Kavala, Macedonia.
War and campaign: Wars of the Second Triumvirate.
Opposing sides: (a) Octavian and Mark Antony commanding the army of the Triumvirate; (b) Marcus Junius Brutus and Gaius Cassius Longinus commanding the Republicans.
Objective: The Triumvirs were hunting down the Republican murderers of Julius Caesar.
Forces engaged: (a) 90,000 infantry and 13,000 cavalry – total 103,000; (b) 90,000 infantry and 20,000 cavalry – total 110,000.
Casualties: Unknown. Cassius commited suicide during the first battle and Brutus did likewise after the second.
Result: The Republicans were defeated. Octavian and Mark Antony assumed respective responsibility for the western and eastern portions of the Empire. The two subsequently quarrelled over Mark Antony's support for Cleopatra VII of Egypt and

> Octavian won a decisive naval victory at Actium (31 BC) which resulted directly in his assumption of autocratic Imperial rule and the name of Augustus.

Piave

Date: 15–22 June 1918.

Location: North of Venice, Padua and Verona along a line following the river Piave, then westwards to Lake Garda.

War and campaign: First World War: Italy.

Opposing sides: (a) Colonel-General Arz von Straussenburg, Chief of the Austro-Hungarian General Staff; (b) General Armando Diaz, Chief of the Italian General Staff.

Objective: The Austrians were attempting to knock Italy out of the war.

Forces engaged: (a) Army Group Conrad (Field Marshal Count Conrad von Hotzendorff) with the Austro-Hungarian Tenth and Eleventh Armies commanded respectively by Field Marshal von Krobatin and Colonel-General Scheuchensteul and Army Group Boroevic (Field Marshal Baron Svetozan Boroevic von Bojna) with the Austro-Hungarian Sixth and Isonzo Armies commanded respectively by the Archduke Joseph and Colonel-General von Wurm – total 50 divisions and 5,005 guns; (b) the Italian Third (the Duke of Aosta), Eighth (Lieutenant-General Caviglia), Fourth (Lieutenant-General Giardino), Sixth (Lieutenant-General Montuori) and First (Lieutenant-General Count Pecori-Giraldi) Armies – total 44 divisions (including British and French) and 2,866 guns.

Casualties: (a) Approximately 70,000; (b) approximately 85,000.

Result: The battle proved that the Italians had recovered from the disaster of CAPORETTO and it also destroyed the offensive capacity of the Austro-Hungarian Army for the rest of the war. See VITTORIO VENETO.

While Conrad made little or no progress, Boroevic succeeded in crossing the Piave on a wide front. However, heavy rains caused the river to rise and several of his bridges were swept away, leaving his leading elements isolated and exposed to counter-attack, and during the night of 22/23 June they were withdrawn.

Pinkie Cleugh

Date: 10 September 1547.

Location: South of Musselburgh, 7 miles east of Edinburgh.

War and campaign: Anglo–Scottish Wars.

Opposing sides: (a) The Duke of Somerset, Protector of England; (b) James, Earl of Arran, Regent of Scotland.

Objective: The English intention was to enforce a marriage treaty between Edward VI and Mary Queen of Scots, the parties then being aged ten and five respectively. As it approached Edinburgh, the invading English army found itself opposed by a superior Scottish force on the banks of the Esk above Musselburgh.

Forces engaged: (a) 4,000 cavalry and 12,000 infantry – total 16,000, with 80 guns (further gunfire support being provided by the English fleet); (b) 23,000 infantry with artillery (the small Scottish cavalry element had been virtually destroyed in a needless engagement the previous day).

Casualties: (a) 500; (b) 10,000, the majority incurred during the pursuit.
Result: The Scottish army was destroyed and the English occupied Edinburgh. Mary, however, had been sent to France where she was married to the Dauphin.

For reasons which have never been fully established, as the English were preparing to advance, the Scots abandoned their strong position, crossed the Esk and mounted an attack of their own. Their schiltrons were shot to pieces by the fire of the English artillery, warships, handguns and archers, and as they disintegrated the survivors were pursued without mercy by the English cavalry. Pinkie Cleugh was the last formal battle to be fought between the national armies of England and Scotland.

Plassey 409

Date: 23 June 1757.
Location: On the Hugli river in central Bengal, 110 miles north of Calcutta.
War and campaign: Bengal, 1756–1757.
Opposing sides: (a) Colonel Robert Clive; (b) Suraj-ud-Daula.
Objective: The British East India Company's army was pursuing that of Suraj-ud-Daula, Nawab of Bengal, who had sided with the French and committed atrocities against the British in Calcutta the previous year.
Forces engaged: (a) 800 European and 2,100 Indian infantry, with eight guns; (b) 35,000 infantry, 15,000 cavalry and 53 guns.
Casualties: (a) 18 killed ad 45 wounded; (b) approximately 500 killed and wounded, plus five guns captured.
Result: Suraj-ud-Daula was decisvely defeated and he was assassinated shortly afterwards. A substantial indemnity was paid by the new Nawab, Mir Jafar, and of this Clive's share amounted to the immense sum of £234,000. In the wider sphere the result of the battle was very significant since it ensured that the British would become the paramount power in India.

Clive's decision to engage his small force against an army so large that it all but encircled him might be regarded as rash were it not for the fact that he already knew that the majority of enemy divisional commanders were plotting against the Nawab, although in the final analysis they provided no practical assistance. The battle commenced with an attack against the British position, but this made little progress. During a heavy monsoon shower at noon the British covered their powder and the Nawab's men did not, with the result that the latter's guns were useless when fighting was resumed. Clive then went over to the offensive and by 17.00 the Nawab's army had disintegrated.

Plataea 410

Date: 479 BC.
Location: 11 miles south of Thivai (Thebes), Voiotia, Greece.
War and campaign: The Graeco–Persian Wars, 499–448 BC.
Opposing sides: (a) Pausanias, Regent of Sparta, commanding the Greeks; (b) Mardonius in command of the Persian army.
Objective: The intention of the Greeks was to destroy the invading Persian army

which, having temporarily occupied Athens, was retreating northwards following the Greek naval victory at Salamis the previous year.

Forces engaged: (a) 32,000 hoplites and 48,000 light infantry – total approximately 80,000; (b) uncertain, but estimated at 120,000 including a contingent of Thebans and other pro-Persian Greeks and a large cavalry element.

Casualties: (a) Probably more than the 1,300 suggested by Plutarch; (b) estimated 50,000 killed, including Mardonius.

Result: The complete destruction of the Persian army.

Both sides had held their positions for eight days, during which Mardonius's cavalry had preyed on the Greek lines of communication and fouled the water supply. Pausanias therefore embarked on a tactical withdrawal. While this was taking place Mardonius launched a general attack but the hoplites, operating on favourable ground, counter-attacked and drove the Persian infantry back into its stockaded camp, which was then stormed with much slaughter. The Greek victory stemmed more from the hoplites' superior discipline, training and equipment rather than Pausanias's generalship.

Plevna, Siege of 411

Date: 19 July to 10 December 1877.

Location: 100 miles north-east of Sofia, Bulgaria.

War and campaign: Russo–Turkish War, 1877–1878: Balkan Campaign.

Opposing sides: (a) Osman Pasha; (b) General Krudener, later Prince Carol of Romania.

Objective: Following the Russian invasion of Bulgaria, the Turks constructed an improvised fortress at Plevna (Pleven), lying on the right flank of the enemy advance, thereby imposing a delay on the Russians while they dealt with the threat.

Forces engaged: (a) 40,000 men and 77 guns; (b) latterly 110,000 Russians and Romanians with 500 guns.

Casualties: (a) Approximately 30,000; (b) approximately 40,000 Russians and Romanians.

Result: Osman succeeded in imposing serious delays on the invading armies but was forced to surrender when his attempted break-out failed during the night of 9/10 December.

The siege of Plevna, like several battles of the American Civil War, revealed the formidable nature of improvised earthwork defences and was an indication of the form major wars would take during the next forty years. In throwing back repeated Russian assaults with heavy losses the incredibly tough Turkish resistance aroused widespread admiration.

Poitiers 412

Date: 19 September 1356.

Location: 4 miles south of Poitiers, Poitou, France.

War and campaign: Hundred Years' War, 1337–1457: the Black Prince's Chevauchée of 1356.

Opposing sides: (a) Edward the Black Prince; (b) John II, King of France.
Objective: The Enlgish had been conducting a *chevauchée* (destructive raid) through central France; the French intention was to intercept them before they could return to their base at Bordeaux.
Forces engaged: (a) 2,000 archers and 4,000 men-at-arms – total 6,000; (b) 3,000 crossbowmen and 500 mounted and 17,000 dismounted men-at-arms – total 20,500.
Casualties: (a) Uncertain, but moderate; (b) 2,500 killed plus 2,000 captured (including John).
Result: A crushing English victory. Following further successful raids, the French requested a truce in 1360; this lasted for seven years.

The English adopted a similar position to that at CRÉCY, along a ridge with their front protected by two sunken lanes and a hedge; the left flank was anchored on the marshy valley of the Miosson stream and the right was reinforced with a wagon leaguer. The French, attempting to profit by their mistakes at Crécy, dismounted the majority of their men-at-arms but, unable to exploit their overwhelming numerical strength because of the narrow English front, attacked in a column of divisions. The first division, containing John's mounted element, masked the fire of its supporting crossbowmen and was defeated by the English archers and men-at-arms, as was the second division. The third division fled but the fourth, commanded by the French king, launched a determined assault which was only defeated when Edward mounted his men-at-arms and made a counter-charge downhill, coupled with a further charge into the enemy left flank by a small mounted reserve. John was captured in the mêlée and the French broke. See also AGINCOURT.

Poltava 413

Date: 28 June 1709.
Location: City on the Vorskla river, 85 miles south-west of Kharkov, Ukraine.
War and campaign: Great Northern War, 1700–1721: Campaign of Charles XII in Russia, 1708–1709.
Opposing sides: (a) Charles XII of Sweden; (b) Peter the Great.
Objective: The Swedes, besieging Poltava, attacked the entrenched camp of a Russian army which had marched to the city's relief.
Forces engaged: (a) Eighteen infantry battalions, twelve cavalry squadrons and a few guns – total 17,000; (b) 30 infantry battalions, 30 cavalry squadrons and 40 guns – total 80,000.
Casualties: (a) 7,000 killed and 2,600 captured; (b) 1,300 killed and wounded.
Result: The Swedish army was effectively destroyed and Charles fled to the protection of the Turks. Poltava, one of the most decisive battles in history, simultaneously marked the beginning of the decline of Sweden and the rise of Russia as European military powers.

Short of supplies and ammunition, Charles sought a quick victory and mounted a night attack which was intended to pass through a line of enemy redoubts and then assault the Russian camp. Incapacited by a recent wound, he was unable to exercise personal control of the battle, so that while his columns on the left and centre succeeded in passing the redoubts by dawn and repulsing a covering force of cavalry beyond, that on the right fell behind and became involved in a struggle for the redoubts themselves. Observing the isolation of this detachment, Peter despatched a 10,000-strong force which quickly surrounded and overwhelmed it. The remainder of the Swedish army re-formed after protracted bickering between its commanders, and the infantry launched a series of determined assaults on the main Russian entrenchments. These were repulsed with such heavy losses that by the end of the day little remained of the assault force. The Swedish cavalry managed to leave the field but it was overtaken and surrendered two days after the battle.

Pork Chop Hill 414

Date: 16–18 April 1953.
Location: Feature in advance of the main UN line, approximately 50 miles north of Seoul.
War and campaign: Korean War, 1950–1953.
Opposing sides: (a) Major-General Arthur Trudeau commanding the US 7th Division; (b) General Peng Teh-huai, *de facto* commander-in-chief of the Communist armies in Korea.
Objective: While the feature itself was of no great tactical significance, its possession was used by the Chinese to test UN resolve while peace negotiations were in progress.
Forces engaged: (a) Initially two platoons, rising to the equivalent of two battalions; (b) initially two companies, rising to the equivalent of one battalion.
Casualties: (a) Uncertain, but heavy; (b) unknown, but heavier.
Result: The Chinese seized the hill by *coup de main* but were driven off after two days of heavy fighting.

Altogether, nine artillery battalions belonging to the US 2nd and 7th Divisions fired a total of 77,349 rounds during the two-day battle. In the ensuing weeks both sides reinforced their respective positions so that, a fortnight before the armistice was signed on 27 July, the five American battalions holding the hill were confronted by a full Chinese division.

Port Arthur (Lu-Shun), Siege of 415

Date: 1 June 1904 to 2 January 1905.
Location: Port and naval base at the tip of the Liaotung Peninsula, Manchuria.
War and campaign: Russo–Japanese War, 1904–1905.
Opposing sides: (a) Major-General Baron Anatoli Stoessel commanding the Russian garrison; (b) General Baron Maresuke Nogi commanding the Japanese Third Army
Objective: The capture of Port Arthur by the Japanese.
Forces engaged: (a) Approximately 40,000 men and 506 guns, excluding naval personnel and warships; (b) approximately 80,000 men and 474 guns, supplemented by siege train in October.
Casualties: (a) 31,306; (b) 57,780.
Result: After six months of severe fighting, during which most of the incomplete defences were captured by the Japanese at heavy cost, Stoessel surrendered the

fortress and the remnants of the Russian fleet in the harbour. This left Nogi's army free for use elsewhere in Manchuria.

In retrospect, the fighting around Port Arthur, involving as it did a combination of entrenchments, barbed wire, machine guns, intense artillery fire and heavy casualties, provided a clear indication of the form the First World War would take, although the beginnings of the process were visible during the American Civil War.

Port Republic   416

Date: 9 June 1862.
Location: 15 miles north of Waynesboro, Virginia.
War and campaign: American Civil War: Shenandoah Valley Campaign of 1862.
Opposing sides: (a) Brigadier-General Erastus B. Tyler; (b) Major-General Thomas ('Stonewall') Jackson.
Objective: Two Federal columns were pursuing Jackson's II Corps as it withdrew southwards down the Valley. Having defeated one with a single division the previous day at Cross Keys, then barred its further progress by burning the only bridge available, Jackson now turned on the vanguard of the second as it approached Port Republic.
Forces engaged: (a) 3,000; (b) 6,000.
Casualties: (a) 500; (b) 800.
Result: The Federals were forced to retreat and Jackson resumed his withdrawal, joining Lee to take part in the SEVEN DAYS' BATTLES.

Jackson's operations in the Shenandoah valley – always a sensitive sector for the North as it provided an easy invasion route – were designed to tie down Federal troops which would otherwise have been sent to reinforce McClellan in the Peninsula, and in this he succeeded brilliantly. With never more than 16,000 men, he marched more than 400 miles between 30 April and 9 June, won five battles (McDowell, Front Royal, First Winchester, Cross Keys and Port Republic), inflicted 7,000 casualties at the cost of 2,500 of his own and absorbed the attention of some 64,000 Union troops.

Port Stanley   417

Date: 11–14 June 1982.
Location: In the hills to the west of Port Stanley, East Falkland.
War and campaign: The Falklands War, 1982.
Opposing sides: (a) Major-General Jeremy Moore; (b) Major-General Mario Menendez.
Objective: The British intention was to defeat the major portion of the Argentine occupation force and liberate Port Stanley.
Forces engaged: (a) 3 Commando Brigade Royal Marines, 5 Infantry Brigade and supporting arms, including naval gunfire and air support; (b) the equivalent of two infantry brigades and supporting arms – total approximately 8,400.
Casualties: (a) 40 killed and 120 wounded; (b) killed and wounded uncertain, but

heavier (the entire garrison, plus Argentine units elsewhere in the Falklands, became prisoners of war).

Result: Menendez surrendered when the last of his defensive positions was captured. His troops were disarmed and repatriated to Argentina.

Menendez had established a concentric system of defence based on the hills to the west of Port Stanley. The outermost and potentially most formidable ring was broken when 42 Commando seized the virtually undefended Mount Kent on 31 May – see GOOSE GREEN. After careful preparation the second ring was attacked during the night of 11/12 June, Mount Longdon falling to 3 Para after a severe struggle during which Sergeant Ian McKay won a posthumous Victoria Cross, while the Two Sisters and Mount Harriet were taken by 45 and 42 Commando respectively. The final defence line was attacked during the night of 13/14 June, 2 Scots Guards capturing Mount Tumbledown while 2 Para pushed the enemy off Wireless Ridge; on Mount William the Argentines fled before the advance of 1/7 Gurkhas, and 2 Welsh Guards encountered little opposition on Sapper Hill. The Argentines abandoned their remaining positions in a disorderly rout, fleeing into Port Stanley, and opened surrender negotiations.

Prague (1419)   418

Date: 30 July 1419.
Location: Vitkov Hill, outside the city.
War and campaign: Hussite Wars, 1419–1436.
Opposing sides: (a) Jan Ziska commanding the Hussites; (b) King Sigismund of Bohemia commanding the Catholics.
Objective: The Hussites were responding to an appeal for assistance by the inhabitants of Prague, who were being besieged by the Catholics; the Catholics reacted by mounting an attack on the Hussite position.
Forces engaged: (a) 9,000; (b) estimated 25,000.
Casualties: (a) Light; (b) uncertain, but heavy.
Result: The attack was decisively repulsed. Sigismund was forced to abandon the siege and retire temporarily from Bohemia.

Ziska was an innovative military thinker who recognized that his largely peasant army was unable to meet armoured feudal cavalry on equal terms and devised suitable tactics to restore the balance. These consisted of mobile leaguers (*wagenburgen*) in which wagons armed with artillery were drawn up in a defensive circle, usually on a hilltop, with mantlets covering the gaps. When the garrison, which was also armed with handguns, bows, bills and pikes, had beaten off the enemy assault, Ziska sent out his own cavalry to pursue. See also KUTNA HORA and NEMECKY BROD.

Prague (1757)   419

Date: 6 May 1757.
Location: 4 miles east of Prague, Czechoslovakia.
War and campaign: Seven Years' War, 1756–1763: Central European Campaign of 1757.

Opposing sides: (a) Frederick the Great; (b) Prince Charles of Lorraine commanding the Austrian army.
Objective: Frederick II of Prussia, having invaded the Austrian province of Bohemia with the object of capturing Prague, was opposed by an Austrian army east of the city.
Forces engaged: (a) 66 infantry battalions, 113 cavalry squadrons and 82 guns – total 67,000; (b) 60 infantry battalions, twenty cavalry regiments and 59 guns – total 60,000.
Casualties: (a) 14,300 killed and wounded; (b) 12,000 killed and wounded, plus 4,500 captured.
Result: The Austrians were routed when a wedge was driven into their right-centre, separating their right wing from the rest of the army.

Frederick went on to besiege Prague. See KOLIN.

Preston (1648) 420

Date: 17–19 August 1648.
Location: Ribbleton Moor to the east of the town and Walton Bridge to the south.
War and campaign: Second Civil War, 1648.
Opposing sides: (a) James, Duke of Hamilton, commanding the Scottish/Royalist army; (b) Oliver Cromwell.
Objective: The Parliamentarians attacked the flank of a Royalist army marching south through Preston.
Forces engaged: (a) 16,000 infantry, 3,600 cavalry and some guns; (b) 6,000 infantry, 3,000 cavalry and some guns.
Casualties: (a) Estimated 1,000 killed and 4,000 captured at Preston, plus larger numbers killed or captured during the pursuit to the south; (b) light.
Result: The Royalists were routed. The Army had now become the dominant power in the country and it imposed its will on Parliament, which was attempting to reach an accommodation with the King. Charles I was tried and executed on 30 January 1649, the Crown was abolished and a Commonwealth established under military control.

Hamilton's army was strung out over many miles of road, so that only a portion of his strength was actually engaged in the fighting at Preston. Hamilton did not support Sir Marmaduke Langdale, commanding the Royalist flank guard, who was forced back into Preston after heavy fighting. Cromwell then stormed the bridge over the Ribble and relentlessly pursued Hamilton's disintegrating army to the south. The Scottish infantry was brought to battle and forced to surrender at Winwick, near Warrington, on 19 August; Hamilton, with 3,000 cavalry, escaped but surrendered at Uttoxeter.

Preston (1715) 421

Date: 13/14 November 1715.
Location: In the centre and to the south of the town.
War and campaign: Fifteen Rebellion, 1715.

Opposing sides: (a) Major-General Wills commanding the Government forces; (b) Thomas Forster, Member of Parliament for Northumberland, commanding the rebels.
Objective: The rebel army had marched south into Lancashire, hoping to attract recruits to the Jacobite cause. At Preston it was intercepted by Government troops who were determined to stamp out the rising before it could gather momentum.
Forces engaged: (a) Approximately 2,500, including five regiments of dragoons; (b) approximately 3,000.
Casualties: (a) 200 killed and wounded; (b) 42 killed and wounded, plus 1,468 captured.
Result: The rebel army was destroyed, ending the rebellion in England. See also SHERIFFMUIR.

Thanks to Forster's inept leadership, Wills was able to box in the rebels in the town centre, although his subsequent attacks were repulsed. The following morning, however, Forster surrendered with the remnants of his force, the rest of his men having evidently escaped through the Government cordon during the night.

Prestonpans 422

Date: 21 September 1745.
Location: 5 miles east of Edinburgh.
War and campaign: Forty-Five Rebellion, 1745–1746.
Opposing sides: (a) Lieutenant-General Sir John Cope commanding the Government forces; (b) Prince Charles Edward Stuart commanding the Jacobites.
Objective: The Government forces were attempting to intercept and destroy the rebel army.
Forces engaged: (a) 2,200 and six guns; (b) 2,450.
Casualties: (a) 1,800, including 1,500 prisoners, plus all guns captured; (b) 30 killed and 80 wounded.
Result: Cope's force was destroyed. Sufficient recruits were attracted to the Jacobite cause for Prince Charles Edward to cross the border into England with an army of 4,500 infantry and 400 cavalry. This penetrated as far as Derby before retreating to Scotland. See FALKIRK (1746).

The previous day Cope had established a front facing south, but during the night the Jacobites marched round his position to the east. Dawn revealed the rebels to be only 200yds from the Government left flank and Cope barely had time to change front before the Highlanders charged. From start to finish the engagement lasted only some ten minutes.

Princeton 423

Date: 3 January 1777.
Location: 2 miles south-west of Princeton, New Jersey.
War and campaign: American War of Independence, 1775–1783: central theatre of operations.

Opposing sides: (a) Lieutenant-Colonel Charles Mawhood; (b) Major-General George Washington.
Objective: Following the American raid on TRENTON, the town was re-occupied on 2 January by a British force under Major-General Lord Cornwallis. For a while there was a confrontation with Washington's army, encamped across Assunpink Creek, but during the night the Americans slipped away, leaving their camp fires burning, and set off for Princeton, twelve miles in Cornwallis's rear. Approaching Princeton, they ran into a British column marching south on a parallel road to reinforce Cornwallis, and an encounter battle ensued.
Forces engaged: (a) 800; (b) 4,600.
Casualties: (a) 28 killed, 58 wounded and 323 captured, including 200 in Princeton; (b) 23 killed and 20 wounded.
Result: Although small in scale, the American victory had important consequences for the Revolution. The British evacuated their outposts in New Jersey, and Washington, incapable of further offensive action, was able to establish his army in winter quarters at Morristown.

Washington's thrust at Princeton came dangerously close to disaster when Mawhood's force, despite being heavily outnumbered, took the initiative and routed two American brigades in succession. It was defeated only after Washington personally rallied the fugitives and brought up a regular brigade.

Pusan Perimeter 424

Date: 5 August to 15 September 1950.
Location: UN defence line south and east of the Naktong river, based on the port of Pusan on the south-eastern coast of the Korean peninsula.
War and campaign: Korean War, 1950–1953.
Opposing sides: (a) General Douglas MacArthur in overall command of the UN forces and Lieutenant-General Walton H. Walker commanding the US Eighth Army; (b) Marshal Choe Yong Gun commanding the NKPA.
Objective: As the invading North Korean People's Army (NKPA) drove south, the UN intention was to create a secure area in which the defeated South Korean army could be rallied while the build-up of UN troops continued.
Forces engaged: (a) Five re-equipped South Korean divisions, three US divisions and one British brigade; (b) fourteen divisions, plus supporting armour.
Casualties: (a) Heavy; (b) killed and wounded unknown, but 125,000 prisoners were taken and virtually all the NKPA's heavy weapons and equipment were destroyed or abandoned.
Result: The Eighth Army's break-out from its perimeter was timed to coincide with the landing at INCHON. Trapped between the two and with its lines of communication cut, the NKPA disintegrated and its remnants were pursued the length of the Korean peninsula. See also CHOSIN RESERVOIR/HUNGNAM.

Walker's command enjoyed the benefit of interior lines and while it became steadily stronger the Communists made determined if unco-ordinated attempts to eliminate the last UN toe-hold in Korea. On 3 September, for example, Choe mounted a three-division attack against the northern defences, compelling Walker to commit the last of his reserves, but the line held.

Pydna

Date: 22 June 168 BC.
Location: Near the mouth of the Aeson river on the western shore of the Gulf of Thessalonika.
War and campaign: Third Macedonian War, 172–167 BC.
Opposing sides: (a) Lucius Aemilius Paulus commanding the Roman army; (b) King Perseus commanding the Macedonians.
Objective: A minor skirmish beside the river escalated into a general engagement.
Forces engaged: (a) Four legions and auxiliaries – total approximately 25,000; (b) 40,000 infantry (including a 20,000-strong phalanx) and 4,000 cavalry – total 44,000.
Casualties: (a) Approximately 500 killed and wounded; (b) at least 20,000 killed and 10,000 captured.
Result: The Macedonian army was destroyed. Perseus escaped but surrendered later and died in captivity. Rome established a virtual protectorate over Greece.

The Macedonian phalanx at first pushed the Romans back but its ranks became disordered when it reached broken ground. The legionaries quickly counter-attacked, breaking into the gaps and slaughtering the now defenceless phalangites to a man. The battle confirmed the lesson of CYNOSCEPHALAE, namely that the flexibility of a legion made it more than a match for the monolithic tactics of the phalanx.

Pyramids, The

Date: 21 July 1798.
Location: Gizeh, near Cairo, Egypt.
War and campaign: French expedition to Egypt, 1798–1801.
Opposing sides: (a) General Napoleon Bonaparte; (b) Murad Bey.
Objective: Having defeated its Continental enemies, the French Directory approved Bonaparte's scheme for an expedition to Egypt, then nominally a province of the Ottoman Empire, as a means of bringing pressure to bear against the British in India. After capturing Alexandria on 2 July 1798, Bonaparte advanced on Cairo, where he was opposed by the Mameluke army.
Forces engaged: (a) 30,000; (b) 60,000.
Casualties: (a) 300; (b) approximately 6,000.
Result: The Mamelukes were defeated. Cairo was entered the following day and the French extended their hold over Egypt. Unfortunately for Napoleon, his entire strategic concept was disrupted when Admiral Horatio Nelson destroyed the French fleet in Aboukir Bay on 1 August (the Battle of the Nile).

The battle was essentially a contest between a modern and a medieval army. The Mameluke cavalry were repulsed by the fire of the French squares, then driven into the Nile, where many drowned, and the entrenched camp of the Egyptians was stormed. See also ABOUKIR.

Quatre Bras

Date: 16 June 1815.
Location: Crossroads and farm on the Charleroi road, 25 miles south of Brussels, Belgium.
War and campaign: Napoleon's Hundred Days: Campaign in Belgium.
Opposing sides: (a) Field Marshal the Duke of Wellington commanding the Anglo-Netherlands army; (b) Marshal Michel Ney commanding the left wing of the French Army of the North.
Objective: Having crossed the Belgian frontier, Napoleon sought to defeat the Prussian and Anglo-Netherlands armies in separate engagements. Attacking the former at LIGNY with his centre and right wing, he ordered his left wing to seize the strategically important road junction at Quatre Bras.
Forces engaged: (a) 7,800, rising to approximately 31,000; (b) approximately 22,000.
Casualties: (a) 4,700; (b) 4,300.
Result: A hard-fought but inconclusive battle. Ney, overawed by Wellington's reputation, did not press his assault when an opportunity existed during the early phases of the engagement. After darkness put an end to the fighting, Wellington commenced an orderly withdrawal to the ridge of Mont St Jean, south of WATERLOO.

Quebec (Plains of Abraham) (1759)

Date: 13 September 1759.
Location: On the Plains of Abraham to the west of the city.
War and campaign: French and Indian War in North America, 1754–1763.
Opposing sides: (a) Major-General James Wolfe; (b) Major-General Marquis Louis-Joseph de Montcalm.
Objective: Following their successes at LOUISBURG and FORT DUQUESNE the previous year, and at Fort Niagara and FORT TICONDEROGA in July 1759, the major British objective had become the capture of Quebec, the centre of French power in Canada.
Forces engaged: (a) 4,441; (b) 4,500.
Casualties: (a) 58 killed (including Wolfe) and 600 wounded; (b) approximately 600 killed and wounded (including Montcalm, mortally wounded).
Result: The French army was defeated and Quebec surrendered on 18 September. A French attempt to recapture the fortress the following spring was defeated and on 8 September 1760 the Marquis de Vaudreuil, Governor of Canada, surrendered at Montreal.

Wolfe's army arrived from Louisburg in June and established itself on the Isle of Orleans, downstream from Quebec. His major problem was that every approach to the fortress was covered by steep river cliffs which were easily defended by the French. After protracted reconnaissance he decided to use a diagonal path up the cliffs at a point west of the city called the Anse au Foulon, now known as Wolfe's Cove. During the night of 12/13 September his troops scaled this and deployed on the Plains of Abraham. Montcalm led out his own army to give battle but during a brief exchange of fire this was worsted by the much superior British musketry, the first volleys of which were not delivered until the two sides were only 40yds apart.

Quebec (1775) 429

Date: 31 December 1775.
Location: The Lower Town, Quebec City.
War and campaign: American War of Independence, 1775–1783: Canadian theatre of operations.
Opposing sides: (a) Major-General Sir Guy Carleton, Governor-General of Canada; (b) Brigadier-Generals Richard Montgomery and Benedict Arnold.
Objective: The Americans intended capturing Quebec in the hope that by defeating the British in Canada they would encourage the Canadians to join them.
Forces engaged: (a) Approximately 1,200, the majority being militia; (b) approximately 900.
Casualties: (a) Five killed and thirteen wounded; (b) 60 killed and wounded (including Montgomery killed), plus 426 captured.
Result: The assault failed disastrously.

Following the arrival of British reinforcements the survivors retreated to Montreal, then abandoned Canada altogether. The Canadians remained loyal to the United Kingdom.

Queenston Heights 430

Date: 13 October 1812.
Location: On the Niagara river, Ontario, Canada.
War and campaign: War of 1812: Canadian front.
Opposing sides: (a) General Sir Isaac Brock; (b) Major-General Stephen van Rensselaer.
Objective: The British and Canadians converged on an American force which had crossed the river and established itself on Queenston Heights.
Forces engaged: (a) 600 regulars, 400 militia and a contingent of Indians; (b) 950 regulars.
Casualties: (a) Fourteen killed (including Brock) and 96 wounded; (b) 250 killed and wounded and 700 captured.
Result: The American force was destroyed.

Van Rensselaer also had 2,270 militia available but they played no part in the battle. To their shame, they claimed their rights and refused to cross from the American side of the river.

Ramillies 431

Date: 22 May 1706.
Location: Village 10 miles north of Namur, Belgium.

War and campaign: War of Spanish Succession, 1701–1714: Spanish Netherlands Campaign of 1706.
Opposing sides: (a) The Duke of Marlborough commanding the Allied army; (b) Marshal Duke François de Villeroi commanding the French army.
Objective: Louis XIV, anxious to restore the prestige of the French army after the defeat at BLENHEIM, had ordered Marshal de Villeroi, his commander in the Spanish Netherlands, to bring Marlborough to battle (the latter had, in fact, been vainly attempting to provoke de Villeroi for some time). The two armies converged near Namur.
Forces engaged: (a) 74 infantry battalions, 123 cavalry squadrons and 120 guns – total 62,000 (British, Dutch, German and Imperial); (b) 70 infantry battalions, 132 cavalry squadrons and 70 guns – total 60,000.
Casualties: (a) 1,066 killed and 3,633 wounded; (b) 8,000 killed and wounded, 7,000 prisoners and 50 guns captured.
Result: The French were decisively defeated and Marlborough overran the Spanish Netherlands, taking a further 14,000 prisoners as one French fortress after another surrendered to him. Villeroi was replaced by Marshal Duke Louis Joseph de Vendôme – see OUDENARDE.

Marlborough began the battle with an aggressive feint against the French left, causing Villeroi to reinforce his threatened flank with infantry from his centre. On Marlborough's left, however, the French cavalry were having the better of a mêlée until he brought up additional squadrons from his centre and right and drove them off the field. The allied cavalry then swung right to roll up the French line while an infantry assault stormed its way into the village of Ramillies in the centre of Villeroi's position. Marlborough's victory was complemented by Eugene's at TURIN (7 September).

Ramleh 432

Date: 6 September 1101.
Location: Near modern Ramla, between Jerusalem and Tel Aviv.
War and campaign: Wars of the Crusader States.
Opposing sides: (a) Baldwin, King of Jerusalem; (b) Saad el-Dawileh.
Objective: The Crusaders engaged an Egyptian army which had been sent into Palestine to expel them.
Forces engaged: (a) 260 mounted knights and 900 infantry – total 1,160; (b) 11,000 cavalry and 21,000 infantry – total 32,000.
Casualties: (a) Estimated 300; (b) unknown, but heavy.
Result: The Egyptians defeated three Crusader charges but broke and fled at the fourth.

A second Egyptian invasion the following year was similarly defeated. While small, the Crusader army was battle-hardened, professional and fighting for survival; much of the Egyptian army, on the other hand, consisted of untrained feudal levies.

Rava Russkaya 433

Date: 3–11 September 1914.

Location: Across Austrian Galicia, now part of south-eastern Poland and the western Ukraine.
War and campaign: First World War: Eastern Front.
Opposing sides: (a) Field Marshal Count Conrad von Hotzendorf, Chief of the Austro-Hungarian General Staff; (b) General Nikolai Ivanov commanding the South-West Front.
Objective: Each side was engaged in a general offensive against the other.
Forces engaged: (a) Austro-Hungarian Second (Bohm-Ermoli), Third (Brudermann), Fourth (Auffenberg) and First (Dankl) Armies; (b) Russian Ninth (Lechitsky), Fourth (Evert), Fifth (Plehve), Third (Ruzsky) and Eighth (Brusilov) Armies.
Casualties: (a) 400,000, including 100,000 prisoners and 300 guns (entire offensive); (b) 250,000, including 40,000 prisoners and 100 guns.
Result: The Austrians were compelled to abandon their base at Lemberg (Lvov) and retreat 100 miles to the Carpathian mountains. The fortress of Przemysl was besieged by the Russians and surrendered on 22 March 1915. Significantly, the defeat at Rava Russkaya led Conrad to seek German assistance, although the war was barely a month old.

A confused, untidy series of actions in which neither commander was aware of his opponent's dispositions until battle was joined. In the south the Austrian Third Army was overwhelmed by the attack of the Russian Third and Eighth Armies. The Russian Third Army, advancing north-west towards Lemberg, then clashed with the Austrian Fourth, marching south-east, at Rava Russkaya. Finally, increasing pressure against his left flank forced Conrad to withdraw in order to escape destruction.

Reichswald, The 434

Date: 8 February to 3 March 1945.
Location: Within Germany's frontier with Holland in the general area Cleve–Reichswald Forest–Goch, extending south-east to the left bank of the Rhine.
War and campaign: Second World War: North-West Europe.
Opposing sides: (a) Field Marshal Sir Bernard Montgomery commanding the 21st Army Group; (b) Colonel-General Johannes Blaskowitz commanding Army Group H.
Objective: To penetrate the northern extension of the Siegfried Line and clear the left bank of the Rhine in preparation for THE RHINE CROSSINGS.
Forces engaged: (a) Lieutenant-General H. D. G. Crerar commanding the Canadian First Army with the Canadian II Corps (Simonds) (initially one infantry division and one armoured brigade) and the British XXX Corps (Horrocks) (initially one armoured division, six infantry divisions, three armoured brigades and specialist armoured teams); (b) General Alfred Schlemm commanding the First Parachute Army with II Parachute Corps (one infantry and one parachute division) and LXXXVI Corps (two infantry and elements of one parachute division), subsequently reinforced with XLVII Panzer Corps (two panzer and one panzergrenadier divisions) from army group reserve.
Casualties: (a) Approximately 15,000; (b) approximately 22,000 killed and wounded and the same number captured.

> **Result:** Despite delays imposed by flooding and heavier casualties than had been anticipated, the Allies attained all their objectives.

The Reichswald battle, codenamed 'Veritable', began with the most concentrated Allied artillery bombardment of the war, over 6,000 tons of shells being fired during the first 24 hours. At first good progress was made, but the Germans breached local dykes to create large flooded areas and this, plus a combination of atrocious weather and stiffening resistance, imposed severe restrictions on the rate of advance. To the south of the main battle area the Germans had also breached the Roer dams to create a large flooded area which delayed the converging advance of the US Ninth Army. By 23 February, however, the water level had fallen and the Americans commenced their attack, codenamed 'Grenade', and on 3 March effected a junction with the Canadians at Geldern. Following this, Schlemm withdrew the remnants of his First Parachute Army across the Rhine.

Rhine Crossings, The 435

Date: 7–31 March 1945.
Location: Rees, Wesel, Rheinberg, Remagen, Boppard, St Goar, Mainz, Oppenheim, Worms and Germersheim.
War and campaign: Second World War: North-West Europe.
Opposing sides: (a) General Dwight D. Eisenhower, Supreme Commander of the Allied forces; (b) Field Marshal Albert Kesselring, Commander-in-Chief West.
Objective: The Allied intention was to cross the Rhine and defeat the remaining German armies in the West.
Forces engaged: (a) US 6th Army Group (Devers), US 12th Army Group (Bradley) and British 21st Army Group (Montgomery) – total 85 divisions; (b) Army Group H (Blaskowitz), Army Group B (Model) and Army Group G (Hausser) – total 60 under-strength divisions.
Casualties: Including REICHSWALD and other operations preparatory to the crossings, and the crossings themselves: (a) 6,570 Americans killed, 15,628 British and Canadians killed and wounded; (b) 60,000 killed and wounded, 250,000 and large quantities of equipment captured.
Result: The great defensive barrier of the Rhine was crossed along its length and in the process such severe casualties were inflicted on the German armies in the West that they were incapable of offering further resistance as the Allies advanced into the heartland of Germany.

On 7 March the leading elements of the US 9th Armored Division (US First Army) captured the Ludendorff Bridge at Remagen by *coup de main*; this was supplemented by pontoons and by 21 March the bridgehead was twenty miles long and eight miles deep. On 22 March Patton's Third Army, also part of Bradley's 12th Army Group, mounted a surprise attack and secured a second bridgehead at Oppenheim. The following day Montgomery's 21st Army Group obtained bridgeheads at Rees, Wesel and Rheinberg after making an assault crossing. On 24 March Patton obtained a further bridgehead at St Goar. On Devers' Sixth Army Group sector in the south the US Seventh Army crossed at Worms on 26 March, followed by the French First Army at Germersheim on 31 March.

Rhodes, First Siege of 436

Date: 23 May to 20 August 1480.
Location: Fortified city at the northern extremity of the island.
War and campaign: The Wars of Mahomet II.
Opposing sides: (a) Masih Pasha commanding the besiegers; (b) Pierre d'Aubusson, Grand Master of the Knights of St John, commanding the garrison.
Objective: The Turkish intention was to drive the Knights of St John from their base on the Island.
Forces engaged: (a) Approximately 70,000; (b) approximately 4,000 knights and local militia.
Casualties: (a) Estimated 9,000 killed and 30,000 wounded; (b) uncertain, but heavy.
Result: Repeated Turkish assaults were repulsed in ferocious fighting. After his losses had become insupportable Masih embarked his troops and left the island, which remained in the Order's possession for a further 42 years. See RHODES, SECOND SIEGE OF.

Rhodes, Second Siege of 437

Date: 28 July to 21 December 1522.
Location: Fortified city at the northern extremity of the island.
War and campaign: Turkish Wars of the Sixteenth Century.
Opposing sides: (a) Sultan Suleiman the Magnificent; (b) Philip Villiers de L'Isle Adam, Grand Master of the Knights of St John.
Objective: The Turkish intention was to drive the Knights of St John from their base on the island.
Forces engaged: (a) Approximately 100,000, including engineers and a powerful artillery siege train, reinforced by a similar number; (b) 700 knights and 6,000 local militia, plus emplaced artillery.
Casualties: (a) Minimum and maximum estimates of Turkish dead were, respectively, 50,000 and 100,000; (b) only 180 knights and 1,500 militia, most of whom were wounded, remained alive at the end of the siege.
Result: The Knights of St John were granted honourable surrender terms and left the island, establishing a new base on Malta.

The ferocity of the fighting equalled that of the earlier siege (q.v.). Suleiman, shaken by his army's terrible losses, offered generous terms which permitted the population to leave or remain on the island with the promise that their religion would be respected. As his ammunition was all but expended and his surviving garrison was too small to man the walls, de L'Isle Adam accepted. It is probable that the Knights could have held their immensely strong fortifications indefinitely had they received some reinforcements and supplies from Europe, but none were forthcoming.

Riga 438

Date: 1–5 September 1917.

Location: City on the coast of Latvia.
War and campaign: First World War: Eastern Front.
Opposing sides: (a) General Oskar von Hutier commanding the German Eighth Army; (b) General Klembovsky commanding the Russian Twelfth Army.
Objective: The Germans wished to eliminate a Russian bridgehead on the west bank of the Dvina and capture Riga as a preliminary to an advance on Petrograd (St Petersburg).
Forces engaged: (a) Fifteen infantry divisions, two cavalry divisions and reinforced artillery support; (b) nine and a half infantry and two cavalry divisions.
Casualties: (a) 4,200; (b) 25,000, including 9,000 prisoners.
Result: Riga was captured and the Russians were forced back 30 miles.

While small in scale by First World War standards, the battle contained a number of tactically important features. Instead of mounting a frontal assault on the Russian bridgehead, Hutier used the indirect approach and crossed the Dvina upstream from Riga; Klembovsky, realizing that his troops were in danger of being encircled, promptly withdrew from the city and the bridgehead. The German infantry employed speed and infiltration to work their way past centres of resistance, while waves of ground-attack aircraft strafed the Russian trenches. Phosgene (mustard) gas shells were used operationally by the German artillery for the first time.

Rivoli 439

Date: 14 January 1797.
Location: Village between Lake Garda and the Adige, 14 miles north of Verona, northern Italy.
War and campaign: War of the First Coalition, 1792–1798: Campaign in Italy, 1796–1797.
Opposing sides: (a) General Napoleon Bonaparte; (b) General Baron Josef Alvintzy.
Objective: Despite their defeats at BASSANO and ARCOLA, the Austrians mounted a fourth attempt to relieve the besieged fortress of Mantua. Once again, however, they divided their forces and the stronger portion attacked the French covering position at Rivoli.
Forces engaged: (a) 23,000; (b) 28,000.
Casualties: (a) 2,500; (b) 10,300, including 7,000 prisoners.
Result: The Austrian attack was decisively defeated.

Mantua surrendered on 2 February and the following month the French invaded Austria.

Rocroi 440

Date: 18/19 May 1643.
Location: Fortified town near the Franco-Belgian frontier, 55 miles north-east of Rheims.
War and campaign: Thirty Years' War, 1618–1648: Campaign of 1643 in France and Belgium.

Opposing sides: (a) Duke Louis d'Enghien commanding the French army; (b) Don Francisco de Melo commanding the Spanish army.
Objective: The French were attempting to relieve Rocroi, which was being besieged by the Spanish.
Forces engaged: (a) Eighteen infantry battalions, 32 cavalry squadrons and twelve guns – total 23,000; (b) twenty infantry *tercios*, 7,000 cavalry and 28 guns – total 27,000.
Casualties: (a) 2,000 killed and 2,000 wounded; (b) 7,500 killed, 7,000 captured and 6,500 missing.
Result: Rocroi was relieved and the Spanish army was destroyed. France replaced Spain as the Continent's leading military power.

Both armies were drawn up with their infantry in the centre and cavalry on the flank, although the Spanish occupied a shorter front as their infantry was massed in depth. During the first day's fighting the French had the worst of an artillery duel and their left-wing cavalry under La Ferté-Senneterre was repulsed when it attempted to ride round the Spanish right into Rocroi. The following morning the French right wing defeated its opponents but on the left La Ferté-Senneterre was again repulsed by Isembourg's Spanish cavalry which, with the leading *tercios*, then attacked the French infantry. After changing hands several times the French artillery was turned on its owners. The French began to give way but were rallied and the position was stabilized by a counter-attack with the reserve. At this point d'Enghien, having defeated the Spanish left, fell on the uncommitted *tercios* and routed them. The remainder of the Spanish infantry abandoned its assault and began retiring slowly, followed closely by the French. During the ensuing firefight both sides suffered severely, but d'Enghien massed his recaptured artillery against an angle of the enemy square and a final attack swept the Spanish army away.

Romani

Date: 3–5 August 1916.
Location: Town in northern Sinai, 15 miles east of the Suez Canal and inland of the Bay of Tina.
War and campaign: First World War: Egypt and Sinai.
Opposing sides: (a) General Sir Archibald Murray, Commander-in-Chief of the British Forces in Egypt; (b) Colonel Freiherr Freidrich Kress von Kressenstein commanding the Turkish forces in Sinai.
Objective: The British intention was to remove the threat to the Suez Canal by pushing the Turks out of Sinai; the Turks were contesting the advance with a major counter-attack.
Forces engaged: (a) ANZAC Mounted Division (Major-General Chauvel) and 52nd (Lowland) Division (reinforced) (Major-General Lawrence); (b) approximately 18,000 men, including German medium and heavy artillery units and a German machine-gun battalion.
Casualties: (a) 1,130; (b) over 5,000 killed and wounded, plus 4,000 captured.
Result: The Turkish counter-attack was decisively repulsed and Kress executed a difficult disengagement.

Murray resumed his advance, the pace of which was dictated by the need to establish a

sound logistic infrastructure, and reached El Arish in December. See GAZA, THIRD
BATTLE OF.

Rorke's Drift   442

Date: 22/23 January 1879.
Location: Mission station on the Buffalo River, 10 miles from Helpmakaar, Natal.
War and campaign: Zulu War, 1879.
Opposing sides: (a) Lieutenant John Chard, Royal Engineers; (b) Dabulamanzi, brother of King Ceteweyo.
Objective: The right wing of the Zulu army which had attacked ISANDHLWANA, having seen little fighting, was determined to wipe out the British post at Rorke's Drift.
Forces engaged: (a) B Company 2nd/24th Regiment (South Wales Borderers), commanded by Lieutenant Gonville Bromhead, plus attached personnel – total 139, including 35 already sick or injured; (b) 4–5,000.
Casualties: (a) 15 killed and 12 seriously wounded; (b) over 500 killed and a comparable number wounded.
Result: During a night of desperate fighting, repeated Zulu attacks were beaten off. The post was relieved by Lord Chelmsford the following morning. See also KAMBULA.

The remarkable defence of the post against seemingly impossible odds went far to deaden
the shock of Isandhlwana. Eleven members of the garrison were awarded the Victoria
Cross. Among the recipients were Chard and Bromhead, who became brevet-majors and
were summoned to a personnal audience with Queen Victoria.

Rossbach   443

Date: 5 November 1757.
Location: Village near Weissenfels, 26 miles south-west of Leipzig, Germany.
War and campaign: Seven Years' War, 1756–1763: Central European Campaign of 1757.
Opposing sides: (a) Frederick the Great; (b) Prince Charles de Soubise and Prince Joseph of Saxe-Hildburghausen commanding the Franco-Austrian army.
Objective: Frederick's army confronted an invading Franco-Austrian army near Rossbach.
Forces engaged: (a) 27 infantry battalions and 45 cavalry squadrons – total 21,000; (b) 62 infantry battalions and 82 cavalry squadrons – total approximately 41,000.
Casualties: (a) 165 killed and 376 wounded; (b) 3,000 killed and wounded, 5,000 prisoners and 67 guns captured.
Result: An overwhelming Prussian victory which dealt a severe blow to French prestige and cleared Frederick's western front at a period when he was closely encircled by his enemies.

The allies planned to encircle the Prussian left with a large-scale turning movement,
carried out in five columns of march. Frederick's artillery and cavalry, the latter

commanded by General Friederich von Seydlitz, quickly redeployed to meet the threat, their movement concealed by Janus Hill. When the allied cavalry appeared it was charged and routed by Seydlitz. The allied infantry columns came under fire from the Prussian artillery on Janus Hill and their right flank was then charged by Seydlitz's rallied troopers. Coming up, the Prussian infantry attacked the left flank of the columns in echelon from the left. The entire allied army broke and fled in disorder. Although credit for the victory is often accorded to Frederick, it was Seydlitz who correctly interpreted the allied move and set the Prussian response in motion. The battle considerably eased the difficult strategic situation in which Frederick had found himself after his defeat at KOLIN. A large Russian army under Marshal Stepan Apraxin had defeated a smaller Prussian force at Gross-Jägersdorf in East Prussia (30 July) but had then retired across the frontier because supply difficulties had induced a mutiny. The remaining allied armies had not pressed their advantage until Soubise and Hildburghausen had resumed their advance. The victory at Rossbach enabled Frederick to deal promptly with a fresh threat which had materialized in Silesia – see LEUTHEN.

Roundway Down 444

Date: 13 July 1643.
Location: 2 miles north of Devizes, Wiltshire.
War and campaign: First Civil War, 1642–1646.
Opposing sides: (a) Lord Wilmot commanding the relief column and Sir Ralph Hopton commanding the force in Devizes; (b) Sir William Waller commanding the Parliamentarians.
Objective: A column of Royalist cavalry was moving to the relief of a force of infantry blockaded in Devizes by a Parliamentary army.
Forces engaged: (a) 1,800 cavalry with Wilmot and 3,000 infantry with Hopton in Devizes; (b) 2,000 cavalry and 2,500 infantry, with eight guns.
Casualties: (a) Light; (b) 600 killed, 800 prisoners and all guns captured.
Result: The Parliamentary army was destroyed. The victorious Royalists went on to capture Bristol on 26 July.

In theory, Waller's army was more than a match for either Royalist force unless the latter acted in concert; this was, in fact, the intention of the Royalist commanders, although in the event it came about more by accident than design. Waller drew up his army in the valley between Bagdon Hill and King's Play Hill, directly across Wilmot's line of march, with his cavalry on the flanks and his infantry in the centre. Wilmot, lacking infantry, charged the Parliamentary cavalry and routed it after a struggle lasting 30 minutes, driving it over a precipitous slope dropping some 300ft to what is still known as Bloody Ditch. Hopton's troops were now debouching from Devizes and, with Wilmot's rallied troopers, they attacked the isolated Parliamentary infantry, who had remained helpless spectators while the cavalry combat raged on either flank; those unable to flee were cut down or captured.

Rouvray ('The Herrings') 445

Date: 12 February 1429.
Location: Village on the Paris–Orléans road.

War and campaign: Hundred Years' War, 1337–1457: Siege of Orléans, 1428–1429.
Opposing sides: (a) Sir John Fastolf commanding the convoy; (b) the Comte de Clermont and Sir John Stewart of Darnley.
Objective: The French intention was to capture a supply convoy destined for the English army besieging ORLÉANS.
Forces engaged: (a) 1,000 mounted archers; (b) 3,000 French and Scots with a number of small guns.
Casualties: (a) Light; (b) approximately 600 killed, including Stewart and 120 knights.
Result: The attackers were routed and the convoy reached the English army.

Fastolf formed his 300 wagons into a defensive leaguer on a ridge above Rouvray. They were carrying barrels of salted herrings which would form the army's staple rations during Lent, and when the French opened fire with their guns, fish began to cascade from damaged vehicles. A premature attack by the Scots was beaten off with heavy losses, as was a supporting attack by the French men-at-arms. Fastolf then led his men in a mounted sortie which routed the attackers.

St Albans, First Battle of 446

Date: 22 May 1455.
Location: Within the town, with the fighting concentrated around the market place and St Peter's Street.
War and campaign: Wars of the Roses, 1455–1485.
Opposing sides: (a) Henry VI commanding the Lancastrians; (b) Richard Duke of York commanding the Yorkists.
Objective: A Yorkist force advancing on London was opposed by a smaller Lancastrian force at St Albans.
Forces engaged: (a) 2,000; (b) 3,000.
Casualties: (a) 75 killed, including the Duke of Somerset; (b) 25 killed.
Result: The Lancastrians were defeated and the King was captured.

Richard resumed his advance on London, where he had himself proclaimed Constable of England, assuming dictatorial powers.

St Albans, Second Battle of 447

Date: 17 February 1461.
Location: Within the town and on Bernard's Heath to the north.
War and campaign: Wars of the Roses, 1455–1485.
Opposing sides: (a) The Duke of Somerset (son of the Duke killed at the FIRST BATTLE OF ST ALBANS) commanding the Lancastrians; (b) the Earl of Warwick commanding the Yorkists.
Objective: The Lancastrians, advancing on London after their victory at WAKEFIELD, outflanked the Yorkist army and attacked it from the rear.

Forces engaged: (a) 12,000; (b) 9,000.
Casualties: (a) 1,000; (b) 1,900.
Result: The Lancastrians were victorious and recaptured King Henry VI. However, they were slow to exploit their victory and Warwick and Edward, Duke of York, the recent victor of MORTIMER'S CROSS, reached London first, the Duke being proclaimed Edward IV. The Lancastrian army then withdrew northwards – see TOWTON.

Warwick's troops possessed some handguns and artillery. However, the Yorkists were shooting into a snow-laden wind which caused their arrows to fall short and extinguished the handgun matches; in addition, several artillery pieces seem to have burst on discharge, which can have done nothing to improve the Yorkists' morale.

St Mihiel 448

Date: 12–16 September 1918.
Location: South-west of Metz and south-east of Verdun.
War and campaign: First World War: Western Front.
Opposing sides: (a) Marshal Ferdinand Foch, Allied Supreme Commander; (b) General Erich Ludendorff, First Quartermaster-General of the German Army.
Objective: To eliminate the St Mihiel salient as a prelude to an Allied attack on Metz.
Forces engaged: (a) General John J. Pershing commanding the US First Army, with seven American and four French divisions; (b) General Max von Gallwitz commanding the German Fifth Army, with eight divisions in the line and four in reserve.
Casualties: (a) 7,000; (b) 5,000 killed or wounded and 15,000 prisoners.
Result: In this, the US Army's first independent operation on the Western Front (and also its largest operation since the Civil War), the Americans gained all their objectives, assisted to some extent by Ludendorff's decision that the salient should be abandoned.

Saipan 449

Date: 15 June to 9 July 1944.
Location: One of the Marianas Islands, Central Pacific.
War and campaign: Second World War: Central Pacific.
Opposing sides: (a) Admiral Chester Nimitz, Commander-in-Chief Central Pacific Theatre; (b) Admiral Chuichi Nagumo commanding Japanese forces in the Marianas and General Hideyoshi Obata commanding the Japanese Thirty-First Army.
Objective: The capture of the Marianas would enable the Americans to launch a bombing offensive against Japan itself and also cut the enemy's communications with his conquests to the south.
Forces engaged: Lieutenant-General Holland M. Smith commanding V Amphibious Corps (2nd and 4th Marine Divisions and 27th Infantry Divisions); (b) Lieutenant-General Yoshitsugo Saito commanding some 24,000 men of the Thirty-First Army and 6,000 naval troops.

Casualties: (a) 3,126 killed, 13,106 wounded and 326 missing; (b) about 27,000 killed (Nagumo, chiefly remembered for his attack on Pearl Harbor, committed suicide, as did Saito).

Result: After the usual fanatical resistance, the island fell to the Americans.

See also TINIAN and GUAM.

Sakaria River

450

Date: 24 August to 16 September 1921.
Location: 50 miles west of Ankara.
War and campaign: Graeco–Turkish War, 1920–1922.
Opposing sides: (a) King Constantine; (b) Mustapha Kemal (known later as Kemal Ataturk).
Objective: The Turks were resisting the Greek advance on Ankara – see INONU.
Forces engaged: (a) 65,000; (b) 55,000.
Casualties: (a) 18,000; (b) 16,000.
Result: A narrow Turkish victory following a protracted struggle in which both armies were fought to a standstill. Constantine ordered his troops to withdraw and the future of modern Turkey was assured.

The Greek army, over-extended, demoralized and riven by political rivalries, retreated towards its distant bases at Bursa and Smyrna, which fell to the Turks in September 1922. Both sides were guilty of atrocities, but the fall of Smyrna, involving the massacre of Greek civilians and the burning of most of the town, was the most horrific episode in a notably bitter war.

Salamanca

451

Date: 22 July 1812.
Location: City on the river Tormes, 100 miles north-west of Madrid.
War and campaign: Peninsular War, 1807–1814; Campaign of 1812.
Opposing sides: (a) General the Earl of Wellington commanding the Allied army; (b) Marshal Auguste Marmont commanding the Army of Portugal.
Objective: Having captured BADAJOZ and CIUDAD RODRIGO, the Allied army advanced on Madrid from the latter but found the French Army of Portugal barring its path near Salamanca. After three weeks of manoeuvring, the French provoked a general engagement.
Forces engaged: (a) 3,254 cavalry, 47,449 infantry and 60 guns; (b) 3,400 cavalry, 46,600 infantry and 78 guns.
Casualties: (a) 5,200; (b) 14,000, including 7,000 prisoners, plus twenty guns captured.
Result: The French sustained a serious defeat which led them to evacuate Madrid temporarily and raise the siege of Cadiz – see BARROSSA. However, as they began to concentrate against his own line of communications in October, Wellington

withdrew to winter quarters in Portugal, intending to renew his offensive the following spring – see VITTORIA.

Marmont, dangerously overconfident despite the fact that he was unable to see the entire battlefield, incorrectly believed that Wellington was withdrawing and instituted a move which bypassed the Allied right wing in the false hope of heading off his opponents. Wellington quickly interpreted his intention and, seeing a chance to inflict a serious defeat, redeployed his troops into an approximate right-angle with a refused right flank parallel to the French line of march. As each division of the French flanking force came up it was routed in detail. Marmont was seriously wounded, as was his successor, General Jean Bonnet, and for twenty minutes the French were without a commander until General Bertrand Clausel restored control. Clausel launched a dangerous counter-attack into the angle of the Allied line, but Wellington had already reinforced this and it was contained. Following the failure of this the French army broke; its defeat would have been even more severe had not a Spanish force holding the bridge at Alba de Tormes, lying directly on the French line of retreat, decided to abandon its positions. Subsequently one of the French divisional commanders, General Maximilien Foy, generously commented that Wellington's conduct of the battle raised him to the level of Marlborough. For his achievements during the Campaign of 1812 Wellington was made a marquess.

Salerno 452

Date: 9–18 September 1943.
Location: Gulf of Salerno, south of Naples, Italy.
War and campaign: Second World War: Italy.
Opposing sides: (a) General Sir Harold Alexander commanding the Allied 15th Army Group; (b) Field Marshal Albert Kesselring commanding the German forces in southern Italy.
Objective: Following the landing of the British Eighth Army in Calabria on 3 September, the Allied intention was to land the US Fifth Army at Salerno and seize the port of Naples, thereby preventing the Germans from establishing a coherent front in southern Italy.
Forces engaged: (a) Lieutenant-General Mark W. Clark commanding the US Fifth Army, consisting of the US VI Corps (Major-General Ernest Dawley, then Major-General John P. Lucas) and the British X Corps (Lieutenant-General Sir Richard McCreery) – total approximately 85,000; (b) General Heinrich von Vietinghoff commanding the German Tenth Army, with four panzer and two panzergrenadier divisions – total approximately 50,000.
Casualties: (a) About 15,000; (b) about 8,000.
Result: A narrow Allied victory in the tactical sense, although Naples was not captured until 1 October, by which time Kesselring had succeeded in establishing a defensive front on the line of the Volturno river.

The Allies seriously underestimated the speed and weight of the German reaction. Their beach-head was quickly contained and subjected to determined counter-attacks which, despite naval gunfire support and air superiority, came dangerously close to driving the landing force into the sea. Alexander, however, rushed reinforcements into the beach-head and, with the approach of Montgomery's Eighth Army from the south, Vietinghoff began breaking contact and conducted a skilful withdrawal to the north.

Samarkand 453

Date: June 1220.
Location: City in Transoxania (now Uzbekistan).
War and campaign: Mongol War against the Kwarezmian Empire, 1218–1224.
Opposing sides: (a) Genghis Khan; (b) Alub Khan commanding the garrison.
Objective: The Mongols intended to capture their opponent's principal city.
Forces engaged: (a) Approximately 120,000; (b) 100,000 Turks and Kwarezmians.
Casualties: (a) Unknown; (b) the garrison and most of the population were massacred – only Alub and 1,000 cavalry escaped.
Result: The Mongols made little progress until the city's gates were treacherously opened by some of its inhabitants in the vain hope that they would be spared pillage and massacre.

See also INDUS, THE.

Sandepu/Heikoutai 454

Date: 26–27 January 1905.
Location: Villages 36 miles south-west of Mukden, Manchuria.
War and campaign: Russo–Japanese War, 1904–1905.
Opposing sides: (a) General Alexi Kuropatkin, Commander-in-Chief of the Russian armies in Manchuria; (b) Field Marshal Marquis Iwao Oyama, Commander-in-Chief of the Japanese armies in Manchuria.
Objective: Having received further reinforcements since SHA-HO RIVER, Kuropatkin attempted to regain the initiative from Oyama before Nogi's Third Army, which had taken PORT ARTHUR, could reach the front.
Forces engaged: (a) Second (Grippenberg), Third (Kaulbars) and First (Linievich) Manchurian Armies – total 300,000 men; (b) the Japanese First (Kuroki), Second (Oku) and Fourth (Nodzu) Armies – total 220,000 men.
Casualties: (a) 20,000; (b) 9,000.
Result: The battle ended in a tactical stalemate.

Kuropatkin had failed to recover the strategic initiative and this, coupled with his heavy losses, further lowered Russian morale. See MUKDEN.

San Juan/El Caney 455

Date: 1 July 1898.
Location: Hill positions covering the approach to Santiago from the east and north-east, Cuba.
War and campaign: Spanish–American War, 1898.
Opposing sides: (a) Major-General William R. Shafter commanding the US V Corps; (b) General Arsenio Linares commanding the Spanish garrison of Santiago.

Objective: Having secured their beach-head, the Americans were advancing on Santiago.
Forces engaged: (a) Approximately 3–4,000 engaged in the assault; (b) 1,200 on San Juan Ridge and 500 at El Caney.
Casualties: (a) 1,572; (b) 850.
Result: The Americans captured both positions. Admiral Cervera's Spanish naval squadron was destroyed during the Battle of Santiago Bay on 3 July and Santiago itself was surrendered by General Jose Toral on 17 July, Linares having been wounded during the fighting at San Juan.

The best-remembered episode in the battle was the dismounted attack of Major-General Joseph Wheeler's Cavalry Division at San Juan, and in particular the part played by the 1st Volunteer Cavalry (Rough Riders) under Lieutenant-Colonel Theodore Roosevelt, the future President. In fact the feature assaulted was Kettle Hill, in front of San Juan Ridge, and the regular 1st and 9th Cavalry played an equally distinguished if less publicized role.

Sanna's Post 456

Date: 31 March 1900.
Location: Waterworks 23 miles east of Bloemfontein, Orange Free State.
War and campaign: Second Boer War, 1899–1902.
Opposing sides: (a) General Christiaan De Wet; (b) Brigadier-General Robert Broadwood.
Objective: The Boers' intentions were to disrupt Bloemfontein's water supply and ambush a heavily escorted convoy.
Forces engaged: (a) 1,500 men and several guns; (b) 1,900 men and twelve guns.
Casualties: (a) Light; (b) 155 killed and wounded, 428 taken prisoner, seven guns and 117 wagons captured.
Result: De Wet achieved both objectives at low cost in a model guerrilla operation.

To some extent the British defeat was redeemed by the exemplary courage displayed by the personnel of Q Battery Royal Horse Artillery.

Saratoga (Freeman's Farm) 457

Date: 19 September 1777.
Location: On the Hudson river, 10 miles south-west of Saratoga, northern New York State.
War and campaign: American War of Independence, 1775–1783: northern theatre of operations.
Opposing sides: (a) Major-General John Burgoyne; (b) Major-General Horatio Gates.
Objective: British strategy in the northern theatre involved converging thrusts along the Hudson valley, with Clinton advancing north from New York and Burgoyne south from Canada, the idea being to isolate the New England states, which were regarded as the epicentre of the rebellion. Clinton's participation

amounted to little more than a demonstration which penetrated as far as the Hudson Highlands then withdrew. Burgoyne, however, fought his way south against steadily increasing opposition until he found further progress blocked by an American army entrenched on Bemis Heights, which he decided to attack.

Forces engaged: Approximately 6,000; (b) Approximately 7,000.

Casualties: (a) Approximately 600; (b) approximately 300.

Result: The British advance was halted near Freeman's Farm.

Both sides held their positions. See SARATOGA (BEMIS HEIGHTS).

Saratoga (Bemis Heights)   458

Date: 7 October 1777.

Location: On the Hudson river, 10 miles south-west of Saratoga, northern New York State.

War and campaign: American War of Independence, 1775–1783: northern theatre of operations.

Opposing sides: (a) Major-General John Burgoyne; (b) Major-General Horatio Gates.

Objective: See SARATOGA (FREEMAN'S FARM). Burgoyne, against the advice of his senior officers, was for renewing the assault. A compromise resulted in a reconnaissance in force against the American left.

Forces engaged: (a) 5,000; (b) 9,000.

Casualties: (a) Approximately 600; (b) approximately 150.

Result: The reconnaissance in force was defeated by an American counter-attack which went on to capture key redoubts, leaving the British right exposed.

Burgoyne withdrew to Saratoga where, surrounded by a force now three times the size of his own, he agreed surrender terms with Gates. This effectively ended formal operations in the northern theatre, but resulted in far wider strategic consequences. France not only recognized the independence of the United States but also declared war on the United Kingdom (1778) and was followed by Spain (1779) and Holland (1780). The battles of Freeman's Farm and Bemis Heights therefore marked a major turning point in the course of the war, which became a global contest. The American success in both engagements resulted largely from the drive and energy displayed by Major-General Benedict Arnold, who was wounded in the closing stages of the second. In the eyes of many Americans his change of sides in 1780 made him the archetypal traitor figure and this has tended to eclipse his many and great services to the colonists' cause. Burgoyne and Gates actually signed a Convention, under the terms of which the former's British and German troops were to be disarmed, marched to Boston and repatriated. To its shame, Congress repudiated the agreement and the men were held in Virginian prison camps for the rest of the war.

Sarikamish   459

Date: 29 December 1914 to 3 January 1915.

Location: Town in Turkish (formerly Russian) Armenia, 50 miles south-west of Kars.

War and campaign: First World War: Trans-Caucasian Front.
Opposing sides: (a) Enver Pasha, Minister of War, in personal command of the Turkish Third Army; (b) General Count Vorontsov-Dashkov (replaced by General Nikolai Yudenich) commanding the Russian Caucasian Army.
Objective: The Turks had invaded Russia and were advancing on the fortress of Kars.
Forces engaged: (a) IX, X and XI Corps – total approximately 95,000; (b) I Caucasian Army Corps and II Turkistan Corps – total approximately 65,000.
Casualties: (a) About 75,000 (including 15,000 frozen to death), plus all the artillery captured or abandoned (only 18,000 of Enver's men completed the withdrawal); (b) 16,000 killed and wounded, plus 12,000 sick (the latter mainly frostbite cases).
Result: A major Russian victory which secured the Trans-Caucasian Front until after the Revolution.

Enver's plans, while attractive on paper, bore little relation to the reality of the situation. The Turkish advance was made through difficult mountainous country in the dead of winter, and the troops were required to bivouac in the open in temperatures of –20C (–36F).

Savannah, Siege of (1779) 460

Date: 16 September to 9 October 1779.
Location: Savannah, Georgia.
War and campaign: American War of Independence, 1775–1783: southern theatre of operations.
Opposing sides: (a) Major-General Augustine Prevost commanding the British and loyalist garrison; (b) Major-General Benjamin Lincoln and Admiral Count d'Estaing commanding, respectively, the American and French contingents.
Objective: Loyalist support was stronger in the south than in the north and in December 1778 Clinton had despatched a force which succeeded in capturing Savannah. The following September the French and Americans mounted a combined operation to recover the city.
Forces engaged: (a) 3,200; (b) 1,500 Americans and 3,500 French.
Casualties: (a) 40 killed and 63 wounded; (b) total 244 killed and 584 wounded.
Result: An assault on 9 October failed disastrously. D'Estaing declined to pursue the operation, embarked his troops and departed.

Loyalist morale soared throughout the south and Clinton, deciding to reinforce success, sailed from New York with an additional 8,500 men on 26 December. See CHARLESTON.

Savannah (1864) 461

Date: 9–21 December 1864.
Location: Savannah, Georgia.
War and campaign: American Civil War: Sherman's Campaign in Georgia.

Opposing sides: (a) Major-General William T. Sherman; (b) Major-General William J. Hardee.
Objective: The city was the ultimate objective of Sherman's march from ATLANTA to the Confederacy's Atlantic coast.
Forces engaged: (a) Up to 68,000 available; (b) 15,000.
Casualties: Light on both sides.
Result: At first Hardee refused to surrender but when Sherman, having established contact with the fleet, deployed siege artillery and prepared to invest the city, he evacuated the garrison before his lines of communication were cut; there was comparatively little fighting.

The eastern states of the Confederacy were now cut in two and its remaining field armies were trapped in a converging strategic pincer between Grant at PETERSBURG in the north and Sherman at Savannah in the south.

Scheldt Estuary 462

Date: 9 October to 8 November 1944.
Location: Area approximately 23 miles wide and 15 miles deep on the south bank of the West Scheldt, including Zeebrugge, Knokke-sur-Mer and Breskens (the Breskens Pocket), and the islands of Walcheren, North Beveland and South Beveland in the Scheldt Estuary.
War and campaign: Second World War: North-West Europe.
Opposing sides: (a) Field Marshal Sir Bernard Montgomery commanding the British 21st Army Group; (b) Field Marshal Walter Model commanding Army Group B.
Objective: It was necessary for the Allies to clear both banks of the West Scheldt before the port of Antwerp, captured on 4 September, could be brought into action, thereby reducing dependence on a supply line stretching back to Normandy.
Forces engaged: (a) Lieutenant-General H. D. G. Crerar commanding the Canadian First Army (reinforced Canadian II Corps and 4th Special Service Brigade (Commandos)); (b) General Gustav von Zangen commanding the German Fifteenth Army with the 64th Division in the Breskens Pocket, the 70th Division on Walcheren, North Beveland and South Beveland and the 719th Division north of Antwerp covering the isthmus connecting South Beveland with the mainland.
Casualties: (a) 12,874 killed, wounded and missing; (b) 41,000 captured (killed and wounded unknown).
Result: The capture of North and South Beveland was completed on 29 October, the Breskens Pocket was finally eliminated on 2 November and German resistance on Walcheren ended on 8 November. After the channel had been swept clear of mines the first Allied ships reached Antwerp on 26 November. The shortened line of communcations enabled Montgomery to plan the Battle of THE REICHSWALD and THE RHINE CROSSINGS on the 21st Army Group's sector of the front, despite the German counter-offensive mounted in December (see BULGE, THE).

The battle involved a complex series of amphibious landings against a determined enemy occupying excellent defensive positions. Allied casualties were kept to the minimum possible by the use of the 79th Armoured Division's amphibious AFVs, including Buffalo LVTs and DD Shermans, supplemented by Crabs and AVREs landed once beach-heads had been secured.

Sedan

Date: 1 September 1870.
Location: Town on the Meuse in northern France.
War and campaign: Franco–Prussian War, 1870–1871.
Opposing sides: (a) Field Marshal Count Helmuth von Moltke commanding the Third and Meuse Armies of the North German Confederation; (b) the Emperor Napoleon II and General Auguste Ducrot commanding the Army of Chalons.
Objective: The French Army of Chalons, marching to the relief of METZ, had been outmanoeuvred and forced back to Sedan, where it was isolated by the converging advance of two German armies.
Forces engaged: (a) 222 infantry battalions, 186 cavalry squadrons and 774 guns – total 200,000; (b) 202 infantry battalions, 80 cavalry squadrons and 564 guns – total 120,000.
Casualties: (a) 2,320 killed, 5,980 wounded and 700 missing; (b) 17,000 killed and wounded, 21,000 missing.
Result: The French army's attempts to break out were repulsed and on 2 September its remnants surrendered. Napoleon III accompanied his troops into captivity and on 4 September the Second French Empire was replaced by the Third Republic. Now confident that METZ could not be relieved, von Moltke ordered his armies to march on PARIS.

Ducrot succeeded to command of the French army when MacMahon was wounded on 31 August; he was succeeded in turn by General Emmanuel de Wimpffen, who effected the surrender. The decisive factor in the battle was the German artillery, ranged in a semi-circle on the hills above Sedan.

Sedgemoor

Date: 6 July 1685.
Location: 4 miles south-east of Bridgewater, Somerset.
War and campaign: The Duke of Monmouth's Rebellion.
Opposing sides: (a) The Earl of Feversham commanding the Government troops; (b) James Scott, Duke of Monmouth (and illegitimate son of Charles II), commanding the rebels.
Objective: Monmouth's rebel army mounted a night attack on the camp of the Government troops which had been sent to crush it.
Forces engaged: (a) Six infantry battalions, four cavalry squadrons and seventeen guns – total 2,500; (b) five infantry battalions, 800 cavalry and four guns – total 3,700.
Casualties: (a) 300 killed and wounded; (b) approximately 1,000 killed, 500 prisoners and three guns captured.
Result: The night attack failed and the rebel army was destroyed when the Government troops counter-attacked at dawn. Monmouth was captured three days later and executed on 15 July.

Subsequently, the savage vengeance imposed on the West Country by Judge Jeffreys and his Bloody Assize added to the unpopularity of James II and contributed to his downfall three years later.

Sempach 465

Date: 9 July 1386.	
Location: 10 miles north-west of Lucerne on the shores of Lake Sempach.	
War and campaign: Swiss Wars of Independence.	
Opposing sides: (a) The Cantonal commanders of Lucerne, Uri, Underwalden and Schwytz; (b) Duke Leopold III of Austria.	
Objective: An Austrian army, having penetrated central Switzerland to put down the rebellion, was opposed by a small Swiss force at Sempach.	
Forces engaged: 1,600 pikemen and halberdiers; (b) 4,000, including a high proportion of cavalry, and several guns.	
Casualties: (a) 200 killed; (b) 1,800 killed, including Leopold.	
Result: A decisive victory which established the Swiss military reputation.	

Leopold led his attack with a formation consisting of dismounted knights and men-at-arms fighting as pikemen. At first the Austrians were successful, then held their own against the pikemen of successive cantons in turn. According to legend, the deadlock was broken by Arnold of Winkelreid, who deliberately impaled himself on several enemy spears, enabling the Swiss halberdiers to hack their way into the Austrian phalanx. Once this had broken the remainder of the Austrian army fled.

Seringapatam, Siege of 466

Date: 6 April to 3 May 1799.	
Location: Fortress in Mysore, south-western India.	
War and campaign: Fourth Mysore War.	
Opposing sides: (a) General George Harris; (b) Tippoo Sahib.	
Objective: The British had decided that they would break the power of the pro-French ruler of Mysore, Tippoo Sahib (who, with his father, Haidar Ali, had been a thorn in their side for many years), and had driven him into his principal fortress.	
Forces engaged: (a) 6,000 British and Indian troops; (b) estimated 30,000.	
Casualties: (a) 1,464 killed and wounded; (b) 8,500 killed and wounded.	
Result: The fortress was stormed after scientific artillery preparation and Tippoo Sahib was killed in the fighting.	

Present at the siege was the then Colonel Arthur Wellesley (later the Duke of Wellington), who became the *de facto* ruler of Mysore for the next four years.

Sevastopol, Siege of (1854–1855) 467

Date: 28 September 1854 to 8 September 1855.	
Location: Fortified city and naval base on the southern coast of the Crimea.	

War and campaign: Crimean War.
Opposing sides: (a) Field Marshal Lord Raglan (General Sir James Simpson from 28 June 1855) and General François Canrobert in joint command of the Allied armies; (b) General Prince Alexander Menshikov (replaced by General Prince Mikhail Gorchakov in February 1855).
Objective: The elimination of the naval base and the destruction of the Russian fleet within was the primary strategic objective of the Allies (Great Britain, France, Turkey and Sardinia).
Forces engaged: (a) Approximately 100,000; (b) approximately 120,000.
Casualties: Siege operations only: (a) 11,000 British and 12,000 French; (b) over 50,000.
Result: The Russians evacuated the fortress after blowing up its remaining defences. Peace talks began in February 1856.

Lacking sufficient resources to encircle the fortress, the Allies invested its southern defences only, being forced simultaneously to guard against attempts by the Russian field army in the Crimea to disrupt or break the siege (see BALAKLAVA and INKERMAN). In June a British attempt to storm the formidable defences of the Redan strongpoint was repulsed with heavy losses and Raglan, worn out, died shortly afterwards. On 8 September, however, the French succeeded in capturing the equally formidable Malakoff, rendering the fortress untenable, and the Russians withdrew; the timing of the assault was governed, perhaps for the first time, by the synchronization of watches. The battle casualties quoted conceal the fact that many more men died of wounds or disease. The British contingent, forced to endure the winter without adequate clothing or shelter, was decimated by cholera, exposure and semi-starvation until the scandalous misman-agement of its logistic services was revealed by William Howard Russell in *The Times*, after which the situation improved.

Sevastopol (1941–1942) 468

Date: 29 October 1941 to 3 July 1942.
Location: Fortified city and naval base on the southern coast of the Crimea.
War and campaign: Second World War: Russian Front.
Opposing sides: (a) Initially Field Marshal Gerd von Rundstedt commanding Army Group South; (b) initially Marshal Semyon Budenny commanding the Soviet armies in the southern USSR.
Objective: The capture of Sevastopol was necessary to complete the occupation of the Crimea, thereby securing the southern flank of the German armies in Russia.
Forces engaged: (a) General Erich von Manstein commanding the German Eleventh Army, consisting of one armoured, one cavalry and thirteen infantry divisions with 120 artillery batteries, including the super-heavy 600mm Thor howitzers and the 800mm Gustav railway gun – total approximately 204,000 (reinforced during the final assault); (b) Major-General I. E. Petrov commanding the Soviet Coastal Army, consisting of seven rifle divisions, four rifle brigades and two marine regiments with 600 guns, an armoured train and 38 tanks – total approximately 106,000 (reinforced during the siege).
Casualties: Including clearing the Crimea and the final assault on Sevastopol, 3 June to 4 July 1942: (a) approximately 80,000; (b) approximately 250,000, including 90,000 captured in Sevastopol.

> **Result:** The Crimea remained in German hands until May 1944. Manstein was rewarded with his Field Marshal's baton.

Petrov and his senior officers were evacuated by sea during the closing stages of the siege.

Seven Days' Battles 469

Date: 25 June to 1 July 1862.
Location: East of Richmond, Virginia, in the peninsula between the York and James rivers.
War and campaign: American Civil War: Peninsula Campaign.
Opposing sides: (a) Major-General George B. McClellan commanding the Army of the Potomac; (b) General Robert E. Lee Commanding the Army of Northern Virginia.
Objective: A Confederate counter-offensive involving a series of actions intended to remove the Federal threat to Richmond. These included Mechanicsville (26 June), Gaines Mill (27 June), Savage Station (29 June), Frayser's Farm (30 June) and Malvern Hill (1 July).
Forces engaged: (a) 100,000; (b) 72,000.
Casualties: (a) 1,734 killed, 8,062 wounded and 6,053 missing (mainly prisoners); (b) 3,478 killed, 16,261 wounded and 875 missing.
Result: Although the Confederates sustained the heavier losses, the Federals were pushed steadily back to Harrison's Landing on the James, where they enjoyed the protection of the US Navy's gunboats.

The strategic initiative in eastern theatre of war now passed to the Confederacy (see CEDAR MOUNTAIN and BULL RUN, SECOND) and the Army of the Potomac was shipped back from the Peninsula to Washington. See also SEVEN PINES (FAIR OAKS).

Seven Pines (Fair Oaks) 470

Date: 31 May to 1 June 1862.
Location: 6 miles east of Richmond, Viginia.
War and campaign: American Civil War: Peninsula Campaign.
Opposing sides: (a) Major-General George B. McClellan commanding the Army of the Potomac; (b) General Joseph E. Johnston commanding the Confederate army.
Objective: A Confederate counter-attack on the left wing of the Federal army, which had been separated from its main body by the Chickahominy river as it closed in on Richmond.
Forces engaged: (a) Approximately 45,000; (b) 60,000.
Casualties: (a) 5,000; (b) 6,100.
Result: While the result of the battle was indecisive, McClellan seriously overestimated the Confederates' strength and halted his advance on Richmond. Johnston was severely wounded and General Robert E. Lee was appointed commander of the Confederate army, which then became the Army of Northern Virginia.

Brigadier-General J. E. B. Stuart raided the rear areas of the Army of the Potomac on 12–15 June, destroying large quantities of stores and obtaining information on the Federal dispositions which enabled Lee to plan the SEVEN DAYS' BATTLES.

Sha-Ho River   471

Date: 5–17 October 1904.
Location: Along a 37-mile front centred at Sha-Ho on the Mukden–Port Arthur railway, north of Liaoyang, Manchuria.
War and campaign: Russo–Japanese War, 1904–1905.
Opposing sides: (a) General Alexei Kuropatkin, Commander-in-Chief of the Russian army in Manchuria; (b) Field Marshal Marquis Iwao Oyama, Commander-in-Chief of the Japanese armies in Manchuria.
Objective: Having been reinforced in the aftermath of LIAOYANG, Kuropatkin was determined the wrest the initiative from Oyama.
Forces engaged: (a) 210,000; (b) the Japanese First (Kuroki), Second (Oku) and Fourth (Nodzu) Armies – total 150,000.
Casualties: (a) 44,351; (b) 20,345.
Result: Indecisive.

Both sides dug in and prepared for the next round. See SANDEPU/HEIKOUTAI.

Sheriffmuir   472

Date: 13 September 1715.
Location: East of Dunblane, 6 miles north of Stirling.
War and campaign: Fifteen Rebellion, 1715.
Opposing sides: (a) John, Duke of Argyll, commanding the Government forces; (b) John Erskine, Earl of Mar, commanding the rebels.
Objective: The Jacobites, advancing from Perth to Stirling, were intercepted by Government troops at Dunblane.
Forces engaged: (a) 2,200 infantry and 960 dragoons; (b) 6,290 infantry and 807 cavalry.
Casualties: (a) 350 killed and wounded; (b) 250 killed and wounded.
Result: The right wings of both armies were victorious but the battle itself was inconclusive. However, while Argyll held his ground, Mar had failed to win the clear-cut victory necessary to attract support for the Jacobite cause and when he withdrew his army melted away.

The battle effectively ended the rebellion in Scotland. See also PRESTON (1715).

Sherpur   473

Date: 23 December 1879.
Location: Fortified cantonment area north of Kabul, Afghanistan.
War and campaign: Second Afghan War, 1878–1880.

Opposing sides: (a) Lieutenant-General Sir Frederick Roberts; (b) Mohammed Jan of Wardak.
Objective: Afghan nationalists, whose mullahs had declared a holy war against the British, were attempting to overwhelm the position.
Forces engaged: (a) 6,500; (b) estimated 100,000.
Casualties: (a) Three killed and 30 wounded; (b) 3,000 killed and wounded.
Result: The attack was decisively repulsed and the Afghan force dispersed. See also CHARASIA, MAIWAND and KANDAHAR.

Roberts had been informed of the enemy's plans and was fully prepared. Starshell was used by his artillery to illuminate the enemy attack when it began just before dawn.

Shiloh (Pittsburg Landing)   474

Date: 6–7 April 1862.
Location: Shiloh, on the Tennessee river, 25 miles north of Corinth, Mississippi.
War and campaign: American Civil War: western theatre of operations.
Opposing sides: (a) Major-General Ulysses S. Grant commanding the Army of the Tennessee and Brigadier-General Don Carlos Buell commanding the Army of the Ohio; (b) General Albert Sidney Johnston commanding the Army of the Mississippi, succeeded by Lieutenant-General Pierre Beauregard.
Objective: Grant, planning to advance on the important railway junction at Corinth, was ordered to await Buell's arrival from Nashville and had encamped his troops around Shiloh Methodist Church. Johnston planned a surprise attack which would destroy Grant's army before Buell arrived.
Forces engaged: (a) 62,000; (b) 44,000.
Casualties: (a) 13,047; (b) 11,694.
Result: The Confederate achieved tactical surprise and pushed the Federals steadily back throughout the day. Johnston, killed during the afternoon, was succeeded by Beauregard. During the night Grant was reinforced by 20,000 of Buell's men and the following morning he took the offensive, forcing the Confederates to abandon their gains. Beauregard disengaged and withdrew.

After Shiloh, the Confederacy never recovered the strategic initiative in the west. Under Federal pressure, CORINTH was evacuated on 29 May; its loss deprived the South of a vital junction connecting the only direct east–west rail link between Richmond and the Mississippi and the north–south axis of the Mobile & Ohio Railroad.

Shrewsbury   475

Date: 21 July 1403.
Location: 3 miles north of Shrewsbury.
War and campaign: English Baronial Wars: Percy's Rebellion.
Opposing sides: (a) King Henry IV and Prince Henry (later Henry V); (b) Sir Henry Percy (also known as Hotspur) and the Earl of Douglas.
Objective: The rebels unwisely chose to engage the royal army before they were reinforced by the Earl of Northumberland and Owain Glyndwr.

Forces engaged: (a) 14,000; (b) 10,000.
Casualties: Estimated 3,000 killed and wounded on each side. Hotspur was killed.
Result: The rebels were defeated and the rebellion collapsed.

The Earl of Northumberland submitted and was pardoned. He rebelled again in 1408 and was defeated and killed at Bramham Moor (20 February).

Sidi Barrani 476

Date: 9–12 December 1940.
Location: Town on the northern coast of Egypt, 60 miles east of the Libyan frontier and 80 miles west of Mersa Matruh.
War and campaign: Second World War: North Africa.
Opposing sides: (a) General Sir Archibald Wavell, Commander-in-Chief Middle East; (b) Marshal Rodolfo Graziani commanding the Italian forces in North Africa.
Objective: The British intention was to mount a heavy spoiling attack which would disrupt Italian plans for a continued advance into Egypt.
Forces engaged: (a) Lieutenant-General Richard O'Connor commanding Western Desert Force, with the 7th Armoured and 4th Indian Divisions, plus corps troops including the 7th Royal Tank Regiment equipped with Matilda II infantry tanks – total approximately 31,000; (b) General Berti commanding the Italian Tenth Army, with the 1st and 2nd Libyan, 4th Blackshirt, 63rd Cyrene and 64th Catanzaro Divisions, plus Gruppo Maletti with one medium tank battalion under command – total approximately 50,000.
Casualties: Including pursuit to Buq Buq: (a) 624; (b) 40,000 (of whom 38,000, including four generals, were taken prisoner), plus 237 guns and 73 medium tanks or tankettes destroyed or captured.
Result: The Italians were completely routed. Wavell immediately developed the spoiling attack into a general offensive which culminated in the destruction of the Italian Tenth Army at BEDA FOMM.

The British spoiling attack, codenamed 'Compass', commenced during the night of 8/9 December when the Western Desert Force penetrated a wide gap in the Italian chain of fortified camps stretching south-westwards from Sidi Barrani. At dawn, while the 7th Armoured Division screened the operation and isolated Sidi Barrani from the west, the 4th Indian Division, spearheaded by Matildas, began storming the camps to the north of the gap in succession. On 10 December Sidi Barrani itself was stormed and next day the Italians evacuated the camps south of the gap. On 12 December the 7th Armoured Division overran the 64th Division's rearguard and artillery at Buq Buq. The remnants of the Tenth Army retreated across the frontier into Libya.

Sinai (1956) 477

Date: 29 October to 5 November 1956.
Location: The Sinai Peninsula.
War and campaign: The Arab–Israeli War of 1956.
Opposing sides: (a) Lieutenant-General Moshe Dayan, Chief of Staff of the Israeli

Defence Force; (b) General Abd el Hakim Amer, Minister of Defence and Commander-in-Chief of the Egyptian armed forces.
Objective: The Israeli intentions were to destroy the Egyptian army in Sinai and to capture Sharm el Sheikh at the southern tip of the peninsula, thereby opening the Straits of Tiran to shipping bound for Eilat.
Forces engaged: (a) One armoured, two mechanized, one parachute and six infantry brigades – total 45,000, with 180 tanks and 150 guns; (b) two infantry divisions, one armoured brigade, one independent infantry brigade and a number of light mechanized units – total 40,000, with 150 tanks and 140 guns (the 1st Mechanized Division was sent to Sinai on the outbreak of hostilities but was withdrawn almost immediately).
Casualties: (a) 181 killed and 25 tanks destroyed; (b) approximately 2,000 killed and 6,000 prisoners, plus 100 tanks and tank destroyers and numerous guns and APCs lost.
Result: The Israelis achieved all their objectives, overrunning Sinai but halting 10 miles short of the Suez Canal, as agreed in joint planning with the British and French. See also SUEZ LANDINGS.

The battle began when one battalion of Colonel Ariel Sharon's 202nd Parachute Brigade was dropped at the eastern exit of the Mitla Pass at 17.00 on 29 October. The remainder of the brigade advanced overland in a motorized column, brushing aside opposition, and by 22.30 on 30 October had reached the isolated battalion. The following day Sharon exceeded his orders and his men sustained serious casualties in an abortive attempt to fight their way through the pass. Further north the 7th Armoured and 4th and 10th Infantry Brigades and part of the 37th Mechanized Brigade were involved in a fierce struggle for the Egyptian fortified complex at Abu Agheila, which did not fall until the night of 1 November. The 7th Armoured then advanced directly across Sinai to a point 10 miles short of Ismailia, without encountering opposition. To its right the 37th Mechanized Brigade, having broken through the Egyptian lines at Rafah in heavy fighting, advanced along the coast road to capture Romani. To all intents and purposes the battle was now over, although mopping-up operations continued. The Gaza Strip was cleared by the 11th Infantry Brigade and part of the 37th Mechanized Brigade. The 9th Infantry Brigade drove down the east coast of Sinai and captured Sharm el Sheikh on 5 November. Simultaneously the 202nd Parachute Brigade, redeployed from the Mitla Pass, advanced down the west coast, having dropped an advance guard at El Tur. The reason for the lack of Egyptian resistance in northern and central Sinai was that British and French aircraft had begun bombing targets in Egypt on 31 October. Amer correctly interpreted this as being a prelude to the Suez landings and decided to withdraw the 1st Mechanized Division and 1st Armoured Brigade to meet the threat; unfortunately, he also withdrew air cover from the Sinai front, so that the Egyptian withdrawal was severely harassed by the IAF.

Sinai (1967)   478

Date: 5–8 June 1967.
Location: The Sinai Peninsula.
War and campaign: Arab–Israeli War of 1967 ('The Six Day War').
Opposing sides: (a) Major-General Yeshayahu Gavish, GOC Israeli Southern Command; (b) General Abd el Mohsen Mortagy, Egyptian Commander-in-Chief in Sinai.

Objective: The Israelis' intention was to destroy the Egyptian army in Sinai and advance to the Suez Canal, thereby obtaining a defensible frontier in the south.
Forces engaged: (a) Three armoured divisions, two independent armoured brigades and one paratroop brigade – total 680 tanks, plus 70 in reserve; (b) the 2nd, 3rd, 7th and 20th Infantry Divisions, 6th Mechanized Division, 4th Armoured Division and Task Force Shazli – total 800 tanks and tank destroyers, plus 150 in reserve.
Casualties: (a) 275 killed and 800 wounded (most battle-damaged tanks were recovered and repaired); (b) estimated 15,000 killed, wounded and captured, and 800 tanks and tank destroyers (including 300 in working order), 450 guns and 10,000 APCs and other vehicles lost.
Result: The Egyptian army was destroyed and the Israelis established a defence line along the Suez Canal. The Egyptians, however, were determined to recover their lost territory – see SUEZ CANAL CROSSING.

The Israeli offensive began immediately after a pre-emptive strike by the IAF had destroyed the Egyptian Air Force on the ground. While one independent armoured brigade supported a paratroop attack on the Gaza Strip, Major-General Tal's armoured division broke through the Egyptian defences at Rafah and again at Jiradi to advance along the coast road and capture El Arish. Further south, Major-General Sharon's division stormed the fortified complex at Abu Agheila in heavy fighting which included the helicopter insertion of paratroops into the Egyptian artillery positions. The Egyptian 4th Armoured Division, advancing to counter-attack during the night, was ambushed by Major-General Yoffe's division at Bir Lahfan and was forced to retreat, badly mauled, when Tal despatched an armoured brigade from El Arish to fall on its flank. The hard shell of the Egyptian defences having been broken, the Israeli strategy now was for the divisions of Tal and Yoffe to advance through the retreating enemy and seize the Mitla, Giddi and Tassa Passes leading from the Sinai plateau to the Suez Canal; Sharon's division, having completed mopping-up tasks in the Abu Agheila area, drove the remaining Egyptians across Sinai before it, thus trapping them between the hammer and the anvil. The entire operation was closely supported by the IAF, which strafed the Egyptian columns without mercy. Only part of Task Force Shazli succeeded in reaching the safety of the west bank of the canal as an operational unit; the remainder of Mortagy's divisions were destroyed where they stood or disintegrated into small groups as they attempted to escape from the trap.

Singapore 479

Date: 8–15 February 1942.
Location: Island off the southern tip of the Malayan peninsula.
War and campaign: Second World War: Malaya.
Opposing sides: (a) Lieutenant-General Tomoyuki Yamashita commanding the Japanese Twenty-Fifth Army; (b) Lieutenant-General Arthur Percival commanding the British garrison.
Objective: The Japanese intention was to crown their conquest of the Malayan mainland with the capture of Singapore itself.
Forces engaged: (a) Japanese 5th and 18th Infantry Divisions, followed by the Imperial Guards Division – total approximately 40,000; (b) the Australian 8th,

Indian 9th, 11th and 17th and British 18th Divisions – total approximately 107,000 (including 27,000 administrative troops).
Casualties: Including the campaign on the Malayan mainland: (a) 9,000, including 3,000 killed; (b) 9,000 killed and wounded, 130,000 prisoners of war.
Result: The worst military disaster in the history of the British Empire. With the capture of the allegedly impregnable fortress island of Singapore, Japanese military prestige reached its zenith.

Following their reverses on the mainland, the morale of Percival's experienced troops was poor and in some units discipline had begun to decline, while many of the most recent arrivals on the island were either untrained or unfit after their time at sea. Furthermore, almost every aspect of Singapore's defence was badly handled. During the night of 8/9 February the Japanese experienced no difficulty in securing a beach-head and by the morning of 15 February they controlled the island's vital water reservoirs. Percival, believing that if they were forced to storm the city the Japanese would massacre the civilian population, as they had at Shanghai and Hong Kong, asked Yamashita for terms. Ironically, the latter had only sufficient ammunition in hand for three days' serious fighting and was considering withdrawal. Nevertheless, he bluffed angrily and demanded unconditional surrender, promising only to safeguard the lives of troops and civilians, and Percival accepted this. Among the myths regarding the fall of Singapore is the suggestion that the island's heavy coast defence guns could not be traversed inland and therefore played no part in the fighting; in fact, they could fire landwards and successfully engaged targets on several occasions.

Smolensk 480

Date: 17 July to 5 August 1941.
Location: City and important railway junction 250 miles west of Moscow.
War and campaign: Second World War: Russian Front.
Opposing sides: (a) Field Marshal Fedor von Bock commanding Army Group Centre; (b) Marshal Semyon Timoshenko commanding the West Front.
Objective: The German intention was to encircle the Soviet armies on the Smolensk sector of the front.
Forces engaged: (a) Field Marshal Gunther von Kluge commanding the German Fourth Army with, under command, Panzer Groups 2 (Guderian) and 3 (Hoth); (b) mainly the Soviet 16th and 20th Armies, with 12–14 divisions trapped in the Smolensk pocket.
Casualties: (a) Total 298,000 killed, wounded and missing (for all three army groups during the relevant period – of these, Army Group Centre sustained the heaviest proportion); (b) (Smolensk sector only) killed and wounded unknown, 309,000 prisoners, 3,205 tanks and 3120 guns captured.
Result: Great as the German victory was, Hitler had become obsessed with the idea of destroying the Soviet Army piecemeal in similar battles of encirclement. While the fighting at Smolensk was in progress he decided that Army Group Centre's drive on Moscow, the major strategic objective of Operation 'Barbarossa', was to be halted while Guderian's Panzer Group 2 went south to assist von Rundstedt's Army Group South in its conquest of the Ukraine. This proved to be the most critical mistake of the entire campaign. See KIEV.

Sobraon

Date: 10 February 1846.
Location: Village in the Punjab below the confluence of the Sutlej and Beas rivers.
War and campaign: First Sikh War, 1845–1846.
Opposing sides: (a) General Sir Hugh Gough; (b) Tej Singh.
Objective: Despite their defeats at MUDKI, FEROZESHAH and ALIWAL, the Sikhs again crossed the Sutlej and established themselves in a strongly fortified position on the river. Following the arrival of their seige train the British assaulted it.
Forces engaged: (a) 15,000 British and Indian troops, with 100 guns; (b) 20,000 with 70 guns.
Casualties: (a) 164 killed and 2,119 wounded; (b) approximately 3,000 killed and 7,000 wounded (many were drowned while fleeing across the Sutlej), plus 67 guns captured.
Result: The Sikhs were driven from their entrenchments and decisively defeated.

Gough marched on Lahore and the Punjab became a British protectorate.

Sohr (Soor)

Date: 30 September 1745.
Location: Village in north-eastern Bohemia (now Czechoslovakia).
War and campaign: War of Austrian Succession, 1740–1748: Central European Campaign of 1745.
Opposing sides: (a) Frederick the Great; (b) Prince Charles of Lorraine.
Objective: Following his victory at HOHENFRIEDBERG, Frederick II of Prussia advanced into Bohemia. After three months of inconclusive manoeuvre he decided to withdraw to Silesia, but at Sohr he found the Austrian army blocking his line of retreat.
Forces engaged: (a) 18,000; (b) 30,000.
Casualties: (a) 3,500; (b) 6,000 killed, wounded and prisoners, plus 22 guns captured.
Result: Frederick overwhelmed the enemy left with an attack in oblique order.

The remainder of the Austrian army withdrew, enabling the Prussians to return to Silesia.

Solferino

Date: 24 June 1859.
Location: Between Brescia and Mantua, 4 miles south-east of Castiglione delle Stiviere, Lombardy, Italy.
War and campaign: Italian Wars of Independence.
Opposing sides: (a) The Emperor Napoleon III and King Victor Emmanuel II commanding the Franco-Piedmontese army; (b) the Emperor Franz Josef commanding the Austrian army.

Objective: The Franco-Piedmontese army was following up its victory at MAGENTA.	
Forces engaged: (a) 217 infantry battalions, 88 cavalry squadrons and 320 guns – total 118,600; (b) 151 infantry battalions, 52 cavalry squadrons and 451 guns.	
Casualties: (a) 2,491 killed, 12,512 wounded, 2,292 missing and prisoners; (b) 3,000 killed, 10,807 wounded, 8,638 missing and prisoners.	
Result: A costly Allied victory.	

Napoleon, sickened by the carnage, concluded a separate peace with Austria under the terms of which Lombardy was ceded to France then ceded in turn to Piedmont in exchange for Nice and Savoy, an outcome which disappointed the Italians, who had hoped that Austria would be forced to relinquish Venetia as well – see CUSTOZZA, SECOND BATTLE OF. The horrible conditions endured by the wounded were a major factor in the founding of the International Red Cross organization.

Somme, The

Date: 1 July to 18 November 1916.
Location: Mainly between the Somme and Ancre rivers along a line stretching from Chaulnes in the south to Beaumont-Hamel in the north.
War and campaign: First World War: Western Front.
Opposing sides: (a) General Sir Douglas Haig, Commander-in-Chief of the British Armies in France and Belgium; (b) General Erich von Falkenhayn, Chief of German Staff.
Objective: The British were attempting to end the deadlock of trench warfare and restore mobility to the Western Front by achieving a major breakthrough.
Forces engaged: (a) General Sir Henry Rawlinson commanding the British Fourth Army, with supporting operations by General Allenby's British Third Army to the north and General Fayolle's French Sixth Army to the south; (b) General Fritz von Below commanding the German Second Army.
Casualties: (a) British 418,000, French 194,000; (b) 650,000.
Result: The Allies gained a strip of territory some 20 miles long and up to 7 miles deep.

The battle was preceded by a colossal bombardment lasting five days in which no fewer than 1,732,873 shells were fired at the German positions. Yet, during the first day's fighting, British losses amounted to 19,240 killed, 35,493 wounded, 2,152 missing and 585 captured, the total of 57,470 representing the highest casualty rate in the history of the British Army; French and German losses on the same day were comparatively light, the former because they adopted a more flexible method of attack and were not overlooked by their objectives and the latter because they were fighting behind their defences. As the battle wore on, German casualties began to exceed those of the Allies when they mounted repeated counter-attacks to recover lost ground. The fighting ended without a conclusive result, although during February 1917 the Germans abandoned their remaining positions and withdrew to the stronger defences of the Hindenburg Line. In the wider sphere, most of the British casualties had fallen on the volunteer formations of Kitchener's New Army, with the result that never again did the British place such confidence in their leaders, military or political. Likewise, the magnificent German Army of 1914 no longer existed after the Somme, the best of its professional junior officers and NCOs having been killed. The battle is often quoted as an example of the folly of launching an offensive against prepared positions when the powers of the defence, including entrenchments, barbed wire aprons, machine guns and supporting artillery, were so much stronger than those of the attack. Conversely, on 15 September the British committed a handful of tanks to battle for the first time on the Flers sector; they were unreliable, underpowered and painfully slow, but they achieved local successes out of all proportion to the numbers employed and revealed something of the shape of things to come. See also CAMBRAI and AMIENS.

Son-Tai (Sontay) 485

Date: 14–16 December 1883.
Location: Fortified city with citadel 20 miles west of Hanoi on the Red River, Tonkin (now Vietnam).
War and campaign: Undeclared War between China and France, 1883–1885.
Opposing sides: (a) Admiral Amedée Courbet; (b) Lin Yung Ku.
Objective: China refused to recognize Vietnamese acceptance of French protectorate status, particularly regarding Tonkin (on which she retained ancient claims), and despatched troops from Yunnan to occupy the fortress. A French expedition was mounted to eject them.
Forces engaged: (a) 7,000, plus eight river gunboats; (b) 25,000 Chinese, including 10,000 Black Flags (Vietnamese pirates and mercenaries).
Casualties: (a) 410 killed and wounded; (b) approximately 1,000 killed and wounded.
Result: The fortress was captured and French control was extended to the Black River valley.

Spicheren 486

Date: 6 August 1870.
Location: 3 miles south of Saarbrucken, Lorraine, France.
War and campaign: Franco–Prussian War, 1870–1871.
Opposing sides: (a) General Karl Friedrich von Steinmetz commanding elements from III, VII and VIII Corps of the First and Second Armies of the North German Confederation; (b) General Charles Auguste Frossard commanding the French II Corps.
Objective: The Prussians were attempting to entrap the French armies on the frontier within a double-envelopment, of which the attack on Spicheren was the northern arm.
Forces engaged: (a) 33 infantry battalions, 33 cavalry squadrons and 108 guns – total 35,000; (b) 39 infantry battalions, 24 cavalry squadrons and 90 guns – total 28,000.
Casualties: (a) 850 killed, 3,650 wounded and 400 missing; (b) 2,100 killed and wounded, approximately 2,000 captured.
Result: After holding his position all day, Frossard withdrew at nightfall when his left flank was in danger of being turned. Steinmetz, however, by prematurely provoking a general action, had compromised the planned German double-envelopment – see WÖRTH. Nevertheless, the strategic initiative had passed to the

> Germans, who were able to separate the French troops under the overall command of Marshal Bazaine, who were withdrawing on METZ, from those of Marshal MacMahon, which regrouped at Chalons.

Shaken by these reverses, Napoleon relinquished the supreme command in favour of Bazaine on 12 August.

Spion Kop   487

Date: 19–24 January 1900.	
Location: Hill feature 20 miles west of Colenso on the north bank of the Tugela river, Natal.	
War and campaign: Second Boer War, 1899–1902.	
Opposing sides: (a) General Sir Redvers Buller; (b) General Louis Botha.	
Objective: A British relief force was attempting to fight its way through to LADYSMITH.	
Forces engaged: (a) 24,000 infantry, 2,600 mounted troops, eight field batteries and ten naval guns; (b) 6–8,000 men, five guns and one heavy machine gun.	
Casualties: (a) 243 killed and wounded, including 300 captured; (b) approximately 335 killed and wounded.	
Result: The attempt to outflank the Boer right was defeated and Buller's troops retired south of the Tugela.	

For the British, the battle was marked by inept command and control, a failure to reinforce initial success, a failure to provide adequate artillery support and the courage of the troops on Spion Kop itself; for the Boers, it was marked by a rapid reaction to the serious threat posed by the British occupation of Spion Kop, together with excellent artillery support. The summit of the hill, the scene of a prolonged and murderous short-range firefight, was abandoned by both sides simultaneously, but the Boers quickly recognized their mistake and took possession. However, many Boers, believing that their victory was decisive, went on leave, seriously depleting Botha's strength. Thus while Buller was again repulsed when he attacked the Val Krantz on 5 February, later that month he captured Hlangwhane Mountain, east of COLENSO, and turned the Boer left. Botha withdrew and Buller relieved LADYSMITH on 28 February.

Spotsylvania Court House   488

Date: 8–18 May 1864.	
Location: South-west of Fredericksburg, Virginia.	
War and campaign: American Civil War: Grant's Virginia Campaign of 1864.	
Opposing sides: (a) Lieutenant-General Ulysses S. Grant, the US Army's General-in-Chief, in the field with Major-General George G. Meade's Army of the Potomac; (b) General Robert E. Lee commanding the Army of Northern Virginia.	
Objective: Following the Battle of THE WILDERNESS, Grant resumed his advance on Richmond until checked again by Lee just north of the village of Spotsylvania Court House.	
Forces engaged: (a) 111,000; (b) 63,000.	

Casualties: (a) 14,267; (b) approximately 10,000.

Result: Once again Lee was unable to halt Grant, who resumed his southward advance by working round the Confederate right in the aftermath of the battle. See YELLOW TAVERN and COLD HARBOR.

The most severe fighting took place at the tip of a salient in the Confederate line, subsequently named the Bloody Angle because of the horrific casualties incurred by both sides within a comparatively small area.

Stalingrad 489

Date: 19 August 1942 to 2 February 1943.

Location: City on the Volga, formerly named Tsaritsyn and now known as Volgograd.

War and campaign: Second World War: Russian Front.

Opposing sides: (a) Field Marshal Freiherr Maximilian von Weichs commanding Army Group B; (b) General Andrei Yeremenko commanding the Stalingrad Front.

Objective: Hitler, despite the reservations of his generals, insisted that it was necessary to capture the city in order to protect the left flank of the German drive into the Caucasus; however, recognizing the nature of this fixation, Stalin and his General Staff decided to exploit it and prepared a counter-offensive with the object of trapping and destroying the German Sixth Army.

Forces engaged: (a) General Friedrich von Paulus commanding the German Sixth Army and part of Fourth Panzer Army – total 22 divisions with approximately 230,000 men; (b) General Vasili Chuikov commanding the Soviet 62nd Army at Stalingrad – total approximately 300,000 men.

Casualties: (a) 120,000 killed, 25,000 wounded evacuated by air and 91,000 captured, of whom only 5,000 eventually returned to Germany (to these figures must be added casualties incurred by the German relief force and the Romanian, Italian and Hungarian armies overrun during the Soviet counter-offensive – total Axis casualties were estimated by the Soviets to be in excess of one million), plus 3,500 tanks and assault guns, 12,000 artillery weapons, 3,000 aircraft and 75,000 motor vehicles; (b) unpublished, but estimated 200,000.

Result: A crushing Axis defeat resulting in the destruction of the Sixth Army and the abandonment of the German drive into the Caucasus. Although the Soviet Army was in turn to be defeated at KHARKOV, Stalingrad nevertheless represented the turn of the tide on the Russian Front.

The first German attacks on Stalingrad were launched on 19 August and soon the Sixth Army had become firmly locked into a bitter struggle among the ruins. The Soviet counter-offensive, codenamed 'Uranus', was planned by Marshal Georgi Zhukov and involved over one million men, 3,500 tanks and self-propelled mountings of various types and 13,500 guns. On 19 November Vatutin's South-West Front and Rokossovsky's Don Front burst through the Axis lines to the north of the city, while Yeremenko's Stalingrad Front did likewise to the south; by 23 November the jaws of the trap had closed and the Sixth Army had been isolated. Paulus requested permission to break out but this was refused when Goering promised Hitler that the Luftwaffe would supply the Sixth Army by air, a boast that proved vain. A relief force named Army Group Don was assembled under Field Marshal von Manstein and by 18 December this had reached a point only 35 miles from the Stalingrad perimeter. Manstein urged Paulus to break out but the latter, short of fuel and unwilling to incur Hitler's displeasure, temporized and the moment was lost. By

29 December the relief force had been pushed back to Kotelnikovo, its starting point, having incurred 16,000 casualties and lost 300 tanks in the process. Throughout January the Soviets continued to launch attacks on the trapped army and by the 23rd had cut it in two. The Germans were now starving and thousands of their untreated wounded lay in the streets. On 30 January Paulus was promoted to field marshal, being simultaneously reminded by Hitler that no German field marshal had ever surrendered. Nevertheless, the following morning Paulus did surrender and on 2 February the last pocket of German resistance was eliminated.

Stamford Bridge 490

Date: 25 September 1066.
Location: On the river Derwent, 8 miles east of York.
War and campaign: Norwegian Invasion of England, 1066.
Opposing sides: (a) King Harold commanding the English army; (b) King Harald Hardrada commanding the Norwegians.
Objective: King Harold's plan was to destroy the Norwegian force before the Normans landed in southern England.
Forces engaged: (a) Approximately 7,000; (b) uncertain, but perhaps 8–10,000.
Casualties: (a) Unknown, but serious enough to matter when Harold needed every man he could muster to meet the anticipated invasion in the south; (b) unknown, although only 24 ships were needed to transport the survivors of an army which had arrived in 300. Harold Hardrada and Harold's treacherous brother Tostig were among those killed.
Result: The Norwegian invasion was decisively defeated. Hardrada's son Olaf made peace with Harold, swearing never to attack England again; the survivors of his army were permitted to sail away.

Strategically, the victory left Harold inconveniently placed to deal with the Norman landing three days later and cost him casualties which he could ill afford. See also HASTINGS.

Standard, The 491

Date: 22 August 1138.
Location: 3 miles north of Northallerton, Yorkshire.
War and campaign: The Anglo–Scottish Wars.
Opposing sides: (a) Archbishop Thurston of York; (b) David I, King of Scotland.
Objective: Taking advantage of the disturbed state of England following the death of Henry I, the Scots mounted a series of raids into the northern counties. Rallied by the Archbishop of York, the northern barons and their levies marched to meet the invaders.
Forces engaged: (a) Numbers uncertain – perhaps 8,000 English and 10,000 Scots.
Casualties: (a) Unknown, although the Scots undoubtedly sustained the heavier losses.
Result: The Scots were defeated and withdrew to Northumberland. The respite

gained, however, was only temporary and Scottish depredations continued for a further eleven years.

The battle took its name from the banners of St Peter of York, St John of Beverley and St Wildred of Ripon, flown on a wagon in the centre of the English position.

Stirling Bridge (Cambuskenneth)   492

Date: 11 September 1297.
Location: Near Abbey Craig to the north-east of Stirling.
War and campaign: The Anglo–Scottish Wars.
Opposing sides: (a) The Earl of Surrey and Hugh de Cressingham commanding the English army; (b) William Wallace commanding the Scots.
Objective: The Scots, rebelling against the rule of Edward I, had assembled an army at Abbey Craig. The English army attempted to cross the river Forth and bring them to battle.
Forces engaged: (a) The overall English strength is said to have been 50,000 but this almost certainly an exaggeration – 15,000 would seem to be a more reasonable estimate but, whatever the true figure, only the 5,400 men of the vanguard were actually engaged; (b) 5,100.
Casualties: (a) Approximately 5,400, including Cressingham killed; (b) uncertain, but moderate.
Result: The English vanguard was annihilated. Surrey hastily withdrew his army to Berwick and the Scots marched south to pillage the border counties. Wallace was knighted for his achievement. See also FALKIRK (1298).

Although a broad ford lay only two miles upstream, Cressingham ignored this and pushed the vanguard across the bridge, which was only wide enough for two mounted men. Once a sufficient number had crossed, Wallace fell on them with his entire army; thus the leading elements of the vanguard, and those who attempted to reinforce them, were overwhelmed by superior numbers.

Stoke   493

Date: 16 June 1487.
Location: 3 miles south of Newark, Nottinghamshire, near the village of East Stoke.
War and campaign: Lambert Simnel's Rebellion, 1487.
Opposing sides: (a) Henry VII; (b) the Earl of Lincoln and the Swiss mercenary Martin Schwarz commanding the rebels.
Objective: On the accession of Henry VII some Yorkists, resenting their loss of power, used Lambert Simnel, the son of an Oxford artisan, to impersonate Edward, Earl of Warwick, and pursue his claim to the crown, despite the fact that Edward was already imprisoned in the Tower. Simnel was taken to Dublin, where his was crowned 'Edward VI', then landed in Lancashire with a largely Irish army stiffened by Swiss and German mercenaries. Crossing the Pennines, the rebels enjoyed some minor successes but were intercepted by the royal army as they began to march south.
Forces engaged: (a) 12,000; (b) 8,000.
Casualties: (a) 3,000; (b) 4,000 killed, including Lincoln and Schwarz.

> **Result:** The rebellion was crushed. Simnel was captured but, thanks to Henry's shrewd political judgement, he was allowed to survive as a scullion in the royal kitchens, thus discrediting the Yorkist conspirators.

The royal vanguard was badly mauled when it launched a premature attack, although the situation was retrieved by the arrival of the main body of Henry's army. Stoke, a harder-fought engagement than BOSWORTH, is regarded by some historians as the last battle of the Wars of the Roses, although as the context differed somewhat from the main thrust of the quarrel it is, perhaps, better seen as a postscript.

Stones River (Murfreesboro) 494

Date: 31 December 1862 to 2 January 1863.
Location: Murfreesboro, Tennessee, 25 miles south-east of Nashville.
War and campaign: American Civil War: western theatre of operations.
Opposing sides: (a) Major-General William S. Rosecrans commanding the Federal Army of the Cumberland; (b) General Braxton Bragg commanding the Confederate Army of Tennessee.
Objective: An attempt by both sides to break the stalemate which had existed in the central Kentucky/Tennessee war zone since PERRYVILLE.
Forces engaged: (a) 44,000; (b) 34,000.
Casualties: (a) 12,906; (b) 11,740.
Result: Bragg drove in Rosecrans' right, capturing prisoners and guns, but was unable to make further progress against the rallied Federal line. As the Federals were being reinforced and the Stones River, which divided the two wings of his army, was rising due to heavy rain, he complied with President Jefferson Davis's instructions to withdraw south to the Tennessee.

Tactically the engagement was a drawn battle, but strategically it left the Federals in a stronger position. See also CHICKAMAUGA.

Stony Creek 495

Date: 6 June 1813.
Location: Near Hamilton, Lake Ontario, Canada.
War and campaign: War of 1812: Canadian Front.
Opposing sides: (a) Brigadier-General John Vincent commanding the British; (b) Brigadier-Generals William Winder and John Chandler commanding the Americans.
Objective: Having opposed an American landing at Fort George on 27 May, the British garrison retired in the direction of Hamilton. The Americans carried out a dilatory pursuit but at Stony Creek the British turned to mount a night attack on their camp.
Forces engaged: (a) 704; (b) approximately 2,000.
Casualties: Uncertain, but the American losses were heavier and included the capture of both generals, artillery and baggage.

> **Result:** The Americans withdrew to Fort George, where complete demoralization set in.

On 24 June, 540 regulars on a raiding mission surrendered to a British lieutenant and a small party of Indians at Beaver Dam, less than 20 miles from the fort; the American area commander, Major-General Henry Dearborn, was dismissed. The Niagara sector was progressively stripped of troops for Wilkinson's abortive offensive against Montreal (see CHRYSLER'S FARM), and on 12 December Vincent recaptured Fort George.

Stormberg 496

Date: 10 December 1899.

Location: Railway junction 50 miles south of the Orange River, Cape Colony (now part of South Africa).

War and campaign: Second Boer War, 1899–1902.

Opposing sides: (a) Lieutenant-General Sir William Gatacre; (b) General J. H. Olivier.

Objective: The British were attempting to recapture the junction from the Boers.

Forces engaged: (a) 3,000 men and supporting artillery; (b) 2,300 men.

Casualties: (a) 135 killed and wounded, 696 captured; (b) trivial.

Result: A humiliating British reverse for which Gatacre was dismissed. Stormberg was the first of the three defeats in six days, known collectively as 'Black Week', which seriously shook British confidence, the others being MAGERSFONTEIN and COLENSO.

Having become lost during his night approach march, Gatacre ordered his men to assault a Boer position surmounting a precipitous rock face. When the attack failed he withdrew, but the order to retreat did not reach over 600 men still on the feature and they were forced to surrender.

Suez Canal Crossing 497

Date: 6–8 October 1973.

Location: The east bank of the Suez Canal.

War and campaign: Arab–Israeli War of 1973 ('Yom Kippur War').

Opposing sides: (a) Major-General Shmuel Gonen, GOC Israeli Southern Command; (b) General Ahmed Ismail Ali, Egyptian Minister of War, and General Saad el Din Shazli, Army Chief of Staff.

Objective: The Egyptian intention was to secure a crossing of the canal along its length, with the ultimate object of breaking out and recovering the Sinai peninsula.

Forces engaged: (a) Initially the regular 252nd Armoured Division with 280 tanks (of which only 100 were deployed close to the canal), plus 436 reservists of the Jerusalem Brigade manning the Bar Lev outpost line, reinforced on 7–8 October by the reserve 143rd and 162nd Armoured Divisions; (b) the Egyptian Third Army (Major-General Abd el Muneim Wassel), comprising the 4th Armoured and 6th Mechanized Divisions, 7th and 19th Infantry Divisions, 22nd and 25th Armoured Brigades and 130th Marine Brigade, and the Egyptian Second Army (Major-General Saad Mamoun), comprising the 21st Armoured and 23rd Mechanized Divisions,

2nd, 16th and 18th Infantry Divisions and 14th, 15th and 24th Armoured Brigades – total 285,000 men and 2,000 tanks.
Casualties: (a) Approximately 500 killed, wounded or captured during the first 36 hours, plus 170 tanks destroyed or in need of major repairs; (b) 208 killed (the Egyptian General Staff had been prepared to accept 30,000 casualties, including one-third killed).
Result: Both Egyptians armies succeeded in crossing the canal, linking their bridgeheads and beating off Israeli counter-attacks. During subsequent operations the Israelis defeated Egyptian attempts to break out, then secured a crossing of their own to the west bank and cut the Third Army's lines of communication. At this point pressure from the United States and the Soviet Union forced Egypt and Israel to accept a UN ceasefire resolution. Nevertheless, the Egyptians felt that they had recovered their military honour and in the peace negotiations which followed Israel agreed to evacuate Sinai in exchange for recognition and a secure southern frontier. See also GOLAN HEIGHTS (1973).

The date chosen for the crossing coincided with Yom Kippur, the holiest day in the Jewish calendar, during which neither public transport nor broadcasting operated in Israel. The choice was a direct reprisal for the pre-emptive air strikes with which the Israelis had begun the 'Six Day War' of 1967 and achieved a similar degree of strategic surprise. The crossing was meticulously planned and employed large quantities of Soviet amphibious and bridging equipment. The troops themselves were thoroughly trained and strongly motivated. Shazli anticipated an immediate response by the IAF and countered this with a strong air-defence umbrella, incorporating SAMs and radar-controlled anti-aircraft artillery, along the west bank of the canal. It took the Israelis some time to solve the technical problems associated with this and in the meantime they sustained serious losses over the combat zone. Shazli also anticipated immediate counter-attacks by the Israeli armour and, worried that insufficient tanks and anti-tank guns could be got across in time for the infantry to secure their bridgeheads, he equipped each infantry division with 314 RPG-7 close-range anti-tank rocket launchers and 48 portable AT-3 'Sagger' wire-guided anti-tank missiles. These inflicted heavy losses on the Israelis' piecemeal counter-attacks, which were often mounted in response to calls for assistance from the trapped garrisons of Bar Lev outposts, only sixteen of which were manned. Shaken, the Israelis were unable to deliver a concentrated counter-stroke until 8 October and this, planned on the incorrect assumption that the Egyptians were already breaking out, first took an axis parallel to the front then degenerated into an inconclusive firefight. In subsequent operations the Israelis solved the 'Sagger' problem by increasing the proportion of infantry and artillery within their armoured formations.

Suez Landings 498

Date: 5–7 November 1956.
Location: Port Said, Port Fuad and the northern half of the Suez Canal.
War and campaign: Suez Canal Crisis of 1956.
Opposing sides: (a) Lieutenant-General Sir Hugh Stockwell; (b) General Abd el Hakim Amer, Minister of Defence and Commander-in-Chief of the Egyptian armed forces.
Objective: The intentions of the United Kingdom and France were to recover control of the recently nationalized canal, thereby undermining the position of

Egyptian President Gamal Abd el Nasser and so restore their prestige in the Middle East.

Forces engaged: (a) British – 3rd Commando Brigade, 16th Parachute Brigade, one armoured regiment and one engineer squadron, plus one infantry battalion in reserve; French – 10th Parachute Division, three commandos, one medium and two light tank squadrons and one engineer company; (b) the Egyptian garrisons of Port Said and Port Fuad – approximately one division.

Casualties: (a) 22 British killed and 97 wounded, 10 French killed and 33 wounded; (b) unknown.

Result: Despite achieving tactical success in the landings and advancing 25 miles along the canal, the Allies were compelled to abandon the operation on 7 October because of intense financial pressure by the United States and political pressure by the United Nations. The international prestige of Great Britain and France was severely damaged by the incident; arguably, that of the United Kingdom was not recovered until the Falklands War of 1982. In contrast Nasser, though defeated at Suez, and in SINAI by the Israelis, emerged the apparent victor and became the leading figure in the Arab world.

The operation began with parachute drops on both the British and French sectors, followed by amphibious landings. The break-out down the canal encountered negligible opposition and could have been completed had not the Allies accepted the UN demand for an immediate ceasefire. The principal reason for the failure was the four-month delay in mounting the operation, during which world opinion hardened against the UK and France.

Suomossalmi 499

Date: 11 December 1939 to 6 January 1940.

Location: Village in central Finland close to the frontier with Russian Karelia.

War and campaign: Second World War: Winter War between the USSR and Finland, 1939–1940.

Opposing sides: (a) Marshal Semyon Timoshenko commanding the Soviet armies in Finland; (b) Marshal Carl Gustav von Mannerheim, Commander-in-Chief of Finland's armed forces.

Objective: The Russians were attempting to relieve one of their divisions which had been cut off by the Finns at Suomossalmi.

Forces engaged: (a) The 163rd Division, trapped at Suomossalmi, and the 44th Division, ambushed while marching to its relief, both belonging to the Soviet Ninth Army; (b) the 9th Division, commanded by Colonel H. J. Siilasvuo.

Casualties: (a) About 27,500 killed or frozen to death and 1,600 taken prisoner, plus 80 tanks, 70 guns and 400 lorries captured; (b) 900 killed and 1,770 wounded.

Result: The most notable of several such defeats inflicted by the Finns on the Russians in the arctic conditions prevailing along their eastern frontier.

See also MANNERHEIM LINE.

Syracuse, Siege of 500

Date: 415–413 BC.

Location: City on the east coast of Sicily.
War and campaign: The Peloponnesian War, 431–404 BC: Sicilian Campaign.
Opposing sides: (a) Nicias, Lamachus and Alcibiades, joined in July 413 by Demosthenes; (b) initially Hermocrates, later Gylippus of Sparta.
Objective: The Athenians wished to extend their influence to Sicily by capturing the rich and powerful city of Syracuse.
Forces engaged: (a) Initially 6,400 infantry and 30 cavalry, reinforced in July 413 by 15,000 infantry and 680 cavalry; (b) uncertain, but at least equal to the Athenians (the Spartan contingent, originally 3,000 strong, was reinforced by a further 1,300 in the spring of 413).
Casualties: (a) Of the entire Athenian force, only 7,000 survived to be sold into slavery; (b) unknown, but heavy.
Result: The destruction of the besieging force marked the beginning of the decline of Athens and the rise of Sparta.

From the outset the Athenians suffered from command problems. Alcibiades, summoned home to answer a charge of sacrilege, deserted to Sparta and the able Lamachus was killed during the early fighting. This left the indecisive Nicias in control and, thanks to the vigorous defence conducted by Gylippus he was unable to complete his wall of circumvallation. By the end of 414 it was apparent that the siege could not succeed but the Athenian government refused to abandon it and promised to reinforce Nicias. At sea, the Athenians began to lose control, although the Syracusans were unable to prevent the arrival of Demosthenes in July 413. After further abortive operations it was decided to withdraw. However, the Athenian fleet was again worsted as it tried to break out and, with their remaining 7,000 men, Nicias and Demosthenes attempted to escape overland. The Syracusans and Spartans pursued and on 20 September the Athenians surrendered; Nicias and Demosthenes were beheaded. It has been estimated that the campaign cost Athens some 34,000 soldiers and seamen, an insupportable loss for a small city-state which had fatally overreached itself.

Taierchwang 501

Date: April 1938.
Location: North-east of Xuzhou (Suchow), Jiangsu province, China.
War and campaign: Sino–Japanese War, 1937–1945.
Opposing sides: (a) General Li Tsung-jen; (b) uncertain.
Objective: An unexpected Chinese counter-attack succeeded in encircling a large Japanese force which had been advancing southwards on Xuzhou. The Japanese intention was to break out of the trap.
Forces engaged: (a) Approximately 200,000 regulars and guerrillas; (b) approximately 60,000.
Casualties: (a) Unknown, but heavy; (b) 20,000 killed and large quantities of equipment abandoned.
Result: After several failed attempts, the Japanese finally broke out to the north at the cost of one-third of their force.

The battle ended with the first major defeat sustained by Japan in modern history and did much to restore Chinese morale after the loss of Shanghai and Nanking the previous year. However, the Japanese quickly regrouped and resumed their advance, capturing Xuzhou on 20 May.

Taku Forts 502

Date: 21 August 1860.
Location: At the mouth of the Hai river, below Tientsin, China.
War and campaign: Second Opium War, 1856–1860.
Opposing sides: (a) Lieutenant-General Sir James Grant and Lieutenant-General Cousin-Montauban; (b) the Chinese governor Hang Foo.
Objective: The Anglo-French intention was to march on Peking by way of Tientsin. This involved capturing the formidable Taku Forts which, on 25 June 1858, had decisively repulsed an attempt by a British squadron of gunboats to fight its way up-river.
Forces engaged: (a) 11,000 British and Indian, 7,000 French; (b) estimated 5,000.
Casualties: (a) 21 British killed and 184 wounded, fewer French casualties; (b) 400 killed and wounded, 2,100 captured, disarmed and released.
Result: The two northern forts were stormed from the landward side; the smaller southern fort was abandoned and the larger southern fort surrendered the following day.

The expeditionary force advanced on Peking, where the Chinese government sued for peace.

Talavera 503

Date: 27–28 July 1809.
Location: Town on the Tagus, 70 miles south-west of Madrid.
War and campaign: Peninsular War, 1807–1814: Allied Invasion of Spain, 1809.
Opposing sides: (a) Lieutenant-General Sir Arthur Wellesley and General Gregorio de la Cuesta commanding, respectively, the British and Spanish elements of the Allied army; (b) Joseph Bonaparte, King of Spain, and Marshal Claude Victor commanding the French army.
Objective: The Allied intention was to advance on Madrid, but at Talavera the French counter-attacked.
Forces engaged: (a) 54,441 including 33,000 Spanish; (b) 46,138.
Casualties: (a) 801 British killed, 3,915 wounded and 645 missing (an exaggerated figure of 1,207 Spanish casualties was claimed, but since the Spanish took little part in the battle the majority can only be classed as missing); (b) 761 killed, 6,391 wounded and 206 missing, plus twenty guns captured.
Result: Although Wellesley repulsed the French attacks and won a tactical victory, his army was too exhausted to follow up. On 3 August he learned that a second French army under Soult was threatening his lines of communication and he withdrew into Portugal. See BUSACO.

The burden of the fighting fell on Wellesley's British troops. Most of the Spanish contingent fled after firing a single volley on the first day; some units did a little better on the second day but after the battle Cuesta decided to go his own way. Wellesley, created Viscount Wellington of Talavera on 26 August, vowed never again to attempt joint operations with such unreliable allies.

Tamai 504

Date: 13 March 1884.
Location: West of Suakin, Sudan.
War and campaign: Sudan Campaigns: Suakin Front.
Opposing sides: (a) Major-General Sir Gerald Graham; (b) Osman Digna, Mahdist Governor of Eastern Sudan.
Objective: The British intended to destroy the Mahdist army in the area, and there was the further possibility of opening communications with Berber on the Nile and establishing contact with Gordon at KHARTOUM.
Forces engaged: (a) 4,000, plus four guns and several Gatling and Gardner machine guns; (b) 12,000.
Casualties: (a) 214; (b) 2,200 killed.
Result: Although Osman Digna was defeated, he could sustain the loss and Suakin remained in a virtual state of siege.

See also EL TEB.

Tannenberg (1410) 505

Date: 15 July 1410.
Location: Between the villages of Tannenberg and Grunfelde, near Soldau, formerly East Prussia and now north-eastern Poland.
War and campaign: Wars of the Teutonic Knights: Campaign against Poland and Lithuania, 1410–1411.
Opposing sides: (a) The Grand Master; (b) Ladislas II, King of Poland, and Witowt, Grand Duke of Lithuania.
Objective: The Knights were resisting an invasion of their territory by the combined Polish/Lithuanian army, which included Bohemian mercenaries under Jan Ziska. See PRAGUE (1419).
Forces engaged: (a) Precise figures uncertain (the number of the Order's knights had fallen below 1,600, of which the important Livonian branch and many individuals were absent – overall strength at Tannenberg 4–6,000); (b) 10,000.
Casualties: (a) The Grand Master, the senior officers of the Order and a minimum of 200 knights were killed and the rest of the army sustained proportionally heavy casualties; (b) uncertain, but probably heavy.
Result: The Order was decisively defeated.

Though the Order was permitted to retain most of its lands, its military power and prestige never recovered and its influence declined steadily.

Tannenberg (1914)

Date: 26–30 August 1914.

Location: Along a 50-mile front between Saldau (Mlawa) and Bishofsburg (Biskupiec), formerly East Prussia and now Poland.

War and campaign: First World War: Eastern Front.

Opposing sides: (a) General Helmuth von Moltke, Chief of the German General Staff; (b) General Yakov Zhilinsky commanding the North-West Front.

Objective: Having intercepted uncoded radio transmissions which confirmed that the Russian Second Army was advancing unsupported, the German Eighth Army was redeployed rapidly to envelop and destroy it.

Forces engaged: (a) Colonel-General Paul von Hindenburg commanding the German Eighth Army (twelve divisions); (b) General Alexander Samsonov commanding the Russian Second Army (ten infantry and three cavalry divisions).

Casualties: (a) Approximately 15,000; (b) approximately 120,000, including 92,000 prisoners and 300 guns captured (Samsonov took his own life in the aftermath of the battle).

Result: Two of Samsonov's five corps were destroyed and the remainder were so severely mauled that the Second Army ceased to exist. Having thus removed half of the threat to East Prussia, Hindenburg was now free to take the offensive against Rennenkampf's Russian First Army. In the wider sphere, the victory created such euphoria in Germany that the strategic failure at the FIRST BATTLE OF THE MARNE was eclipsed. See also MASURIAN LAKES.

Although Ludendorff is sometimes credited with the rapid redeployment of the Eighth Army after GUMBINNEN, his orders had already been anticipated by Lieutenant-Colonel Max Hoffmann, the army's senior operations staff officer. The use of the strategic railway system and requistioned motor transport enabled the move to be made with such speed that Samsonov was unaware that his troops were marching into a trap. Rennenkampf, whose tardy advance after Gumbinnen was further delayed by a single German cavalry division, was ordered by Zhilinsky to move to Samsonov's assistance on 27 August, but his response amounted to little more than a token effort.

Tarawa Atoll

Date: 20–23 November 1943.

Location: Part of the Gilbert Islands, Central Pacific (the fighting took place on Betio Island).

War and campaign: Second World War: Central Pacific.

Opposing sides: (a) Admiral Chester Nimitz, Commander-in-Chief Central Pacific, and Vice-Admiral Raymond Spruance, with overall responsibility for the capture of Tarawa; (b) Rear-Admiral Keichi Shibasaki commanding the Tarawa garrison.

Objective: The capture of Tarawa was the first step in the American drive across the Central Pacific towards Japan. It provided the airfields necessary to support the next phase of the advance.

Forces engaged: (a) Rear-Admiral Richmond Kelly Turner in tactical command of the operation, Major-General Holland M. Smith commanding V Amphibious Corps and Major-General Julian Smith commanding the 2nd Marine Division with approximately 20,000 men. (b) 7th Special Naval Landing Force and 3rd Special Base Force plus attached naval personnel and a technically non-combatant labour force – total 4,836, of whom 2,619 were fighting troops.

Casualties: (a) 2nd Marine Division – 997 killed, 88 missing presumed killed, and 2,233 wounded; US Navy – 30 killed and 59 wounded; (b) with the exception of 146 prisoners, all but seventeen of whom were Korean labourers, the entire garrison were killed.

Result: Although the operation was successful, American public opinion was seriously shocked by the heavy casualties incurred in securing such an apparently insignificant objective. In fact, the lessons of Tarawa were quickly absorbed and put to good use in subsequent amphibious operations.

The heavy preliminary bombardment left the formidable Japanese fortifications largely untouched. Many landing craft grounded on the reef so that their occupants were forced to wade ashore in the teeth of the enemy's fire. On the other hand, the use of armoured amtracs (LVTs) in the combat role for the first time undoubtedly saved many American lives and was a critical factor in the success of the operation.

Telamon 508

Date: 225 BC.

Location: Near Cape Talamone, between Rome and Pisa.

War and campaign: Gallic Invasion of Italy, 225–222 BC.

Opposing sides: (a) The Consuls Lucius Papas and Gaius Regulus; (b) Kings Concolitanus and Aneroestus commanding the Gauls.

Objective: The Roman intention was entrap and destroy the Gallic army.

Forces engaged: (a) 41,600 legionaries and 30,000 allied infantry, plus 2,400 legionary and 2,000 allied cavalry – total 76,000; (b) 50,000 infantry and 20,000 cavalry – total 70,000.

Casualties: (a) 6,000, including Regulus killed; (b) 40,000 killed and 10,000 captured.

Result: A decisive victory which removed the Gallic threat to Rome.

Tel-el-Kebir 509

Date: 13 September 1882.

Location: On the Sweet Water Canal between Cairo and Ismailia, Egypt.

War and campaign: Achmet Arabi Pasha's Rebellion.

Opposing sides: (a) Lieutenant-General Sir Garnet Wolseley; (b) Achmet Arabi Pasha.

Objective: The British intention was to defeat the rebel army and advance on Cairo, thereby restoring the stability of Egypt and the security of the Suez Canal.

Forces engaged: (a) 17,000 men and 67 guns; (b) 22,000 men and 60 guns.

Casualties: (a) 58 killed, 379 wounded and 22 missing; (b) 2,000 killed, 500 wounded and all guns captured.

> **Result:** The rebels were driven from their positions and Arabi surrendered when Wolseley's troops entered Cairo the following day.

Wolseley's attack was delivered at first light after a difficult night approach march across the desert, achieving complete surprise.

Teutoburger Wald 510

Date: September/October AD 9.
Location: The Grotenburg, south-west of Detmold.
War and campaign: Germanic Wars of the Roman Empire.
Opposing sides: (a) Publius Quintilius Varus, Governor-General and Commander-in-Chief; (b) Arminius (Hermann), a chief of the Cherusci.
Objective: The intention of the rebellious German tribes was to ambush and destroy the Roman army as it withdrew to its winter quarters at Aliso (Haltern) on the Lippe.
Forces engaged: (a) XVII, XVIII and XIX Legions, plus auxiliaries – total approximately 20,000, including 1,500 cavalry, accompanied by 10,000 camp followers; (b) unknown, but well in excess of the Roman fighting strength.
Casualties: (a) Approximately 18,000 legionaries and most of the camp followers were killed (the few survivors were enslaved;) (b) unknown.
Result: The Roman army was wiped out and Varus committed suicide. Subsequent punitive expeditions inflicted heavy losses on the German tribes but failed to subdue them and the northern frontier of the Empire was fixed along the Rhine. Both Sir Edward Creasy and Major-General J. F. C. Fuller regard the defeat of Varus as being one of the world's most decisive battles, commenting that if Arminius had failed the history of Germany would have been radically altered by prolonged contact with Graeco-Roman influences and that the Saxon migration to Britain would not have taken place.

Varus allowed himself to be lured into the broken, heavily forested and trackless Teutoburger Wald where the going was rendered even more difficult by torrential rain. The Germans closed in, cutting the struggling column into sections and slaughtering the camp followers. Varus ordered the construction of an earthwork fort on the Grotenburg, but this was stormed after several days' fighting; the Roman cavalry was cut to pieces when it attempted to fight its way out. Only a handful of Romans escaped the disaster. The remainder were put to the sword, the tribunes and centurions being offered as human sacrifices to the tribal gods.

Tewkesbury 511

Date: 4 May 1471.
Location: Immediately south of Tewkesbury, Gloucestershire, beside the river Severn.
War and campaign: Wars of the Roses, 1455–1485.
Opposing sides: (a) Edward IV commanding the Yorkists; (b) Edmund Beaufort, Duke of Somerset (brother of the Duke killed at HEXHAM), commanding the Lancastrians.
Objective: On receiving news of the Lancastrian defeat at BARNET, Queen

Margaret, who had landed at Weymouth the same day, attempted to march north and recruit support. Edward IV, anticipating her intention, pursued closely and brought the Lancastrians to battle.
Forces engaged: (a) 9,000; (b) 7,000.
Casualties: (a) Uncertain, but moderate; (b) approximately 2,000, including the young Edward, Prince of Wales, Somerset and most of the Lancastrian nobility, either killed in the fighting or captured and executed after the battle.
Result: A Yorkist victory which secured Edward IV's hold on the throne until his death in 1483. Queen Margaret was captured and Henry VI was put to death in the Tower; this all but destroyed the Lancastrian branch of the royal family, with the exception of Henry Tudor – see BOSWORTH.

Following an artillery exchange, Somerset led an attack against the Yorkist left flank but lost direction and was thrown back in disarray. The Yorkists then made a general advance and after a short mêlée the Lancastrian army disintegrated.

Thames, The   512

Date: 5 October 1813.
Location: Near Moravian Town (now Fairfield) on the Thames river, Ontario, Canada.
War and campaign: War of 1812: Canadian Front.
Opposing sides: (a) Brigadier-General Henry Proctor commanding the British; (b) Major-General William Harrison commanding the Americans.
Objective: The Americans caught up with a British force which was retreating into Canada from Detroit. See FRENCHTOWN.
Forces engaged: (a) 880 regulars and approximately 1,000 Indians; (b) 4,500 regulars and militia.
Casualties: (a) British – twelve killed, 22 wounded and 477 captured; Indians – 35 killed, including Chief Tecumseh; (b) Americans – seven killed and 22 wounded.
Result: Proctor's demoralized regulars surrendered after offering a token resistance. His feeble performance resulted in a court martial, but far more serious than the defeat of his battalion-sized force of regulars was the death of Tecumseh, without whom the pro-British Indian Confederacy could not survive. However, the full potential of Harrison's victory was largely squandered by the American War Department. The regular element of his army was sent to the Niagara sector (see CHIPPEWA and LUNDY'S LANE), but when his militia units were disbanded and sent home he resigned in disgust and retired to civilian life. In 1841 Harrison was elected President of the United States, an office he held for only one month before his death.

Thermopylae   513

Date: 480 BC.
Location: Pass 10 miles south of Lamia, Greece.
War and campaign: Graeco–Persian Wars, 499–448 BC.

Opposing sides: (a) Leonidas, King of Sparta, commanding the Greek forces; (b) Xerxes, King of Persia.
Objective: The Greeks hoped to halt the Persian invasion by holding the pass.
Forces engaged: (a) 7,000; (b) approximately 100,000.
Casualties: (a) 4,500 killed including Leonidas; (b) estimated 20,000 killed and wounded.
Result: The Persians eventually succeeded in forcing the pass, but the heroic defence by Leonidas and his men inspired Greek resistance to the invaders – see PLATAEA.

Leonidas detached 1,000 men to hold a secondary track through the mountains to his left while, with the main body of his troops, he repulsed repeated Persian attempts to break through the pass. After three days a Greek traitor named Ephialtes informed Xerxes of the existence of the secondary track and the latter despatched his guard, known as the Immortals, along it. Learning that the Immortals had broken through, Leonidas sent back half his troops to contain the flank attack. The Persians, however, brushed them aside and the survivors retreated to Elatea. Leonidas now found himself simultaneously attacked from the front and the rear inside the pass. The Thebans and other Greeks with him surrendered but the King and his 300-strong bodyguard of Spartans refused to give up and fought to the death; it is thought that the Persians, overawed by the Spartans' superiority in hand-to-hand combat, destroyed the little group with a continuous rain of arrows.

Tinian 514

Date: 24–31 July 1944.
Location: One of the Marianas Islands, Central Pacific.
War and campaign: Second World War: Central Pacific.
Opposing sides: (a) Admiral Chester Nimitz, Commander-in-Chief Central Pacific Theatre; (b) General Hideyoshi Obata commanding the Japanese Thirty-First Army.
Objective: The capture of the Marianas would enable the Americans to launch a bombing offensive against Japan itself and also sever the enemy's communications with his conquests to the south.
Forces engaged: (a) Lieutenant-General Holland M. Smith commanding V Amphibious Corps (2nd and 4th Marine Divisions) – total about 40,000; (b) Colonel Keishi Ogata commanding the Japanese garrison – total about 9,000.
Casualties: (a) 394 killed and 1,961 wounded; (b) the entire garrison fought to the death.
Result: The capture of Tinian was described by General Holland Smith as the finest amphibious operation of the Pacific War.

See also SAIPAN and GUAM.

Tippermuir 515

Date: 1 September 1644.
Location: North-east of Stirling.

War and campaign: First Civil War, 1642–1646: operations in Scotland.
Opposing sides: (a) James Graham, Marquis of Montrose, commanding the Royalists; (b) Lord Elcho commanding the Covenanters.
Objective: Following the intervention of Scottish troops in the Civil War, the Marquis of Montrose had mobilized a number of Highland clans for the King. At Tippermuir the advance of his troops was opposed by a Covenanter army.
Forces engaged: (a) 3,000; (b) 5,000.
Casualties: (a) Uncertain, but moderate; (b) estimated 2,000 killed, plus an unknown number of wounded.
Result: The Covenanter army was destroyed.

Montrose captured Perth and Aberdeen. See also INVERLOCHY.

Tobruk, First Battle of   516

Date: 21–22 January 1941.
Location: Fortified town and harbour on the coast of Cyrenaica, Libya.
War and campaign: Second World War: North Africa.
Opposing sides: (a) Lieutenant-General Richard O'Connor commanding XIII Corps; (b) General Pitassi Mannella commanding the Italian garrison.
Objective: The British capture of Tobruk.
Forces engaged: (a) Reinforced 6th Australian Division (Major-General Iven MacKay), plus one squadron of Matilda II tanks (7 RTR); (b) the 61st Division, a 2,000-strong naval detachment and 9,000 stragglers from previous engagements – total 32,000, supported by 200 guns and 90 AFVs.
Casualties: (a) Light; (b) 25,000 captured, together with all the garrison's equipment.
Result: A major Italian defeat.

See BARDIA, BEDA FOMM and SIDI BARRANI; also TOBRUK (OPERATION 'CRUSADER') and GAZALA.

Tobruk (Operation 'Crusader')   517

Date: 18 November to 7 December 1941.
Location: Area to the south and east of Tobruk, a fortified port on the coast of Cyrenaica, Libya.
War and campaign: Second World War: North Africa.
Opposing sides: (a) Lieutenant-General Sir Alan Cunningham (until 26 November, then Major-General Neil Ritchie) commanding the British Eighth Army; (b) General Erwin Rommel, *de facto* field commander of the Axis army in North Africa.
Objective: The British intention was to relieve the besieged garrison of Tobruk and destroy the Axis army in Libya.
Forces engaged: (a) XIII Corps (Godwin-Austen) – 2nd New Zealand Division, 4th Indian Division and 1st Army Tank Brigade; XXX Corps (Norrie) – 7th

Armoured Division, 1st South Africa Division and 22nd Guards Brigade; Tobruk garrison – 70th Division, Polish Carpathian Brigade and 32nd Army Tank Brigade; total British tank strength – 201 infantry tanks and 523 cruiser/Stuart. (b) Afrika Korps (Crüwell) – 15th and 21st Panzer Divisions and one motorized division; Italian XX Mobile Corps (Gambara) – Ariete Armoured and Trieste Motorized Divisions (technically outside Rommel's command); Italian XXI Corps (Navarini) – five infantry divisions; total Axis tank strength – 35 PzKpfw IVs, 139 PzKpfw IIIs and 146 M.13s.
Casualties: (a) 18,000 killed, wounded and missing and 278 tanks lost (many subsequently recovered and repaired); (b) 38,000 killed, wounded and missing plus about 300 tanks lost.
Result: 'Crusader' succeeded in relieving Tobruk and forcing Rommel to abandon Cyrenaica, but only after a far tougher struggle than had been anticipated. The Axis garrisons at Bardia, Sollum and Halfaya Pass, isolated by Rommel's retreat, were attacked in turn and forced to surrender.

The Eighth Army crossed the Libyan frontier on 18 November and did not encounter serious opposition until the following day. By 21 November, however, a confused and hard-fought series of actions had developed on and around Sidi Rezegh airfield, in which the Tobruk garrison had begun to break out against opposition from the Afrika Division (later known as the 90th Light), which was itself trying to defend the airfield against the 7th Armoured Brigade and the 7th Armoured Division Support Group; the latter were in turn under attack from the south-east by the Afrika Korps, whose anti-tank gunners were holding off pursuit by the 4th and 22nd Armoured Brigades. This phase of the battle ended with the 7th Armoured Division's three armoured brigades in disarray and on 24 November Rommel decided to lead his armour eastwards in a lightning foray to the frontier, believing that this would unsettle Cunningham and induce him to withdraw. In Cairo General Sir Claude Auchinleck, Commander-in-Chief Middle East, was aware of the danger and on 26 November he replaced the Eighth Army's commander with his own Deputy Chief of Staff. For the Axis, Rommel's foray – sometimes referred to as the 'Dash to the Wire' – proved to be a disaster, for during his absence XIII Corps continued its advance and during the night of 26/27 November the 2nd New Zealand Division effected a junction with the Tobruk garrison. Rushing back from the frontier, Rommel was briefly able to reimpose the siege, but he was now faced with a revitalized 7th Armoured Division and in a series of actions against both British corps his strength was steadily eroded. By 5 December the Eighth Army had re-established contact with Tobruk and Rommel reluctantly accepted that if he did not retreat his army would be destroyed. On 7 December he commenced an orderly withdrawal to El Agheila, abandoning Cyrenaica and his garrisons on the Egyptian frontier.

Torgau 518

Date: 3 November 1760.
Location: Town on the Elbe, 65 miles south of Berlin.
War and campaign: Seven Years' War, 1756–1763: Central European Campaign of 1760.
Opposing sides: (a) Frederick the Great; (b) Marshal Leopold von Daun.
Objective: Following LIEGNITZ, Austrian and Russian troops had temporarily occupied and partially burned Berlin (9–12 October). Frederick II of Prussia marched

north to relieve his capital but found the main Austrian army holding a strong defensive position at Torgau.
Forces engaged: (a) 44,000; (b) 65,000.
Casualties: (a) 13,120 killed and wounded; (b) 4,200 killed and wounded and 7,000 prisoners.
Result: The Austrians were narrowly defeated and withdrew east of the Elbe. Both sides, exhausted, went into winter quarters.

Frederick's intention was that Ziethen should mount a holding attack against the Austrian front with half the army while he, with the remainder, made a wide march round the enemy right with the object of attacking it from the rear. However, Ziethen became engaged prematurely and Frederick's approach march was disorganized, with the result that the Prussian flank attack forfeited surprise, was delivered piecemeal and sustained serious casualties. However, Frederick persisted, and when Ziethen finally came into action against the principal objective the Austrians retreated.

Toulon, Siege of   519

Date: 27 August to 19 December 1793.
Location: City and naval base on the Mediterranean coast of France.
War and campaign: War of the First Coalition, 1792–1798.
Opposing sides: (a) Admiral Lord Hood in overall command; (b) latterly General Jacques Dugommier.
Objective: Disaffected citizens had handed over the base to an Allied naval and military expedition and the Revolutionary Government of France was determined to recapture it.
Forces engaged: (a) 16,000 (including 2,200 British, 6,900 Spanish and 1,600 émigré Royalists); (b) 11,500.
Casualties: (a) Unknown.
Result: Once the French had captured Fort Mulgrave and the promontory of L'Eguillette (16 December), they were in a position to command the Inner Harbour with their guns and Hood ordered the evacuation of the city and naval base. Of the 30 French warships which had been captured in the harbour, half were destroyed or sailed away by the Royal Navy, but the remainder were negligently left intact by the Spanish to be recovered by the besiegers.

Toulon marked an important step in the rise of the young Napoleon Bonaparte, who served as Dugommier's principal artillery adviser and was, in fact, the architect of his victory. Beginning the siege as a captain, Bonaparte was quickly promoted to colonel and, following the capture of the base, to brigadier-general as a reward for his services.

Toulouse   520

Date: 10 April 1814.
Location: Fortified city on the Garonne river, southern France. The battle was fought on a range of hills to the east.
War and campaign: Peninsular War, 1807–1814: Campaign of 1814.
Opposing sides: (a) Field Marshal the Marquess of Wellington commanding the

Allied army (b) Marshal Nicolas Jean-de-Dieu Soult commanding the French Army of Spain.
Objective: After eliminating the last French garrisons in Spain, Wellington fought his way through the Pyrenees and on to French soil. Soult, commanding the reorganized French army, withdrew across the Garonne but chose to offer battle outside Toulouse.
Forces engaged: (a) 50,000, including 10,000 Spanish; (b) 42,000.
Casualties: (a) 4,500, including 2,000 Spanish; (b) 3,200.
Result: The French abandoned the city and withdrew.

This, the last battle of the war, was fought without either side being aware that Napoleon had already agreed to capitulate. Two days after the battle a local armistice was concluded between Wellington and Soult.

Tours 521

Date: 10 October 732.
Location: Probably at Cenon, between Tours and Poitiers.
War and campaign: Moslem Invasion of France, 732.
Opposing sides: (a) Charles Martel commanding the Franks; (b) Abd er-Rahman, Moslem Governor of Spain.
Objective: The Franks were attempting to defeat the invasion.
Forces engaged: (a) Estimated 30,000 (b) estimated 80,000.
Casualties: (a) Estimated 1,500; (b) unknown, but severe – Abd er-Rahman was among those killed.
Result: Charles won a decisive victory which removed the Moslem threat to western Europe. The Moslems withdrew, abandoning most of their plunder; by 759 they had been driven from France altogether.

Few details of the battle exist but it is evident that Charles formed his army into a solid infantry phalanx which repeated Moslem cavalry attacks were unable to penetrate. Heavy fighting continued until dusk and during the night the Moslems, dishearted by heavy casualties and the death of their leader, abandoned their camp and fled south.

Towton 522

Date: 29 March 1461.
Location: South of Towton village, between Pontefract and Tadcaster, north Yorkshire.
War and campaign: Wars of the Roses, 1455–1485.
Opposing sides: (a) The Duke of Somerset commanding the Lancastrians; (b) King Edward IV commanding the Yorkists.
Objective: Following their failure to capture London after the SECOND BATTLE OF ST ALBANS, the Lancastrians withdrew into Yorkshire. The Yorkists followed and both sides accepted a pitched battle at Towton.
Forces engaged: (a) Estimated 20,000; (b) estimated 16,000.

Casualties: (a) Towton has the reputation of being the bloodiest battle ever fought on English soil, but accurate casualty figures remain a matter of conjecture. The overall estimate of 28,000 produced by the Yorkist heralds must be regarded as an exaggeration. Paston's figure of 8,000 for the Yorkist casualties seems reasonable and, given the nature and outcome of the engagement, comparable Lancastrian losses would have been in the region of 10,000. This would give each side a loss ratio of 50 per cent, of whom not less than one-third would be killed and, while high by any standard, it is compatible with so hard-fought an encounter in which Edward had ordered that quarter should neither be offered nor accepted. The majority of the Lancastrian leaders died in the battle.

Result: A Yorkist victory, following which Edward was crowned in London. Henry VI, Queen Margaret and Edward Prince of Wales fled to Scotland. See HEXHAM.

The battle was fought in a blizzard which blew directly into the faces of the Lancastrians. Lord Thomas Fauconberg, commanding the Yorkist archers, ordered his men to fire a volley of heavy-shafted arrows and then withdraw a short distance. The Lancastrians, blinded by the snow, responded, but because of the wind their supply of arrows was expended on empty space. The arrows were then collected by the Yorkists, who opened so galling a fire that the Lancastrians were provoked into charging downhill to engage in a fiercely contested, six-hour mêlée which was only decided when the Duke of Norfolk arrived with Yorkist reinforcements and fell on Somerset's left flank. The Lancastrians then broke, most streaming westward across what is still known as Bloody Meadow to cross the river Cock. Although little more than a stream, the Cock was in spate and presented an obstacle to exhausted, fully armed men. Many of the fugitives, therefore, were cut down by the Yorkist cavalry as they converged on a bridge and ford. Nevertheless, the slaughter at this stage of the engagement was probably less than some accounts suggest as the Lancastrian flight was covered by nightfall and Edward's army was in no condition to mount an immediate pursuit. The following day Edward entered York, only to find that his royal rivals and Somerset had already fled to Newcastle.

Trebbia, The

Date: December 218 BC.

Location: On the east bank of the Trebbia close to its confluence with the Po, south-west of Piacenza.

War and campaign: The Second Punic War, 219–202 BC.

Opposing sides: (a) The Consul Tiberius Sempronius; (b) Hannibal.

Objective: Having crossed the Maritime Alps and won a skirmish at the Ticinus river, Hannibal continued his advance into Italy and established a camp near Piacenza (ancient Placentia). His intention was to destroy the Roman army which had concentrated against him.

Forces engaged: (a) 40,000; (b) 36,000.

Casualties: (a) Approximately 20,000; (b) approximately 5,000.

Result: The Roman army was routed. Hannibal was able to augment his strength by recruiting among the Cisalpine Gauls. See also LAKE TRASIMENE.

Hannibal concealed 2,000 of his best infantry and cavalry, commanded by his brother Mago, in a ravine to the south of the area he had selected as the main battlefield. Then, by raiding the Roman camp, he provoked Sempronius into fording the Trebbia and mounting a full-scale attack. The Roman cavalry on the wings, inferior in numbers, was driven off and when the two armies were fully engaged Hannibal signalled Mago to attack into the Roman rear. About 10,000 legionaries reached safety by fighting their way through the Carthaginian centre but the rest of Sempronius' army was destroyed.

Trenton   524

Date: 26 December 1776.
Location: Town on the New Jersey bank of the Delaware River.
War and campaign: American War of Independence, 1775–1783: central theatre of operations.
Opposing sides: (a) Colonel Johann Rall commanding the garrison of Trenton; (b) Major-General George Washington.
Objective: Washington's intention was to raise his army's morale by carrying out a successful raid in strength against a British outpost.
Forces engaged: (a) 1,400 Hessians in British service; (b) 2,400.
Casualties: (a) 22 killed (including Rall) and 918 captured; (b) four killed and eight wounded.
Result: Most of the Hessians, outnumbered and surrounded, surrendered.

The Hessian garrison of a neighbouring outpost at Bordentown also withdrew. Encouraged, Washington decided to advance deeper into New Jersey – see PRINCETON.

Turin   525

Date: 7 September 1706.
Location: West of the old city, between the Stura and Dora Riparia rivers, north-western Italy.
War and campaign: War of Spanish Succession, 1701–1714: Italian Campaign of 1706.
Opposing sides: (a) Prince Eugene of Savoy commanding the Allied army; (b) Marshal Count Ferdinand de Marsin and the Duke of Orleans commanding the French army.
Objective: Prince Eugene was attempting to break the French siege of Turin.
Forces engaged: (a) 18,000 infantry, 12,000 cavalry, 5,000 militia and some artillery – total 35,000; (b) 8,500 infantry, 6,000 cavalry and twenty guns – total 17,000.
Casualties: (a) 3,000 killed and wounded; (b) 3,000 killed and wounded (including de Marsin mortally wounded), 6,000 prisoners and siege guns captured.
Result: The siege was raised and the French abandoned all their previous gains in Italy.

Eugene's victory complemented that of Marlborough at RAMILLIES (23 May).

Ulm, Capitulation of   526

Date: 20 October 1805.

Location: Town at the confluence of the Iller and Danube rivers, 48 miles south-east of Stuttgart, Bavaria.
War and campaign: War of the Third Coalition, 1805–1807: Campaign in Germany, 1805.
Opposing sides: (a) The Emperor Napoleon I; (b) nominally the Archduke Ferdinand, *de facto* General Mack von Leiberich.
Objective: Having learned that he was to be attacked by the combined armies of the Continental members of the Coalition, Napoleon abandoned his plans to invade England and marched secretly eastwards with the intention of destroying the Austrian army in Bavaria before it could be joined by the Russians.
Forces engaged: (a) 200,000; (b) approximately 72,000.
Casualties: (a) 6,000; (b) 50,000 killed, wounded, missing and prisoners, plus 65 guns captured.
Result: In a series of concentric wheels from the north, the six columns of the Grand Army crossed the Danube and isolated Mack from further support before he could react. Only one Austrian corps managed to escape briefly from the encirclement and, after making a half-hearted attempt to break out of the trap at Elchingen, Mack surrendered on 20 October.

Without the necessity of having to fight a major battle, Napoleon had disposed of an entire Austrian army. He went on to occupy Vienna, then turned north to meet the Allied army at AUSTERLITZ.

Ulundi 527

Date: 4 July 1879.
Location: Central Zululand, north of the White Umvolosi river.
War and campaign: Zulu War, 1879.
Opposing sides: (a) Lieutenant-General Lord Chelmsford; (b) King Cetewayo.
Objective: The British sought a decisive action which would break the military power of the Zulus.
Forces engaged: (a) 4,166 British and colonial troops (including one cavalry brigade), 958 native troops, twelve guns and two Gatling machine guns; (b) 20,000.
Casualties: (a) Thirteen killed and 78 wounded; (b) estimated 1,500 killed and a similar number wounded.
Result: The Zulu army was destroyed. Cetewayo escaped but was captured on 8 August.

Chelmsford's advance on Cetewayo's capital was made in square. Faced with overwhelming firepower, the Zulus were unable to press home their attacks and were routed when Chelmsford unleashed his cavalry in pursuit.

Valmy 528

Date: 20 September 1792.
Location: Village between Chalons-sur-Marne and Ste Menehould, approximately 100 miles east of Paris.

War and campaign: War of the First Coalition, 1792–1798: Campaign in North-Eastern France, 1792.
Opposing sides: (a) General François Kellermann commanding the French Army of the Centre, reinforced by General Charles Dumouriez with part of the Army of the North; (b) Karl Wilhelm, Duke of Brunswick, commanding the Prussian army.
Objective: The Prussians' intention was to destroy the French revolutionary army and advance on Paris.
Forces engaged: (a) 36,000, with 40 guns; (b) 34,000, with 36 guns.
Casualties: (a) 300 killed and wounded; (b) 180 killed and wounded.
Result: The Prussians failed to defeat the French and withdrew into Germany. The morale of the French soared and the full fury of their revolutionary fervour was unleashed on Europe, initiating a world war that would last for 23 years. For this reason Valmy is regarded by such distinguished historians as Sir Edward Creasy and Major-General J. F. C. Fuller as one of the most decisive battles in world history.

In essence the battle consisted of a protracted artillery duel culminating in a stalled Prussian assault. It marked a watershed between the formal limited wars of the eighteenth century and the concept of total war fought with armies raised by *levée-en-masse* or conscription. The view is sometimes expressed that if Kellermann and Dumouriez had lost the battle, Revolutionary France was doomed and the subsequent history of Europe would have taken a different course. Fuller, on the other hand, offers a different opinion. While scathing in his comments on Brunswick's generalship, he suggests that for logistic reasons Paris had ceased to be a viable Prussian objective before the battle began, and that the decision to retire was therefore correct. What is certain is that the motivation of the French was higher, that they did not break under fire as had been anticipated, and that Brunswick and his professionals were psychologically dominated by the enthusiasm of their opponents from the outset.

Verdun 529

Date: 21 February to 18 December 1916.
Location: Fortified city on the upper Meuse, eastern France.
War and campaign: First World War: Western Front.
Opposing sides: (a) General Joseph Joffre, Commander-in-Chief of the French armies; (b) General Erich von Falkenhayn, Chief of the German General Staff (replaced by Hindenburg/Ludendorff on 29 August).
Objective: The German intention was to impose a ruinous battle of attrition on the French Army, thereby destroying its limited manpower reserves.
Forces engaged: (a) General Henri Philippe Pétain commanding the French Second Army with overall responsibility for the defence of Verdun, succeeded by General Robert Nivelle on 1 May (almost every French division on the Western Front served by rotation in the Verdun sector); (b) Crown Prince Wilhelm commanding the German Fifth Army (fewer German divisions served at Verdun, but they too were rotated with those on quieter sectors of the line).
Casualties: (a) 362,000 killed and wounded; (b) 337,000 killed and wounded.
Result: Inconclusive. The Germans failed to take Verdun and, while they succeeded in inflicting heavy losses on the French, their own casualties were comparable.

Although the German attacks captured ground in their early stages, by the end of March

Falkenhayn had recognized that attrition was a two-edged weapon and would have abandoned the offensive had it not been for the insistence of the Crown Prince. However, the Battle of THE SOMME and THE BRUSILOV OFFENSIVE also made demands on German resources and in midsummer fifteen divisions left the Verdun sector for other fronts. By the end of August the German strategy had become defensive. Verdun became a symbol of French determination, inspired by Pétain's declaration *'Ils ne passeront pas!'* The French were seriously handicapped by the fact that they were forced to rely on a single road, later known as *La Voie Sacrée*, for supplies and reinforcements, but this was kept open by Herculean efforts. On the other hand, they rotated their divisions in the line more quickly than the Germans, so that the attacks of the latter were always met by comparatively fresh troops. The entire battlefield became a hideous artillery killing ground which still bears the scars of the fighting. On 24 October Nivelle opened a counter-offensive which succeeded in recovering much of the lost ground; during the last phase of this (15–18 December) over 11,000 prisoners were captured, together with 115 guns, 44 trench mortars and 107 machine guns. The success of his counter-attacks led Nivelle to claim, groundlessly, that he had unlocked the secrets of trench warfare. On 15 December he replaced Joffre as Commander-in-Chief, with baleful consequences for the French Army the following year. See NIVELLE OFFENSIVE, THE.

Verneuil   530

Date: 17 August 1424.
Location: Town on the Arve 50 miles west of Paris.
War and campaign: Hundred Years' War, 1337–1457: English consolidation in northern France, 1422–1428.
Opposing sides: (a) John, Duke of Bedford; (b) the Duke of Alençon and the Earls of Douglas and Buchan commanding the Franco-Scottish army.
Objective: The English intention was to break the French siege of the town.
Forces engaged: (a) 9,000; (b) 15,000, including 900 mounted crossbowmen and 1,000 mounted men-at-arms.
Casualties: (a) Approximately 1,000; (b) 5,000, mainly Scots (Alençon was captured and Douglas and Buchan were killed).
Result: An English victory which virtually destroyed the Scottish contingent fighting with the French army.

Verneuil was the English archers' last strategic victory and was more fiercely contested than AGINCOURT. Having completed his consolidation, Bedford advanced south to the Loire – see ORLÉANS, SIEGE OF, and ROUVRAY.

Vicksburg, Siege of   531

Date: 19 May to 4 July 1863.
Location: Vicksburg, Mississippi.
War and campaign: American Civil War: western theatre of operations.
Opposing sides: (a) Major-General Ulysses S. Grant commanding the Army of the Tennessee; (b) Lieutenant-General John C. Pemberton commanding the Confederate garrison.

Objective: The capture of the Confederate fortress controlling the southern Mississippi.	

Forces engaged: (a) Approximately 75,000; (b) approximately 30,000.

Casualties: (a) 9,362; (b) approximately 1,000 killed and wounded, 29,000 captured and paroled and 172 guns captured.

Result: Pemberton, desperately short of food and with half his garrison sick, surrendered on 4 July. The fall of Vicksburg, followed by the surrender of the smaller fortress of Port Hudson on 9 July, won control of the Mississippi for the Union and effectively split the Confederacy in two. It was, therefore, one of the most decisive actions of the war, and one which further enabled large numbers of Federal troops to be redeployed against eastern Confederate states. Occurring the day after GETTYSBURG, it also destroyed Southern hopes of ultimate victory. See also CHATTANOOGA.

Having advanced down the right bank of the Mississippi, Grant crossed the river at Bruinsburg on 30 April. Relying on heavily escorted wagon trains rather than conventional lines of communication, he circled Vicksburg from the south to approach the fortress from the east, defeating his opponents at Port Gibson (1 May), Jackson (14 May) and Champion Hill (16 May), simultaneously out-thinking General Joseph E. Johnston, the Confederate Commander-in-Chief in the West, and Pemberton, who was forced to retire within the Vicksburg defences. During its indirect approach march the Army of the Tennessee advanced 200 miles, living off the land and its own resources, and inflicted 8,000 casualties in exchange for 4,400 of its own. An assault was mounted against the fortifications on 19 May but this was beaten off with heavy losses and Grant settled down to let bombardment and starvation take their toll.

Vienna, First Siege of (1529)   532

Date: 23 September to 15 October 1529.

Location: Around the perimeter of the old (inner) city.

War and campaign: Turkish Wars of the Sixteenth Century.

Opposing sides: (a) Marshal William von Roggendorf in effective command of the garrison; (b) Sultan Suleiman the Magnificent.

Objective: The Hungarian defeat at MOHACS had opened central Europe to Turkish invasion, and in 1529 Suleiman decided to extend his conquests in that direction, advancing on the Hapsburg capital.

Forces engaged: (a) 17,000; (b) 80,000, plus a large siege train and a flotilla of warships.

Casualties: Uncertain, although the Turkish army's losses were far heavier and were aggravated by the loss of much equipment during its withdrawal.

Result: Unable to make headway against the defences, Suleiman withdrew rather than expose his army to a harsh winter in its siege lines. This reverse set the limit on his advance into central Europe.

Roggendorf's garrison conducted an energetic defence, levelling buildings close to the fortifications to give their artillery a clear field of fire, digging additional trenches, maintaining a heavy counter-bombardment, making repeated sorties and raids, counter-mining and breaking up Turkish assault concentrations. After three weeks Suleiman accepted that, with the premature onset of winter, further progress was impossible and he gave the order to withdraw, killing all his adult male prisoners as he did so. The retreat was vigorously harassed by the Austrians and the Turkish flotilla carrying the siege train was severely battered as it passed under the guns of the fortress of Pressburg (Bratislava).

Vienna (1683) 533

Date: 12 September 1683.
Location: The present-day north-western suburbs of the city and the Wiener Wald.
War and campaign: Great Turkish War, 1683–1699: Turkish Invasion of Austria, 1683.
Opposing sides: (a) King John Sobieski of Poland commanding the relieving army; (b) Kara Mustapha, Grand Vizier of the Ottoman Empire, commanding the Turks.
Objective: The United Christian Army intended to relieve Vienna, which was being besieged by the Turks.
Forces engaged: (a) Approximately 76,000 (Austrian, Saxon, Bavarian and Polish), plus 16,000 within the defences; (b) approximately 107,000, plus 31,000 in the siege lines.
Casualties: (a) Approximately 2,000 killed and wounded; (b) approximately 10,000 killed and wounded.
Result: The Turks were defeated and forced to abandon the siege; Kara Mustapha was executed for his failure.

This was the last occasion on which a Turkish army posed a serious threat to Central Europe. See MOHACS (1687).

Vimeiro (Vimiero or Vimiera) 534

Date: 21 August 1808.
Location: Between Torres Vedras and Lourinha, 32 miles north-west of Libson, Portugal.
War and campaign: Peninsular War, 1807–1814: Campaign in Portugal, 1808.
Opposing sides: (a) Lieutenant-General Sir Arthur Wellesley commanding the Allied army; (b) Marshal Andoche Junot, Duke of Abrantes, commanding the French Army of Portugal.
Objective: After completing its landing at Mondego Bay, the Allied army advanced on Lisbon but was confronted by the French at Vimeiro.
Forces engaged: (a) 18,712, including 2,000 Portuguese; (b) 13,050.
Casualties: (a) 160 killed and 505 wounded; (b) 3,000 killed, wounded and prisoners and thirteen guns captured.
Result: The French were defeated in a battle which demonstrated that their assault columns could not prevail against the superior firepower produced by British linear tactics.

Junot surrendered his army to Wellesley's recently arrived superiors, Generals Sir Harry Burrard and Sir Hew Dalrymple, on 30 August. The agreement, known as the Convention of Cintra, provided for the repatriation of the French troops in British ships, and its leniency caused such outrage that all three British commanders were called to account for their actions at a court of enquiry; Wellesley was exonerated of blame. See also CORUNNA.

Vinegar Hill 535

Date: 12 June 1798.
Location: Near Enniscorthy, County Wexford, Eire.
War and campaign: Rebellion in Ireland, 1798.
Opposing sides: (a) Lieutenant-General Gerard Lake commanding the Government troops; (b) Father John Murphy, leader of the rebellion in Wexford.
Objective: The rebel army holding the hill was attacked by Government forces.
Forces engaged: (a) Approximately 10,000; (b) approximately 16,000.
Casualties: (a) Light; (b) approximately 4,000 killed and wounded.
Result: The rebels were routed and the back of the rebellion was broken. See also BALLINAMUCK.

Although folklore sometimes presents the battle as an Anglo–Irish contest, the greater part of Lake's troops belonged to Irish yeomanry and militia regiments. During the course of the rebellion horrific atrocities and reprisals were committed by rebels and loyalists alike, leaving an enduring legacy of bitterness.

Vittoria (Vitoria) 536

Date: 21 June 1813.
Location: Town south of the Zaborra river, 40 miles south-east of Bilbao, northern Spain.
War and campaign: Peninsular War, 1807–1814: Campaign of 1813.
Opposing sides: (a) General the Marquess of Wellington commanding the Allied army; (b) Joseph Bonaparte, King of Spain, and Marshal Jean-Baptiste Jourdan commanding the concentrated Armies of the South, Centre and Portugal.
Objective: After his defeat at SALAMANCA the previous year, followed by the destruction of the Grand Army in Russia, the overall strategic situation rendered Joseph Bonaparte's position in Spain untenable, and when Wellington, reinforced, again seized the initiative, he abandoned Madrid, concentrated his armies and withdrew north towards France. At Vittoria Wellington caught up with him and, intending to crush the French forces in the Peninsula once and for all, promptly launched an attack.
Forces engaged: (a) 8,317 cavalry and 27,372 British, 27,569 Portuguese and 6,800 Spanish infantry, with 90 guns – total 75,152; (b) 7,000 cavalry and 43,000 infantry with 153 guns – total 57,000.
Casualties: (a) 740 killed, 4,174 wounded and 266 missing – total 5,180; (b) 756 killed, 4,414 wounded and 2,829 missing – total 7,999, plus 151 guns, 415 ammunition wagons and a huge quantity of equipment captured.
Result: The French were routed, losing practically all their artillery and baggage, and driven back through the Pyrenees – see TOULOUSE. Encouraged by the scale of the Allied victory, Austria joined the Sixth Coalition.

Wellington's mutually supporting assault columns, assisted by the enemy's failure to destroy the bridges over the Zaborra, pressed the Armies of the South and Centre steadily back towards Vittoria; an Allied flanking move did not produce all the dividends Wellington had hoped for but it tied down the Army of Portugal north of the town. When the French broke only those on foot or horseback were able to escape; their guns and other wheeled vehicles remained locked in an inextricable tangle in and around Vittoria. This inhibited the Allied pursuit when some 5,000 men stopped to plunder the treasures which the French had themselves looted in Spain. One item of booty was Jourdan's baton, which Wellington despatched to the Prince Regent; in return, he received the baton of a British field marshal.

Vittorio Veneto 537

Date: 24 October to 4 November 1918.
Location: Along the river Piave between Grave di Papadopoli and Vidor.
War and campaign: First World War: Italy.
Opposing sides: (a) General Armando Diaz, Chief of the Italian General Staff; (b) Field Marshal Arz von Straussenburg, Chief of the Austro-Hungarian General Staff.
Objective: The Italians' intention was to separate the Austro-Hungarian armies on the Piave sector from those in the Trentino, then eliminate the former.
Forces engaged: (a) The Italian Third (the Duke of Aosta), Tenth (General the Earl of Cavan) and Eighth (Lt-General Caviglia) Armies – total available (entire front) 57 divisions, including three British, two French, one Czech and an American regiment, support by 7,720 guns. (b) Army Group Boroevic (Field Marshal Baron Svetozan Boroevic von Bojna) with the Austro-Hungarian Sixth (General von Schönburg-Hartenstein) and Isonzo (Colonel-General von Wurm) Armies – total available (entire front) 58 divisions, supported by 6,030 guns.
Casualties: (a) Approximately 40,000; (b) approximately 330,000, including an estimated 300,000 prisoners, plus 5,000 guns captured.
Result: After offering fierce resistance, the Austrian armies suddenly broke. Vittorio Veneto was captured on 30 October and on 4 November an armistice came into effect.

The defeat led to the final collapse of the Austro-Hungarian Empire.

Volturno River 538

Date: 12 October to 14 November 1943.
Location: Approximately 15 miles north of Naples.
War and campaign: Second World War: Italy.
Opposing sides: (a) General Sir Harold Alexander commanding the Allied 15th Army Group; (b) Field Marshal Albert Kesselring, Commander-in-Chief of the German force in southern Italy.
Objective: Having broken out of the SALERNO beach-head, the Allies were advancing north towards Rome; the Germans' intention was to halt the advance with a series of prepared defence lines.
Forces engaged: (a) Lieutenant-General Mark W. Clark commanding the US Fifth Army, with the US VI Corps (Lucas) and the British X Corps (McCreery); (b)

Colonel-General Heinrich von Vietinghoff (until 5 November, then Lieutenant-General Joachim Lemelsen) commanding the German Tenth Army, with XIV Panzer Corps (Hube) on the Volturno sector.
Casualties: (a) Severe, particularly among the infantry divisions; (b) severe.
Result: Although the Allies succeeded in crossing the river and breaching the German defences, the achievement was at heavy cost and left the troops exhausted. The Germans were able to withdraw to the much stronger defences of the Gustav Line, including CASSINO.

The fighting on the Volturno set the pattern for subsequent battles throughout the Italian Campaign.

Vyazma-Bryansk 539

Date: 5–20 October 1941.
Location: 100–175 miles west and south-west of Moscow.
War and campaign: Second World War: Russian Front.
Opposing sides: (a) Field Marshal Fedor von Bock commanding Army Group Centre; (b) Marshal Semyon Timoshenko (later General Ivan Konev) commanding West Front.
Objective: The Germans were initiating their drive on MOSCOW, the final phase of Operation 'Barbarossa', and had split the main portion of the Soviet West Front into two pockets.
Forces engaged: (a) Panzer Groups 2, 3 and 4 (commanded by, respectively, Guderian, Hoth and Hoepner) and the Fourth Army (von Kluge); (b) the Soviet 19th, 24th, 29th, 30th, 32nd and 43rd Armies in the Vyazma sector and the 3rd, 13th and 50th Armies in the Bryansk sector.
Casualties: (a) Unknown; (b) 663,000 prisoners, plus 1,242 tanks and 4,512 guns captured.
Result: The Vyazma pocket, closed by Hoth and Hoepner, was eliminated on 14 October; the Bryansk pocket, closed by Guderian and Kluge, was eliminated on 20 October.

Had the advance on MOSCOW been maintained after the fighting at SMOLENSK, it is probable that the Soviet capital would have fallen. As it was, Hitler's KIEV diversion consumed priceless time before Army Group Centre's drive was resumed. Thus while Vyazma-Bryansk was yet another stunning victory in the series won by the German Army since it invaded the USSR, it was the last before the onset of the autumn rains, followed by an extremely severe winter and a Soviet counter-offensive, brought the advance to a standstill.

Wagon Box Fight, The 540

Date: 2 August 1867.
Location: Between Big and Little Piney Creeks, 5 miles north-west of the site of Fort Phil Kearny, Wyoming.
War and campaign: American Indian Wars.

Opposing sides: (a) Colonel John E. Smith commanding Fort Phil Kearny; (b) Chief Red Cloud.
Objective: The Sioux and Cheyenne attacked a portion of the garrison of Fort Phil Kearny engaged in cutting timber.
Forces engaged: (a) Captain James W. Powell with one officer, 26 soldiers and four civilians; (b) 1,500–2,000 Sioux and Cheyenne.
Casualties: (a) Six killed and two wounded; (b) 60 killed and 120 wounded.
Result: The attack was beaten off and the Indians were scattered by a relief column from the fort.

Powell and his men fought from the cover of a compound formed from wagon bodies, originally intended to corral mules. The outcome of the fight was undoubtedly influenced by the recent issue of Springfield breech-loading rifles to the troops. After THE FETTERMAN MASSACRE in December 1866, the Wagon Box Fight, together with a smaller engagement the previous day near Fort C. F. Smith on the Big Horn River, known as the Hayfield Fight, restored the morale of the Bozeman Trail garrisons. In 1868 the forts were abandoned following the conclusion of a treaty with Red Cloud. However, the subsequent discovery of gold on Indian territory made a resumption of the conflict inevitable. See LITTLE BIG HORN.

Wagram 541

Date: 5–6 July 1809.
Location: Village 10 miles north-east of Vienna.
War and campaign: War of the Fifth Coalition, 1809: campaign against Austria.
Opposing sides: (a) The Emperor Napoleon commanding the Grand Army; (b) the Archduke Charles commanding the Austrian army.
Objective: Having failed to destroy the Austrian army at ASPERN-ESSLING, Napoleon re-planned the battle and again forced a crossing of the Danube from Lobau Island.
Forces engaged: (a) 130,800 infantry, 23,300 cavalry and 554 guns – total 154,100; (b) 139,500 infantry, 18,600 cavalry and 480 guns – total 158,000.
Casualties: (a) 34,000; (b) 45,000.
Result: A French victory which resulted in Austria requesting an armistice on 10 July, effectively ending the Fifth Coalition.

Although Napoleon again used Lobau Island as his base, he employed a night crossing and bridge sites downstream of that used at ASPERN-ESSLING, achieving complete surprise. During 5 July he consolidated his position and pushed the Austrians back towards Wagram. The following morning Charles mounted counter-attacks against both flanks, hoping to isolate the French from their bridgeheads, but these were contained. At noon Napoleon smashed through the Austrian centre with an 8,000-strong column and Charles began to withdraw from the battlefield, beaten but not routed.

Wake Atoll 542

Date: 8–23 December 1941.

Location: Central Pacific.
War and campaign: Second World War: Central Pacific.
Opposing sides: (a) Commander Winfield Scott Cunningham in overall command of the Wake garrison; (b) Rear-Admiral Sadamichi Kajioka commanding the invasion force.
Objective: The Japanese' intention was to add Wake, with its airstrip and flying boat base, to their conquests.
Forces engaged: (a) Major James Deveruex commanding the US Marine Corps' 1st Defense Battalion (400 men) with six 5in guns, twelve 3in AA guns and 48 machine guns, Major Paul Putnam commanding Marine Fighter Squadron 211 with twelve Wildcat fighters, and 1,100 technically non-combatant civilian construction workers; (b) first attempt – one light cruiser, two older cruisers, six destroyers, two destroyer transports, two transports, two submarines and a 450-strong naval infantry landing force; second attempt – two fleet carriers, six heavy cruisers, six destroyers, one seaplane tender and transports, 1,000-strong naval infantry landing force with 500 seamen in immediate reserve and a final reserve consisting of the crews of two destroyers to be run aground.
Casualties: (a) 49 Marines, three seamen and 70 construction workers killed, plus at least five Marines and 100 construction workers murdered while prisoners in Japanese hands; (b) one light cruiser seriously damaged, four destroyers, one destroyer transport and one submarine sunk, numerous aircraft destroyed or damaged and a minimum estimate of 900 killed and 1,100 wounded.
Result: The Japanese were so humiliated by the failure of their first attempt to capture the atoll (11 December) that when they returned (23 December) they did so with an absurdly large force, given the size of the garrison. Although Cunningham was forced to surrender once the enemy had established himself ashore, his remarkable stand inspired an American public depressed by Pearl Harbor and other recent setbacks in the Pacific.

Wakefield 543

Date: 30 December 1460.
Location: North and west of Sandal Castle, 2 miles south of Wakefield, West Yorkshire.
War and campaign: Wars of the Roses, 1455–1485.
Opposing sides: (a) Richard Duke of York commanding the Yorkists; (b) the Duke of Somerset commanding the Lancastrians.
Objective: The Yorkists, having advanced north from London to meet a Lancastrian threat, were enticed out of their position at Sandal Castle and ambushed.
Forces engaged: (a) 8,000; (b) 10,000.
Casualties: (a) 2,000, including Richard and his eldest son Edmund killed during the fighting and the Earl of Salisbury murdered in captivity; (b) uncertain, but moderate.
Result: A Lancastrian victory.

Following their victory the Lancastrians advanced on London – see the SECOND BATTLE OF ST ALBANS. Leadership of the Yorkist cause passed to Richard's second son, the formidable Edward, Earl of March, who succeeded to the York title and was later crowned

Edward IV – see MORTIMER'S CROSS and TOWTON. Wakefield initiated one of the most brutal aspects of these wars, neither side being inclined to show mercy to the captured nobility of the other.

Warburg   544

Date: 31 July 1760.
Location: Village on the Diemel 20 miles north-west of Kassel, Germany.
War and campaign: Seven Years' War, 1756–1763: Campaign in Western Germany of 1760.
Opposing sides: (a) Duke Ferdinand of Brunswick; (b) the Chevalier du Muy.
Objective: The advance guard and cavalry of an Anglo-Prussian army was blocking the march of a detached French corps towards Hanover.
Forces engaged: (a) 24,000; (b) 21,500.
Casualties: (a) 1,200 killed and wounded; (b) 1,500 killed and wounded, 1,500 prisoners and twelve guns captured.
Result: The French were defeated and retired towards the Rhine. The decisive charge of the British cavalry, commanded by Lieutenant-General the Marquess of Granby, restored its reputation, which had been unfairly tarnished by the conduct of Lord George Sackville at MINDEN the previous year.

Granby, who was bald, lost both his hat and his wig while leading the charge, giving rise to the expression 'going for it bald-headed'. He later provided taverns for some of his NCOs who had been disabled at Warburg so that they could earn a decent living. Both events are commemorated by the many public houses in England named after him; most of the inn signs show a representation of him leading the attack.

Warsaw (1920)   545

Date: 16–25 August 1920.
Location: A 200-mile front north-east, east and south-east of Warsaw.
War and campaign: Russo–Polish War of 1920.
Opposing sides: (a) Marshal Jozef Pilsudski, Commander-in-Chief of the Polish Army, advised by the French General Maxime Weygand; (b) Mikhail Tukhachevsky commanding the Bolshevik Army of the West.
Objective: A Polish counter-offensive intended to destroy the invading Russian armies.
Forces engaged: (a) Southern Group comprising the 7th and 6th Armies and Northern Group comprising the 2nd, 3rd, 4th and 1st Armies – total 178,500 Poles and Ukrainians; (b) 4th, 15th, 3rd, 16th, 12th and 14th Armies, plus 1st Cavalry Army – total 177,900 Bolsheviks.
Casualties: (a) Approximately 50,000; (b) approximately 150,000, including 66,000 prisoners and over 30,000 disarmed and interned in East Prussia, plus 231 guns and 1,023 machine guns captured.
Result: Although further fighting followed, the Bolsheviks never recovered from the defeat and on 12 October an armistice was concluded; the following year the Soviet government agreed to Polish territorial claims in the Treaty of Riga.

Tukhachevsky's troops had outrun their supplies and were living off the country. Pilsudski perceived that in such circumstances any check would be fatal; his counter-offensive took the form of a pincer movement directed against the enemy centre and the Bolshevik army collapsed. The battle was regarded by Major-General J. F. C. Fuller as one of the most decisive in the history of the Western World in that it checked the spread of Bolshevism into Europe. The Soviets never forgave the defeat and were determined that, sooner or later, they would destroy the Polish military establishment – a policy they put into effect during the Second World War, notably at Katyn Wood, where 4,500 captured Polish officers were massacred in 1943, and at WARSAW in August 1944, where the Polish Home Army was cynically allowed to fight itself to destruction.

Warsaw (1944)   546

Date: 1 August to 2 October 1944.
Location: In the centre of the Polish capital, mainly in the Old Town, Zoliborz, Mokotow and Sielce.
War and campaign: Second World War: Russian Front.
Opposing sides: (a) General Tadeusz Bor-Komorowski commanding the Home Army; (b) SS Major-General Erich von dem Bach-Zelewski commanding German forces responsible for putting down the rising.
Objective: A rising by the Polish Home Army, timed to coincide with the approach of the advancing Soviet armies during the closing stages of Operation 'BAGRATION'.
Forces engaged: (a) About 38,000, including 4,000 women; (b) unknown, but mainly SS formations supported by heavy artillery, reinforced throughout the fighting.
Casualties: (a) 150,000, including civilians; (b) 26,000, including 10,000 killed.
Result: Bor-Komorowski surrendered on 2 October and Warsaw was then systematically looted and destroyed. In the wider sphere, however, the defeat of the Home Army created serious stresses in the alliance between the Soviet Union on the one hand and the United Kingdom and the United States on the other.

Although the rising had been requested by the Soviets, they made no attempt to assist the Polish Home Army and actually took steps to prevent the Western Allies from giving air support until Britain threatened to stop sending Arctic convoys to the USSR, when limited overflight facilities were granted, too late, on 10 September. Russian historians claim that the rising was premature and that the Soviet armies had outrun their supplies because of the tremendous efforts they had made during Operation 'BAGRATION', a view which receives limited support from Guderian, who believed that the Germans had themselves brought the Soviet advance to a halt. That, however, does not explain why Home Army units trying to reach Warsaw were surrounded and disarmed by Soviet troops. The Kremlin's attitude to the Warsaw rising was based on self-interested cynicism; no matter who won, the continued existence of a Polish army loyal to the government-in-exile was not acceptable to Stalin, who intended imposing his own Communist puppet regime.

Waterloo   547

Date: 18 June 1815.

Location: The battlefield lies 12 miles south of Brussels on the Charleroi road, 3 miles south of Waterloo village.
War and campaign: Napoleon's Hundred Days: Campaign in Belgium.
Opposing sides: (a) Field Marshal the Duke of Wellington commanding the Anglo-Netherlands army and Field Marshal Prince Blücher commanding the Prussian army; (b) the Emperor Napoleon I commanding the French Army of the North.
Objective: After defeating Blücher's Prussians at LIGNY, Napoleon turned his attention to Wellington's Anglo-Netherlands army, intending to force it off its position on Mont St Jean and so open the way to Brussels.
Forces engaged: (a) Anglo-Netherlands army: 50,000 infantry, 12,500 cavalry and 156 guns – total approximately 68,100; Prussian army: approximately 50,000; (b) French Army of the North: 49,000 infantry, 15,750 cavalry and 246 guns – total approximately 72,000.
Casualties: (a) Anglo-Netherlands army – 15,100 killed and wounded; Prussian army – approximately 7,000; (b) French Army of the North – 25,000 killed and wounded, 8,000 prisoners and 220 guns captured.
Result: The Allies were victorious and Napoleon, his power finally broken, abdicated on 22 June. The battle, one of the most decisive in history, established the framework of European politics for the next century.

Because of heavy rain the previous night, Napoleon waited for the ground to dry out before he commenced his attack. At 11.20 he launched Reille's corps against the Château of Hougoumont, covering Wellington's right, intending this to be a feint which would absorb the Allied reserves while he attacked in the centre with D'Erlon's corps. In the event the feint was allowed to escalate into a major action which absorbed far more French troops than Allied. D'Erlon's attack, delivered at about 14.00, was repulsed but during the Allied counter-attack two British cavalry brigades overreached themselves and were badly cut up. Meanwhile the Prussians had begun entering the battle from the east and Napoleon detached Lobau's corps from the centre to hold them off at Plancenoit. At this point Ney observed what he mistakenly took to be a retrograde movement on Mont St Jean and, believing that Wellington's army was on the point of disintegration, mounted a series of unsupported cavalry attacks against the Allied centre. In fact, Wellington was simply moving his units behind the crest for better protection against the French artillery, and by 17.30 the French cavalry had been virtually destroyed. Of this aspect of the battle, it has been said that the outcome might have been different had the French provided themselves with a hammer and a bag of nails, for while each of the twelve separate cavalry charges overran the British artillery, no one thought to spike the guns; thus, as the attacks receded, the gunners were able to emerge from the shelter of the infantry squares and man their weapons. Simultaneously, despite a successful counter-attack by the Young Guard at Plancenoit, Prussian pressure on the French was increasing inexorably. Nevertheless, Napoleon believed that he still had time to beat Wellington. The farm of La Haye Sainte, covering the left-centre of the Allied position and held throughout the day by a stubborn garrison of the King's German Legion, was finally taken. A number of units were destroyed when the young and inexperienced Prince of Orange, Wellington's deputy, launched an ill-conceived counter-attack, and at 19.00 a yawning gap suddenly appeared in the centre of the Allied line. Napoleon was slow to react and with every minute that passed Wellington pushed fresh troops into the gap. When, shortly after 19.30, Napoleon did commit the Middle Guard, it was decisively repulsed. The rest of the French army, now exhausted and aware that the Prussians had again broken through at Plancenoit, saw a symbolic significance in the Guard's defeat and broke at once when Wellington ordered a general advance from the ridge. With the exception of the infantry battalions of the Old Guard, which saw Napoleon safely off the field, the Army of the North degenerated into a panic-stricken, undisciplined mob, hounded southwards through the night by the vengeful Prussian cavalry. Wellington was to comment on the battle: 'In all my life I have not experienced such anxiety, for I must confess that I have never been so close to defeat. Never did I see such a pounding match. Napoleon did not manoeuvre at all. He just moved forward in the old style, in columns, and was driven off in the old style.' Of the Prize Money awarded by the British Government for Waterloo, Wellington's share as Commander-in-Chief amounted to £61,000; general officers received £1,274 10s.10d., colonels and majors £443 2s.4¼d., captains £90 7s.3¾d., subalterns £34 14s.9½d., sergeants £19 4s.4d., and corporals, drummers and privates £2 11s.4d.

Waxhaws 548

Date: 29 May 1780.
Location: Near Waxhaws settlement on the North/South Carolina border, north-west of Camden.
War and campaign: American War of Independence, 1775–1783: southern theatre of operations.
Opposing sides: (a) Lieutenant-Colonel Banastre Tarleton commanding the British Legion; (b) Colonel Abraham Buford commanding the Americans.
Objective: Following the surrender of CHARLESTON, a British column was despatched in pursuit of an American force attempting to withdraw into North Carolina.
Forces engaged: (a) 270 and one gun; (b) 380 and six guns.
Casualties: (a) Five killed and twelve wounded; (b) 113 killed, 150 wounded, 51 prisoners and all guns captured.
Result: The American force was destroyed. Reports that a massacre had taken place generated anti-British feeling over a wide area. Tarleton was hated and feared more than any other British commander, and the phrase 'Tarleton's Quarter' became synonymous with cold-blooded butchery.

The British Legion was a loyalist unit containing cavalry and infantry elements, with a troop of regular light dragoons attached for stiffening; on this occasion the entire Legion was mounted although the infantry fought on foot during the battle. Tarleton had carried out a remarkable 150-mile pursuit before he caught Buford, who rejected a call for his surrender, then attempted to surrender while the attack was in progress, then escaped, leaving his men to their fate. Clearly, the Legion behaved with unusual savagery even by the standards of a civil war; for a while they were out of hand and one explanation for this is that they believed Tarleton, lying pinned beneath his horse, had been killed. 'Bloody Tarleton', as the Americans called him afterwards, was a brilliant cavalry leader whose character was marred by a sadistic steak. The sobriquet was justified, yet ironically not for Waxhaws, where he exercised no control after his horse had been shot under him. See also CAMDEN and COWPENS.

White Hill (Weisser Berg) 549

Date: 8 November 1620.
Location: Feature to the west of Prague, Czechoslovakia.

War and campaign: Thirty Years' War, 1618–1648.
Opposing sides: (a) Prince Christian of Anhalt-Bernberg commanding the Protestant forces; (b) Maximilian I of Bavaria and Count John Tzerklaes de Tilly commanding the army of the Catholic League.
Objective: A Catholic army had invaded Bohemia with the object of removing the recently installed Protestant king, Frederick V of the Palatinate.
Forces engaged: (a) Approximately 15,000; (b) approximately 25,000.
Casualties: (a) 5,000 killed, wounded or captured; (b) uncertain, but light.
Result: The Protestants were surprised and routed when the Catholics attacked through the morning mist under cover of an artillery bombardment.

Frederick was forced to abandon Prague and flee, and his lands in the Palatinate were confiscated. The conflict between the Catholic and Protestant factions in central Europe, hitherto mainly confined to Bohemia, now became general.

White Plains 550

Date: 28 October 1776.
Location: On the Bronx river, approximately 25 miles north of New York.
War and campaign: American War of Independence: central theatre of operations.
Opposing sides: (a) Major-General William Howe; (b) Major-General George Washington.
Objective: Having captured New York (see LONG ISLAND), the British were seeking to destroy the principal American army.
Forces engaged: (a) 14,000; (b) 14,500.
Casualties: (a) Approximately 300 killed and wounded on each side.
Result: Howe captured a hill dominating the American right flank, compelling Washington to withdraw.

After probing the strong American position at Harlem Heights on 16 September, Howe decided to use his amphibious capability to bypass this and effected a landing at New Rochelle on Long Island Sound, forcing the Americans to withdraw to White Plains. Following the battle, Howe turned his attention to Fort Washington on the Hudson, the 2,800-strong garrison of which surrendered on 16 November; Fort Lee, opposite, was evacuated two days later. Washington retreated across New Jersey, his rear covered by Major-General Charles Lee, who was captured with many of his men near Morristown. The American army, now reduced to a mere 3,500 men, crossed the Delaware into Pennsylvania. Howe, who had consistently outmanoeuvred Washington but lacked the killer instinct, could have put an end to the campaign but chose instead to go into winter quarters. For his part Washington recognized that only a successful riposte could keep the American cause alive – see TRENTON and PRINCETON.

Wilderness, The 551

Date: 5–6 May 1864.
Location: 10 miles west of Fredericksburg, Virginia, overlapping the old CHANCELLORSVILLE battlefield.

War and campaign: American Civil War: Grant's Virginia Campaign of 1864.
Opposing sides: (a) Lieutenant-General Ulysses S. Grant, the US Army's General-in-Chief, in the field with Major-General George G. Meade's Army of the Potomac; (b) General Robert E. Lee commanding the Army of Northern Virginia.
Objective: Grant's intention was to advance directly on Richmond, the capital of the Confederacy, engaging Lee's army in a series of attritional battles which he knew the South could not afford; the Wilderness was the first of these encounters.
Forces engaged: (a) 118,769; (b) 62,000.
Casualties: (a) 18,000; (b) 10,800.
Result: Despite inflicting heavy casualties, Lee was unable to halt Grant, who slipped past his right flank. See SPOTSYLVANIA COURT HOUSE.

The Wilderness, fourteen miles wide and ten deep, was a densely wooded area choked by secondary undergrowth. Senior commanders were unable to exercise effective control in a soldier's battle fought of necessity at close range because of the limited visibility. An horrific aspect of the battle was the outbreak of forest fires in which many of the wounded were trapped.

Wittstock   552

Date: 4 October 1636.
Location: Village on the Dosse river, 58 miles north-west of Berlin.
War and campaign: Thirty Years' War, 1618–1648: German Campaign of 1636.
Opposing sides: (a) Field Marshal Count Johan Baner commanding the Swedish army; (b) John George I of Saxony commanding the Imperialist/Saxon/Bavarian army.
Objective: The Imperialists were attempting to sever Swedish communications with the Baltic.
Forces engaged: (a) Nine infantry brigades and 50 cavalry squadrons – total 15,000; (b) thirteen infantry brigades, 75 cavalry squadrons and 33 guns – total 20,000.
Casualties: (a) 3,000 killed and wounded; (b) 5,000 killed, wounded and prisoners and all guns lost.
Result: The Imperialist army was destroyed. Swedish morale, seriously damaged by the disastrous FIRST BATTLE OF NÖRDLINGEN, was restored.

Baner enticed the overconfident Imperialists out of their strong entrenched position with a feint frontal attack made with only a portion of his force. The rest he sent on a wide encircling march under two Scottish officers, Alexander Leslie and James King, and at the critical moment they fell on the flank and rear of the Imperialist army, routing it.

Worcester   553

Date: 3 September 1651.
Location: To the south and east of the city.
War and campaign: Third Civil War, 1650–1651.
Opposing sides: (a) Charles II commanding the Royalist army; (b) Oliver Cromwell commanding the Parliamentary army.

Objective: After Dunbar both sides had manoeuvred inconclusively in central Scotland. In August 1651, however, Charles crossed the border with the intention of marching on London, but he attracted little support for his cause. Cromwell set off in pursuit, simultaneously concentrating Parliamentary forces in England. At Worcester the Royalists were compelled to give battle.
Forces engaged: (a) 8,000 infantry, 4,000 cavalry and some guns – total 12,000 (including 10,000 Scots); (b) 18,000 infantry, 9,000 cavalry and some guns – total 28,000.
Casualties: (a) 3,000 killed, up to 7,000 prisoners and all guns captured; (b) undoubtedly greater than the 300 killed suggested by Cromwell.
Result: A decisive Parliamentary victory which destroyed the Royalist army and consolidated Cromwell's hold on power. Charles became a fugitive for six weeks before escaping to the Continent. See DUNES, THE.

Cromwell's opening attack against the Royalist right was directed across the Severn and its tributary the Teme but was contained. Charles responded by attacking the Parliamentary centre and made some progress until Cromwell returned to break the Royalist horse and drive his opponents back into the city, where the majority of them surrendered.

Wörth (Fröschwiller) 554

Date: 6 August 1870.
Location: 10 miles south-west of Wissembourg, Lorraine, France.
War and campaign: Franco–Prussian War, 1870–1871.
Opposing sides: (a) Crown Prince Friedrich Wilhelm commanding the Third Army of the North German Confederation; (b) Marshal Edmé-Patrice-Maurice MacMahon commanding the French I Corps.
Objective: The Prussians were attempting to entrap the French armies on the frontier within a double-envelopment, of which the attack at Wörth was the southern arm.
Forces engaged: (a) 89,000 infantry, 7,750 cavalry and 342 guns; (b) 42,800 infantry, 5,750 cavalry and 167 guns.
Casualties: (a) 10,500 killed and wounded; (b) approximately 11,000 killed and wounded, 9,200 prisoners and 28 guns captured.
Result: After a stubborn defence lasting eight hours, the French were overwhelmed by numbers. The double-envelopment sought by the Prussians did not materialize, largely because the trap was sprung prematurely at SPICHEREN. MacMahon withdrew his troops to Chalons.

The nature of the fighting in the interconnected battles of Wörth and SPICHEREN set the pattern for the entire war, namely with the Prussians emerging the tactical victors yet sustaining losses in killed and wounded as high as, or higher than, the French. The French Chassepot rifle was much superior to the Prussian Dreyse 'needle gun' and the German infantry, attacking in close order, suffered severely because of it. On the other hand, the Prussian artillery possessed more modern guns and shell-fuzes than the French and easily dominated the battlefield. The French forfeited the benefit of their numerous mitrailleuses (machine guns) by deploying them in the manner of artillery batteries, so providing easy targets for the longer-ranged Prussian field guns. Faced with such firepower, the cavalry of both armies all but lost its capacity for shock action.

Yalu River

Date: 30 April to 1 May 1904.
Location: Near Wiju on the lower reaches of the Yalu river, dividing Korea from Manchuria.
War and campaign: Russo–Japanese War, 1904–1905.
Opposing sides: (a) General Alexei Kuropatkin, Commander-in-Chief of the Russian army in Manchuria; (b) Field Marshal Marquis Iwao Oyama, Commander-in-Chief of the Japanese armies in Manchuria.
Objective: The Russian orders were to resist the Japanese invasion with a delaying action; however, these were ambiguous in their phrasing and were interpreted as the need to conduct the static defence of fixed positions along the Yalu.
Forces engaged: (a) Lieutenant-General Zasulich with 15,000 infantry, 5,000 cavalry and some 60 guns; (b) Major-General Baron Tamesada Kuroki commanding the Japanese First Army with 40,000 men.
Casualties: (a) About 3,000, including some 1,400 killed and 600 prisoners, plus eleven guns and eight machine guns captured; (b) about 1,000.
Result: The Japanese crossed the river successfully and invaded Manchuria.

The victory of an Oriental over a European army seriously damaged Russian prestige and raised Japanese morale.

Yellow Ford, The

Date: 14 August 1598.
Location: Ford across the river Callan, 3 miles north of Armagh, Ulster.
War and campaign: Tyrone's Rebellion, 1598–1603.
Opposing sides: (a) Sir Henry Bagenal commanding the Government forces, succeeded by Sir Thomas Wingfield; (b) the Earl of Tyrone and Hugh O'Donnell commanding the rebels.
Objective: The rebels ambushed a Government column marching to relieve the Blackwater Fort.
Forces engaged: (a) One cavalry and six infantry regiments with four guns – total 4,220; (b) approximately 5,000 infantry and 600 cavalry.
Casualties: (a) 2,000 killed, wounded and missing, including Bagenal killed; (b) unknown, but light.
Result: The column was destroyed, although its remnants managed to withdraw into Armagh; Tyrone permitted the survivors, and the garrison of the Blackwater Fort, to march out.

The defeat, the worst ever sustained by English troops in Ireland, led to the rapid spread of the rebellion, which was not finally put down until 1603. See also FORD OF THE BISCUITS, THE, and KINSALE.

Yellow River, The

Date: 1226.

Location: On the Yellow River (Hwang Ho) near Yingchwan (formerly Ning-sia), north-western China.
War and campaign: Rebellion of the Hsia Empire against Mongol rule.
Opposing sides: (a) Genghis Khan; (b) the Hsia Emperor.
Objective: The Mongol intention was to crush the rebellion.
Forces engaged: (a) 180,000; (b) over 300,000.
Casualties: (a) Unknown; (b) Mongol claims to have counted 300,000 Hsia dead were almost certainly exaggerated.
Result: The Mongols won a complete victory then simultaneously invested Ning-sia, invaded the Chin Empire and advanced into south-eastern China.

Genghis Khan died the following year and was succeeded by his son Ogatai.

Yellow Tavern 558

Date: 11 May 1864.
Location: 10 miles north of Richmond, Virginia.
War and campaign: American Civil War: Grant's Virginia Campaign of 1864.
Opposing sides: (a) Major-General Philip H. Sheridan commanding the cavalry corps of the Army of the Potomac; (b) Lieutenant-General J. E. B. Stuart commanding the Confederate cavalry.
Objective: While the battle of SPOTSYLVANIA COURT HOUSE was in progress, Grant sent his cavalry on a raid against Lee's lines of communication.
Forces engaged: (a) 10,000; (b) 4,500.
Casualties: (a) 400; (b) 1,000.
Result: Sheridan's men drove their opponents off the field, killing Stuart, whose death was a serious blow to the Confederacy. A number of recently captured Federal prisoners of war were released.

Yorktown, Siege of 559

Date: 28 September to 19 October 1781.
Location: Yorktown, near the mouth of the York river, Virginia, and Gloucester, opposite.
War and campaign: American War of Independence, 1775–1783: southern theatre of operations.
Opposing sides: (a) Major-General Lord Charles Cornwallis; (b) Lieutenant-General George Washington and Lieutenant-General Count Jean-Baptiste de Rochambeau, the latter commanding the French contingent but subordinate to Washington.
Objective: Cornwallis, having unwisely advanced north into Virginia, had received orders to despatch 3,000 men to New York (subsequently countermanded) and withdraw his army into a secure deep water sea port which would provide an anchorage for the fleet. His choice of Yorktown would have been sound had the Royal Navy retained naval superiority, but at the critical period this was temporarily lost to the French at the Battle of the Capes (5–9 September) and he was isolated. In

the meantime, Washington had already begun concentrating a superior number of American and French troops with which he intended to administer the *coup de grâce* to the last British army in the field, and on 28 September Yorktown was invested.

Forces engaged: (a) 8,000; (b) 9,500 Americans and 7,800 French.

Casualties: (a) 156 killed and 326 wounded; (b) 20 Americans killed and 56 wounded, 52 French killed and 134 wounded.

Result: Cornwallis asked for terms on 17 October and surrendered two days later. The war was unpopular in the United Kingdom and the capitulation convinced Parliament that a favourable military solution was impossible. Peace negotiations were opened in April 1782 and concluded in September 1783, culminating in British recognition of the independence of the United States. No major military operations took place after Yorktown.

Cornwallis' decision to advance into Virginia was made without the authority of Lieutenant-General Sir Henry Clinton, the British Commander-in-Chief in North America, in the mistaken belief that it would consolidate his hold on the southern states. In fact, although he enjoyed a number of minor tactical successes, his move not only resulted in the loss of most of the previous year's gains in the south (see EUTAW SPRINGS), but also placed his own army firmly inside a strategic trap. It can be argued that, rather than sending him to the coast, Clinton might profitably have ordered him to withdraw south into the Carolinas, but he was himself under intense political pressure from London to support operations in Virginia. Cornwallis was normally a competent commander, but the enormity of the mistake, coupled with his own isolation, the superiority of his opponents' artillery, an ammunition shortage and an outbreak of smallpox, contributed to his lacklustre defence of Yorktown. The outer works, which would have delayed the besiegers for some weeks, were abandoned prematurely, enabling the French and American artillery to engage the inner defences, and the loss of two key redoubts on 14 October made the position untenable. Five days after the surrender Clinton arrived in Chesapeake Bay with 7,000 reinforcements but, realizing he was too late, returned to New York.

Ypres, First Battle of   560

Date: 18 October to 30 November 1914.

Location: Semi-circular salient to the north, east and south of the city of Ypres, Flanders.

War and campaign: First World War: Western Front.

Opposing sides: (a) General Joseph Joffre, Commander-in-Chief of the French armies; (b) General Erich von Falkenhayn, Chief of the German General Staff.

Objective: The last German attempt of 1914 to break through the Allied line and capture the Channel ports.

Forces engaged: (a) Field Marshal Sir John French commanding the British Expeditionary Force (I, III, IV and Cavalry Corps, reinforced by Joffre with the French IX and XVI Corps); (b) Duke Albrecht of Württemberg commanding the German Fourth Army and Crown Prince Rupprecht of Bavaria commanding the German Sixth Army, both heavily reinforced during the battle.

Casualties: (a) 58,155 British and approximately 50,000 French; (b) approximately 130,000.

Result: The German drive was halted, albeit at heavy cost.

Following the battle of THE AISNE, each side made repeated attempts to turn the other's northern flank until the lines eventually reached the coast, and First Ypres was the culmination of this process, which was known as the 'Race to the Sea'. Initially an encounter battle, it quickly assumed the form of continuous German attacks on the salient which had been formed around the city. The original BEF is said to have died at Ypres and many of its units were indeed reduced to a mere handful. For the Germans, who employed young, idealistic but inexperienced recruits, including a high proportion of university students, in the newly raised Reserve corps which formed Württemberg's army, the battle was known as the 'Massacre of the Innocents' because of the horrific casualties sustained. Conversely, on 11 November the repulse of several regiments of the crack Prussian Guard, the élite of Imperial German Army, provided convincing proof that the offensive had failed. See also YPRES, SECOND BATTLE OF.

Ypres, Second Battle of   561

Date: 22 April to 25 May 1915.
Location: Semi-circular salient to the north, east and south of the city of Ypres, Flanders.
War and campaign: First World War: Western Front.
Opposing sides: (a) Field Marshal Sir John French commanding the British armies in France; (b) General Erich von Falkenhayn, Chief of the German General Staff.
Objective: The Germans' intention was to eliminate the Ypres salient, partly because of the threat it presented to Brussels, partly to renew the threat to the Channel ports and partly to straighten an inconvenient bulge in the line.
Forces engaged: (a) General Sir Horace Smith-Dorrien (replaced by Lieutenant-General Sir Herbert Plumer on 27 April) commanding the British Second Army, with V Corps in the salient and two French divisions covering its northern sector; (b) Duke Albrecht of Württemberg commanding the German Fourth Army.
Casualties: (a) 59,275 British and approximately 10,000 French; (b) approximately 35,000.
Result: The Germans made some gains but were unable to eliminate the salient altogether.

This was the first occasion on which the Germans used poison gas on the Western Front, although they had used it in the East three months previously. Their gas attack on 22 April enabled them to break through the French sector, although they were slow to exploit their success and in the long term the use of gas was a tactical error as the prevailing westerly winds favoured the Allies. One reason why the Allied casualties were so heavy was that the more numerous German artillery dominated the battlefield. The principal cause of Smith-Dorrien's being relieved of command was a clash of personalities with Sir John French.

Ypres, Third Battle of (Passchendaele)   562

Date: 31 July to 6 November 1917.
Location: The Ypres Salient, Flanders.
War and campaign: First World War: Western Front.
Opposing sides: (a) Field Marshal Sir Douglas Haig commanding the British armies

in France and Belgium; (b) Crown Prince Rupprecht of Bavaria commanding the northern group of German armies.

Objective: Following the capture of MESSINES RIDGE, the British plan was to launch an offensive out of the Ypres salient with the ultimate object of clearing the Belgian coast and advancing to the Dutch border.

Forces engaged: (a) General Sir Herbert Plumer commanding the Second Army and General Sir Hubert Gough commanding the Fifth Army, and General Anthoine commanding the French First Army to the north of the salient; (b) General Sixt von Arnim commanding the Fourth Army and General Otto von Below commanding the Sixth Army.

Casualties: (a) 80,000 British killed and missing, 230,000 wounded and 14,000 captured, and approximately 50,000 French casualties; (b) 50,000 German killed and missing, 113,000 wounded and 37,000 captured.

Result: No breakthrough was obtained, although the salient was expanded. The battle relieved pressure on the French armies, which were still recovering from THE NIVELLE OFFENSIVE and its consequences.

Years of shellfire had destroyed the drainage system of the countryside over which the battle was fought so that heavy rain in August, and again later in the offensive, turned the whole area into a bog in which men vanished and tanks sank up to their roofs. On 6 November the capture of Passchendaele ridge and village, a mere seven miles from Ypres, concluded the offensive. The name Passchendaele has since come to epitomize the misery of trench warfare on the Western Front.

Zama   563

Date: 202 BC.

Location: Modern Zowareen, 60 miles south-west of Tunis.

War and campaign: Second Punic War, 219–202 BC: Roman invasion of North Africa.

Opposing sides: (a) Publius Cornelius Scipio commanding the Roman army; (b) Hannibal.

Objective: Hannibal succeeded in drawing the Romans away from Carthage by marching inland and at Zama turned to offer battle.

Forces engaged: (a) 34,000 infantry and 9,000 cavalry – total 43,000; (b) 45,000 infantry, 3,000 cavalry and twenty war elephants – total approximately 48,000.

Casualties: (a) 1,500 killed and about 4,000 wounded; (b) 20,000 killed and 15,000 captured.

Result: Hannibal was decisively defeated and Carthage sued for peace. She was forced to hand over all her warships and elephants and agreed to pay Rome a huge indemnity over a 50-year period. Scipio was awarded the title of Africanus.

With the exception of 18,000 veterans with whom he had returned from Italy, Hannibal's infantry consisted of untrained levies and foreign mercenaries, and his cavalry was but a shadow of the formidable force it had once been. Scipio's army, on the other hand, was thoroughly trained and well equipped. The Carthaginian cavalry was quickly driven off on both flanks, and when Hannibal's war elephants attacked they were simply herded down lanes between the Roman maniples which Scipio had left for the purpose. The Roman infantry then advanced, easily defeating the mercenary troops and levies which formed the Carthaginian first and second lines. The third line, however, consisted of Hannibal's veterans and this stood its ground until the Roman cavalry, returning from its pursuit, fell on its rear. Hannibal and the survivors of his army fled to Carthage.

Zenta (Senta) 564

Date: 11 September 1697.

Location: Town on the Theiss (Tisza) river, 80 miles north of Belgrade, Yugoslavia.

War and campaign: Great Turkish War, 1683–1699: attempted Turkish invasion of Hungary, 1697.

Opposing sides: (a) Prince Eugene of Savoy commanding the Austrian army; (b) Sultan Mustapha II in personal command of the Turkish army.

Objective: The Turks, having marched north from Belgrade towards the Hungarian frontier, were intercepted by an Austrian army as they attempted to cross the Theiss.

Forces engaged: (a) 50,000; (b) uncertain, but larger.

Casualties: (a) 500 killed and wounded; (b) an estimated 20,000 killed, wounded, captured or drowned while trying to escape.

Result: The Turks on the west bank were annihilated and the Ottoman Empire's capacity for further offensive action was destroyed. The victory led to the Treaty of Karlowitz, as a result of which Austria received Hungary and Poland recovered Podolia.

Eugene allowed the Turkish cavalry to reach the west bank, then launched his assault while the infantry were still crossing by means of a temporary bridge. When this was destroyed, those in the bridgehead were isolated and overwhelmed.

Zorndorf 565

Date: 25 August 1758.

Location: Hamlet north of Kostrzyn (Kustrin), north-western Poland.

War and campaign: Seven Years' War, 1756–1763: Central European Campaign of 1758.

Opposing sides: (a) Frederick the Great; (b) Count Wilhelm Fermor.

Objective: Frederick II's Prussian army was threatening the lines of communication of a Russian army besieging Kustrin, only 45 miles from Berlin. The Russians abandoned the siege and turned to give battle.

Forces engaged: (a) 36,000; (b) 42,000.

Casualties: (a) 13,500; (b) 21,000.

Result: After a bloody attritional struggle, the Russians withdrew eastwards to Königsberg (Kaliningrad).

With the Russian threat removed for the time being, Frederick was free to march against the Austrians – see HOCHKIRCH.

Zutphen

Date: 11 November 1586.	
Location: Town 17 miles north-east of Arnhem, Holland.	
War and campaign: Eighty Years' War (War of Dutch Independence), 1568–1648: Campaign of 1586.	
Opposing sides: (a) The Earl of Leicester commanding the Anglo-Dutch besieging force; (b) Alexander Farnese, Duke of Parma, commanding the relief force.	
Objective: The Spanish intention was to break the Anglo-Dutch siege of Zutphen.	
Forces engaged: (a) Approximately 10,000; (b) approximately 15,000.	
Casualties: (a) Uncertain, but heavy; (b) light.	
Result: Leicester was defeated and forced to abandon the siege.	

The battle is best remembered for the selfless act of the dying Sir Philip Sidney, who insisted that a wounded man nearby should receive the water he had been offered.

APPENDIX A: LIST OF BATTLES BY WARS, WITH ENTRY NUMBERS

APPENDIX B: LIST OF PROMINENT COMMANDERS, WITH ENTRY NUMBERS

commander during the Franco–Prussian War, 203, 340, 351

Beauharnais, Prince Eugene de, Viceroy of Italy and French commander during the Napoleonic Wars, 325

Beaulieu, General, Baron Jean-Pierre de, Austrian commander during the French Revolutionary Wars, 301

Beauregard, Lieutenant-General Pierre, Confederate commander during the American Civil War, 86, 180, 403, 474

Bedford, John, Duke of, English commander during the Hundred Years' War, 530

Bela IV, King of Hungary, 357

Benedek, Field Marshal Ludwig von, Austrian commander during the Austro–Prussian War in 1866, 270

Bennigsen, General Levin, Russian commander during the Napoleonic Wars, 162, 187

Beresford, General Viscount William, British commander of Portuguese troops during the Peninsular War, 17

Bergonzoli, General, Italian commander in the Western Desert during the Second World War, 55

Bernadotte, Marshal Jean Baptiste, French commander during the Napoleonic Wars, latterly King of Sweden, 288

Berwick, Marshal, Duke James of, natural son of James II of England, French commander during the eighteenth century, 24

Blaskowitz, Colonel-General Johannes, commander of German Army Group H in 1945, 434, 435

Blücher, Field Marshal, Prince Gerhard von, Prussian commander during the French Revolutionary and Napoleonic Wars, 60, 288, 298, 316, 547

Bock, Field Marshal Fedor von, German commander in the Second World War, 154, 183, 262, 369, 480, 539

Bohemond, Duke of Taranto, Christian commander during the First Crusade, 29, 149

Botha, General Louis, Boer leader during the Second Boer War, 124, 145, 487

Boufflers, Marshal, Duke Louis de, French commander during the War of Spanish Succession, 326

Bourbaki, General Charles, French commander during the Franco–Prussian War, 63

Braddock, Major-General Edward, British

commander during the French and Indian War in North America, 362

Bradley, General Omar, American commander in the Second World War, 1, 85, 163, 435

Bragg, General Braxton, Confederate commander during the American Civil War, 116, 117, 402, 494

Brauchitsch, Field Marshal Walter von, commander-in-chief of the German Army in the Second World War until dismissed by Hitler in 1941, 91, 183, 369

Brihtnoth, Ealdorman, English leader opposing the Danish invasion of 991, 324

Brock, General Sir Isaac, British commander during the War of 1812, 430

Brown, Major-General Jacob, American commander during the War of 1812, 119, 313

Browne, Field Marshal Count Maximilian von, Austrian commander during the Seven Years' War, 300

Brunswick, Ferdinand, Duke of, Prussian commander during the Seven Years' War, 353, 544

Brunswick, Karl Wilhelm, Duke of, Prussian commander during the French Revolutionary and Napoleonic Wars, 244, 528

Brusilov, General Alexei, commander of the Russian South-West Front in the First World War, 83, 433

Buckingham, Humphrey Stafford, Duke of, Lancastrian commander during the Wars of the Roses, 387

Buckner, Lieutenant-General Simon, commander of the US Tenth Army in the Pacific during the Second World War, 388

Budenny, Marshal Semen, commander-in-chief of the Soviet armies in the Ukraine in 1941, 262, 468

Buell, Major-General Don Carlos, Union commander during the American Civil War, 402, 474

Buller, General Sir Redvers, British commander during the Second Boer War, 124, 487

Bulow, General Karl von, commander of the German Second Army during the First World War, 209, 338

Bureau, Jean, French Master of Artillery during the final phase of the Hundred Years' War, 100

Burgoyne, Major-General John, British commander during the American War of

26, 219, 310, 311, 312, 338, 339, 352, 448

Franchet d'Esperey, General, commander of the French Fifth Army during the First World War, 209, 338

Francis I, King of France, 337, 399

Franklyn, Major-General H. E., commander of Frank Force at Arras in 1940, 36

Franz Josef, Emperor of Austria, 483

Frederick II, the Great, King of Prussia, 220, 223, 269, 272, 291, 297, 300, 359, 419, 443, 482, 518, 565

Freissner, Colonel-General Johannes, commander of the German Army Group South Ukraine in the Second World War, 241

French, Field Marshal Sir John, British commander in the First World War, 13, 287, 304, 338, 363, 560, 561

Freyberg, Major-General Bernard, New Zealand commander in the Second World War, 132

Friedrich Karl, Prince, Prussian commander during the Austro–Prussian and Franco–Prussian Wars, 270, 340, 351

Friedrich Wilhelm, Crown Prince of Prussia, Prussian commander during the Austro–Prussian and Franco–Prussian Wars, later Emperor of Germany, 270, 554

Fritigern, Gothic commander in, 378, 8

Frossard, General Charles Auguste, French commander during the Franco–Prussian War, 486

Gage, Major-General Thomas, British commander during the American War of Independence, 89

Galway, Henri de Massue de Ruvigny, Earl of, Huguenot commander of British troops during the War of Spanish Succession, 24

Gamelin, General Maurice, French and Allied commander-in-chief in France in 1940, 183

Gatacre, Lieutenant-General Sir William, British commander in the Second Boer War, 496

Gates, Major-General Horatio, American commander during the American War of Independence, 94, 457, 458

Gavish, Major-General Yeshayahu, GOC Israeli Southern Command in 1967, 478

Geiger, Major-General Roy S., commander of the US III Amphibious

Corps in the Pacific during the Second World War, 207, 401

Genghis Khan, 231, 453, 557

George II, King of England, 144

Giap, General Vo Nguyen, Communist commander-in-chief during the Vietnam War, 146, 261

Ginkel, General Godert de, Dutch commander of Williamite troops in Ireland in 1689–1691, 46

Godfrey de Buillon, Crusader leader, 39, 149, 245

Golikov, Colonel-General, Soviet commander in the Second World War, 259

Goltz, Field Marshal Baron Colmar von der, German commander of Turkish forces in Mesopotamia in 1915, 134, 274

Gonen, Major-General Shmuel, GOC Israeli Southern Front in 1973, 497

Gorchakov, General, Prince Mikhail, Russian commander in the Crimean War, 467

Gordon, Major-General Charles, British commander in the Sudan in 1884–1885, 260

Gort, Field Marshal Lord John, commander of the British Expeditionary Force in France in 1939–1940, 154, 183

Gough, General Lord Hugh, British commander during the Sikh Wars, 118, 167, 210, 371, 481

Graham, Major-General Sir Gerald, British commander during the Sudan Campaigns, 158, 504

Graham, Major-General Sir Thomas, British commander during the French Revolutionary and Napoleonic Wars, 57

Grant, General Ulysees S., Union commander during the American Civil War, latterly the US Army's General-in-Chief, later President of the United States, 31, 116, 123, 170, 177, 403, 474, 488, 531, 551

Graziani, Marshal Rodolpho, commander of the Italian forces in Libya in 1940–1941, 62, 476

Greene, Major-General Nathanael, American commander during the American War of Independence, 160, 208

Guderian, General Heinz, German commander of armoured troops during the Second World War, later Chief of General Staff, 262, 480, 539

Gustavus Adolphus, King of Sweden, 25,

Leopold III, Duke of Austria, 465

Leopold William, Archduke, Imperialist commander during the Thirty Years' War, 80

Leslie, David, Scottish soldier who served in the Civil and Thirty Years' Wars, 152, 405

Linares, General Arsenio, Spanish commander in the Spanish–American War, 455

Lincoln, Major-General Benjamin, American commander during the American War of Independence, 113, 460

Lohr, Colonel-General Alexander, German commander during the battle for Crete, 1941, 132

Louis II, King of Hungary, 355

Louis IX, King of France, 333

Lucas, Major-General John P., commander of the US VI Corps in Italy in the Second World War, 30, 452, 538

Ludendorff, General Erich, First Quartermaster-General of the German Army during the First World War, 26, 37, 93, 219, 309, 310, 311, 312, 339, 349, 352, 384, 448, 506, 529

Luxembourg, Marshal François, Duke of, French commander during the seventeenth century, 171, 379

MacArthur, General Douglas, American and Allied commander in the Pacific theatre of war during the Second World War and Korean War, 59, 230, 294, 424

MacDonnell, Colonel George, British commander in the War of 1812, 114

MacMahon, Marshal, Count Edme-Maurice-Patrice, French nineteenth century commander, later President of France, 319, 463, 554

McClellan, Major-General George B., Union commander during the American Civil War, 28, 469, 470

McCreery, General Sir Richard, British commander in the Second World War, 452

McDowell, Major-General Irvin, Union commander during the American Civil War, 86

McPherson, Major-General James B., Union commander during the American Civil War, 45, 256

Mack, General Karl von Lieberich, Austrian commander during the Napoleonic Wars, 526

Mackay, Major-General Hugh, commander of Government troops during the Jacobite Rebellion of 1689, 263

Mackensen, General Eberhard, commander of the German Fourteenth Army in Italy in the Second World War, 30

Mahdi, the, Mohammed Ahmed, Sudanese religious leader and ruler, 157, 260

Mahomet II, Sultan of Turkey 1451–1481, also known as the Conqueror, 125

Malinovsky, Marshal Rodion, commander of the Soviet 2nd Ukrainian Front during the Second World War, 241

Mannerheim, Marshal Carl Gustav, commander-in-chief of Finland's armed forces during the Second World War, 331, 496

Mansfeld, Count Ernst von, 143

Manstein, Field Marshal Erich von, German commander in the Second World War, 183, 251, 259, 273, 468, 489

Mardonius, Persian commander during the Graeco–Persian Wars, 410

Marlborough, John Churchill, Duke of, British commander during the War of Spanish Succession, 71, 148, 326, 393, 431

Marmont, Marshal Auguste, French commander during the Napoleonic Wars, 397, 451

Marsin, Marshal, Count Ferdinand de, French commander during the War of Spanish Succession, 525

Massena, Marshal André, Duke of Rivoli, French commander during the Napoleonic Wars, 90, 188

Maude, General Sir Frederick Stanley, British commander in Mesopotamia during the First World War, 49

Maximilian I, Elector of Bavaria, Catholic commander during the Thirty Years' War, 25, 549

Meade, Major-General George G., Union commander during the American Civil War, 123, 130, 170, 194, 403, 488, 551

Melas, Field Marshal Baron Michael von, Austrian commander during the French Revolutionary Wars, 335

Melo, Don Francisco de, Spanish commander during the Thirty Years' War, 440

Menelek, Emperor of Abyssinia during the war against Italy in 1895–1896, 7

chief of the French armies in 1917, 384, 529

Nixon, Lieutenant-General Sir John, British commander in Mesopotamia during the First World War, 134, 274

Noailles, Marshal Adrien, Duke of, French commander during the War of Austrian Succession, 144

Nogi, General Baron Maresuke, commander of the Japanese Third Army during the Russo–Japanese War, 414

Nur-ed-Din Pasha, Turkish commander in Mesopotamia during the First World War, 134

O'Connor, General Sir Richard, British corps commander in the Western Desert and Europe during the Second World War, 55, 62, 476, 516

Obata, General Hideyoshi, commander of the Japanese Thirty-First Army in the Second World War, 449, 514

Osman Digna, Dervish commander during the Sudan Campaigns, 44, 158, 504

Osman Pasha, Turkish commander during the Russo–Turkish War in 1877–1878, 411

Otozo, General Yamada, Japanese army group commander in Manchuria in 1945, 328

Otto IV, Holy Roman Emperor, 75

Oyama, Field Marshal Marquis Iwao, Japanese commander in Manchuria during the Russo–Japanese War, 295, 372, 375, 454, 471, 555

Pakenham, Major-General Sir Edward, British commander during the War of 1812, 382

Pappenheim, Count Gottfried zu, Catholic commander during the Thirty Years' War, 318

Parma, Alexander Farnese, Duke of, 566

Patch, Major-General Alexander, commander of the US XIV Corps on Guadalcanal and later the US Seventh Army in Europe in the Second World War, 206

Patton, Lieutenant-General George S., American commander in the Second World War, 85, 255

Paulus, Field Marshal Friedrich von, German commander in the Second World War, 489

Paulus, Lucius Aemilius, Roman commander during the Third Macedonian War, 425

Pausanias, Regent of Sparta, Greek commander during the Graeco–Persian Wars, 410

Pavlov, General, Soviet commander during the Spanish Civil War and Second World War, 205

Pemberton, Lieutenant-General John C., Confederate commander during the American Civil War, 531

Peng Teh-huai, General, Chinese Communist commander during the Korean War, 228, 414

Percival, Lieutenant-General Arthur, British commander in the Second World War, 479

Percy, Sir Henry, also known as Hotspur, 392, 475

Pershing, General John J., American commander in the First World War, 352, 448

Pescara, Fernando, Marquis of, sixteenth century Imperialist commander, 399

Pétain, Marshal Henri Philippe, French commander in the First World War, President of France in 1940, 529

Peter the Great, Tsar of Russia, 413

Philip II, King of Macedonia, 106

Philip IV, King of Macedonia, 138

Philip IV, King of France, 131

Philip Augustus, King of France, 75

Pickett, Major-General George E., Confederate commander during the American Civil War, 170, 194

Pilsudski, Marshal Joseph, Polish commander during the Russo–Polish War, 545

Plautius, Aulus, Roman conqueror of Britain, 345

Pleasanton, Major-General Alfred, Union commander during the American Civil War, 77

Pompeius, Gnaius, Pompey the Great, Roman soldier and triumvir, 404

Pope, Major-General John, Union commander during the American Civil War, 87

Prevost, Major-General Augustine, British commander during the American War of Independence, 460

Proctor, Brigaider-General Henry, British commander in the War of 1812, 186, 512

Putnam, Major-General Israel, American commander during the American War of Independence, 302

Qutuz, Sultan of Egypt, Mameluke commander, 12

Raglan, Field Marshal Lord, British commander during the Crimean War, 23, 51, 232, 467
Rameses II, King of Egypt, 248
Rawlinson, General Sir Henry, commander of the British Fourth Army during the First World War, 26
Raymond, Count of Toulouse, Crusader leader, 149
Rennenkampf, General Pavel, commander of the Russian First Army in the First World War, 211, 343, 506
Rensselaer, Major-General Stephen van, American commander during the War of 1812, 430
Reynier, General Jean, French commander during the Napoleonic Wars, 321
Riall, Major-General Sir Phineas, British commander during the War of 1812, 119
Richard I, King of England, Christian commander during the Third Crusade, 38
Richard III, King of England, 73
Ritchie, Lieutenant-General Neil, British commander in the Second World War, 192, 517
Robert the Bruce, King of Scotland, 54
Roberts, Field Marshal Earl Frederick, British commander in colonial wars and the Second Boer War, 112, 145, 252, 322, 394, 473
Rokossovsky, Marshal Konstantin, Soviet commander in the Second World War, 50, 273
Rommel, Field Marshal Erwin, German commander in North Africa and Europe during the Second World War, 14, 15, 16, 36, 92, 141, 192, 255, 344, 517
Rose, Major-General Sir Hugh, British commander during the Indian Mutiny, 67, 212
Rosecrans, Major-General William S., Union commander during the American Civil War, 117, 127, 494
Ross, Major-General Robert, British commander in the Peninsular War and North America in 1814, 53, 70
Rundstedt, Field Marshal Gerd von, German commander during the Second World War, 81, 85, 141, 154, 183, 262, 468
Rupert, Prince, nephew of Charles I and Royalist commander during the Civil War, 108, 341, 377
Rupprecht, of Bavaria, Crown Prince, German commander in the First World War, 562

Saint-Arnaud, Marshal Armand de, French commander during the Crimean War, 23
Saddam Hussein, President of Iraq, commander-in-chief of Iraqi armed forces during the war against Iran and the Gulf War in 1990–1991, 276
Saladin (Salah-al-din Yusuf ibn-Ayub), Sultan of Egypt, 38, 217
Sale, Brigadier-General Sir George, British commander during the First Afghan War, 242
Salisbury, Thomas de Montacute, Earl of, English commander during the Hundred Years' War, 390
Samsonov, General Alexander, Russian commander in 1914, 506
Sanders, General Liman von, German commander of Turkish troops in the First World War, 189, 348
Santa-Anna, General Antonio Lopez de, Mexican soldier, President and Dictator, 84, 105, 111, 126, 358.
Saxe, Marshal, Count Maurice de, French commander in the eighteenth century, 174, 279
Saxe-Coburg, Frederick Josias, Prince of, Austrian and Allied commander during the French Revolutionary Wars, 172
Schmidt, Major-General Harry, commander of the US V Amphibious Corps in the Pacific in the Second World War, 240
Schofield, Major-General John M., Union commander during the American Civil War, 45, 256
Schorner, Field Marshal Ferdinand, German commander during the Second World War, 66
Scipio, Publius Cornelius, Roman commander during the Second Punic War, 563
Scoones, Lieutenant-General G. A. P., commander of the British IV Corps in Burma during the Second World War, 229
Scott, General Winfield, American commander in the US–Mexican War, 105, 111, 119, 126, 358
Schwarzenberg, Field Marshal Prince Karl von, Austrian commander during the

342

Napoleonic Wars, 150, 288, 397

Schwarzkopf, General Norman, Allied commander during the Gulf War in 1990–1991, 276

Shafter, Major-General William R., American commander during the Spanish–American War, 455

Shazli, General Saad el Din, Egyptian Army Chief of Staff in 1973, 498

Sher Singh, Sikh leader in the Second Sikh War, 118, 210

Sheridan, Major-General Philip, Union commander during the American Civil War, 102, 170, 558

Sherman, Major-General William T., Union commander during the American Civil War, 45, 256, 461.

Shibasaki, Rear Admiral Keichi, commander of the Japanese garrison at Tarawa, 507

Shrewsbury, John Talbot, Earl of, English commander in the Hundred Years' War, killed in 1453, 100

Slim, Field Marshal Viscount William, British commander in Burma during the Second World War, 229, 268, 329

Smigly-Rydz, Marshal Edward, Commander-in-Chief of the Polish Army in 1939, 91

Smith, Major-General Sir Harry, British commander during the First Sikh War, 21

Smith, General Holland M., commander of the US V Amphibious Corps, then Commanding General Fleet Marine Force Pacific in the Second World War, 277, 449, 507, 514

Smith, Major-General Oliver, commander of the US 1st Marine Division in the Korean War, 120

Smith, Senator Samuel, responsible for the defence of Baltimore 1814, 53

Smith-Dorrien, General Sir Horace, British commander in the First World War, 287, 363

Somerset, Edmund Beaufort, Duke of, English commander during the Hundred Years' War and Lancastrian supporter in the Wars of the Roses, killed in 1455, 446

Somerset, Edmund Beaufort, Duke of, Lancastrian commander in the Wars of the Roses, executed in 1471, 511

Somerset, Henry Beaufort, Duke of, Lancastrian commander in the Wars of the Roses, executed in 1464, 218, 447, 522, 543

Soubise, Marshal Prince Charles de

Rohan, French commander during the Seven Years' War, 443

Soult, Marshal Nicolas Jean-de-Dieu, Duke of Dalmatia, French commander during the Revolutionary and Napoleonic Wars, 17, 128, 520

Stalin, Iosef, Soviet dictator, 369

Steinmetz, General Karl Friedrich von, Prussian commander during the Franco–Prussian War, 486

Stockwell, Lieutenant-General Sir Hugh, British commander of Allied landing force at Suez 1956, 498

Stoessel, Major-General Baron Anatoli, Russian commander at Port Arthur during the Russo–Japanese War, 375, 415

Straussenburg, Field Marshal Arz von, Chief of Austro–Hungarian General Staff in 1918, 407, 537

Stuart, Prince Charles Edward, The Young Pretender, Jacobite commander during the Forty-Five Rebellion, 135, 422

Stuart, General Sir John, British commander during the Napoleonic Wars, 321

Stuart, Major-General J. E. B., Confederate cavalry commander during the American Civil War, 77, 558

Subotai, Mongol leader, 249, 357

Suleiman I (the Magnificent), Sultan of Turkey, 355, 437, 532

Sulla, Lucius Cornelius, Roman soldier and politician of the first century BC, 107

Suraj-ud-Daula, Nawab of Bengal, 409

Surenas, Parthian commander in the first century BC, 98.

Surrey, Thomas Howard, Earl of, later Duke of Norfolk, English commander during the early sixteenth century, 173

Suzuki, Lieutenant-General Sosaku, commander of the Japanese Thirty-Fifth Army in the Philippines during the Second World War, 294

Takashina, Lieutenant-General Takeshi, Japanese garrison commander on Guam during the Second World War, 207

Tallard, Marshal Count Camille de, French commander during the War of Spanish Succession, 71

Tamerlane, 253, 396

Tantia Topi, rebel leader in the Indian Mutiny, 67, 101, 212

Tarleton, Lieutenant-Colonel Banastre, British cavalry commander during the

American War of Independence, 129, 548

Taylor, Major-General Richard, Confederate commander during the American Civil War, 332

Taylor, Major-General Zachary, American commander in the US–Mexican War, 84, 365, 395

Thomas, Major-General George H., Union commander during the American Civil War, 45, 256, 378

Thutmosis III, King of Egypt, 347

Tilly, Count John de, Catholic commander during the Thirty Years' War, 79, 221, 314, 318, 549

Timoshenko, Marshal Semyon, Soviet commander during the Second World War, 258, 331, 369, 480, 499, 539

Tolbukhin, Marshal F. I., commander of the Soviet 3rd Ukrainian Front during the Second World War, 241

Tortensson, Field Marshal Lennart, Swedish commander during the Thirty Years' War, 80

Townshend, Major-General Sir Charles, British commander in Mesopotamia during the First World War, 134, 274

Trochu, General Louis, French commander during the Franco–Prussian War, 398

Tukhachevsky, Marshal Mikhail, Bolshevik commander during the Russian Civil War and Russo–Polish War, later murdered on the orders of Stalin, 545

Turenne, Marshal Viscount Henri de, French commander during the Thirty Years' War and Louis XIV's Dutch War against Spain, 153, 185

Tyrone, Hugh O'Neill, Earl of, leader of rebellion in Ireland against Elizabeth I, 267, 556

Ushijima, Lieutenant-General Mitsuru, Japanese commander of Okinawa in 1945, 388

Valens, joint Roman Emperor in AD 364–378, 8

Vallette, Jean de la, Grand Master of the Knights of St John, 327

Vandergrift, Lieutenant-General Alexander A., American commander in the Solomon Islands during the Second World War, 206

Van Doorn, Major-General Earl, Confederate commander during the

American Civil War, 127

Van Fleet, Lieutenant-General James, commander of the US Eighth Army during the Korean War, 228

Varro, Terentius, Roman commander and consul during the Second Punic War, 96

Varus, Publius Quintilius, Roman commander-in-chief in Germany in AD 9, 510

Vasilevsky, Marshal Alexandr, Soviet commander in the Second World War, 328

Vatutin, General Nikolay, Soviet commander in the Second World War, 259, 273

Vendôme, Marshal, Duke Louis Joseph de, French commander during the War of Spanish Succession, 393

Vercingetorix, Gallic commander during the war against Julius Caesar, 18

Victor, Marshal Claude, Duke of Belluno, French commander during the Napoleonic Wars, 57, 503

Vietinghoff, Colonel-General Heinrich von, commander of the German Tenth Army in Italy in 1943–1945 and subsequently Army Group South-West, 99, 200, 452, 538

Villars, Marshal, Duke Claude de, French commander during the War of Spanish Succession, 222, 326

Villeroi, Marshal, Duke François de, French commander in the late seventeenth and early eighteenth centuries, 431

Vincent, Brigadier-General John, British commander in the War of 1812, 495

Voroshilov, Marshal Klimenti, Soviet commander in the Second World War, 289

Wainwright, Lieutenant-General Jonathan M., American commander in the Philippines in 1941–1942, 59

Walker, Lieutenant-General Walton H., commander of the US Eighth Army in the Korean War, 424

Wallace, Major-General Lewis, Union commander during the American Civil War, 361

Wallace, Sir William, Scottish patriot, 164, 492

Wallenstein, General Albrecht von, Imperialist/Catholic commander during the Thirty Years' War, 25, 143, 315

Waller, Sir William, Parliamentarian

commander during the Civil War, 133, 444

Ward, Major-General Artemis, American commander during the American War of Independence, 89

Warwick, Richard Neville, Earl of, also known as 'The Kingmaker', fought for both factions during the Wars of the Roses, 50, 387

Washington, General George, American commander during the American War of Independence, subsequently President of the United States, 78, 179, 193, 360, 423, 524, 550, 559

Wavell, Field Marshal Sir Archibald, British and Allied commander in the Second World War, 476

Weichs, Field Marshal Freiherr Maximilian von, German commander during the Second World War, 489

Wellington, Field Marshal Arthur Wellesley, Duke of, British commander in India, the Peninsular War and the Waterloo campaign, later Prime Minister, 43, 48, 90, 122, 188, 427, 451, 503, 520, 534, 536, 547

Westmoreland, General William C., Head of the US Military Assistance Command during the Vietnam War, 247

Weygand, General Maxime, French and Allied commander-in-chief in France in 1940, 183, 545

White, Lieutenant-General Sir George, British commander during the Second Boer War, 278

William, Duke of Normandy, later William I, King of England, 216

William III, King of England, 76, 379

Wilson, Major-General Archdale, British commander during the Indian Mutiny, 142

Winchester, Major-General James, American commander in the War of 1812, 186

Winder, Major-General William, American commander during the War of 1812, 70, 495

Wittgenstein, Field Marshal Prince Ludwig, Russian commander during the Napoleonic Wars, 60, 65, 316

Wolfe, Major-General James, British commander during the French and Indian War in North America, 428

Wolseley, General Lord Garnet, British commander in colonial wars, 4, 5, 27, 509

Wurmser, Field Marshal Count Dagobert, Austrian commander during the French Revolutionary Wars, 58

Xenophon, Athenian soldier, 136

Xerxes, King of Persia, 513

Yamashita, General Tomoyuki, Japanese commander in Malaya and the Philippines during the Second World War, 294, 330, 479

Yeremenko, General Andrei, Soviet commander in the Second World War, 489

Yudenich, General Nikolai, Russian commander in the First World War, 459

Zhilinsky, General Yakov, commander of the Russian North-West Front during the First World War, 343, 506

Zhukov, Marshal Georgi, Soviet commander during the Second World War, 66, 251, 257, 273, 289, 369, 489

Ziska, Jan, Hussite leader, 275, 380, 418

APPENDIX C:
TACTICS AND WEAPONS

SELECT BIBLIOGRAPHY

Atteridge, A. Hilliard, *Famous Land Fights*, 1914

Catton, Bruce, *Centenniel History of the Civil War Vols 1–3*, 1965

Chandler, David, *A Traveller's Guide to the Battlefields of Europe, Vols 1 and 2*, 1965

Chandler, David, *Battles and Battlescenes of World War II*, 1989

Dupuy, R. Ernest, and Dupuy, Trevor N., *The Encyclopedia of Military History From 3500 BC to the Present*, 1970

Edwardes, Michael, *Battles of the Indian Mutiny*, 1963

Forbes, Archibald; Henty, G. A.; Griffiths, Major Arthur; and others, *Battles of the Nineteenth Century, Vols 1 and 2*, 1896

Fuller, Major-General J. F. C., *The Decisive Battles of the Western World 480 BC – 1944*, 1954

Hackett, General Sir John, (Ed.), *Warfare in the Ancient World*, 1989

Haythornthwaite, Philip J., *A Napoleonic Source Book*, 1990

Holmes, Richard, (Ed.), *The World Atlas of Warfare – Military Innovations that Changed the Course of History*, 1988

Howard, Michael, *The Franco–Prussian War*, 1961

Kennedy, Frances H., (Ed.), *The Civil War Battlefield Guide*, 1990

Lloyd, Alan, *The Scorching of Washington – The War of 1812*

Lloyd, Alan, *The Zulu War 1879*, 1973

Macksey, Kenneth, *The Guinness History of Land Warfare*, 1973

Montgomery of Alamein, Field Marshal Viscount, *A History of Warfare*

Oman, Charles, *A History of the Art of War in the Middle Ages* 1924

Oman, Charles, *A History of the Art of War in the Sixteenth Century*, 1937

Packenham, Thomas, *The Boer War*, 1979

Pemberton, W. Baring, *Battles of the Crimean War*, 1962

Perrett, Bryan, and Hogg, Ian, *Encyclopedia of the Second World War*, 1989

Pitt, Barrie, (Ed.), *Purnell's History of the First World War Vols 1–7*

Pitt, Barrie, (Ed.), *Purnell's History of the Second World War Vols 1–6*

Smurthwaite, David, *The Ordnance Survey Complete Guide to the Battlefields of Britain*, 1984

Rogers, Colonel H. C. B., *The British Army of the Eighteenth Century*, 1977

Sweetman, John, *A Dictionary of European Land Battles From the Earliest Times to 1945*, 1984

Symonds, Craig L., *A Battlefield Atlas of the American Revolution*, 1986

Thompson, Sir Robert, (Ed.), *War in Peace – An Analysis of Warfare Since 1945*, 1981

Walder, David, *The Short Victorious War – The Russo–Japanese Conflict 1904–5*, 1973

Wedgewood, C. V., *The Thirty Years War*, 1956

Wise, Terence, *The Wars of the Crusades 1096–1291*, 1978

OTHER BOOKS BY BRYAN PERRETT

Last Stand! Famous Battles Against the Odds
Tank Tracks to Rangoon: The Story of British Armour in Burma
Desert Warfare
The Czar's British Squadron
A History of Blitzkrieg
Canopy of War: Jungle Warfare from Forest Fighting to Vietnam
Knights of the Black Cross: Hitler's Panzerwaffe and its Leaders
Tank Warfare
Liverpool: A City at War
Weapons of the Falklands Conflict
Soviet Armour Since 1945

With Ian V. Hogg:
Encyclopedia of the Second World War